Running the Family Firm

MANCHESTER
1824

Manchester University Press

Running the Family Firm

How the monarchy manages its image and our money

Laura Clancy

Manchester University Press

Published by Manchester University Press
Altrincham Street, Manchester M1 7JA
www.manchesteruniversitypress.co.uk

British Library Cataloguing-in-Publication Data
A catalogue record for this book is available from the British Library

ISBN   978 1 5261 5875 8   paperback
ISBN   978 1 5261 4933 6   hardback

First published 2021

The publisher has no responsibility for the persistence or accuracy of URLs for any external or third-party internet websites referred to in this book, and does not guarantee that any content on such websites is, or will remain, accurate or appropriate.

Typeset
by New Best-set Typesetters Ltd
Printed in Great Britain
by TJ Books Ltd, Padstow

For Mum, Dad, Sam, Abby and Ruby
And in memory of Paul Stewart

Contents

Figures

Figures

Preface

'I hate it when people moan about how much money royal weddings cost – this country has more important problems to worry about.'

This is a conversation I overhear at my local gym. It is 12 October 2018, and Princess Eugenie has married Jack Brooksbank at Windsor Castle, funded by the Sovereign Grant. The ceremony aired live on ITV but to significantly less fanfare than other contemporary royal weddings, such as those of Prince William and Kate Middleton, and Prince Harry and Meghan Markle.

This is a sentiment I have battled throughout my research on the royal family, and I have been regularly asked why the monarchy is important and worthy of study. *Running the Family Firm* aims to demonstrate why the 'more important problems' described above are not detached from the institution of monarchy. In fact, it is not that we *might* talk about the monarchy when we talk about growing inequalities in Britain but that we *have to* in order to understand how inequality works. I would go further to suggest that we cannot talk about inequalities in Britain without talking about the monarchy. *Running the Family Firm* argues that the principles by which monarchy works are key principles by which the whole system works, and in understanding monarchy we can begin to make sense of the system.

Laura Clancy
February 2021

Acknowledgements

This book has been a long time in the making. Every day, the project became bigger and bigger, and it is a research project that could go on for ever. This book is one iteration of my attempt to piece all of this together.

This research was funded by the ESRC and the AHRC, and then an ESRC Postdoctoral Fellowship which relieved me from teaching and administrative duties and allowed me the time to lock myself inside (COVID and lockdown did somewhat prompt that) and write this thing.

Thank you to everyone who has contributed to this book, and/or to my sanity, in a variety of ways: Amy Calvert and Flynn, Anne Cronin, Anne-Marie Fortier, Bev Skeggs, Claire Kelly, Daisy Barker, Debra Ferreday, Elmer Fernandes, Emily Hoyle, Emily Pugh, Emily Winter, everyone at the FSA, the FINER team, Georgia Newmarch, Hannah Yelin, Jo Littler, Jonny Beacham, Karen Gammon, Kim Allen, Lizzie Houghton, Maarten Michielse, Miranda Barty-Taylor, Sara De Benedictis, Tom Whittle, Tracey Jensen, Vicky Singleton and all the brilliant students I've had the privilege to teach. An extra special thanks to Imogen Tyler, Bruce Bennett (plus Bonnie) and Helen Wood, without whom this book would not exist.

This book is dedicated to my parents and siblings, and thank you also to the rest of my family.

Acknowledgements

Thanks to the team at Manchester University Press. Tom Dark, in particular, has been enthusiastic about the book from the beginning, and I am very grateful.

Towards the end of writing this book, I got two kittens, Agnes and Ginny. My keyboard promptly became a toy, so any typos in this manuscript are firmly their responsibility. Any other mistakes or inaccuracies are my own.

Some of Chapter 2 has been published in amended form as 'The Corporate Power of the British Monarchy: Capital(ism), Wealth and Power in Contemporary Britain' in *The Sociological Review* (2020).

A section of Chapter 3 has been published in amended form as '"Queen's Day – TV's Day": The British Monarchy and the Media Industries' in *Contemporary British History* (2019).

Some of Chapter 4 has been published in amended form as '"Queen of Scots": The Monarch's Body and National Identities in the 2014 Scottish Independence Referendum' in *European Journal of Cultural Studies* (2020).

Introduction: Why does monarchy matter?

On 5 November 2017, leaked documents from two offshore tax havens in the Cayman Islands revealed that the Duchy of Lancaster – the Queen's private estate – had used offshore private equity funds to avoid paying tax on its holdings.[1] The so-called 'Paradise Papers' were 13.4 million leaked documents revealing how more than 120,000 people and companies globally used offshore investments to avoid paying tax. The papers showed that the Duchy of Lancaster's investments had put funds into an array of businesses, including the retailer BrightHouse, Britain's largest rent-to-own company which has been 'criticised for exploiting thousands of poor families and vulnerable people' by charging huge interest rates on purchases using cost credit.[2] The Duchy responded to the Paradise Papers by claiming that 'our investment strategy is based on advice and recommendation from our investment consultants and appropriate asset allocation', essentially shifting accountability.[3] On 7 November 2017, the Chair of the Duchy, Sir Mark Hudson, was knighted by the Queen at Buckingham Palace in a pre-planned ceremony the monarchy seemingly saw unfit to cancel.[4] The Queen has never publicly apologised for investments made on her behalf that investigative journalists have argued contribute to exploitative practices leading to poverty in debt.

Later on 7 November 2017, another leak from the Paradise Papers revealed that Prince Charles's private estate, the Duchy of

Cornwall, had invested millions of pounds in offshore companies, including Sustainable Forestry Management, a Bermuda-registered business run at the time by Charles's best friend Hugh van Cutsem.[5] The investment was put into land to protect it from deforestation in mid-2007. In January 2008, Charles featured in a charity video discussing tactics for protecting rainforests. As the *Guardian* commented, 'the Duchy should have publicly declared the investment in a company that might have indirectly benefited from the impact of the Prince's longstanding support for conservation projects'.[6] In response to the scandal, the Duchy claimed that Charles had no 'direct involvement in investment decisions', and again Charles has never publicly apologised for investments made on his behalf that potentially exploit conflicts of interest.[7]

In the days following the Paradise Papers revelations, the then Labour Shadow Chancellor John McDonnell called for the monarchy to publish full financial and tax records for 'complete openness and transparency'.[8] Buckingham Palace has never directly responded to this request. In July 2018, the Duchy of Lancaster's Annual Report made no direct reference to the Paradise Papers or the investments revealed within. Instead, in a section on 'Strategic Risk', the Keeper of the Privy Purse Alan Reid reiterated that management of the investment portfolio was made independently: 'the Duchy employs an investment consultant to advise overall and an investment manager to manage the financial portfolio on a day-to-day basis'.[9] This could be seen as an attempt to absolve the Duchy of responsibility for the investments. In September 2018, the *Guardian* revealed that HM Revenue and Customs would block individuals involved in tax avoidance schemes from receiving knighthoods or honours, because 'poor tax behaviour is not consistent with the award of an honour' and these individuals will 'bring the system into disrepute'.[10] No mention was given to the monarchy's involvement in 'poor tax behaviour', given its obviously pivotal role in the honours system.

Introduction: Why does monarchy matter?

The representation of the Paradise Papers as a 'scandal' was a rare moment for the British monarchy, where it faced (temporary) overt public criticism and (temporary) attention drawn to its means of accumulating wealth. On 6 November 2017, the *Guardian* represented the findings on its front page, using the iconic etching of the Queen's profile on British coins next to the headline 'Queen's cash invested in controversial retailer accused of exploiting the poor', to make critical connections between the monarchy, wealth accumulation and class-based exploitation.[11] Three weeks later on 27 November 2017, very different representations emerged when Clarence House (Prince Charles's Communications Offices) announced that Prince Harry would marry Meghan Markle. The couple's relationship and marriage dominated royal news, due primarily to Meghan's status as a bi-racial, self-identified feminist, divorced, American actor. According to Google Trends, UK searches for the term 'British royal family' at the time of the engagement announcement were more than double those around the time of the Paradise Papers leak:[12] the engagement announcement foregrounded familial relationships – the royal *family* – rather than the *institution* of monarchy and the investors caught up in the Paradise Papers 'scandal'. That is, media representations of Harry and Meghan's engagement – such as the *Daily Express*'s 'The Look of Love' and the *Sun*'s 'She's the One', all including photographs from the couple's staged engagement photocall – obscured (whether intentionally or not) political-economic issues of monarchy and capital, through moral economies of familialism and (heteronormative) love.[13]

Running the Family Firm is about the British monarchy, media culture, power, capital and inequalities. It probes conventional understandings of *what monarchy is* and *why monarchy matters* by exposing the systemic relations between the media culture of monarchy and its political and economic formations: how it looks versus how it makes its money and power. Academic anthropological accounts often position royalty as superficial, and nothing more than symbolic.[14] In media and public commentary, the contemporary British monarchy is typically positioned as an archaic institution, an anachronism to corporate forms of wealth and power, and therefore irrelevant. However, the relationship between monarchy and capitalism is as old as capitalism itself. Whilst most academic books on monarchy have had a historical focus, *Running the Family Firm* centres monarchy in debates about culture and economy in contemporary Britain. In academic terms, it uses a British Cultural Studies approach to read political economy through culture, and argues that media representations of the royal *family* are staged as affective and ideological projects to distance the monarchy from issues of capital and inequalities, and 'produce consent' for monarchy in the public imagination, as illustrated in the Paradise Papers moment.[15]

Running the Family Firm works with concepts of the 'frontstage' and the 'backstage' of monarchy. It argues that media representations (of, for instance, familial intimacies or spectacular royal events) constitute the 'frontstage'; that is, *this is what we see*. Meanwhile, 'backstage' there are a host of political-economic functions, infrastructures and modes of production that reproduce the institution. This is what *we typically don't see*. This book aims to pull back the stage curtain and expose those systemic relations that are usually obscured. To do this, I conceptualise the monarchy as a capitalist corporation, oriented towards, and historically entrenched in, processes of capital accumulation, profit extraction and forms of exploitation – processes that the Paradise Papers made temporarily hypervisible. 'The Firm' is a longstanding nickname for the British monarchy (see Chapter 1), but I use this name more literally to refer to the monarchy as a corporation, using 'Firm' and 'corporation' as analogous. This enables me to describe an institution and its corporate investments, wealth, assets, operational tactics and actions.

The central thread of *Running the Family Firm* is how these processes of capital accumulation occur alongside our emotional investment in the monarchy as a 'family': what I call the Family Firm. It describes how the reproduction of power and privilege happens in tangent with, and through, affective notions of family and other forms of benevolence, belonging and identity in media culture. In sum, the corporate power of monarchy (the Firm) is disguised through media representations of the royal *family* (the Family Firm). By analysing five key royal figures from across Elizabeth II's reign (1953 to present) – the Queen, Prince Charles, Prince Harry, Kate Middleton and Meghan Markle – I ask what are representations of these figures doing to conceal capital relations and reproduce monarchical power? What might a wide-ranging analysis of these figures reveal about how the Firm represents itself as a successful family over time? What forms of capital, both 'old' and 'new', are being mobilised by the Firm? How does the Firm seek to (re-)establish forms of social hierarchy, belonging and exclusivity, which help to reproduce global inequalities and ideologically reinforce inequality as a necessary system? These are not easy, stable or frictionless relations. Indeed, I argue that media representations of monarchy are often highly contradictory, constantly shifting and reactive. But in drawing out the economic, political, social and cultural functions of monarchy, I ask what our investments in monarchy are investments for; what is reproduced in media representations of tradition and family; and how revisiting these historical issues sheds light on processes of division and difference in Britain today.

Britain and class inequalities

In 2019 the world's richest 26 people owned equivalent wealth to the poorest 3.8 billion, and in 2017 the UK's wealthiest one thousand people owned more wealth than the poorest 40 per cent of households.[16] These growing inequalities leave the poorest worse off, as 1.6 million UK people used a food bank in 2019, and in 2017/18 around 14.3 million people lived in poverty.[17]

In this context, sociologists have returned to questions of class to understand economic disadvantage and poverty.[18] Alongside this, academic research on 'the elites' has also experienced a significant resurgence. The sociologists Mike Savage and Karel Williams's *Remembering Elites* was amongst the first recent studies to identify the 'glaring invisibility of elites' in sociological research.[19] The economist Thomas Piketty's influential volume *Capital in the Twenty First Century* concluded that the richest were disproportionately benefiting from neoliberal capitalist regimes, and the geographer Danny Dorling's *Inequality and the 1%* demonstrated how social mobility is stagnating.[20] Other research has explored how elite wealth is maintained, the forms it takes and the systems perpetuating such unequal access to elite lifestyles.[21]

Much of this research focuses on transnational, 'meritocratic', neoliberal corporate power and the 'new rich', overlooking older, inherited forms of wealth, and 'old' forms of political and institutional power in reproducing economic and cultural dis/advantage in Britain. Despite claims that landed power is in decline,[22] the investigative journalist Guy Shrubsole demonstrates that long-established, land-based wealth holding (by, for example, the Crown, the aristocracy and the church) remains central to systems of power.[23] Seventy per cent of British and Irish land is owned by 0.28 per cent of the population, illustrating an enduring landed elite.[24] Almost one-third of UK wealth is inherited, and a social mobility study found wealth has remained within a select few British families for a thousand years.[25] These forms of 'old wealth' increasingly intersect with capitalist logics of 'new' wealth elites. 'New' global elites often own international property portfolios, reflecting the model of 'landed' wealth.[26] Meanwhile, aristocrats are expanding their investments, perhaps best exemplified by the Duke of Westminster, whose original land holdings have now broadened into sixty cities globally, and incorporate forms of rentier capitalism in tourist or entertainment attractions, shopping centres leased to businesses, privately owned public spaces, and asset management services.[27] This expanding portfolio demonstrates how 'old' traditions of landownership facilitate 'new' capital forms, and how 'putting land to work' in new ways ensures the persistence and mutability of aristocratic commercial activities in contemporary Britain. Various forms of elite wealth intersect and converge through comparable cultural, political, social and economic behaviours.[28] Whilst this is not to overstate the aristocracy's endurance, it does demonstrate the persistence of the aristocracy as a privileged class, and the ongoing importance of kinship and inheritance as a form of wealth accumulation.[29]

One possible explanation for competing narratives that aristocratic power is in decline versus their interactions with new forms of capital is that the aristocracy tends to remain invisible to avoid public scrutiny. Whilst centuries ago power was linked to spectacular forms of visibility (see Chapter 2), now 'gate-keepers' curb access to this demographic.[30] These range from managers of stately homes, National Trust employees and journalists at 'elite' magazines such as *Tatler* and *Country Life*, and aristocratic lifestyles tend to include 'exclusive' sporting activities such as polo or shooting.[31] In an increasingly networked world, the aristocracy's invisibility in contemporary Britain is incredibly powerful.

An exception to this invisibility is in institutionalised and/or ceremonial forms, such as the House of Lords, or the British monarchy.[32] Indeed, these visual spectacles are so visible they disguise invisibility through theatrical masquerade. The co-constitutive and co-dependent relationship between invisibility, visibility and power is one key theme of *Running the Family Firm*. As I explore, the monarchy promises access to aristocratic cultures: royal events are media spectacles for public consumption (Chapter 2) and key royal figures are represented as 'modern' and 'progressive' through mediated public intimacies (Chapter 5), representations of 'ordinary family' life (Chapter 6) and claims of multiculturalism and postracialism (Chapter 7). However, I argue that this access is limited and carefully stage-managed, seemingly concealing monarchy's vast wealth, hidden tax arrangements, corruption, unspoken political influence, labour relations and trans/national relationships (Chapter 1).

Running the Family Firm argues that we must invest in the language of monarchy and Marxist notions of class inequality to understand inequality today. Elite studies must recognise how forms of power intersect and converge. It is only by revealing these relations and placing the monarchy at the centre of class analysis, which *Running the Family Firm* aims to do, that its importance to British socio-political life is revealed.

The cultural politics of monarchy

Growing divides between Britain's rich and poor were illustrated viscerally in June 2017, when a reported eighty people died in a fire in the high-rise, social-housing building Grenfell Tower in the London Borough of Kensington and Chelsea. This is an area with extreme inequalities between the poorest and the richest, who live in close proximity. The cladding covering Grenfell Tower's exterior so it looked more appealing to wealthy neighbours was highly flammable, used by the management company instead of fireproof alternatives because it was cheaper.[33] As the sociologist Tracy Shildrick notes, 'the disaster ... epitomises so much that is unfair and divisive with neoliberal capitalism'.[34]

Various royal family members visited the Grenfell Tower site in the aftermath as part of their philanthropic engagements (see Chapter 5 for a discussion of royal 'work').[35] Following the Queen's visit, the *Daily Mirror* published the headline 'A Tale of Two Leaders', which contrasted a photograph of the Queen talking to Grenfell Tower residents with one of the then Prime Minister Theresa May at the site flanked by police officers to avoid local and national public anger at the role of government in the incident. This commentary seems to present the Queen as the antithesis of the policies that many blame for causing the fire: the austerity policies of the state, and the elite power of global investors gentrifying the London property market. Here, the Queen represents a paternalistic and patronising morality in opposition to the immorality of the 'new elites', embodying values of history, heritage and protection against external threats. Yet, Grenfell Tower is less than two miles from Kensington Palace, the official London residence of royals including Prince William and Kate Middleton. This demonstrates a physical proximity between the monarchy, its property portfolio, the casualties of austerity policies and the greed of financial capitalism. Indeed, whilst Tracy Shildrick describes the visceral visual comparisons between 'luxury tower blocks and the haunting images of the burnt out shell of the Grenfell Tower', the opulence of nearby Kensington Palace provides an equally stark visual contrast.[36]

In 'A Tale of Two Leaders', the left-of-centre *Daily Mirror* fails to identify the Queen as part of the systems of class greed and inequality that facilitated the Grenfell incident. Similarly, many people's response to the monarchy's exposure in the Paradise Papers, and its involvement in tax avoidance schemes, was one of surprise. The Labour MP Margaret Hodge said she was 'furious' with the Queen's advisers for bringing her 'reputation into disrepute', and claimed the Queen would be 'completely shocked' to learn of the schemes.[37] She continued, the 'monarchy is one of the most trusted, loved and respected institutions in Britain and it symbolises the integrity of Britain in the world, and to see it sullied by these sort of activities is outrageous'.[38] Such bewilderment that the monarchy might engage in immoral practices to accumulate wealth is revealing of its positioning in the public imagination as the opposite of corporate forms of wealth and power. Yet, as the American politician Bernie Sanders argued, the Paradise Papers evidence an 'international oligarchy'.[39] In this new order of elites, 'old' and 'new' wealth intersects through interest, debt, capital gains, tax schemes and entangled family relationships.[40]

One argument of this book is that the inequalities inherent to monarchical systems of rule combine with those of financial capital. I argue that the monarchy acts as a façade, through which the mechanisms of inequality are disguised and naturalised. Another explanation for sociological research's overlooking of the aristocracy is that there has been a 'turn away' from earlier Marxist debates about the ruling class and economic class struggle. Because of this, Marxist frameworks like those of Silvia Federici and Ellen Meiksins Wood exploring how late capitalism remains rooted in historical forms of exploitation, extraction and class-based inequality are overlooked.[41] Meiksins Wood argues that:

> there has been no fatal disjuncture between a capitalist economy and a political-cultural ancient regime suspended in time somewhere around 1688. On the contrary, the formation of state and dominant culture has been inextricably bound up with the development of capitalism, conforming all too well to its economic logic and internal contradictions. Britain may even be the most thoroughly capitalist culture in Europe.[42]

It then follows that the monarchy, the aristocracy and the gentry *have always been* capitalistic, while premodern forms of status, privilege and prerogative continue in our understandings of class, belonging and national identity.

Economic theories on royal power further demonstrate the monarchy's capitalist logics. Academic anthropological accounts of 'inalienable possessions', such as Annette Weiner's work, focus on what she calls 'the paradox of keeping-while-giving', where 'inalienable possessions' (things that cannot be traded and are conserved through inheritance; the Crown Jewels are one example) are hoarded, while symbolic replacements are offered as a form of exchange, even while it reproduces inequalities.[43] Similarly, the anthropologist David Graeber argues that contemporary capitalist economic relations are organised around (im)moral logics of exchange and reciprocity.[44] Debt repayment, for example, is positioned as a moral imperative. But there are still hierarchies of precedence and privilege which order moral relations of inequality.

In Chapter 1, I argue that royal funding and/or wealth is offset in public discourse against notions of monarchy's wider cultural, historical or economic 'value' to British society (for example, that oft-repeated mantra 'the monarchy is good for tourism'). Monarchy is understood here as a form of Weiner's 'keeping-while-giving', where monarchy may be accumulating wealth but the royals are represented as socially responsible and 'giving back' through, for example, philanthropic activity or notions of royal 'work'. The historian Frank Prochaska argues that, whilst monarchs like Henry VIII were seen to rule by divine right, after the English Civil War it was generally believed that 'privilege entailed responsibility to the less fortunate'.[45] That is, monarchy had to be seen as 'giving something back'.

Such discourses also position royal figures as productive, and active in capitalist labour markets (Chapter 5). This reflects forms of 'philanthrocapitalism', which describes how philanthropy functions as a form of capital to make corporations and/or wealthy individuals 'look good' which then offsets inequalities, as well as generating more capital from customers drawn to a 'socially responsible' company.[46] Visiting Grenfell Tower in the fire's aftermath makes the royals appear to be 'giving', even while the monarchy 'keeps' its power, and 'keeps' its privileged position in the very London borough that facilitated the unequal conditions for the fire.[47] Royals reproduce inequalities in the very act of appearing to mitigate them.

Moral economies are further reproduced through 'categories' of wealth. New forms of capital in Britain get caught in a contest over legitimate possession and belonging. In Chapter 1, I describe how Victorian industrialists were seen as 'vulgar' compared to the 'respectable' landed gentry. 'Family Firms' were promoted at the time because they drew on moralising language of 'the family', and gestured towards a form of inheritance reflecting the model of the aristocracy. Likewise, I will demonstrate how notions of history, heritage, national identity and familialism structure our emotional investments in monarchy. The Firm becomes the Family Firm. This is not a corporation but a bastion of Britain's heritage.

The monarchy is important because it symbolises national identity. Hence, the Firm's wealth is depoliticised through these moral economies.

Running the Family Firm describes the monarchy as a corporation, the Firm, in order to look behind the moralising economies and expose capitalist logics. As the Paradise Papers demonstrate, the reproduction of the monarchy's wealth is partly dependent on the monarchy being run as a corporate business, exploiting procedural loopholes to maximise profit and avoid taxation, alongside corporate giants such as Apple, Nike and Facebook, who were also embroiled in the Paradise Papers 'scandal'. Considering the Firm as a corporation allows new ways of understanding the monarchy's wealth, assets, operational tactics and actions. For instance, in 1992 the Queen's self-identified 'annus horribilis' ('horrible year') – one of her reign's most sustained periods of public criticism – was partly characterised by anger at 'public funds' being used to restore Windsor Castle after a fire.[48] The fallout was so dramatic that some royal scholars predicted the end of the monarchy.[49] Instead, 1992 concluded with the monarchy paying 'voluntary' income tax to assuage public criticism, and the monarchy's cost to the taxpayer has not raised substantial public concern since.[50] Indeed, the Republican movement has all but disappeared into fringe campaigning, despite the rising social inequalities outlined above, and despite the exact sum of this 'voluntary' income tax, as well as the size of the wealth the income is taxable from, remaining undisclosed.

It is interesting to reflect on the similarities between the Firm and the taxation of global corporations such as Starbucks. In 2012, responding to public anger that it had paid no UK corporation tax for three years, the managing director of Starbucks, Kris Engskov, announced 'we will propose to pay a significant amount of corporation tax during 2013 and 2014 regardless of whether our company is profitable during these years'.[51] Admitting that 'the tax authorities were unaware' of these plans, Engskov's announcement is essentially 'voluntary corporation tax' because it is not based on official profit calculations.[52] The tax lawyer Conor Delaney said this 'made a mockery' of the tax system, because it skirts the laws of taxation for good publicity.[53] We could ask whether the Firm is doing the same.

Whilst the journalist Nicholas Shaxson describes tax havens as offering 'escape routes from the duties that come with living and obtaining benefits from society – tax, responsible financial regulation, criminal laws, inheritance rules and so on', I argue that the Firm has been doing this for centuries by being legally exempt from taxation. Meanwhile, it presents 'voluntary' taxation as benevolent giving (or, as Weiner would say, 'keeping-while-giving').[54] Likewise, whilst scholars such as Nadine El-Enany and Ida Danewid have described how the Grenfell Tower fire reflects colonial logics of racial capitalism because the inequalities in global cities like London are built on institutional racism and racialised dispossession (and, indeed, the majority of the Grenfell victims were people of colour), the Firm has been invested in racial capitalism for centuries through the British Empire: from providing charters to imperial corporations like the East India Company, to continuing to use goods stolen during colonisation (such as the Koh-i-Noor diamond from India used in the Crown Jewels), even while sympathising with Grenfell victims (again, what Weiner calls 'keeping-while-giving').[55]

It is notable in this context that global corporations are often nicknamed 'empires' (for example, 'Mark Zuckerberg's Facebook Empire'). This plays on the language of imperial empires to describe how 'a non-state body such as a corporation or a religious order can also establish control over peoples and nations'.[56] But describing the Firm as a global business empire is more than a metaphor. Rather, it is recognising how contemporary corporate capital works similarly to historical forms of racial capital, how they remain co-dependent and how this is embodied in the sovereign body of the British monarch(y).

The monarchy is a model for the capitalist regime. *Running the Family Firm* argues that there are in/consistencies in how the monarchy historically exploited its legal status to its advantage, and has adapted to various periods of capitalism to sustain power and accumulate wealth. For example, long before offshore tax havens, the aristocracy and the monarchy were avoiding tax by investing landed estates in trusts.[57] Likewise, as the social scientist Guy Standing argues, 'rentier capitalism' – the monopolisation of property – historically began with the monarchy's attempts to raise capital through fee extraction, from the patent system and copyright laws, to landlordism and the enclosure of public space.[58] In medieval times, the Crown collected rent – called 'landgable' or 'hawgable' – on urban property where it owned the land.[59] Where autonomy over rent was granted to local authorities, the town paid an annual payment – the 'fee-farm' – to the Crown.[60] Indeed, the negative reaction in 1992 to 'public funds' restoring Windsor Castle was misplaced, given that *all* monarchical wealth comes from public funds at some point, via different extraction tactics.

A popular mythology of monarchy is that it is apolitical. Constitutionally it is banned from being involved in party politics, and as the constitutional scholar Walter Bagehot wrote, 'the Crown is … the "fountain honour"; but the Treasury is the spring of business'.[61] In February 2021, the *Guardian* released documents which countered understandings of the monarchy as apolitical. The documents showed that the historical procedure of the 'Queen's consent' – where government ministers ask the Queen's permission to debate laws and bills which will privately or personally affect her, such as those relating to her private assets or position as landowner – was not merely a formality as widely understood, but rather the monarchy had used the procedure to persuade government ministers to alter laws in its favour. This included a 'transparency law' which would have revealed the Queen's wealth, and road safety laws which would have affected the royal estates.[62] The constitutional law scholar Thomas Adams said the documents revealed 'the kind of influence over legislation that lobbyists would only dream of', demonstrating again how monarchy's power goes beyond other corporate, state or political actors.[63] *Running the Family Firm* also counters this mythology of the monarchy as apolitical, and argues that the monarchy is a deeply political institution which ensures the social, political, cultural and economic order. The monarchy is involved in 'shoring up an *ancien régime*', and as such is central to understanding rising inequalities.[64]

Researching the media monarchy: notes on research practice

Britain is invested in monarchy as a family: the royal *family*. The sociologist Michael Billig's important work *Talking of the Royal Family* used discourse analysis to explore how British families spoke about the monarchy, and found that comparisons were often drawn between 'ordinary' families and their royal counterparts.[65] Such framing allowed the families to negotiate the monarchy's wealth and power, because the royals were seen as 'ordinary' and 'just like us'. More recently, the cultural theorist Jo Littler argued how elite figures like the royals contradictorily draw on ideas of meritocracy to position their wealth as 'earned', and therefore we, too, can be rich and privileged if we 'work hard enough'.[66]

I argue that these ideas are re/produced in media culture. If the reproduction of (corporate) monarchical power happens alongside, and through, emotional investments in the royal *family*, media representation is how this is maintained. *Running the Family Firm* draws on the academic work of British Cultural Studies, particularly Stuart Hall, to read the political economy through culture and argue that media culture is a key site through which class power is exercised and understood.[67] Hall notes the importance of 'conjunctural analysis': situating the present in historical trajectories and mapping power relations as they change over time.[68] Considering 'the conjuncture' means we can attend to the specificity of the present, and consider how we got here. In *Running the Family Firm*, this means asking what it means to study the British monarchy *at this socio-political moment.* Hall's work also recognises the important role of media culture in shaping practices of state and society: the media is one 'mechanism of consent' for securing power.[69] 'Culture' and 'society' are not separate; rather, British social, political, cultural and economic life is staged through media culture. Whilst media representations are *what we usually see* of monarchy (for example, royal ceremonies or royal babies), *Running the Family Firm* turns this narrative on its head *to expose what we don't see*. This is a complex process of cultural politics to reveal what is usually concealed. To use the metaphor of theatre again, it uses the 'frontstage' of monarchy to expose the 'backstage'.

In a broader historical sense, representations of monarchy have always been ways of 'producing consent' for royal power.[70] Monarchies have been considered as theatrical productions, from court masques as literal stagings of royal power (see Chapter 3) to the royal court as a dramaturgy of ritual, etiquette and hierarchy (see Chapter 1) and the royal event as spectacular ceremony (see Chapter 2).[71] Historians have analysed representations of global monarchies through portraits, artefacts, coinage, plays and performances.[72] Developments in print and electronic media accelerated this further. Queen Victoria's reign was represented in print, news media and newsreel coverage, and interwar monarchs used radio to communicate directly with their subjects.[73]

The contemporary monarchy is telegenic and digitised (see Chapter 2). *Running the Family Firm* draws together a range of materials on monarchy since 1953, including newspapers, magazines, books, films, television productions, portraiture and paintings, websites, social media outputs, public opinion polls, government reports, cartoons, political commentary, historical archive material and memorabilia. I have also undertaken ethnographic fieldwork at royal tourist sites, events, galleries and museums. This material ranges from 'official' representations produced by the monarchy to activist or republican texts, commentary from journalists and commentators, entertainment texts, fandom materials and public commentary on social media. This multi-textual analysis illustrates the complexity of monarchy as a social form and cultural representational system. I use investigative research methods to map monarchy across various media, physical and embodied sites, to explore how the cultural political economy of monarchy works across varied textual spaces.

Running the Family Firm explores the relationships between the corporate power of the Firm and representations of the royal *family* using analysis of five key royal figures: the Queen, Prince Charles, Prince Harry, Kate Middleton and Meghan Markle. In describing them as 'figures', I draw on Celebrity Studies approaches of celebrities as collections of images, discourses and narratives, or, as Richard Dyer writes, 'a complex configuration of... signs'.[74] These signs can be (re)contextualised within their social and material conditions of production. Figurative methodology has also been developed in feminist work.[75] This describes how particular figures are brought into being through representations across a range of cultural sites, with figuration operating as 'a constitutive effect and generative circulation'.[76] Claudia Castañeda describes how 'unpack[ing]' these figures reveals details about both the figures themselves and the cultural, political, social and economic relations they 'body forth'.[77] Crucially, this book is about *the representation of royal figures*. It is not about them as individual people. Indeed, the Queen's 'real' personality is irrelevant for our purposes. Not everything that is represented in media culture is 'true', and nor am I claiming such. Likewise, this is not a book that systemically addresses specific media forms, nor does it undertake ethnographic or qualitative analysis about people's responses to monarchy, although these contribute towards the argument. What matters are the representations circulating about royal figures, and how these representations work alongside, through and in service of broader structural relations that keep monarchy in place.

For my five royal figures, I ask how and where is this royal figure represented? What work does this figure do? What is the

meaning of this figure? Using a figurative method, each royal
figure embodies the various ways in which the Firm remakes itself
as a successful family over time. That includes through national
identity or identities, (geo)politics, sovereignty and landscape (the
Queen in Chapter 3), through landownership, conservatism and class
hierarchy (Charles in Chapter 4), through 'philanthrocapitalism',
masculinities and the military-industrial complex (Harry in Chapter
5), through the (social) reproduction of conservative, 'middle-class',
nuclear 'family values' (Kate in Chapter 6) and through ideologies of diversity, post-imperialism and post-racialism (Meghan in
Chapter 7). Each royal figure makes up the (Family) Firm. I do not
cover every royal, and I have chosen case studies which reveal key
themes in the Firm's reproduction. This selective approach reflects
representations of monarchy in wider media culture, where the
wider royal family is displayed on and hidden from the royal stage
when relevant. Prince Edward, for example, is absent from this
book as he is absent from royal events focusing on the 'core' family
members, usually including the Queen and (until his death in 2021)
Prince Philip, Prince Charles and Camilla Parker-Bowles, Prince
William, Kate Middleton and their children, and (prior to their
resignation) Prince Harry, Meghan Markle and Archie. In this book,
'unpack[ing]' these royal figures demonstrates not only how systems
of representation 'produce consent' for the monarchy but also how
the everyday construction, mediation and consumption of these
representations 'produce consent' for, and reveal something about,
various phenomena across British social, political and cultural life.[78]

Academic scholarship on monarchy has focused on accounts of
historical royal figures or families,[79] the monarchy on film,[80] other
media representations of monarchy,[81] audience reception,[82] monarchy
and gender,[83] monarchy and social class,[84] monarchy and national
identity,[85] royal wealth,[86] monarchy and Empire,[87] monarchy and
British politics,[88] royal events[89] and anti-monarchism.[90] There are
many popular biographies about monarchy, from those within the
institution and journalists and/or commentators outside.[91] *Running*

the Family Firm is the first to connect the culture and the economy; that is, it is the first account of the cultural politics of monarchy. I have chosen to largely discount the royals' official titles, and instead use their colloquial names: the Queen, Charles, Harry, Kate and Meghan. This was purposeful, both because the full titles are so unwieldy that it is impractical to use them throughout, and to reflect the construction of the royals in the public imagination. As Michael Billig writes in his analysis of people talking about monarchy, people demonstrated a 'cheeky familiarity' rather than a 'hushed reverence'.[92] *Running the Family Firm* is interested in how this 'ordinariness' is established.

The outline of *Running the Family Firm*

Chapters 1 and 2 explore the 'backstage' and 'frontstage' of monarchy, respectively, and the co-dependence of invisibility and visibility. Chapter 1, 'The (Family) Firm: Labour, capital and corporate power', outlines my conceptual framework of the monarchy as a corporation: the Firm. It maps the mechanics, technologies and industries involved in 'backstage' labour of the Firm's reproduction. The chapter also argues there are a web of capital relations: the exploitation of low-paid workers through ideologies of class subservience; the 'revolving door' between the Firm and global corporations; the murky rules of royal financing; the secrecy of royal wealth; the networks of contacts; the exploitation of political relationships for profit; and the abuse of political privileges. I unpack the historical relations between 'family' and 'firm' to consider how ideas of 'the family' moralise wealth.

Chapter 2, '"The greatest show on earth": Monarchy and media power', focuses on the 'frontstage', and how representations reproduce public consent for the monarchy. The Queen has reigned during a period of rapid technological expansion: from the emergence of television, through tabloid newspapers and paparazzi, to social media and citizen journalism. The Firm has consistently faced new challenges in how the public engages with monarchy. Starting with the Queen's 1953 coronation – the first royal ceremony to be televised live – the chapter traces 'the media monarchy' to the present day. It argues that all royal representations are stage-managed and precisely manufactured, and indeed royal visibility is balanced with a paradoxical but co-dependent *in*visibility, to ensure monarchy retains its mystique.

The subsequent chapters each use a royal figure as their case study to unpack what the Family Firm looks like. Chapter 3, '"Queen of Scots": National identities, sovereignty and the body politic', explores the relationship between the monarch(y) and national identities. On 20 September 2014, following the Scottish Independence Referendum, the British broadsheet the *Daily Telegraph's* front page featured a photograph of the Queen in the grounds of her Balmoral Estate in the Scottish Highlands, under the headline 'Queen's pledge to help reunite the Kingdom'. This chapter uses this to explore how the Queen's body becomes a site of symbolic struggle over discourses of national identity and citizenship during the referendum, embodying interrelations of 'Britishness', 'Englishness' and 'Scottishness'. I argue that when British status quo was under threat, representations of the Queen shifted from banal to purposeful symbols of authority and historical legitimacy. The photograph reveals the Firm's violent history, usually obscured in representations of the *Family* Firm.

In Chapter 4, 'Let them have Poundbury! Land, property and pastoralism', I analyse Poundbury, a 400-acre urban extension to Dorchester in Dorset, England, built on Duchy of Cornwall land using the architectural principles designed by Prince Charles in his book *A Vision of Britain*.[93] Charles's vision rejects modernism, and Poundbury recreates a conservative blend of 'familiar, traditional, well-tried and beautiful' architectural styles.[94] I propose that Charles links architectural trends to society and culture, and his *vision of Britain* is concerned not only with the architecture but also with managing the citizens populating it. Poundbury stages a traditional understanding of monarchy based on relations of feudalism, imperialism, pre-industrialisation, anti-urbanisation and classed, raced and gendered hierarchies; while contradictorily functioning as part of Charles's 'property empire' and reproducing forms of capitalist wealth.

Chapter 5, '"I am Invictus": Masculinities, "philanthrocapitalism" and the military-industrial complex', uses Prince Harry's involvement with the Armed Forces and the Invictus Games to consider the Firm's relation to global military capital and philanthropy. It argues that representations of Harry narrate his redemption through philanthropy, both through the redemptive masculinities of his royal figure (from the 'playboy prince' to the 'philanthropic prince', via the 'soldier prince'), and in the redemption of a 'good soldier' from a 'bad war' in the 'War on Terror'. Harry's performances of intimate address and talk of royal 'duty' represent the Firm as socially responsible, as the younger royals perform a populist and progressive version of monarchy. More broadly, Harry's persona condenses and disguises the neocolonial complexities of recent global conflicts in the Middle East, ambiguities in ideas of state responsibility versus individual rehabilitation, and the role of corporate capital.

Chapter 6, 'The heteromonarchy: Kate *Middle*ton, "*middle*-classness" and family values', considers how the Firm is reproduced through patriarchal, nuclear, conservative, heteronormative family values, which are contextualised in authoritarian neoliberalism and rising global anti-gender movements. It suggests that the monarchy's power is dependent on the subjugation of women's bodies through reproducing an heir. The chapter also considers relations of social class. Due to her non-aristocratic background, Kate Middleton has been represented as 'middle class'. I argue that this is strategic for the Firm to appear to open aristocratic cultures to the middle classes through performing 'ordinariness' in, for example, the Kensington Palace Instagram account. However, this 'openness' is merely a gesture, and the monarchy is becoming even more remote through Kate's indeterminate persona and staged photoshoots.

In Chapter 7, 'Megxitting the Firm: Race, postcolonialism and diversity capital', I explore Meghan Markle's introduction into the monarchy as a bi-racial, divorced, self-proclaimed feminist, American actor with a working-class background. Harry and Meghan's wedding was represented as a feminist, post-racial, meritocratic utopia, with Meghan's identity 'diversifying' the monarchy and illustrating its 'progressive' values. In the context of a monarchy built upon racism, colonialism and sexism, and in the broader contexts of Brexit, growing global far-right movements, increasingly factional political ideologies and widening global inequalities, I describe representations of Meghan as 'diversity capitalism', used to extend and diversify the Firm's markets. The couple's resignation from the Firm less than two years after the wedding illustrates how Meghan carried *too much* symbolic weight, and, rather than resolving royal histories of racism, (post-)colonialism, gender and social injustice, representations of Meghan merely pulled these inequalities into view.

The conclusion, 'The post-royals', expands upon Harry and Meghan's departure and uses these emerging representations to tease out the key themes of *Running the Family Firm*. Their resignation temporarily disturbed the monarchy's careful balance of visibility and invisibility, and emphasised issues of commercialisation and corporate capital, the media/monarchy relationship, and interrelations between the elites and the monarchy. This makes their departure an interesting point for me to leave this research, and going forward, to continue asking the key question 'why does monarchy matter?'

The (Family) Firm: Labour, capital and corporate power

The 2011 wedding of Prince William and Kate Middleton was a key moment for the contemporary British monarchy. It attracted two billion television viewers in 180 countries, and one million visitors to London.[1] As has become tradition for royal events since Queen Victoria's reign as a way for royals to manufacture intimacy with audiences,[2] the royal family appeared for now-famous photographs on Buckingham Palace balcony (Figure 1.1).

Although predominantly unnoticed, a host of Buckingham Palace staff were involved in staging the balcony: laying out and vacuuming the iconic red velvet drape (Figure 1.2). The cleaner doing this labour is just one staff of over a thousand working for the monarchy behind the scenes, largely rendered invisible behind the mediated royal spectacle. This chapter explores this backstage labour. It will pull back the stage curtain of monarchical spectacle to reveal the mechanics, technologies, infrastructures and actors behind.

To do this, I introduce a key term used to describe the monarchy in this book: the Firm. This name has a long and debated royal history, seeming to originate with Prince Albert / George VI. The historian Denis Judd claims that in 1920, when accused of behaving inappropriately for the royal family, Prince Albert replied 'we are not a family, we are a firm', which Judd suggested demonstrated disillusionment with his uncaring parents.[3] In the film *The King's Speech* (2010), he says directly to his father George V, 'Papa, we are

1.1 The royal family on Buckingham Palace balcony, 29 April 2011

1.2 Buckingham Palace cleaner vacuums the balcony, 29 April 2011

not a family, we're a firm', to note a lack of familial intimacy.[4] This demonstrates how the language of 'the Firm' has entered into accepted myths about the royal family. However, a more widely cited usage suggests a different meaning. During the Second World War, George VI reportedly stated 'we are the Family Firm' in reference to himself, Queen Elizabeth and Princesses Elizabeth and Margaret.[5] This usage was positive, celebrating the royals' enactment of 'ordinary' British family values to inspire strength and proximity between the monarchy and 'the people' during wartime.[6] This framing has reportedly been adapted by the Queen to refer colloquially to the monarchy as 'the Family Firm',[7] and multiple articles, reports, books and documentaries have used the designation uncritically.[8] The historian Edward Owens uses it to describe the public relations strategy of monarchy in the mid-twentieth century, suggesting it uses ideas of 'the family'.[9]

Whilst 'the *Family* Firm' softens institutional operations through ideas of familial intimacy, *Running the Family Firm* takes the name more literally to describe the monarchy as a corporation: the Firm. This chapter attempts to map the main features of the Firm's infrastructures, labour relations, modes of production, political economies, financial arrangements, inter/national relationships and networks, and the legal status of the Crown and its components. The empirical data take a classic journalistic approach of investigative research, consolidating a mass of material that was difficult to source due to the monarchy's reliance on secrecy. This material ranges from media representations (newspapers, books, documentaries, social media, blogs); statistical data (surveys); government, constitutional and legal documents; material goods (merchandise); and critical academic material on monarchy. It incorporates 'official' representations produced by the monarchy, activist or republican critiques, 'objective' commentary by journalists or commentators, entertainment texts, fandom materials and public commentary on social media. The story of corporate power and labour described here will reappear in later chapters.

I opened this chapter with the photograph of the Buckingham Palace cleaner vacuuming the balcony to illustrate the 'backstage', and each of these sections peels back another layer of the Firm's power. Analysing the Firm is comparable to a tapestry: from afar it appears a complete picture, but upon closer inspection its threads are tightly woven together, and the process of unweaving is near impossible. The Firm's history is so complex, and so bounded in unwritten privileges, that it is extremely difficult to undo its logic – if, indeed, it has any logic. I demonstrated in the Introduction how the monarchy is a key player in financial capitalism, but, whilst the Paradise Papers made this (temporarily) hyper-visible, on the whole *the very invisibility of the Firm's social and economic power is its power.*

Defining the Family Firm

Representations of the monarchy as an 'ordinary' family are commonplace in contemporary Britain. The feminist scholars Michelle Barrett and Mary McIntosh argue, 'it is not the institution of monarchy that is popular, it is the royal *family*',[10] illustrating the separation of the royal figures from the institution. The ex-Director of Royal Communications Sally Osman said 'there is a distinction between what we do to articulate the Monarchy ... and then the role that each of the individuals play within that story'.[11] Osman demonstrates how royal representations are often organised strategically, and indeed many royal biographies[12] and academic studies[13] highlight the importance of a monarchy built on ideologies of quasi-nuclear familialism and 'ordinariness'. In 1917, a royal proclamation renamed the monarchy the House of Windsor, replacing the hereditary surname Saxe-Coburg and Gotha after concerns about anti-Germanism following the First World War. The marketing scholars C.C. Otnes and Pauline Maclaran term this 'brand repositioning', realigning the monarchy with British 'family values'.[14]

'A Family Firm' is a business with 'a family member [as] chief executive officer'.[15] Although they still exist, such firms played an important role in mediating new forms of capital in the Victorian industrial era.[16] At each shift of capitalism, particular figures emerge as 'vulgar' faces of capitalist wealth, 'contaminating' the 'natural' economic order headed by the aristocratic landowner.[17] The historian Nicholas B. Dirks, for example, describes how the eighteenth-century dominance of the East India Company led to moral panics about so-called 'nabobs': mercantile elites returning from India who would then marry into aristocratic families, buy positions in Parliament, and disrupt established economic norms.[18] Likewise, the historian Stana Nenadic argues that new Victorian middle-class commercial business owners were seen to compromise a social class order grounded in the morality of the family and inherited wealth.[19] To counter this, early business organisation was modelled on 'the family'. 'The Family Firm' mimicked the landed estate, which organised enterprise around family relationships.[20] As Nenadic summarises, 'the public integrity of the firm was built on the public integrity of the family'.[21]

This led to corporate exploitation of ideologies of 'the family' to appeal to public morality, and make new capitalist forms appear respectable.[22] In the 1930s and 1940s, the American car manufacturers General Motors advertised itself as a family organisation, claiming 'the word corporation is cold, impersonal … "Family" is personal, human, friendly'.[23] A 2014 YouGov survey found 'managers of big businesses' and 'entrepreneurs' scored a net negative rating on trustworthiness, while 'managers of small businesses' received a net positive rating.[24] In contemporary popular culture, 'family brands' such as the Beckhams and the Kardashians commercialise family relations for profit.[25]

The contemporary monarchy seems to draw on a family model propagated by Queen Victoria. The Industrial Revolution created new commercial business owners and entrepreneurs, while advancements in print cultures and transport expanded prospects.[26] The result was a new 'middle class', differing from the aristocracy above and the working classes below.[27] The sociologist Steph Lawler argues that middle-classness was differentiated through claims to 'culture, morality, and modernity', which since have become social 'norms'.[28] That is, 'middle-classness [became] the benchmark against which other groups are measured'.[29]

The development of the 'separate spheres' of work and home meant that the nuclear, heteronormative family (looked after by the wife or mother) was key to Victorian middle-class respectability.[30] The aristocracy drew on this 'ordinary' bourgeoisie sensibility to distance themselves from classed associations with greed and debauchery – Queen Victoria included.[31] While previously 'the court' was the centre of political power, Victoria's reign was characterised by portraits of interior domestic scenes.[32] Of course, these representations erased the background labour of nannies, governesses and servants.[33] But royal palaces were depicted as family homes, with Victoria and Albert as bourgeois parents.[34] This played out globally with Victoria depicted as grandmother of the nation, the Empire and – after most of her children married into European royalty – Europe.[35] Margaret Homans suggests that these were affective representations when monarchies across Europe were being dismantled under parliamentary democracy.[36] By modelling the monarch on middle-class wives, who were required to act as public symbols of their husband's values and status, monarchy could act as a public symbol of the nation's values and status, and avoid political accountability.[37]

As this book demonstrates, the contemporary monarchy's performance of Victorian-inspired, middle-class 'family values' is a strategic project. It is a prism, distancing the Firm from wealthy oligarchs and capitalist dynasties such as the Bransons and the Trumps – with whom the Firm arguably has more in common than with a typical, middle-class family. Indeed, keeping the royal family clean of associations with capitalist vulgarity is a central ideological project to produce consent for the monarchy in the public imagination, and to preserve a higher moral order that has become untethered from divine right under changing forms of sovereign power. Elsewhere, monarchy and corporation are more visibly interrelated. The Princely Family of Liechtenstein, for example, owns Liechtenstein's biggest financial group, LGT, with Prince Maximilian acting as CEO.[38] That family's estimated worth is $5 billion, and LGT's corporate strategy draws on discourses of both monarchy and family.[39] It describes itself as a 'family-run company', and the LGT Code of Conduct is embedded in 'rules' established in the seventeenth century by Prince Gundaker.[40] The political economist Adam Hanieh explores connections between Gulf state monarchies and circuits of global capital in oil industries, agriculture, construction and banking.[41] In *Royal Capitalism*, Puangchon Unchanam argues that the Thai monarchy has embraced global capitalism by, for example, forming relationships with business elites and global corporations, patronising local industries and selling material goods.[42]

Defining the corporate Firm

I frame the monarchy as a corporation to distinguish from existing work that considers monarchy as a brand.[43] Contemporary marketing literature understands branding as 'distinguish[ing] a particular product or service from its competitors', which means differentiating products from other (similar) items.[44] A brand operates externally. To examine the royal brand is, to be blunt, analysing *what they want you to see*. The Firm has developed some 'public facing' brands, such as the 'Royal Collection Trust' (manages the Royal Collection and tourism at royal residences), 'Duchy Originals' (Prince Charles's organic food range), 'Highgrove' (Prince Charles's garden tours and home products shop) and the 'Windsor Farm Shop' (organic produce shop).[45] Prince William, Kate Middleton and Prince Harry have created companies – 'APL Anglesey', 'CE Strathearn' and 'Tsessebe', respectively – to protect their brands and 'intellectual property rights'.[46] Royal brand visibility is ensured through official merchandise sold at royal tourist sites and other stores such as Waitrose and Harrods.[47] Branding is certainly not irrelevant. But to understand the monarchy's material practices, we must consider its complex historical, economic, political, social and cultural infrastructures; infrastructures often rendered invisible behind the royal spectacle.

'The Firm' is analogous to 'corporation', referring to a company with distinct legal personhood and deriving from the Latin 'corporare', meaning 'combine in one body'.[48] Corporations can 'acquire assets, employ workers, pay taxes and go to court'.[49] The Crown is legally a common law corporation. Medieval law used Roman ideas of the body politic as '*universitas*, a corporation of the polity', to distinguish between the Crown and the monarch's natural body, meaning that laws made regarding, and assets belonging to, the monarch(y) will pass to the succeeding monarch.[50] Historically, the Crown used private corporations to manage public services, such as municipalities, universities or the Corporation of London, and to manage colonisation projects across the Empire.[51] The Bubble Act 1720 decreed that chartered companies must be granted through Royal Charters – documents issued by the Crown – and many monarchs benefited directly from trade deals through custom duties.[52] The Companies Act 1862 granted limited liability joint-stock companies the same rights as humans, and negated Royal Charters.[53] The Industrial Revolution initiated large-scale corporations, with multidivisional organisational structures.[54] Finally, the period since Elizabeth II's 1953 coronation has shifted from the postwar welfare state to financial capital, neoliberal deregulation, free markets and privatisation.[55] In the Global North corporate values are embedded in practices of everyday life.[56] Corporate and civic citizenship increasingly intersect,[57] and corporate accumulation through dispossession, exploitation and extraction expands.[58]

Often monarchy operates similarly to corporations to sustain itself in a networked world market. Yet rather than (or, perhaps, in addition to) corruption, it uses 'extra-juridical' forms of precedence rooted in the (uncodified) British constitution and political custom. The legal bases for monarchical privileges are entrenched in historical laws, policies and/or loopholes. The Firm is embedded in the institutions of the British state as a guarantor of the British constitution with an executive political role. The Queen appoints and dismisses Prime Ministers, has weekly private meetings with them (the contents of which are undisclosed) and receives a daily 'red box' of government documents; the monarch's signature allows Bills to take effect legally under royal assent.[59] The monarch's advisory body, the Privy Council, comprises 650 members including all Cabinet Ministers. The Council approves government decisions but can also create 'Orders' enforceable by law under royal prerogative.[60] In 2021, the *Guardian* revealed that the procedure of the 'Queen's consent', previously considered a formality where government ministers would seek the Queen's permission before debating bills or laws which would affect her, had actually been used to lobby government ministers to alter more than a thousand laws, from the Brexit trade deal to laws on inheritance.[61] The cultures of secrecy surrounding the monarchy are upheld by various state actors, and the Firm has tangible powers. Yet, as I demonstrated in the Introduction, many global corporations also rely on governmental protection and legal loopholes. As the political economist David Ciepley has argued, 'corporations are government-like in their powers'.[62]

Working for the Firm

Royal staff

The Firm draws extensively on the time and energy of others to reproduce its power. Whilst civil servants, military personnel and ministers could be considered employees of the Crown,[63] my narrative of domestic employment defines staff as those working in royal palaces. The Firm employs around 1,200 staff across the Royal Households, the largest being the Household of Elizabeth II at Buckingham Palace.[64] This Household is overseen by the Lord Chamberlain, and work is departmentalised: the Lord Chamberlain's Office (ceremonies, public events); the Private Secretary's Office (constitutional and political duties, communications); The Privy Purse and Treasurer's Office (finance); The Master of the Household's Department (catering, hospitality, housekeeping); and the Royal Collection Trust (maintaining the Royal Collection of artwork and artefacts).[65] I argue that this personnel organisation reflects bureaucratic multidivisional corporations, with the Queen equivalent to Vice President, the Lord Chamberlain as Chairman, the Queen's Private Secretary as Managing Director or Chief Executive, and Heads of Department as sector managers.

Inside accounts suggest a strictly demarcated staff hierarchy usually built around proximity to the royals and policed by a dramaturgy of ritual and etiquette.[66] Reports recount segregated dining locations and timings, whereby 'junior members' (butlers, housekeepers) eat self-service meals using plastic seats and plastic cutlery; 'officials' (long-serving staff, dressers, chauffeurs) dine on upholstered chairs with silver cutlery; 'senior officials' (personal secretaries, press officers) are permitted alcohol, and 'members' (ladies-in-waiting, Private Secretary) are served by junior staff.[67] This shows the Firm merging corporate structure and historical royal etiquette or hierarchy. Reports also show inconsistent hiring practices and enormous variations in wages and benefits. Whilst senior staff are typically headhunted and often employed without formal interview,[68] lower-level staff complete an application form, undertake an interview, and some attend an Assessment Day.[69] Stephen P. Barry's interview for Valet in the 1960s involved being judged 'entirely on appearance', particularly height.[70] Now, all staff must have relevant experience, such as in hospitality.[71]

Salaries also vary. A Housekeeping Assistant position was advertised in 2015 at £14,513.16 per annum,[72] which, presuming a

37.5 hours per week contract (it advertises for 'five days'), is barely above the 2015 London living wage of £9.40 per hour.[73] Pay scales for senior staff are not advertised, but the biographer Brian Hoey suggested that in 2011 the Queen's Private Secretary was paid £146,000 and the Keeper of the Privy Purse £180,000.[74] In 2011–12, pay was seemingly frozen for staff earning over £21,000,[75] but reports suggested that some top earners saw increases of up to 6.4 per cent regardless.[76] This reflects how UK elite wages continue rising after the North Atlantic financial crash and austerity economics, despite average UK household income decreasing.[77] Meanwhile, reflecting the global 'gig economy' model, the Royal Households use temporary contracts. According to reports, some cleaners are agency staff; footmen from elite colleges apparently undertake unpaid 'internships' at state banquets; and 350 part-time staff worked on zero-hour contracts for Buckingham Palace's 2013 summer opening.[78] Some staff are Public and Commercial Services Union members, and in 2015 they threatened industrial action over working conditions and pay.[79]

Benefit packages seem to operate hierarchically. Reports say that junior staff are offered accommodation within Buckingham Palace – typically single rooms with gendered and hierarchical segregation – costing 17.5 per cent of wages.[80] Meanwhile, many senior staff receive 'grace-and-favour' (either reduced rent or free) apartments in other royal buildings.[81] Brian Hoey claims that staff sign a confidentiality agreement, forbidding them to discuss their work.[82] The consequences of breaking these agreements were revealed in 2003, when the *Daily Mirror* journalist Ryan Parry posed as a footman to work at Buckingham Palace for two months, before documenting his experiences in the newspaper. Buckingham Palace sued Parry for breach of contract, and his stories were redacted.[83]

White male employees seem to dominate. The government's 2018 gender pay gap report showed that women in the Royal Household are paid 12.39 per cent less than men,[84] and the first Black equerry was hired only in 2017.[85] Although the official Royal website has a 'diversity and inclusion' policy stating that the monarchy attempts to 'raise awareness of diversity and equal opportunities throughout our workforce', and hire on merit, it does not detail *how* this occurs (indeed, the gender pay gap suggests it does not).[86] Statistics on racial diversity are not available. In 1997, the *Independent* revealed that UK statutory policies on ethnic monitoring of staff were not being used by the Firm.[87] In response, the Firm claimed that 'the number of current employees from an ethnic minority background is about 5 per cent ... in line with ethnic minority representation across the Civil Service'.[88] The Civil Service figure was actually 18.4 per cent in Greater London, and the Firm did not seem to undertake any ethnic monitoring of current staff by position, making calculations on BAME employees' distribution across pay grades impossible.[89] In 2001, Elizabeth Burgess, a Black woman and former personal assistant to Prince Charles, went to tribunal over discrimination and racist bullying by other staff. Her claims were dismissed.[90]

These findings demonstrate the Firm's reliance on underpaid, under-rewarded 'domestic' staff, who are often unidentified. Meanwhile, senior members – although still operating under the Firm's veil of secrecy – often have status, capital and elite connections.

The 'revolving door'

Mapping the senior members reveals networked labour relations between the Firm and other institutions and corporations, and how 'old' and 'new' forms of wealth intersect in the Firm's operations. Table 1.1 illustrates current occupiers of key posts within each department, plus additional information about their employment and personal histories according to the reports and sources listed. Due to significant staff changeovers since 2015, the table also includes some previous longstanding holders of these positions. Table 1.1 shows how gender and race remain problematic, as white males dominate. Likewise, over-representation from elite schools,

Table 1.1   The Royal Household[91]

Household members	Description
<u>Lord Chamberlain</u> William James Robert Peel, 3rd Earl Peel, 2006-	House of Lords Peer. Shareholder at JP Morgan Fleming Overseas Investment Trust, ETFS Metal Securities Limited, Moonpig.com PLC, amongst others. Landowner in North Yorkshire. Married to Hon. Charlotte Clementine Soames, granddaughter of Winston Churchill.[92]
<u>Private Secretary's Office</u> Sir Edward Young, Private Secretary, 2017-	Promoted from Deputy Private Secretary.[93] Former employment: Barclays Bank as Deputy Head of Corporate Public Relations (1997-2000). Adviser to William Hague as Leader of the Opposition (2000-2001). Head of Communications at Granada (2001-2004).[94]
Previous position holder: Christopher Geidt, Private Secretary, 2007-2017	Attended elite prep and boarding schools, owns a 365-acre sheep farm, served in the Scots Guards and as army intelligence officer, undertook diplomatic roles for the Foreign and Commonwealth Office.[95] Married to daughter of Baron Neill of Bladen.[96]
Tom Laing-Baker, Assistant Private Secretary, 2018-	Former employment: Mergers and Acquisitions for KPMG. Member of the Great Britain Rifle Team.[97]
Matthew Magee, Assistant Private Secretary, 2017-	Promoted from Prince Edward's Private Secretary.[98] Former employment: PricewaterhouseCoopers, Accounting for International Development.[99]
Donal McCabe, Director of Royal Communications, 2019-	Former employment: Director of Corporate Communications at Ladbrokes Coral plc, senior communications positions at Landsec plc, Boots and Railtrack.[100]

Table 1.1 The Royal Household (Continued)

Household members	Description
Previous position holder:	
Sally Osman, Director of Royal Communications, 2014-2019	Former employment: Director of Corporate Communications for Sony, Director of Communications for BBC, Director of Press and PR for Channel 5, Director of Press and PR for British Sky Broadcasting.[101]
Julian Payne, Communications Secretary to Charles and Camilla, 2016-	Former employment: Vice President of PR and Corporate Relations for Burberry, Director of Communications for the BBC, Senior Publicist for Sky, partner at PR company Henry's House with clients such as Honda and the Beckhams.[102]
Christian Jones, Communications Secretary to William and Kate, 2019-	Former employment: Chief Press Officer to the Chancellor of the Exchequer, Press Secretary and Speechwriter to the Secretary of State at the Department for Exiting the European Union, Head of News at the Department for Exiting the European Union, Senior Policy Adviser at the Cabinet Office.[103]
Previous position holder:	
Jason Knauf, Communications Secretary to William and Kate, 2015-2019	Former employment: Director of Corporate Affairs for RBS, press officer at HM Treasury, Advisor to New Zealand's Prime Minister.[104] Left to become CEO of the Royal Foundation.[105]
Privy Purse	
Sir Michael Stevens, Keeper of the Privy Purse, 2018-	Former employment: KPMG.[106]
Previous position holder:	
Sir Alan Reid, Keeper of the Privy Purse, 2002-2017	Former senior partner with KPMG.[107]
Lord Chamberlain's Office	

Table 1.1   The Royal Household (Continued)

Household members	Description
Lieutenant-Colonel Michael Vernon, Comptroller, 2019-	Served with the Coldstream Guards in the British Army.[108]
Lieutenant-Colonel Sir Andrew Ford, Comptroller, 2006-2018	Trained at Sandhurst, served with the Grenadier Guards in the British Army.[109]
Master of the Household	
Vice-Admiral Anthony Johnstone-Burt, Master of the Household, 2013-	Member of the Royal Navy, served in Falklands.[110] Former Chief of Staff at NATO.[111]
Lieutenant-Colonel Charles Richards, Deputy Master of the Household, 1999-	Served in the British Armed Forces.
Royal Collection	
Sir Jonathan Marsden, Director, 2010-	Former curator for the National Trust.[112]

landowners and titled families seems to suggest accumulations of class privilege, and the significance of inherited wealth. There are also cross-institutional relationships: this 'revolving door' between networks is typical of elite institutions to preserve privilege and affluence.[113] As the sociologist Andrew Sayer writes, 'the plutocracy make use of a dense lattice of relationships between businesses, trade and professional organisations, think-tanks, lobbying firms, politicians, political party researchers and special advisers to politicians', which reproduces nepotism and profit.[114]

According to these data, the Royal Household has four key previous and/or future employers: corporations, military, broadcasters and the civil service. Sir Alan Reid, Sir Michael Stevens and Tom Laing-Baker all worked for the finance corporation KPMG, and the former Keeper of the Privy Purse Sir Michael Peat retained his KPMG partnership upon joining the Household in 1990,[115] demonstrating how elites employ experts from 'a handful of firms' that dominate the sector.[116] Corporate banks Barclays and RBS also feature. These affiliations seem to demonstrate 'old' money and 'new' money merging, as corporate businessmen appeal to the Firm's strategies.

The military recurs throughout Table 1.1, reflecting interlinked military and monarchy histories (see Chapter 5). The current Master of the Household (who is always from the Armed Forces), Anthony Johnstone-Burt, notes similarities between military values and Royal Household values, as both emphasise 'the pursuit of excellence, and … teamwork'.[117] They also share value systems to 'serve the Queen'. Equerries are Armed Forces officers, seconded as personal attendants to royals for three years. The Armed Forces continue to pay them, apparently costing the military around £500,000 annually.[118]

Finally, there are several connections to broadcasters, particularly in the Communications Office: Granada, Sony, BBC, Channel 5 and British Sky Broadcasting all feature. This could suggest that the Firm has access to broadcast institutions through interdependent relationships, and that the Firm's communications team have skills in packaging royal events for the news cycle.

Court culture in the Firm

As early modern courts were formed by aristocrats and noblemen as the centre of government and society,[119] the Firm's court remains populated by senior members with political, economic and social influence. Sally Osman and Jason Knauff were listed in the *Evening Standard*'s 'Progress 1000: London's most influential people 2017' in the category of 'Communicators: Media'.[120] Their inclusion alongside key media figures such as Paul Dacre, Editor-in-Chief of the UK's largest newspaper the *Daily Mail*, and BBC's political editor Laura Kuenssberg, seems to demonstrate the Royal Household's power in shaping British media culture. Osman was further awarded Communications Professional of the Year in 2018 by CorpComms magazine.[121]

The Royal Communications Office has undergone structural development in response to changing media landscapes. The Palace Press Secretary position was initially instituted in 1918 in response to growing tabloid print cultures.[122] Sally Osman said the change from Press Secretary to Communications Secretary was a purposeful decision: 'we are a communications office and we deal with all sorts of media'.[123] In 2014, the previously separate Communications Offices of each senior royal merged into one department in Buckingham Palace, headed by Osman.[124] This could suggest attempts to streamline and cohere royal public relations before Charles's succession; as Osman says 'we are all working in the interests of the institution'.[125]

The Sovereign's Private Secretary forms part of a 'golden triangle' of senior royal courtiers and civil servants, alongside the Cabinet Secretary and the Prime Minister's Private Secretary.[126] The Private Secretary communicates between the monarch and the government, arranges official correspondence, and organises the Queen's programme (including writing her speeches).[127] Although the holder of this office is officially a neutral liaison figure, the biographer Paul H. Emden suggested in 1934 that 'to prescribe the limits of his activities, to fix once and for all the sphere of his influence, is impossible', and little seems to have changed since.[128] Indeed, the historian David Cannadine asks, 'how far is the political history of the modern British crown, not so much the history of particular monarchs, but rather the history of successive private secretaries?'[129] Despite its importance, the position evolved organically and is unelected – indeed, many citizens seem unaware of its existence.[130]

Some roles are always filled by aristocrats, such as Ladies-in-Waiting.[131] According to reports, this position is not advertised and relies on personal contacts, and Ladies-in-Waiting are unpaid (aside from travel expenses) and work two-weeks-on-four-weeks-off.[132] With no pay, this is unpaid gendered domestic labour. The role seemingly functions as a mark of honour, and as an aristocratic classed dedication to reproducing royal power.[133] As an aside, these aristocratic–royal relationships are further preserved through god-parents for royal and/or aristocratic children. Many key aristocratic families, such as the Knatchbulls, descended from Prince Philip's uncle Louis Mountbatten,[134] and the van Cutsems, who own a 4,000-acre estate in Norfolk,[135] seem to be repeated as godparents or godchildren across multiple generations, which could indicate commitment to hereditary power and maintaining social networks. Aristocratic institutions and events – for example elite schools or exclusive sporting activities like hunting and polo – further nurture these relationships.[136]

Questions are raised about staff's investment in reproducing the Firm when they seem to experience poor wages and living conditions. Stephen Barry, Prince Charles's valet, said that many staff 'are natural royalists who work for the monarchy for the same romantic reasons I did', and this motivation pivots on moral economies of class subservience.[137] Even senior household members are paid less than in comparable corporate institutions, which could suggest that the networks, privileges and status the Royal Household affords are important across the employment divide. The workforce seems to be essentially bifurcated, with low- to middle-income 'domestic workers' doing the essential, daily, unglamorous work of maintaining the Firm, and then symbolically and politically important senior and honorary staff linked into broader British elites. Various levels of in/visibility permeate across these groups, from those honoured in prestigious, national 'most influential people' lists (although, the intricacies of their daily work remain unknown) to the silent, impersonal figures walking beside state carriages in ceremonial dress during state events.[138] The structure of royal staff appears anachronistic, yet it is maintained, and including royal staff in prestigious lists suggests that these forms of status have value amongst 'the elites'.

Are these staff best considered 'domestic workers' or 'service workers'? Many live in-house, and perform like domestic serv-ants in aristocratic households.[139] Alternatively, if we understand the monarchy as the Firm, staff are not just providing domestic support for a family but labouring within a corporation. This again illustrates the blurring of 'old' and 'new' wealth. In her study of luxury hotels, the sociologist Rachel Sherman notes that rather than the Marxist view of labour processes alienating the worker from themselves, in service work alienation occurs in every interaction.[140] That is, workers and guests (or, workers and royals) 'perform class in their appearance and demeanor ... [and] interactions', and in so doing '*normalise* class entitlements' so they are taken for granted.[141] Sherman calls this 'service theater', where class is 'performative but not necessarily inauthentic; rather, this 'acting' of class can feel genuine and natural'.[142] Of course, for the royals, class hierarchy is more powerful because it functions on inter/national levels, as we all enact the role of loyal subject. I am not suggesting that all staff accept their inferior position or even consider the royals superior. But in many published staff accounts (Paul Burrell, Brian Hoey, Stephen Barry, Dickie Arbiter), deference and class subservience structure their experiences. This is especially notable when the historian Florence Sutcliffe-Braithwaite argued that deference is declining following the postwar welfare-state ethos of equality, and neoliberalism's emphasis on individualisation.[143] The Firm does not appear to have fallen victim to this decline. I argue this is partly attributable to histories of sovereignty and divine right, which although not widely believed today, continue to impact our understandings of monarch(y) (see Chapters 2, 3 and 4). It is also partly attributable to symbolic power: representations and discourses in media and public culture celebrating the Firm as, for example, the embodiment of national identity (Chapter 3) or an idealised 'middle-class' family (Chapter 6), which circumvent questions of inequality.

In Chapter 2, I discuss how media representations of the royals actively bring the mystique of monarchy into being. Likewise, in enacting class subservience, I argue that royal staff are actively 'doing' class in every interaction, and reaffirming labourer/owner, servant/master binaries. All staff reproduce the Firm as a national institution, *and* reproduce corporate power across the 'revolving door' of the elites.[144] The connections described here between staff and other institutions begins to reveal the complex threads weaving together the Firm and other spheres. This is complicated further when considering how historical precedencies inform present economics.

The economics of the Firm

The feudal monarchy accumulated wealth through land: royal estates, feudal rights (feudal aids and reliefs from the tenant to the lord), rent ('landgable', 'hawgable' and the 'fee-farm'), and taxation.[145] The Crown *still* owns all British land, as the Land Registration Act 2002 states: 'The Crown is the only absolute owner of land ... [A]ll others hold an estate in land', with 'estate' meaning 'derive[d] from feudal forms of tenure'.[146] Indeed, the story of twenty-first-century royal wealth has distinct similarities to the eleventh century, and it remains embedded in 'old' forms of wealth and privilege. This section maps the Firm by exploring its economics: funding, wealth and value.

Funding

The British government has provided funds to the monarch since 1688.[147] A fixed payment seemed to give Parliament more control over expenditure, where previously it fluctuated with each monarch's whims. Between 1760 and 2011, this was the Civil List: an annual payment, rising with inflation, in return for the Crown Estate profits – a portfolio of land and property belonging to the Crown.[148] The last Civil List payment in March 2011 was £7.9 million.[149] This was supplemented by grants-in-aid, which funded official engagements, travel (including helicopter, chartered flights and the royal train) and property maintenance.[150] In 2015, royal travel cost £4 million.[151] Only the Queen claimed from the Civil List. The Dukes and Duchesses of Cornwall and Cambridge (and previously Sussex) use profits from the Duchy of Cornwall, and other members receive income from the Privy Purse.[152] The Privy Purse comprises surplus income from the Duchy of Lancaster, another portfolio of Crown land and property, which totalled £20 million in 2017 (the Duchy is valued at £534 million).[153] Funding was completed by the Queen's 'personal income' from her 'private' investment portfolio (including the Balmoral and Sandringham Estates).[154] As this book argues, the concept of 'personal wealth' is questionable considering the monarchy's history of extraction, enclosure and exploitation.

In October 2011, the Civil List and grants-in-aid were replaced with the Sovereign Grant (the Duchy of Cornwall, the Privy Purse and 'personal' funding remain).[155] This restructure seemed to be aimed at improving accountability: the annual payment is calculated from a percentage of the Crown Estate's net income, with the National Audit Office and Public Accounts Committee undertaking regular examinations.[156] However, as the anti-monarchy campaigners Republic argue, concerns arising from examinations are routinely dismissed by the government.[157] Furthermore, although the *Financial Times* used financial capitalist language to describe the Sovereign Grant as 'performance-related pay', the payment does not reflect actual profits or losses of the Crown Estate.[158] A House of Commons Research Paper stated that this was merely 'a means of arriving at a figure'.[159] This lack of accountability is reflected in payment increases. In 2011, the Firm received 15 per cent of the Crown Estate's net income surplus, but in 2017 the Royal Trustees (the Prime Minister, the Chancellor of the Exchequer and the Keeper of the Privy Purse) agreed to 25 per cent, plus an additional 10 per cent annually to fund the ten-year 'Reservicing of Buckingham Palace' project.[160] This amounted to £82.2 million in 2018–19,[161] up from £40 million in 2014–15.[162] As the royal commentator David McClure writes, paraphrasing the *Financial Times*, this bears 'a remarkable resemblance to the generous performance-related pay packages granted to business executives by their indulgent boards' (except that these do occasionally make the news).[163]

Since 1993, after the 1992 fire at Windsor Castle which seemed to prompt public concern about royal funding (see Introduction), the Firm has published annual finance reports purporting to encourage financial accountability.[164] However, figures appear to be obscured. For the Sovereign Grant increase described above, the 2017–18 report first highlighted a 'core' Sovereign Grant of £45.7 million, with the additions in the subsequent paragraph.[165] Likewise, the Queen's report includes only Sovereign Grant income, ignoring other operational costs 'cross-subsidis[ed]' by government departments.[166] The Department for Digital, Culture, Media and Sport funds ceremonials; the Foreign and Commonwealth Office funds state visits; the Ministry of Defence pays equerries' and orderlies' wages; the Home Office provides security and police support;[167] and the Queen's country estates receive European Union farming subsidies of over £1 million (Brexit could end this agreement).[168] Journalists also uncovered that the Firm attempted to claim funds to heat Buckingham Palace under an energy-saving scheme designed for low-income families.[169] A Sovereign Grant clause states that funding can never decrease even if Crown Estate profits do, but can increase when profits go up (especially pertinent given the austerity cuts to public institutions like the NHS), reflecting a more pervasive neoliberal practice which socialises losses and privatises profits.[170]

Discourses of accountability, then, seem merely to assuage public opinion around elite privilege,[171] and could reflect the corporate accounting of global companies like Amazon which 'manipulate results' to appeal to shareholders.[172] In 2018, Republic published 'Fat Cat Monarchy', a report claiming that the monarchy earned the equivalent of the average UK annual salary within the first 43 minutes of 1 January.[173] This played on 'Fat Cat Thursday', research by the Chartered Institute of Personnel and Development, which claimed that the chief executives of FTSE 100 companies earn the equivalent of the average UK annual salary by 4 January.[174] Here, Republic makes explicit connections between monarchy and corporate capital, and demonstrates how the monarchy surpasses this elite wealth.

Since 1910, the Crown seems to have been gradually exempt from a number of taxes, including annuities paid to the royals: Princess Margaret and the Queen Mother paid no tax on annuities and Princess Anne has 95 per cent exemption.[175] By law, the Crown is exempt from taxation, and the Sovereign Grant exempt from income tax.[176] In 1993, responding to the aforementioned public anger over royal spending, the Firm agreed to pay 'voluntary' income and capital gains tax on the Privy Purse and private investments (see Introduction), but only 'to the extent that the income is not used for official purposes'.[177] Prince Charles pays income tax on the Duchy of Cornwall to the same caveat,[178] but pays no corporation tax.[179] The Crown is also exempt from inheritance tax on 'sovereign to sovereign bequests'.[180] The Queen does pay council tax on her properties: £1.4 million in 2018.[181] Whilst corporations like Amazon move their headquarters to avoid paying tax in the countries where their wealth is accumulated, the Firm relies on 'extra-juridical' forms of precedence rooted in the (uncodified) British constitution and political custom to play the same game as corporations – stitching together historical customs with financial capitalist logic, and reminding us of the complexities and interdependency of these overlapping infrastructures.

Wealth

Estimations of the Firm's wealth differ substantially depending upon calculations. The *Sunday Times* Rich List estimated the 'personal net worth' of the Queen as £340 million,[182] news agency Reuters claims the monarchy has nominal assets of £22.8 billion,[183] and consultancy firm Brand Finance combined tangible and intangible asset values to suggest the monarchy 'brand' is worth £44 billion.[184] David McClure argues that these disparities are partly down to royal wills being sealed, probate details kept hidden, senior royals being exempt from Freedom of Information requests, and the tax exemption on sovereign-to-sovereign bequests, which makes accurate calculations impossible.[185] In 2021, the *Guardian* revealed that the monarchy had used the arcane parliamentary procedure of 'Queen's consent' to lobby the government to alter a draft law which would have revealed her private wealth, which could suggest concerted attempts by the monarchy to conceal royal worth.[186]

Discrepancies are also perhaps attributable to misunderstood differences between the Queen's 'personal investments' and property of the Crown. The Queen's 'personal investments' are assets legally hers to maintain, use or sell, including the Balmoral and Sandringham Estates, 'personal possessions' and 'personal investment portfolios'.[187] Properties of the Crown, meanwhile, are held in trust for the nation by the Sovereign, passing to the new Sovereign upon succession. These include the Crown Estate, the Duchy of Lancaster, Royal Collection artwork,[188] most palaces and castles, jewellery (including the Crown Jewels) and land. Because the Queen is not entitled to these profits, they are often omitted from 'official' calculations, although Republic argues that citizens lose profits accruing from them.[189]

The Crown Estate is a land and property portfolio belonging to the Crown, whilst the Duchy of Lancaster is owned by the sovereign as the Duke of Lancaster, and the Duchy of Cornwall by the Duke of Cornwall, currently Prince Charles (see Chapter 5 for the latter). The Crown Estate incorporates UK residential and commercial property, including (at the time of writing) London's Regent Street, some of St James's Park, some of Regent's Park, Kensington Palace Gardens, Eltham, Richmond, Egham and Hampton; three shopping centres; fourteen retail parks; much of the UK's seabed and foreshore including wind, wave and tidal power, marine aggregates and minerals, cables and pipelines; and 336,000 acres of agricultural land and forestry.[190] In 2018, it announced a capital value of £14.1 billion.[191] In 2021, reports suggested that energy companies such as BP had made huge bids for the Crown Estate's offshore windfarm plots, which could sell for up to £9 billion.[192] The Crown Estate is described as an 'independent commercial business', which suggests that it is separate from monarchy but run on its behalf.[193] However, as Andrew Duncan argues, much of its portfolio was 'stolen from the Church at the time of the Reformation' or conquered by historical monarchs.[194] In 2019, the *Guardian* revealed that over five years 113 Crown Estate tenants were evicted so the homes could be sold for profit, and over a hundred complaints from tenants (about leaks, faulty electrics etc.) were received in two years, prompting questions about the management's morality considering the Crown Estate is a custodian, not a commercial estate agent.[195] These misunderstood differences in ownership could demonstrate how the Firm's corporate interests are masked under historical precedence of inherited landownership.

Value

When laid bare, these figures are staggering. However, I argue that royal funding and/or wealth are offset in public discourse against notions of wider cultural, historical or economic royal 'value' to British society, and moral economies of social responsibility. Newspaper headlines such as 'Thank you Ma'am: Royals earn Britain nearly £2 billion a year',[196] 'The Queen costs her subjects 6op each a year'[197] and 'Monarchy attracts £500 million a year from overseas tourists'[198] use mathematics to appeal to capitalist logics of 'value' and exchange.[199] In the Introduction, I described this as 'keeping-while-giving'.[200] Likewise, the Firm's initiatives suggest the production and distribution of broader economic value, such as endorsing goods, practices or places. This is exemplified in three separate royal activities: Royal Warrants, the honours system, and royal visits and/or patronages.

Royal Warrants are awards given to traders providing goods or services to the Queen, Prince Philip (prior to his death in 2021) and/or Prince Charles.[201] Recipients can display a Royal Arms (each royal has a personalised Arms) on their product and premises, meant to function as a marker of value, authority and 'a commitment to the highest standards of service, quality and excellence'.[202] There are currently around eight hundred Warrant holders, and most are members of the Royal Warrants Association, which promotes networking.[203] The award seems to provide both symbolic and economic value, and Otnes and Maclaran liken it to celebrity endorsement, which benefits marketing strategy for the endorser and endorsee by 'transfer[ring] a celebrity's symbolic and aesthetic assets to the promoted brand'.[204] Concomitantly, I argue that the Warrant system provides value for the Firm. The Royal Warrant Holders Association liaises directly with the Royal Household, suggesting that the Firm has or could have access to a network of corporate contacts. In 2013, Buckingham Palace hosted the Coronation Festival, where two hundred Royal Warrant holders displayed their goods for sixty thousand visitors.[205] Additionally, the Arms functions as 'branding' for the Firm through its global display. This is a distribution of symbolic value which reinforces modalities of exchange, whereby the monarchy appears to be generating wealth. The Firm's achievements and profits from this are arguably masked behind notions of patronage and social responsibility.

The British honours system is the awarding of medals, decorations and/or titles to individuals to recognise achievement or service.[206] The system has an internal hierarchy with various 'classes' of honours awarded to individuals according to their achievements. Since 2005 the Honours Committee has operated within the Cabinet Office, with eight sub-committees composed of independent experts and senior civil servants (Arts and Media; Community, Voluntary and Local Services, Economy; Education; Health; Parliamentary and Political Service; Science and Technology; Sport; and State).[207] The system has an imperial history, and the language of Empire remains in its titles: OBE stands for 'Officer of the Most Excellent Order of the British Empire'. In 2004, a Public Administration Committee condemned the honours system as 'anachronistic, dominated by secrecy, riddled with class prejudice and biased against ethnic minorities and women', and recommended altering the names to remove imperialist connotations, for example, 'Officer of the Order of British Excellence'.[208] The then Labour government rejected all of the recommendations.[209] This could be in part, as the historian Tobias Harper suggests, because it encourages public loyalty.[210] That is, recipients could 'buy into … a formal social hierarchy', consenting to monarchy because they felt included in an elite social system.[211] Like the Royal Warrants, the honours system also seems to give the Firm a network of elite contacts. The Order of the Merit – described as 'the story of our country over the last 100 years' – has only twenty-four holders at once and the Queen hosts a gathering every five years.[212] As of 2020, current recipients range from the inventor (and key Brexiteer) Sir James Dyson, the former Australian Prime Minister John Howard, the broadcaster Sir David Attenborough and Sir Tim Berners-Lee, who invented the World Wide Web.[213] Whilst the honours system is presented as 'gift giving', with the Firm bestowing status and privilege on those deemed 'deserving' (we may also question the logics of 'deserving'), it also benefits the monarchy, both by (re)producing loyalty and by creating networks of contacts. It is another form of 'keeping-while-giving'.[214]

Finally, royal visits and patronages provide value for particular places and organisations. Constituting the bulk of royal 'duties', in 2019 the fifteen 'working' royals undertook 3,567 official engagements.[215] Visits are organised by a team of staff, and royal figures visit civic, commercial or charitable sites, open buildings, undertake themed activities (for example, cheese tasting at a cheese factory), chat with members of the public chosen to be presented to them and do a 'walkabout' on local streets to greet the general public.[216] Protocol dictates that royals are met on arrival by local dignitaries, including the Mayor and the Chief Constable.[217] This draws on 'old' forms of social hierarchy, where royals are greeted by those with 'status' according to traditional precedence. Although visits enact values of royal 'access' and intimacy, security is tightly managed: road traffic is rerouted, admission to buildings that the royal is visiting is prohibited, and crush barriers along the street regulate public viewing.[218] Only those invited to meet the royals are given access and – like the honours system – this seems to be only those deemed 'worthy'. Meeting royalty is the reward for an achievement. This imbues monarchy with a symbolic sense of value: it is so special it is accessible only to those important enough.

Royal patronages are when royals become associated with chosen charities, military associations, professional bodies or public service groups. The official royal website lists over three thousand patronages across the 'working' royals.[219] Various foundations organise these patronages. In 2009, the Royal Foundation was launched to manage William's and Harry's charitable initiatives.[220] Kate Middleton and Meghan Markle were later absorbed, before Harry and Meghan launched their own foundation, Sussex Royal (this has since been closed following their resignation). The Foundations typically theme their programmes: as of 2020, the Royal Foundation focuses on mental health, early years, wildlife conservation and emergency responders.[221]

These visits and patronages function as symbolic markers of value for the place or organisation, connoting worthiness and attracting public interest. They are also markers of value for the Firm. The monarchy appears to 'donate' time to a cause, and, as Andrew Sayer writes, philanthropy can legitimise elite wealth because it is '*symbolic capital* in the form of a legacy that evokes admiration'.[222] In fact, the sociologists Jessica Sklair and Luna Glucksberg argue that philanthropy is particularly used by elite family firms as a way to associate themselves with discourses of social responsibility akin to their values of kinship.[223] Many royal visits are commemorated with a plaque: a physical marker of legacy for the Firm. These visits and patronages could be considered as strategic forms of self-presentation.[224] Locations and organisations are organised systematically for regularity and fairness, and are typically matched with individual royals' represented 'interests' in order to maximise audiences (for example, Prince Harry has many military patronages, see Chapter 5).[225] Key journalists are invited to cover the events (according to the Royal Rota, see Chapter 2), and their travel, accommodation and itinerary are organised by Buckingham Palace, with the aim of generating coverage from key media outlets.[226] Royal events are quantified: all royal engagements are recorded in the *Court Circular*, and these are then calculated annually by the royal fan Tim O'Donovan and published in *The Times*.[227] This suggests the reproduction of royal popularity around the globe through strategic and calculated activity.

In these events and patronages, who is 'keeping' and who is 'giving'? The charity campaigner Giving Evidence found that royal patronages have little effect on the charity's work: 74 per cent of charities with royal patrons received no visits from their patron in 2019, and Giving Evidence found no evidence that a royal patron increased a charity's revenue, or increased the public's likelihood to donate.[228] Although these initiatives arguably suggest the production and distribution of value which offsets the 'cost' of monarchy, this is not exchange among equals at all. Rather, as the anthropologist David Graeber argues of broader economic histories, while economic relations are embedded in ideologies of morality – for instance, debt repayment as a moral imperative – in fact moral relations of inequality are ordered hierarchically.[229] Indeed, as this chapter argues, the legal bases for monarchical privileges are based on past actions informing present propriety, whilst emotional investments in the royal *family* – across public and media cultures – offset monarchy's cost. The monarchy undertakes 'keeping-while-giving'.[230] The sociologist Beverley Skeggs suggests that 'ideas such as equivalence and propriety inform the mechanisms of valuation such as calculation and are performative; that is they enable particular processes of valuation, such as judgment, evaluation and expectations, to come into effect and occlude others'.[231] Notions of value seem to allow the monarchy to *perform* and hence *embody* a sense of worth(iness). Skeggs also reminds us that ideas of value are difficult to evaluate because they are symbolic.[232] Vague ideas of being 'good value' allows the monarchy to make claims about its contributions. The ongoing debate about royal tourism is one example. Republic has repeatedly rejected claims that the monarchy attracts millions of pounds in overseas visitors, arguing that the attractions that tourists enjoy (palaces, castles) will still exist even if monarchy is gone.[233] Yet, the claim that 'the monarchy is good for tourism' continues in public and media discourse, becoming what Stuart Hall would call a form of 'common sense'.[234] I argue the intangibility of value works in the Firm's favour here as a form of producing consent.

Symbolic moral codes act as the 'frontstage' of monarchy, while 'backstage' consists of historical precedence and contemporary enterprise, woven tightly together. Again, we see how the Firm connects with other spheres in contemporary Britain. We can now peel back another layer by accounting for longer, global histories.

The global Firm

Contemporary financial capitalism is transnational.[235] Marxist work describes capitalism's (historical and present) dependency on exploitation, extraction, conquest, displacement and slavery.[236] The Firm has always been global: corporations undertook colonisation projects across the British Empire, run on behalf of the British state and the monarch.[237] The East India Company was granted a Royal Charter in 1600, and used its private army to rule and establish monopolies over global trade.[238] The British Empire implemented violent regimes of genocide, famine, enslavement, indentured labour, imprisonment and torture.[239] The Company of

Royal Adventurers Trading to Africa, of which the Duke of York was the governor, was given royal monopoly to trade in the mid-1600s.[240] It transported over three thousand Africans to Barbados, many with the initials 'DY' burned into their chests to signify their belonging to the Duke of York.[241] The Firm seems to continue to use, and extract value from, goods stolen during colonisation, such as the Koh-i-Noor diamond from India used in the Crown Jewels.[242] Hence I argue it continues to benefit from 'old' forms of wealth vested in extraction and exploitation.

As the historian Nicholas B. Dirks contends, today Empire has transformed into global, corporate forms of power using international banking systems to achieve domination under so-called free trade.[243] Post-Second World War decolonisation saw the formation of international institutions such as the World Bank, the International Money Fund and the World Economic Forum: global elites representing the interests of major international, cross-border corporations.[244] These shifts map on to the Firm's development since the 1953 coronation. Analysing the Firm's global interests – the Commonwealth and British Empire, the Queen's sovereignty in other realms, and its role in international trade, commerce and sponsorship – reveals how the Firm reshapes itself in response to changes in capital and global governance, moving from the household to the globe.

The Commonwealth and the British Empire

The Commonwealth is a transnational organisation of fifty-two 'independent and equal' member states headed by the Queen, promoting principles of peace and security, human rights, tolerance and access to health, education, food and shelter through the Commonwealth Charter.[245] These 'shared values' have been contentious. The historian Philip Murphy describes the Charter as 'so poorly drafted that it leaves the nature of [the nations'] commitment [to particular values] completely unclear'.[246] This is illustrated in some member states' apparently poor human rights records, such as criminalising homosexuality despite the Charter's 'discrimination clause'.[247] The Commonwealth also has imperial origins. Many of the fifty-two member states are former colonies of the British Empire, and Murphy describes the 'haphazard' way '"Imperial" became "Commonwealth"'.[248]

David Cannadine notes that the British Empire was royal.[249] It was unified by representations of the British sovereign – Queen Victoria as the Empress of India, for example – and numerous everyday references to royalty, such as coins, stamps, rituals and place names. In 1949, the Commonwealth was formally constituted for former colonies to give 'constitutional and symbolic expression to their independence'.[250] This remains invested in the British monarchy. The Australian Studies scholar Holly Randell-Moon argues that 'the secular autonomy of settler states is buttressed by Crown sovereignty' with regular royal visits to promote ties.[251] At one occasion in 1947, the then Princess Elizabeth visited South Africa and declared she would devote her life to 'the service of our great imperial family to which we all belong'.[252] Randell-Moon argues that, when royals are treated like celebrity visitors, histories of colonialism are transformed into 'a shared endorsement of the divinity of Crown presence'.[253] If, as I argued above, royal visits (re)inscribe royal popularity through strategic activity, this has particular importance in producing consent for the monarchy in Commonwealth countries.

As Head of the Commonwealth, the Queen is supported by intergovernmental agency the Commonwealth Secretariat, and biennial Commonwealth Heads of Government Meetings.[254] There are hundreds of Commonwealth-wide non-governmental organisations, such as the Royal Commonwealth Society (a charity supporting Commonwealth citizens), CPU Media Trust (promoting ethical and free media) and the Commonwealth Forestry Association (encouraging sustainability).[255] Perhaps most notable for this book is the Commonwealth Enterprise and Investment Council (CWEIC), an organisation promoting intra-Commonwealth trade and investment between government and private sectors.[256] Although its remit focuses on small businesses, the multinational corporations Tesco and Rolls Royce attended the 2017 CWEIC first trade ministers' meeting.[257] Although it is not a trading bloc, the Commonwealth Secretary-General said that trade 'is the lifeblood of the Commonwealth', and in 2013 intra-Commonwealth trade was calculated at $592 billion.[258] Despite claims of equality, intra-Commonwealth trade arguably relies on an imperialist framework: 57 per cent of imports to developed countries were sourced from developing countries.[259] This seems to further demonstrate systems of Commonwealth hierarchy.

The Firm's association with Commonwealth and Empire raises key issues of British citizenship, national identity and migration. During the British Empire, all newly acquired colonies assumed the status of 'Subject of the British Crown'.[260] Thus, in theory, UK citizen status belonged to anyone able to travel.[261] Upon establishment of the Commonwealth, the Nationality Act 1948 distinguished between 'Citizens of the UK and Colonies', 'British Subjects without Citizenship' and 'Citizens of Commonwealth Countries'.[262] The Nationality Act 1981 has since replaced this, but these histories demonstrate how notions of national belonging and migration have emerged directly from racialised, gendered and classed histories of colonialism.[263] The use of 'Subject' in these histories means they are inseparable from British monarchy. Not until 1983 did British passports alter from 'British Subject: Citizen of UK and Colonies' to 'British Citizen',[264] and the category of 'British Subject' still refers to those who were considered 'British Subjects without Citizenship' *before* the Nationality Act 1981 and who are not considered citizens of any other country.[265] This means that some individuals living in ex-colonies still have their official immigration status defined by a foreign monarch(y), which I argue continues histories of colonial oppression.

The Firm's power seems to be interwoven, then, with complex historical and legal formations of belonging, borders and dominion. Commonwealth symbolism, connected to histories of Empire, acts as a form of expansionism whereby the Firm's power is extended through imaginaries of global dominance. This is also articulated through notions of 'the family'. As Princess Elizabeth gestured towards in 1947, collective belonging to an international family was key to British imperial ideology.[266] The current Queen may not be 'grandmother of Empire' like Victoria, but elements of familalism remain: the Queen's Christmas speech is broadcast across the Commonwealth, for example. This hierarchical relationship to monarchy is even more complex in countries where the Queen remains sovereign.

Sovereignty in other realms

Whilst the London Declaration 1949 permitted Commonwealth countries – as 'free and equal members' – to adopt republicanism, sixteen remain constitutional monarchies with Elizabeth II as a legally distinct Head of State.[267] These include Caribbean islands like Barbados, African states such as Ghana, and Canada and Australia.[268] Canada was unified in 1867 and Australia in 1901, when each developed independent constitutions as self-governing dominions, while vesting 'executive power' in the British Crown.[269] The Royal Style and Titles Act 1972 permitted the Queen's realms to erase UK references in her overseas titles to highlight their independence, thus making her, for example, 'Elizabeth the Second, by the Grace of God Queen of Australia and Her Other Realms and Territories, Head of the Commonwealth'.[270] Since 1842, each country has nominated a local governor-general as the Queen's representative, with the power to propose legislation, (dis)prove bills and dissolve parliament.[271] Although the Queen has no 'direct' political control in these realms, governor-generals could be interpreted as ongoing monarchical administrative power. Likewise, as the sociologist Ty Salandy argues, the British Empire was partly established by 'the violence of "knowledge" ... spreading a narrow and ideological system of values, culture and information' to form a 'global model of civilization'.[272] Adopting 'God Save the Queen/King' as the national or royal anthem, for example (still used in Australia, Jamaica, Grenada, Saint Lucia, Tuvalu and Barbados, amongst others), could instil British values and subservience to colonial authority.

Discussions around dominion status are ongoing, seemingly with various degrees of public consent. Although 1999 saw enough popular disapproval of monarchy in Australia to trigger a referendum on republicanism, 54 per cent of citizens voted to keep monarchy.[273] Since then, despite enduring republican sentiment, most famously from the Australian Prime Minister Malcolm Turnbull (2015–2018), republicanism has waned.[274] Meanwhile, Canada has had no mainstream republican debates, and public understanding of the role of monarchy in Canada seems to remain minimal.[275] The Firm has played these relations carefully. There have been attempts to use the term 'Sovereign' for the Queen as opposed to 'Head of State', and to depersonalise the role by emphasising the Crown as a symbol rather than individual monarchs, which as Philip Murphy argues allows the Realms to act as 'Crowned Republics'.[276]

Shore and Williams suggest that the Crown's presence in global realms is built upon balancing visibility and invisibility, where despite intense prominence it usually goes unnoticed because people tend not to understand its role.[277] If I argue throughout *Running the Family Firm* that media representations produce consent for the monarchy in Britain, this works on a global scale in the Commonwealth and other sovereign realms. And, as in Britain, this means that the Firm's functions and infrastructures are not addressed in global public and media cultures. One issue that media representations mask, for example, is the Firm's connections to global trade, commerce and sponsorship. I argue that these are built on imperial dominance *and* draw on neoliberal models of global enterprise.

International trade, commerce and sponsorship

Alongside Commonwealth trade, the Firm seems to have other interests in international trade and commerce. There have, for instance, arguably been multiple cases where royals use their connections for personal commercial gain. The Queen's grandson Peter Phillips founded the Patron's Fund charity to arrange her ninetieth birthday celebrations in 2016, but then apparently gave the contract for staging the event to his own for-profit company, SEL UK Limited.[278] Companies House accounts revealed that SEL UK received a £750,000 fee.[279] In 2020, a Chinese television advertisement featured Peter Phillips promoting Jersey Milk to audiences using royal iconography, such as a country estate and a state carriage.[280] His sister, Zara Phillips, has multiple commercial promotional details for the luxury watch brand Rolex, horse auction house Magic Millions, outdoor clothing brand Musto, iCandy prams and a personalised jewellery collection for Calleija.[281] Monarchy's symbol is used to sell commercial products and generate profit. I explore this further in the Postscript, with Harry and Meghan's resignation from royal duties and their attempts to trademark the brand 'Sussex Royal', which was allegedly prohibited by the Firm.[282] As I argue, this is contradictory considering the other deals described above.

The Firm has multiple connections to multinational conglomerates through sponsorship for its charitable initiatives. Heads Together, the mental health charity headed by William and Kate, has four corporate partners: the retail bank Virgin Money, telecommunications company Dixons Carphone, consumer goods company Unilever, and investment management corporation BlackRock.[283] As the sociologist Imogen Tyler writes, this means that Heads Together is sponsored by corporations who benefit from the neoliberal economics 'that are eroding state welfare and social care, and in doing so are exacerbating mental distress' among citizens.[284] The Prince's Trust regional awards are sponsored by a range of corporate actors, including banks HSBC, Royal Bank of Scotland, Ulster and Natwest, technology company Dell, Delta Air Lines, supermarket Tesco, security service G4S and arms dealer BAE Systems.[285] The Duke of Edinburgh Award Scheme is supported by partners including the bank Lloyds Banking Group, travel company Stagecoach Group plc, legal firm Legal and General, car manufacturer Aston Martin Lagonda Ltd and energy provider British Gas.[286] These connections could demonstrate that royal–corporate partnerships are not anomalies but rather strategically sought, providing philanthropic opportunities for both businesses and monarchy, offering the Firm a network of loyal corporate contacts, and demonstrating the blurring of 'old' and 'new' forms of capital accumulation.

Business and trade values are emphasised in some royal charities, particularly those supporting young people. The Queen's Young Leader Award rewards 'exceptional' young people across the Commonwealth with a 'mentoring and networking package';[287] the Prince's Trust 'Youth Can Do It' campaign helps young people gain employment skills;[288] the Duke of Edinburgh Award scheme encourages young people to undertake self-improvement exercises;[289] and Prince Andrew's 'Pitch@Palace' initiative gives young technology entrepreneurs opportunities to pitch to investors.[290] The sociologists Eva Bendix Petersen and Gabrielle O'Flynn argue that the Duke of Edinburgh Award promotes responsibilisation, encouraging young people to align with neoliberal ideology.[291] In fact, all of these royal initiatives emphasise neoliberal enterprise and self-management for young people as vehicles for social mobility. As the media scholars Anita Biressi and Heather Nunn have argued, this obscures material experiences of inequality that limit the opportunities available to young people.[292] The conflation of neoliberal entrepreneurial logic with royal initiatives again demonstrates the merging of 'old' and 'new' wealth, and enterprise and heritage cultures, whereby monarchy gives the schemes and its participants a form of status.[293]

Royal symbolism as status also seems to have been wielded by the UK government. Prince Andrew 'worked' for ten years in the Department for Business, Innovation and Skills as the United Kingdom's Special Representative for International Trade and Investment, promoting the UK at international trade fairs and conferences. This ended in 2011, after reports surfaced about his connections with corrupt Middle Eastern regimes and his personal profiting from trade deals.[294] For instance, he allegedly exploited his personal relationship with the Kazakh oligarch Kenges Rakishev to broker a £885 million deal between a Greek and Swiss consortium and the Kazakhstan government, for which he apparently received £4 million commission.[295] In 2007, he purportedly sold his country estate Sunninghill Park in Berkshire to the Kazakh oligarch Timur Kulibayev for £3 million above the asking price, and in 2011 he allegedly tried to arrange for the British wealth manager Coutts to accept Kulibayev as a client.[296] The former Foreign Office Minister Chris Bryant claimed that 'it was very difficult to see in whose interests [Andrew] was acting'.[297]

The Firm also seems to have questionable connections with British arms trader BAE Systems. In 2016, Charles's tenth visit to Saudi Arabia at the Foreign Office's request, where he danced with members of the House of Saud regime, apparently coincided with the sale of 72 BAE Typhoon fighter jets to the dictatorship.[298] The South African MP Andrew Feinstein has further claimed that the Firm was key to persuading South Africa to buy BAE Hawk jets.[299] The spokesman for the Campaign Against the Arms Trade, Andrew Smith, said 'it is clear that Prince Charles has been used by the UK government and BAE Systems as an arms dealer'.[300] These examples seem to demonstrate how the government–monarchy relationship is used to further trade investments. I argue that the royal figures act as symbols of capital and status, wielded in the pursuit of profit. Due to the royals' nationalist symbolism, and the classed respectability associated with them, they could be used as forms of morality to shield against accusations of crony capitalism or abuse of political privileges.

The Firm is not just an important national institution. Rather, the international relevancy of the Firm indicates its potential global political-ideological significance in terms of reproducing inequalities: normalising elite wealth and shoring up racial capitalist structures and (neo)colonial exploitation both economically (goods stolen during Empire) and culturally (patronage visits to Commonwealth nations). The Queen no longer oversees 'the Empire on which the sun never sets', but the shift to global, multinational conglomerates seems to suggest that the Firm is able to adapt and maintain its international influence. The British monarch's presence as sovereign in other realms, in particular, deserves further research to understand how this could be underpinned by neocolonial ideologies, but also how this relies on capital and commercial interests. What global commercial investments does the Firm have? How are members of the Firm represented internationally? A project using the framework of *Running the Family Firm* but on a global scale would be useful future research.

Conclusion

This chapter aimed to expose the infrastructures of the Firm – the version of monarchy not usually visible. I have attempted to unravel a complex and multi-layered tapestry, ranging from the daily operations and financing of royal households to the global connections that maintain economic and symbolic privilege. We have seen the exploitation of low-paid workers through ideologies of class subservience; the 'revolving door' between the Royal Household and corporations, the military, broadcasters and the civil service; the murky rules of royal financing; the secrecy of royal wealth; the networks of contacts; the relationships to post/colonialism; the exploitation of political relationships for profit; and the abuse of political privileges. This picture is complicated further because the legal bases for monarchical privileges seem to be based in historical precedence, many of which apparently have no discernible logics. These privileges then appear to be reworked in a corporate image. The example of the Paradise Papers in the Introduction precisely encapsulates this: I argued that the Firm's tax exemptions vested in historical privilege allow it to act similarly to contemporary corporations, evading accountability. This is not suggesting that connections between monarchy and capital are new. Rather, the Firm continually adapts to various periods of capitalism, and various 'types' of ('old' and 'new') wealth work together; stitched through the constitutional fabric of Britain. From capitalists, rentiers, aristocrats, the famous, the titled, the idle rich, these are all entangled together, shoring up a highly stratified classed infrastructure.

The Firm seems to evade accountability by preserving symbolic and moral codes. If corporations are organised around (im)moral logics of exchange, where they seem to be contributing to society,[301] the Firm achieves this through (im/material) ideas of patronage, philanthropy, heritage, stability and nationalism. This chapter discussed this through the lens of the Family Firm: a particular ideology of 'middle-class' family values as performed by Queen Victoria. These representations obscure capitalist relations behind mediated royal spectacle, emotional investments in 'the family' and notions of social responsibility and value. In subsequent chapters, I outline what form these representations take, and what they might be obscuring. Before this, the next chapter outlines how these battles are waged in, and through, media culture.

2

'The greatest show on earth': Monarchy and media power

I have to be seen to be believed. – Queen Elizabeth II, circa 2015[1]

We princes ... are set on stages in the sight and view of all the world. – Queen Elizabeth I, 1586[2]

Four hundred years apart, Elizabeth I and Elizabeth II articulate the importance of visibility and performance to the monarch(y). As *Running the Family Firm* argues, for monarchy's power to be reproduced, monarchy must be represented. Elizabeth I's statement about 'princes' on 'stages' reflects this book's framing of monarchy as theatre. Theatrics feature more literally in histories of the early-modern royal court, where the monarch's daily schedule was a hyper-visible performance of ceremonial and sovereign power, from waking, dressing, dining and worshipping.[3] Elsewhere, court masques with allegorical plots would glorify the monarch to reproduce their sovereignty (see Chapter 3).[4]

The royal image has always been mediated, and royal history is a history of representations in different forms. The monarch's profile has been depicted on banknotes, stamps and coins for hundreds of years.[5] The historian Kevin Sharpe argued that 'Tudor authority was constructed and enhanced' through portraits, artefacts and courtly performances, whilst Peter Burke analysed how France's Louis XIV was 'fabricated' through portraits, bronzes, plays and court rituals.[6] More recently, Queen Victoria's reign was mediated by newspapers and early film technology, and interwar monarchs used radio to speak directly to the nation.[7] The historian Edward Owens mapped the relationship between monarchy, mass media and the British public in the early to mid-twentieth century.[8] He argues that monarchs in the twentieth century used photographic portraits which were mass produced as souvenirs, and official and unofficial biographies gave readers behind-the-scenes glimpses at royal life.[9] The case studies in *Running the Family Firm* illustrate varying, expanding forms of mediation: portraits, photographs, physical and material space, newspapers, magazines, television, films and social media, amongst others.

One particular point of interest about the quotations from the two Queen Elizabeths is that both presided over periods of rapid change in media cultures, shifting how monarchy engaged with the citizenry. For Elizabeth I, the emergence of a market society and new consumer cultures in the late sixteenth century created what scholars have identified as a 'public sphere'.[10] Readers consumed royal news like never before, sharing information using new print cultures. As Sharpe suggests, these changes brought both challenges and opportunities.[11] It gave greater scope for distributing the royal image, but also made the reproduction and mis/uses of this image harder to contain.

Elizabeth II has reigned (1952 to present) over even more rapid technological expansion and socio-political change. From the emergence of television, through tabloid newspapers and paparazzi, to social media and citizen journalism (processes related to democratisation), the Firm has consistently faced new challenges in public engagement with monarchy. Due to expanding media forms, we now have more access to monarchy than ever before. I am interested here in the effects of this access. What differences do particular media forms make to the (re)production of monarchy? And what challenges might these new media forms pose to royal representation? Whilst some scholars have explored the media monarchy historically[12] and contemporarily,[13] this chapter is the first detailed analysis of the media monarchy for Elizabeth II's reign, which coincides with seismic technological shifts in the media apparatus from broadcasting to social media.

Debates about the place of monarchy in a contemporary mediated society are given context within wider histories of sovereign power. The philosopher Michel Foucault argues that in the Middle Ages 'the king was the central character in the entire Western juridical edifice' and sovereign power functioned through 'great state apparatus'.[14] The sovereign controlled the army and police, the law was understood to represent the sovereign's will and the sovereign had the right to take life as punishment.[15] This shifted after the English Civil War in 1642–1651 between Parliamentarians and Royalists, and the Glorious Revolution in 1688 where James II was overthrown and the Bill of Rights abolished the monarch's absolute power.[16] Foucault argues that, in the seventeenth and eighteenth centuries, sovereign power as it was known was replaced by 'hierarchical observation [and] normalising judgment', where power was exercised through 'social production and social service'.[17] Productive, disciplinary forms of power circulate through society. This relies, in part, upon theatre and spectacle to engage and inspire the citizenry, and produce consent.[18]

But what does it mean to negotiate with sovereign power – a monarchy – at the level of social media? Monarchy still relies on a form of invisibility, a form of divine right (although not identical to Middle Ages monarchs), and being above or beyond 'ordinary life'. As Chapter 1 demonstrated, the Firm cannot be *too* visible to public scrutiny, or it loses its mystique and its complex infrastructures are unmasked. Therefore, visibility must be tightly stage-managed, and balanced with a paradoxical but co-dependent *in*visibility. Or, as Bagehot famously wrote, 'we must not let in daylight upon magic'.[19] How does this play out when live television offers audiences an opportunity to engage, in real time and across time and space, with royal ceremony? How does this play out when social media offers direct, public contact with the Firm (or at least with its social media team), such as royal Instagram accounts that abound on the same platform as their subjects'?

We have seen rapid technological and socio-political advancements from the Queen's 1953 coronation to today, that have (perhaps permanently) altered how the monarchy and the public engage with one another. In 1953, for the first time, the coronation was produced as live televisual spectacle. These new mediated intimacies posed significant challenges for coronation organisers in terms of how much access to allow audiences. As the *Observer* commented on 7 June 1953, 'the Coronation must not only be the greatest show on earth but it must also be done with taste'.[20] The debate over this offers us a moment where the labour of royal representations was made unusually visible as they navigated new terrain. Changes in modes of production allow us to see how the monarchy can be understood *as* mediated and *as* an event.

It is not only the coronation that is 'the greatest show on earth but … must also be done with taste'. This dilemma haunts royal representations throughout Elizabeth II's reign, as new mediated forms are subject to judgements over access, intimacy and 'taste'. The chapter goes on to explore key moments in the media–monarchy relationship since 1953, including forays into reality television, engagements with celebrity cultures, and social media (Instagram, Facebook, YouTube, Twitter), which all facilitate audience participation. This is not an exhaustive account: other case studies would illustrate similar arguments, or develop them further. My examples illustrate how various modes of production affect how the Firm engages with its publics over time, how intimacy/distance and visibility/invisibility are carefully managed, and the consequences of this balance being fractured.

Staging the coronation as televisual spectacle

Television was a relatively new media form in 1953. Whilst some television existed before the Second World War, the BBC was suspended during wartime before relaunching in 1946. By March 1952 there were 1.45 million UK television licence holders.[21] It was two further years before commercial television – ITV – was established, and the Television Advisory Committee Report in 1953 prompted debate about the impact of commercialisation on British viewers.[22] These debates were concerned with television's perceived 'low-brow' qualities, due to derogatory meanings associated with the term 'popular'. The cultural theorist Raymond Williams notes that one connotation of 'popular' was (and, sometimes, still is) 'inferior kinds of work', where television was seen as '"bad taste"'.[23] The media scholar Helen Wood describes how television was perceived as 'feminised' (and therefore inferior) due to its domesticity, and its initial targeting of the housewife through household management advertisements.[24]

It is unsurprising, then, that, upon commencing coronation preparation, television immediately became contentious. The then Prime Minister Winston Churchill argued that 'modern mechanical arrangements' should be banned from the coronation, and 'religious and spiritual aspects should [not] be presented as if it were a theatrical performance'.[25] This statement suggests that the coronation has a purity of performance that should not be tainted by television as a 'low-brow' cultural technology. In so doing, it misunderstands royal spectacle as a form of power, whereby monarchy *is* performance and representation. Churchill established a narrative that would define commentary of the coronation: the 'risks' of new television technologies in relation to the magic of monarchy.

Initially, cameras were going to be permitted to film the exterior coronation procession but banned from Westminster Abbey's interior.[26] In response, the *Daily Express* and the BBC lobbied for live coverage by subverting Churchill's language and claiming that it would invest monarchy with 'a new kind of legitimacy' if the public felt a sense of proximity and intimacy.[27] After intense pressure, coronation organisers acquiesced to television footage, but debates continued over the precise details. Churchill declared on 10 October

1952 that close-up shots would give too much access, but an archived report from the Coronation Executive Committee (one of the groups responsible for organisation) bears scribbled pencil marks deleting the line 'it is agreed that there should be no "close-up" shots in the television programme'.[28] Eventually, the BBC and organisers compromised: no so-called 'Peeping Tom' close-ups, but a zoom lens could capture 'very special shots', such as four-year-old Prince Charles watching the ceremony.[29]

Camera positions in Westminster Abbey were precisely staged. Five cameras were in restricted positions with the camera operators boxed in cubicles to disguise their work, demonstrating adherence to keeping 'modern mechanical arrangements' away from areas of religious importance.[30] A ban remained on shots of religiously significant parts of the ceremony – the anointing, the communion service and anyone kneeling in worship – and symbolic shots of the Abbey's architectural features were broadcast during these times.[31] On the procession route, 21 cameras were positioned at five different sites; and eleven different commentary positions catered for a hundred commentators from around the Commonwealth and the world.[32]

The sheer scale of the coronation makes it a watershed moment in the history of television as a medium. Simultaneously it was the first royal event broadcast live; was the largest production undertaken by the BBC;[33] saw UK TV licence holders increase in number from 1.45 million in March 1952 to 3.25 million in 1954;[34] was the first time TV audiences (56 per cent of people) overtook radio audiences (32 per cent);[35] and was the first outside, live, multiple-language broadcast transmitted internationally within hours of its occurrence.[36] The historian Roy Strong estimated the total cost of the coronation to be around £912,000 (over £25 million in 2020), and the BBC alone spent £40,000 (£1.1 million in 2020) to deal with the broadcasting complexities of its largest ever production when it was still learning how to stage outside broadcasts.[37] Its unprecedented scale is demonstrated in the lack of facilities: circuit capacities could not handle so large an audience, so the BBC borrowed 1,300 circuits from the General Post Office, while three new television transmitters in the UK provided coverage to Pontop Pike, Glencairn and Truleigh Hill, which were previously uncovered.[38] In a perfect, ironic manifestation of the mediated spectacle of monarchy, horse-drawn carriages were loaned from an Elstree film studio.[39]

Coronation-themed televisual broadcasts began in the months before the event. In keeping with Reithian values of public service broadcasting – to inform, educate and entertain, after John Reith, first director-general of the BBC – educational programmes taught viewers about key coronation iconography, from Westminster Abbey's history to the origin of 'God Save the Queen'.[40] The event's international significance – across the Commonwealth in particular – was highlighted with concerts by Pakistani and Canadian bands, and variety programmes such as *The Commonwealth Gala*.[41] Television transmission on coronation day began at the earlier-than-usual time of 10.15am and included the procession, the ceremony, speeches from Churchill and the Queen and the Westminster firework display, before concluding at 10.20pm.[42] To respond to international demand to view the coronation, telefilm recording was flown across the Atlantic by the RAF and edited in-flight to air on NBC and ABC in the United States, and CBS in Canada on the same day, which cost each institution around $1 million.[43] This was what the theorists Daniel Dayan and Elihu Katz have identified as a 'media event', staged as a large, historical occasion and transmitted live to inter/national audiences.[44] Televising an event does not just re-mediate what already exists, rather 'the nature of public ritual itself … fundementally change[s]' because people's engagements alter.[45]

For the coronation, people's engagement altered because of the particular promise of intimacy that television promoted. Located in the home, television is bound to the politics of domesticity, personal relationships and their correlation(s) to the social, and this was particularly prominent when broadcast television meant a singular family set, usually situated in the family living room for all to gather around.[46] As the communications scholar Paddy Scannell argues, live television's 'presencing' effect unites disparate viewers, and alters understandings of time and space.[47] Feelings of intimacy at the coronation were described in media commentary and personal testimonies. The *Observer* commented on 7 June 1953 that '[i]n experiencing television we have experienced a new extension of our senses – and a major new factor in our public life'.[48] A participant in Mass Observation (a long-term social research project recording everyday UK life) commented on how this access is historically important: 'we are fortunate today in being able to see and hear the actual service, and so the Queen is brought nearer to us, which is different to the old days, when we only read about these things'.[49] They directly compare their experience of watching the coronation to seeing Queen Victoria in person. For this viewer, television afforded comparable intimacy to physical proximity to royalty, and the Queen is 'brought nearer' to them through the television set. But what does 'access' to monarchy mean? How might this alter subjects' engagement with sovereign power?

(Royal) publics, the 'mediated centre' and stage-managing 'magic'

In 'The Meaning of the Coronation', Edward Shils and Michael Young use conceptualisations of the Durkheimian sacred to understand the coronation.[50] The French sociologist Emile Durkheim deploys religious concepts of the 'sacred' and 'profane' to explore individuals uniting in society under a single moral law.[51] Australian Native Tribes, for example, worshipped sacred 'totems' (usually plants or animals) as 'collective sentiments' symbolic of group membership.[52] Everything outside of the sacred, meanwhile, is profane, and must be regulated. Shils and Young employ these terms to understand the coronation as 'the ceremonial occasion for the affirmation of the moral values by which the society lives

… an act of national communion'.[53] Television only enhanced this, they argue, forming a 'national family' watching the coronation across Britain.

Shils and Young's work has been criticised. The political theorist Tom Nairn calls it a 'slavering eulogy' and the American sociologist Norman Birnbaum accuses it of 'sociological generalizations of universal scope' because it overemphasises the power of monarchy.[54] But Shils and Young identify the power of television in representing and constructing a collective participatory event, which has been extensively developed by other media theorists. In *Media Events*, Dayan and Katz argue that television affords new ways of participating in ritual and increases the spectacular power of the event.[55] They take a similar neo-Durkheimian approach in referring to society's 'sacred centre', which comprises a stable set of values shared by the citizenry.[56] A successful media event integrates society around this 'sacred centre'. Dayan and Katz's discussion of this process as *mediated*, and moreover that this mediation alters the event's *meaning*, emphasises the media's role in not just disseminating information but shaping our experiences of it. Indeed, as the media scholar John Fiske argues, the distinction between the 'real' event and its mediation has been eroded, because representation is central to an event's meaning.[57] Or, as Stuart Hall would say, media does not just represent; it reproduces.[58]

The limitations to Dayan and Katz's reading are in the assumption that there are already-existing, stable moral values at society's centre. As Nick Couldry argues in *Media Rituals*, these are neither stable nor coherent.[59] Rather, Couldry theorises this as 'the myth of the mediated centre': 'the belief, or assumption, that there is a centre to the social world, and that, in some sense, the media speaks "for" that centre'.[60] There is an assumption that the media is a 'social frame' showing us what's happening in society, and media institutions sustain that myth to reproduce their legitimacy.[61] Couldry challenges the media's claim to centring, and instead argues that 'media rituals are the mechanism through which that assumed legitimacy is reproduced'.[62] Again, mediations are positioned as active: (re)producing meaning and shaping experiences. The 'centre' of society is constructed, both by the media and in the audiences (re)actions.

Couldry does not theorise the *success* of media texts in binding audiences together; rather he is interested in the 'mediated centre' as a strategic action, helping to formalise media's ritual functions. The queer theorist Michael Warner's work is an interesting addition to consider media affects on audiences, which he calls 'publics'.[63] Warner describes 'publics' as discursive spaces: 'a public is a space of discourse organised by nothing other than the discourse itself'.[64] A 'public' is an active process of spectatorship, 'potent' discursive spaces which 'exist ... by virtue of being addressed' (re)produced through connected and concentrated representations.[65] 'Publics' are not pre-existing or independent, then, but are brought into being through active engagement with media texts. What Couldry's and Warner's work does in combination – linking with Stuart Hall's work – is demonstrate how media texts do not just *reflect* society but rather *construct* it through representation. Publics are constructed around a particular event, and in engaging they give 'consent' for the monarchy to continue in its theatrical form.

This is useful for analysing the media–monarchy relationship, specifically the importance of in/visibility. Due to its scale, the coronation is typically narrated as the occasion when television was anchored and popularised as a national cultural form.[66] It features, for example, as a key case study in multiple critical histories of broadcasting industries, including at the Science Museum in London.[67] In 'Media and Memory in Wales', a study archiving memories of television in the twentieth century, the coronation played a formative role in many participants' recollections.[68] The day after the coronation, the *Daily Express* ran the headline 'Queen's Day – TV's Day' to suggest that, on coronation day, the Queen became Queen and television became television.[69] This is mirrored in television manufacturers such as Sobell advertising their sets with specific reference to the day: the tagline to one advertisement was 'a crowning achievement for coronation year'.[70]

Some scholars such as Joe Moran have convincingly argued that the coronation is merely part of a longer history of television's gradual emergence since the Second World War. But regardless of whether the headline 'Queen's Day, TV's Day' is actually 'true', what matters is the *perceived* importance of television to constructing the coronation as a national event across the historical imaginary, in critical commentary and in television studies, and the effect of this on public experiences of the coronation and the monarchy since.[71] As the sociologist David Chaney argues, televising the coronation established the royal family as a key feature of the new medium.[72] Media institutions like the BBC often use their coronation coverage to document their history, and in so doing claim their own legitimacy 'as privileged interpreters of the social "centre" ... by recalling that event and how they told the story'.[73] The monarchy and the media form are linked, and both take their place in history.[74]

Likewise, an active process of representation positions the monarchy as the antithesis to 'popular' television. In being cited as exemplifying the 'risks' of 'low-brow' television technologies, the monarchy is positioned as comparatively superior. Rather than television fracturing the 'magic' of monarchy, then, the very act of representing monarchy as superior (re)created this 'magic'. This argument is partly rehearsed by Michael Billig in his analysis of popular attitudes towards monarchy. One participant noted her surprise when, upon Princess Margaret meeting her infant daughter, Margaret 'waved and ... said "what a beautiful baby", you know, just like a normal person would'.[75] Billig responds, 'only because the mother accepts the Princess as extraordinary is the normality worthy of comment. No normal person would be described as holding a baby just like a normal person.'[76] As Warner would say, Margaret's extraordinariness is brought into being 'by virtue of being addressed'.[77]

For the coronation, this is illustrated neatly in one example: banning shots of religiously significant parts of the ceremony. Upon anointing, the Queen symbolically becomes, as Shils and Young write, 'something more and greater than the human being [she was]'.[78] Television aired footage of Westminster Abbey's architectural features during the anointing to fulfil the agreed ban. This transmission 'blackout' makes the Queen's transformation more tangible: monarchy's magic is created in the gesture of hiding it, rather than existing independently, since it implies there is magic to hide. The status and hierarchy between sovereign and viewers was (re-)established by cutting live coverage, and the 'myth of the mediated centre' was reified. Essentially, this act connotes 'monarchy doesn't belong here'.

The access that television afforded creates what can be read as a democratised event, where the public were invited into the Abbey and included in state ceremonial. This is not the same, however, as democratising the monarchy. As *The Times* commented afterwards, 'yesterday, for the first time in perhaps a thousand years, the Sovereign was crowned in the sight of many thousands of the humblest of her subjects'.[79] Rather than erasing the hierarchy between Sovereign and subject, television merely confirmed these boundaries by, as the Archbishop of Canterbury wrote, bringing 'to the viewers a realisation of the Queen's burden, the Queen's dedication, God's presence and God's consecration, of religion and of themselves'.[80] Whilst Couldry theorised the 'mediated centre' as a myth, upheld by media institutions to reinforce their legitimacy, this has a new imperative when discussing the monarchy. In some ways, the monarchy *is* the centre: of the British state, the constitution and hereditary power in Britain. Likewise, as I have described, the monarchy preserves the stage set of monarchies past by precisely strategising its mediations (although these might not always translate as intended).[81] The debates about intimacy/distance reify the monarchy as the 'centre' by highlighting its superiority, and reinforcing that any access permitted to the royals is more precious because it is limited. These debates take an interesting turn as media forms expand and develop throughout the twentieth century.

Reality television, royal 'soap opera' and the (classed) politics of taste

If the coronation illustrates the Firm's first, tentative forays into television, over the next few decades this developed as television matured its technological capacities, in the context of 'publics' transforming their relationships to democracy. The historian David Cannadine suggests that these demonstrate the continued 'invention of tradition' in royal cultural forms, as boundaries between 'tradition' and 'modernity' are negotiated in response to changing societies.[82] By the 1960s, there were extended television hours, more choice of channels, colour television, new filming techniques and growing audiences.[83] The Queen's Christmas message was first televised in 1957, giving audiences annual access to their sovereign as part of a mediated ritual. Again, ordinary and extraordinary coalesced through direct contact with the Queen from inside Buckingham Palace, who said 'I very much hope ... that this new medium will make my Christmas message more personal and direct ... I welcome you to the peace of my own home'.[84]

Developments in monarchy's relationship to television are best illustrated in the 1969 BBC–ITV documentary *Royal Family*, directed by Richard Cawston and commissioned by Buckingham Palace.[85] By the late 1960s – perhaps due to the decade's new subcultures, shifting attitudes towards sexual politics and growing consumerism – the popularity of monarchy during the coronation had waned. In 1965, the *Sunday Telegraph* claimed that the Queen was seen as 'the arch-square' among young people, who felt the monarchy was old-fashioned.[86] In response, the then Press Secretary William Heseltine initiated a project to modernise public perception of monarchy by promoting Prince Charles's Investiture in 1969 (which, itself, was broadcast on television) using two 'informal'

2.1 Still from *Royal Family* documentary, BBC/ITV, 1969

documentaries: one interview with Charles, and the documentary *Royal Family*.[87] In contrast to the precisely positioned coronation cameras, *Royal Family* used new techniques of 'cinéma vérité, using hand-held 16-millimetre cameras with synchronized sound recording' to follow the monarchy for one year.[88] The result was the 'first fly-on-the-wall royal reality-TV programme', offering intimate glimpses of domestic scenes, such as family mealtimes (Figure 2.1), a family barbecue and the Queen taking the infant Prince Edward to a sweet shop.[89] Despite its popularity, and the film-maker Alan Rosenthal claims that it is the most widely seen documentary ever made, the programme was controversial.[90] Many were concerned that the voyeuristic style fractured the mystique of monarchy too far. Using language mirroring Shils and Young's account of the 'sacred' and Foucault's on sovereign power, the then BBC controller David Attenborough argued:

> the whole institution depends on mystique and the tribal chief in his hut … If any member of the tribe ever sees inside the hut, then the whole system of the tribal chiefdom is damaged and the tribe eventually disintegrates.[91]

Seemingly thinking similarly, Buckingham Palace redacted the 90-minute documentary and 43 hours of unused footage, forbidding all airings except short clips used in exhibitions and documentaries.[92] *Royal Family* has since become a mythological watershed in royal representational history. Its redaction illustrates how precisely the line between visibility and invisibility is toed in royal media texts. Reality television as a genre has claims to 'realism': representing something that 'actually happened'.[93] Contemporary media scholarship contests this to suggest that it actually 'manipulates and constructs "the real"', and indeed *Royal Family* was distilled from 43 hours of footage into a two-hour documentary.[94] But if reality television connotes 'realism', this complicates royal representations in this form: viewing the Queen preparing salad for a barbecue is more intimate than a close-up of her face during a religious ceremony. The carefully crafted mystique of monarchy is fractured by representations that make claims to 'the real', to which monarchy is necessarily positioned as superior. In a discussion of using social media, the scholars Alice Marwick and danah boyd use the phrase 'context collapse' to describe how social media collapse distinct contexts of time and space and unite otherwise discrete audiences (e.g. celebrity and fan), who all abound on the same platform.[95] I suggest that *Royal Family* failed precisely because it was 'context collapse', whereby the 'distance' the monarchy relies upon and the 'centre' it represents – which distinguishes monarchy from celebrity – disappears. And so monarchy collapses into media.

Reality television attracts further criticism from cultural commentators for having 'low' cultural value, as part of the shift to 'spectacular' television over the perceived 'substance' of earlier documentaries.[96] These derogatory associations are both gendered and classed: reality television has subsumed associations with femininity and domesticity,[97] and so-called 'trash TV' can 'be located as a judgment which justifies its moral and aesthetic criteria within ideological discourses' embedded in class hierarchy.[98] For the Firm to engage with this genre becomes – like original debates about the coronation – an issue of class, taste and respectability.

Some scholars and commentators have associated the Firm with another televisual genre associated with connotations of 'low' cultural value. In a 1984 essay, Rosalind Coward referred to the monarchy as *The Royals*: 'the longest-running soap opera in Britain'.[99] Coward argued that the rise of the soap opera genre in the 1950s coincides with shifting attitudes to monarchy in media culture, which has provided more intimate coverage of the royals.[100] *The Royals*, she argues, follows 'the conventions of a family melodrama … preoccupied with sexual relations, marriage, the unity of the family, internal conflict … and the disintegration of the family'.[101] The narrative form of soap opera as a 'continuous serial' mirrors the 'continuous serial' of monarchy.[102] I document this process in this book, as new figures come and go from the royal stage and give the Firm access to new markets.

Coward describes how this works positively for the Firm:

> the ways in which the story is told means that we never have to deal with the Royal family as a political institution; we only have to think about human behaviour, human emotions, and choices restricted to the family[103]

Here, melodrama is a form of distraction, and of 'producing consent'.[104] It becomes, as we saw previously from the ex-Director of Royal Communications Sally Osman, about 'a distinction between what we do to articulate the Monarchy, and its purpose and value, and then the role that each of the individuals play within that story'.[105] Indeed, the pantomime of royal 'scandal', criticism and resolution is a recurring trope of royal representations (see Chapter 6). For other commentators, the royal soap becomes an issue of taste. In a controversial piece for the *New Statesman* in 1955, entitled 'The Royal Soap Opera', the journalist Malcolm Muggeridge claimed 'this is history, not *The Archers*, and their affairs ought to be treated as such'.[106] Here, 'the royal soap opera' is sensationalist and undignified: in direct opposition to traditionalist, 'substantive' history. Indeed, soap opera as a genre is often associated with low-culture.[107] For Muggeridge, describing monarchy as such demystifies it too far.

The year 1987 brought another example of the Firm subject to what I have called 'context collapse'.[108] *It's a Royal Knockout* was a BBC charity event, based on the slapstick television gameshow *It's a Knockout*, which featured celebrities undertaking games and tasks in fancy dress.[109] The episode included Princes Andrew and Edward, Princess Anne and Sarah Ferguson (then Prince Andrew's wife; they divorced in 1996), each captaining a celebrity team while dressed in mock-Tudor costumes (Figure 2.2). As with *Royal Family*, the audience figures of 18 million suggested a success.[110] Yet, reactions were critical, drawing again on language of access and intimacy; specifically, in this case, 'the irruption of showbiz into the royal world'.[111] The royal historian Ben Pimlott claimed that 'one of the mistakes of *Knockout* was that it gave the impression of the Royal Family using their privileged access to the media to sell themselves'.[112] Of course, all royal representation sells monarchy. Yet because *It's a Royal Knockout* specifically used the tenets of celebrity culture and earlier variety performances (similarly associated with low culture),

2.2 The royals on *It's a Royal Knockout*, BBC, 1987

this marketing ploy was exposed. The journalist Daniel Roseman writes that 'the young royals inadvertently mocked the real costumes and ceremonies of their own House of Windsor'.[113] The show became a type of metatheatre (*the metamonarchy*), where the royals emphasised how all monarchy is a stage show with costumes, crews and equipment. The 'context collapse' here, then, extends to the institution itself being revealed as gimmick.[114] The 'centre' was, once again, erased.

An interesting addition to royal soap opera is the Netflix drama *The Crown*.[115] *The Crown* is a historical television series about the reign of Elizabeth II, with events from 1947 (the wedding of the Queen and Philip) onwards (including the coronation and the *Royal Family* documentary) dramatised as part-fictional retellings with actors. The series has received multiple Emmy and Golden Globe nominations, and, as of January 2020, 73 million global households with a Netflix account (out of 158 million) had watched it.[116]

The Crown is not 'official', hence it is not part of the Firm's public relations package in the same way as *Royal Family* or *It's a Royal Knockout*. Yet, similar debates about in/visibility are used by commentators to debate its place in popular culture. The political journalist John Sergeant claimed that *The Crown* is 'dangerous' for the Firm because it erodes distance and mystique, and monarchy is not a 'multi-million blockbuster' (again, implying issues of taste and respectability).[117] Others argue that *The Crown* functions as royal 'propaganda'.[118] The royal biographer Robert Lacey claims that *The Crown* humanises the royals, and the historian Greg Jenner says it 'depicts [their life as] a soap opera, which... makes them seem more like celebrities'.[119] Analysing a comparable royal melo-drama biopic, the 2006 film *The Queen*, Mandy Merck argued that the 'transfer of spectatorial sympathy represents a political coup de théâtre', whereby real criticisms of the Queen's lack of public response to Princess Diana's death in 1997 were rewritten and reclaimed in filmic scenes depicting the monarch as quietly emo-tional.[120] Likewise, moments such as intense debates over television at the coronation, and the redaction of *Royal Family*, are dramatised in *The Crown* in ways which prompt sympathy, and circumvent political questions of accountability, funding or access.

Whilst Sergeant argued 'there used to be clear rules about depicting people who are still alive' – referring to laws stating that no monarch could be depicted in restagings until a hundred years after their death[121] – to justify his criticism of *The Crown*, this also works in contention of Sergeant's position. Dramatic restagings of present monarch(ie)s can influence and shape public responses. Whilst *The Crown* does sometimes critique monarchy – Series Four was particularly critical of Charles's treatment of Diana, for example – it also glamorises it. Netflix is central to the shift to digital television – 'television after TV' – where high-budget, serialised television narratives like *Game of Thrones*[122] and *Stranger Things*[123] display filmic aesthetics and transcend historical connotations of television as 'low taste'.[124] For the monarchy to feature in this transition is a powerful representational tool. Whilst *The Crown* blurs the in/visibility line by offering intimate 'access' to monarchy (albeit a contrived version), Netflix is vital to its 'success' as a representational tool. David Cannadine points towards Shakespeare plays, a similar form of dramatised royal biography to *The Crown*, as historical representations of monarchy which focus upon royal drama and disputes.[125] Yet, they do not damage monarchy's majesty because they are within boundaries of cultural 'taste'. Like *The Crown*, they humanise royals while simultaneously mythologising and canonising them. *The Crown* also functions as what the scholar Andrew Higson and others term a heritage production, where history is marketed and consumed through media texts.[126] *Downton Abbey*, a comparable television period drama about an aristocratic family, has been critiqued as romanticising a conservative, nostalgic version of Englishness which glamorises classed, gendered and racialised hierarchies.[127] In *The Crown*, monarchy's class hierarchies are (re)produced as entertainment for viewing publics.

Tabloid and celebrity cultures

Other media technologies have expanded during the Queen's reign, which further develop the in/visibility debate. The author Ryan Linkof argues that, upon emerging as cultural intermediaries in the early 1900s, tabloid press photographers established a new style of celebrity photography aiming to capture unposed, apparently authentic images with a sense of immediacy.[128] Like television, then, tabloid cultures posed challenges to the Firm's in/visibility. The scholars Adrian Bingham and Martin Conboy track the monarchy–tabloid relationship, arguing that it shifts between reverence and lampooning. Whilst George IV (1820–1830) and William IV (1830–1837) were satirised in news media to protest against hereditary wealth, by Victoria's reign monarchy was associated with a global Empire, prompting years of effusive coverage.[129]

This shifted upon Edward VIII's relationship with the American socialite Wallis Simpson. Edward was 'Britain's answer to the Hollywood stars of the 1920s', with his public and private activities reported as new 'human-interest journalism'.[130] But despite extensive international reports, Edward and Wallis's affair was absent from the UK press until Edward's abdication in 1936 was imminent, due to attempts to shelter the royals from new mass media technologies.[131] Post-abdication, press photographers – whom we now recognise as paparazzi – were central to exposing their affair, harbingering tabloid behaviour in the twenty-first century. A long-lens photograph of Edward and Wallis on holiday, for example, is now a common trope of celebrity culture.[132] Like live televising the coronation, monarchy was again key in establishing popular media practices. Photojournalism also illustrates the blurring of royalty with celebrity culture, where deference weakened and the public wanted access to royal drama. This is perhaps best illustrated through Princess Margaret and Princess Diana.

From the 1940s onwards, Margaret was the subject of intense tabloid speculation. In 1949, aged eighteen, she was photographed wearing a bathing suit on holiday in Capri, prompting arguments between journalists about in/appropriate royal images.[133] Inter/national magazines and newspapers covered her clothing, her potential boyfriends, her celebrity friends and her partying.[134] Whilst intimate shots of the Queen at the coronation were controlled, a tabloid reporter spotted an intimate moment during the ceremony between Margaret and Captain Peter Townsend, a former adviser of her father King George VI and a divorced man, when she brushed lint from his jacket.[135] The coverage of this as gossip in international newspapers directly contradicted the 'mystique' of monarchy at the coronation, raising questions about which royals must be 'invisible' to public scrutiny.

Margaret married Antony Armstrong-Jones, a society photographer, demonstrating a union of the royals and celebrity culture.[136] In 1976, Margaret was photographed on the luxury private island of Mustique with Roddy Llewellyn, a landscape gardener and aristocrat seventeen years her junior, with whom tabloids reported she was having an affair.[137] The blurry long-lens photographs, of a kind now commonplace in celebrity gossip magazines, drew attention to the party lifestyle Margaret was enjoying using taxpayers' money.[138] Her eventual divorce from Armstrong-Jones in 1978 again became a tabloid 'scandal'.[139] The personal details of Margaret's life made her the first royal manufactured for the tabloid and celebrity era.

Diana's life and death were also extensively documented by the popular media. Much has been written about Diana and the media, from analysis of representations of her as the 'people's princess' to the power of media ritual at her funeral.[140] I will not dwell on these arguments here. More relevant is how Diana *used* the media, particularly after divorcing Charles, to differentiate herself from the Firm, and how this meant that the monarchy lost control of the narrative. Once again, losing stage-management coincides with emerging media forms, to which the Firm must respond reactively. Diana's candid 1995 interview on BBC's *Panorama* programme, in which she accused Charles of an affair and the monarchy of exploiting her, reified representations of Diana as 'the people's princess', used and bullied by a heartless institution (see Chapter 5 for an analysis of this as a 'confessional').[141] This influenced public responses to her death, after which the monarch(y) was accused of being heartless.[142] Her death fundamentally shifted the tabloid media's relationship with monarchy, after paparazzi were blamed for causing her fatal car crash in Paris. The Royal Editor of the *London Evening Standard*, Robert Jobson, said:

> For the media [Diana's death] certainly changed the way reporting would be done around the royal family ... It's certainly less free than when I started doing the job in the early '90s, when really it was the media that saw the story, wrote the story, ran the agenda, and really were not controlled in any way[143]

Jobson's description of increasingly curtailed freedoms in UK reporting of the monarchy reflects the changing codes of conduct for paparazzi since Diana's death, as well as unspoken yet taken-for-granted norms about royal privacy that have developed in discussions between the Buckingham Palace Communications Office and UK media outlets. In the weeks following Diana's death, the Newspaper Society[144] held a meeting of newspaper editors to address reporting and privacy, resulting in 'the rules of press engagement [being] rewritten'.[145] This included extending definitions of privacy to spaces 'where people might have a reasonable expectation of privacy', addressing privacy for young people and children, and introducing the notion of 'persistent pursuit' for paparazzi. The Firm's attempts to protect the privacy of Diana's then-young sons also introduced new rules of engagement specifically for the royals. Known as 'the pressure cooker agreement', the Firm negotiated a deal where the paparazzi would leave William and Harry alone during their education, in return for intermittent occasions when 'the valve would be released' and they would be invited to staged photograph opportunities (for William's eighteenth birthday at Eton College, for example).[146]

The 'pressure cooker agreement' proved contentious for some newspaper editors, who protested against the restrictions when they often *knew* news stories about the young princes but were dissuaded from publishing them. In November 1998, for example, the *Mirror* published the headline 'Harry's had an accident: but we're not allowed to tell you', with the story claiming that 'St James's Palace last night banned all newspapers from revealing what happened to Harry' at school.[147] The newspaper was asked by Buckingham Palace to apologise, to which it responded with another front-page headline 'we're unable to apologise for a story we didn't publish'.[148] In so doing, the *Mirror* lampooned the curtailing of press freedoms on royal news.

The Royal Rota System also manages media coverage of key royal events. This is a system where key journalists are invited to cover royal engagements (for example, a royal visit to a UK town) on the proviso they share their material with other journalists. Members of the Royal Rota include the *Daily Mail*, the *Sun*, *The Times*, the *Telegraph*, Wire Picture Agency, Independent Photographers Association, BBC, Sky News and ITV. The News Media Association says this was introduced 'due to space restrictions and security'.[149] However, it essentially means that the Firm can cultivate relationships with particular organisations, while banning direct access for others. This raises serious questions about journalistic integrity and democracy.

Paparazzi and tabloid exposure raise issues around the blurring line of royal/celebrity cultures. Because the royals are represented in media texts alongside celebrities, they are often categorised as such. Scholars and commentators have debated this.[150] The sociologist Chris Rojek defines three 'types' of celebrity: achieved celebrity based upon talent (sports stars, actors); attributed celebrity manufactured by media representation (reality television stars); and ascribed celebrity stemming from inheritance and bloodline (royalty).[151] Aristocrats and royalty were the 'original celebrities', dominating gossip columns in the early twentieth century.[152] But celebrity in the era of reality television and online stardom (e.g. YouTubers) is increasingly positioned as a democratised, meritocratic space, offering power to 'ordinary people'.[153] In this context, to describe monarchy as 'just' celebrity is to simplify, and depoliticise, the monarchy's structural, constitutional and state privileges. As Tom Nairn writes, 'the Queen and her family are never merely stars, or celebrities. They possess in addition a "secret" … an element of mystique whose glamour is in the end far greater than that of any media personality.'[154] The scholars Heather Mendick, Kim Allen, Laura Harvey and Aisha Ahmed's work on young people's responses to celebrity, and Hannah Yelin and Michele Paule's work on young girls' responses to female stars, has highlighted how royals are compared with celebrity figures.[155] As Yelin and Paule write, although the girls they interviewed recognised royals as part of celebrity culture, they engaged critically with notions of royal celebrity to draw attention to inherited wealth.[156] Monarchy must retain some elements of mystique, and the intimacy of celebrity cultures – particularly social media celebrity – challenges this.

Rather than simply describing monarchy as celebrity, then, some scholars discuss how the monarchy *uses* celebrity to appeal to new royal 'publics'. In 'Everyday Royal Celebrity', for example, Nick Couldry argues that 'royalty are exceptional by virtue of their position in both a social hierarchy and a media hierarchy', where two 'types' of celebrity intersect but both produce royal representation.[157] Likewise, Rosalind Brunt describes the investment of monarchy with 'charisma', a word used to describe the appeal of stars and celebrities but here drawing on mythologies of sovereign power.[158] Again, we see here how the 'magic' of monarchy is being (re)produced in positioning monarchy as superior. There is no 'context collapse', because monarchy is not reduced to *merely* celebrity.[159] In being represented as somehow 'more than', monarchy's superiority is brought into being 'by virtue of being addressed'.[160] Monarchy is simultaneously ordinary and extraordinary.

The Firm 2.0: social media and participation

In the twenty-first century, 'postnetwork, postpublic service media systems' complicate how television is experienced as a communal activity, as there is typically no longer one television set in the family living area, but rather multiple platforms containing thousands of programmes.[161] The 1953 decision to ban coverage of the anointing ceremony would be near impossible now due to camera phones and social media; nor could organisers map the precise position of all filming equipment. As Couldry and Hepp argue, in a global age 'media events are certain situated, thickened centering performances of mediated communication' which reach wide audiences through multiple platforms.[162] Whilst television at the coronation brought monarchy into people's homes, the participatory qualities of digital media mean that the event is interwoven with the everyday lives of audiences.[163] If Couldry argues that 'liveness' is key to the mediated centre, this is established using new forms in digital media culture.[164] The shift from analogue to digital media poses new challenges, but also new affordances, for the Firm. This section describes, briefly, some of these changes.

Prince William and Kate Middleton's 2011 wedding was the first large-scale royal event staged in the digital age. The Foreign and Commonwealth Office (keen to present William as the future Head of the Commonwealth) devised a communication plan for the wedding, specifically requesting 'please use social media' but including guidelines on *how*, illustrating again an embracement of new media but an attempt to control staging of the event.[165] On the day, the event was watched live, worldwide, by two billion people on a multitude of channels and platforms, including the official 'Royal Family' YouTube channel, demonstrating a proliferation of broadcasts (each with different presenters, editing, formatting).[166] YouTube announced 'we've been working to make as much of the big day as possible accessible to everyone', including – much like the coronation footage being flown to the USA and Canada, but digitised – having the footage publicly available after the live stream for those in different time zones.[167]

Direct participation was also encouraged. Facebook users could click an 'I'm attending' button to share their interest with others (and provide a staged sense of intimacy, as though watching on television was equal to physical attendance), the Twitter hashtag #rw2011 synthesised public commentary and an official YouTube 'Wedding Book' allowed users to submit congratulatory videos.[168] Facebook estimated that ten million people worldwide mentioned the wedding in 24 hours.[169] As the media scholar Espen Ytreberg argues in an analysis of Couldry's work, whilst the proliferation of media texts might *appear* to destabilise the 'myth of the mediated centre', actually multi-platform media forms enhance the sense of the event being pervasive.[170] That is, the wider dissemination of the event makes the 'mediated centre' appear more legitimate, as it dominates more of our cultural experiences. No matter what platform we engage with, we will likely see the event.

At Prince Harry and Meghan Markle's wedding in May 2018, digital media had expanded even further. Television remained a key platform with 18 million UK viewers for the ceremony, but television's globalisation meant that it was also watched live by 22 million US viewers, and the BBC commentary included a live link-up to the presenter Richard Bacon staged at a viewing party in Los Angeles, where Meghan was born, creating a 'global' event.[171] The Firm's social media accounts released regular updates prior to the day, making wedding planning part of the public consumption of the event: for example, Twitter was used to announce William as Harry's best man.[172] On the day, @theroyalfamily Instagram posted regular updates on their 'stories' feed, using the informal language of social media: 'Today is Prince Harry and Ms Markle's Wedding Day!' with a tagged location.[173] This is a significant departure from the formalities and hierarchies of the coronation, illustrating the shifting media–monarchy relationship in new socio-political contexts. The use of new platforms suggests attempts to engage new demographics: teen audiences, for example, might be more likely to participate over social media than on 'traditional' channels.

In 2020, the global COVID-19 pandemic gave the media monarchy new challenges. The Queen's motto, 'I have to be seen to be believed', was complicated by the virus being particularly dangerous for older people, meaning that she had to self-isolate for her safety.[74] Royal engagements were cancelled, and crowds of people could not gather at royal events. Like many other UK businesses, the Firm moved online. Royals undertook engagements via the online video platform Zoom, including an appearance from William and Kate playing Bingo with residents in a Welsh nursing home.[75] These events courted the boundaries of visibility/invisibility, ordinary/extraordinary. The royals were seen to be 'working from home' like millions of others around the world. The video backgrounds were interiors of royal palaces, with carefully curated framing: the Queen had a grander backdrop of luscious floral arrangements and chintz antique furniture, Kate and William a simpler (and 'middle-class') cream door, grey wall and single painting. Such concentrated footage of the Queen speaking to subjects is rarely seen, and her interactions with Princess Anne, seen explaining to the Queen how Zoom works, invested the appearances with an intimacy reminiscent of *Royal Family*; albeit more controlled considering it was on the Firm's terms.[76] These Zoom appearances illustrated the importance of keeping monarchy visible, and how technology can be mobilised for the project of 'seeing is believing'.

On one hand, much like television before it, the cultivation of official social media profiles gives the Firm more control. Instagram in particular facilitates images connoting intimacy because they are positioned as 'direct' contact with the monarchy, yet are actually carefully choreographed to depict precise meaning (more in Chapter 6). On the other hand, the social media scholars Alice Marwick and danah boyd undertake an analysis of celebrities' use of social media using similar notions of 'frontstage' and 'backstage', arguing that a celebrity's identity is 'traditionally ... navigated with the help of assistants, public relations personnel, bodyguards, and other mechanisms that broker access between famous person and fan'.[177] On social media, however, such infrastructure is not available, and fans have direct access while co-existing on the same platform: this is 'context collapse'.[178] This argument applies to the Firm; however, it takes on new imperative for a sovereign institution.[179] How can monarchy maintain distance if its mediations abound on the same platform as its subjects'? How can the Firm be seen to represent the 'centre' if everyone has access to the same platform? This is an ongoing challenge for the Firm as it negotiates new media platforms.

Conclusion

In 2017, the *Guardian* released secret plans held by Buckingham Palace, the BBC and the government relating to the Queen's death.[180] One anonymous television director told the journalist Sam Knight, 'I have got in front of me an instruction book a couple of inches thick ... everything in there is planned'.[181] For many years, the BBC was informed of royal deaths first, but now an announcement will go to the Press Association and international media at the same time as a footman in mourning clothes pins a black-edged notice to the Buckingham Palace gates. News organisations will choose from pre-prepared news pieces and obituaries to immediately release online. Regular programming on BBC 1, 2 and 4 will cease immediately and merge to display one newsreader, who will announce the death before the national anthem is played. The television schedules will be altered for the next nine days, with no satirical comedy being aired on BBC for the duration. The funeral itself is meticulously planned, down to the number of seconds the cortège takes to travel between locations. When the coffin reaches Westminster Abbey at exactly 11am, the country will observe a collective silence: railway stations will halt announcements and buses will remain stationary. The ceremony will be televised in its entirety, followed by the cortège procession to Windsor Castle. There will be no footage from inside the royal vault as the coffin is lowered, but the commentator will describe the event to viewers.

Staging a royal death is certainly not new. In 1936, George V's physician injected morphine to initiate the king's death after a long illness to ensure that it coincided with the print deadline for the next morning's papers, which were considered more respectable than the low-culture evening ones.[182] But plans for the Queen's death encapsulate the precision of manufacturing spectacular royal events in a global, digital media age. Whilst, like twenty-first century royal weddings, social media mean that mediation cannot be entirely controlled, the plans demonstrate intent to inspire collective public feeling, as people's daily rituals are interrupted. This can be read as a strategic attempt to create what Couldry called a 'centre'. As one of the Queen's courtiers told Knight, 'it's history', and it is precisely constructed to be.[183] The story of the Queen's death is immediately positioned as more important than all others, and indeed more important than daily life itself. In the initial announcements, the BBC newsreader will begin 'this is the BBC from London', rallying a feeling of national emergency and national identity: this is an announcement from the state's centre, and the media provide access.

Negotiating sovereign power at the level of expanding and democratising media forms has posed significant challenges, where the balance of the paradoxical but co-dependent visibility and invisibility is continually under review. The film historian Jeffrey Richards argued that Bagehot's famous quotation 'we must not let in daylight upon magic' was written 'before cinema, television and wireless transformed the world and made the letting in of light inevitable'.[184] In fact, as I show, letting in *some* light is useful to facilitate public engagement with the Firm. Perhaps a more useful analysis of Bagehot's quotation is to ask *how much* light to let in.

This is a dilemma negotiated throughout the Firm's history, and, as media forms continue expanding, will undoubtedly continue to be.

The monarchy needs the media more than the media need the monarchy. I opened this chapter with a quotation from the Queen: 'I have to be seen to be believed'.[185] Using the framework of British Cultural Studies wielded in this book, we might reformulate this quotation as: 'I have to be seen to produce consent'. Indeed, individual royals must be represented as the Family Firm in order to produce consent for the Firm, and these narratives are fought for in media culture. The remaining chapters in *Running the Family Firm* explore representations of various royal figures to follow this logic.

3

'Queen of Scots': National identities, sovereignty and the body politic

On 20 September 2014, in the wake of the Scottish Independence Referendum, the pro-union, right-wing British broadsheet the *Daily Telegraph*'s front page was dominated by a photograph of Queen Elizabeth II in the grounds of her Balmoral Estate in the Scottish Highlands, under the headline 'Queen's pledge to help reunite the Kingdom' (Figure 3.1).[1] The photograph, entitled *Queen of Scots, Sovereign of the Most Ancient and Most Noble Order of the Thistle and the Chief of Chiefs*, was taken in 2010 as an official portrait by the photographer Julian Calder. It is given context in the *Daily Telegraph* by its caption, which highlights the role of Scottish culture in its composition: 'The Queen wears the robes of the Most Ancient and Most Noble Order of the Thistle, beside Gelder Burn on her Balmoral Estate, for a portrait in 2010'.

The accompanying story by the journalist Mick Brown narrates the polling day and its aftermath, including voting statistics and political reaction. The tagline, 'we have in common an enduring love of Scotland, which is one of the things that helps to unite us all', is excerpted from the Queen's post-referendum press release, a longer version of which opens the article. It continues:

> As we move forward, we should remember that ... we have in common an enduring love of Scotland, which is one of the things that helps unite us all. Knowing the people of Scotland as I do, I have no doubt that Scots, like others throughout the United Kingdom,

3.1 'Queen's pledge to help reunite the Kingdom', *Daily Telegraph* cover, 20 September 2014

are able to express strongly-held opinions before coming together again. My family and I will do all we can to help and support you in this important task.[2]

Here, the Queen asserts the importance of moving forward together and (re)uniting, referencing the 'strongly-held opinions' of pro-independence campaigners before suggesting these can be revoked and the status quo can resume, supported by herself and 'her family'. As a central symbol of British national identity, the Queen's statement constitutes a key moment in the independence debate, particularly when reproduced by the pro-union *Daily Telegraph*. The Queen's tangible delight at the 'no' result works towards producing consent for it in the public imagination.[3]

Representations of the Queen's body become a site of symbolic struggle over discourses of monarch(y) and national identities during the 2014 Scottish Independence Referendum. By reading *Queen of Scots* in historical context, we see that there are multiple representational struggles, over the meaning of the referendum *and* the meaning of the Queen's body, particularly when represented by the *Daily Telegraph*. As a symbol of national identities, the Queen represents complex interrelations of 'Britishness', 'Englishness' and 'Scottishness'. Reading the photograph exposes the power relations of the referendum, the British monarchy and the United Kingdom, and how these are (re)produced in media culture when the hegemony of British national identity was temporarily fractured.

The Queen is the most represented person in British history.[4] One cannot make a cash purchase without encountering her image, and such banality demonstrates monarchy's interweaving into Britain's fabric. Echoing Michael Billig's 'banal nationalism',[5] Andrezej Olechnowicz describes this as 'banal monarchism',[6] ubiquitous in people's lives. Dominant representations of the Queen depict her as moral, respectable and 'ordinary': an ordinary elderly woman clutching a handbag; an ordinary (grand)mother; an ordinary British citizen; an ordinary working woman.[7] Even representations of her undertaking spectacular ceremonies of state rely on motifs of tradition, with an annual programme of activities undertaken by the Firm as a family. The importance of 'family' was exposed following Princess Diana's death. The Queen's (lack of) response to the death of her former daughter-in-law was perceived as so inappropriate that the monarch(y) reached a crisis point of legitimation, because the monarch(y) who represents 'the people' was understood as failing to represent public opinion. The *Express*, for example, published the headline 'Show us you care: mourners call for the Queen to lead our grief'.[8] Eventually, she gave a televised speech which mitigated her silence by emphasising her role as grandmother, busy 'helping' William and Harry address their grief.[9] Official photographs taken by Annie Leibovitz for the Queen's ninetieth birthday in 2016 depicted the monarch as (great-)grandmother, as opposed to Head of State. In one photograph, she sits in a domestic (yet opulent) setting surrounded by her youngest grandchildren and great-grandchildren, with Mia Tindall (Zara Phillips's daughter) clutching her iconic handbag.[10] This models the portraits of Queen Victoria's 'middle-class' family values used to contain royal privilege (see Chapters 1 and 6).

In contrast to using 'ordinariness' as a tool of legitimation, representations seeking to subvert monarchy often depict the Queen's body as monstrous. The republican punk anthem 'God Save the Queen' by the Sex Pistols used Cecil Beaton's portrait of the Queen, but superimposed swastikas on her eyes, a safety pin through her lips and the name of the band displayed as ransom letters across her face.[11] The artist and left-wing political campaigner Artist Taxi Driver satirised public and media reaction to Prince George's birth by referring to her as the 'hairy goat-legged Queen', galloping around the hospital as Kate Middleton births the dynasty's next 'spawn'.[12] The conspiracy theorist David Icke claims that the royal family are shape-shifting reptilian aliens, part of a secret global society of Establishment elites called the Babylonian Brotherhood.[13] This was later used by the jazz band Sons of Kemet, whose song 'Your Queen Is a Reptile' criticised colonialism, Empire and racial inequalities, and suggested alternative women-of-colour monarchs, such as 'My Queen Is Harriet Tubman'.[14] Depicting the Queen as a 'goat' or a 'reptile' evokes images of monstrous human–animal hybrids which, as the feminist theorist Margrit Shildrick describes, signals 'the corruption of the human form'.[15]

This *Queen of Scots* image, perhaps in less obvious ways than those detailed above, depicts the Queen as monstrous. The Firm comes from a violent, autocratic and authoritarian history, and this chapter explores *when* this history becomes visible, and *what form* this visibility takes. The use of *Queen of Scots* by the *Daily Telegraph* is one such moment, where British hegemony is temporarily fractured by the independence vote, and representations of the Queen shift from banal to purposeful, regulated symbols of authority and historical legitimacy, constructing belonging through language of bodies, territory and kinship.

The chapter begins with some contextualisation of the Scottish Independence Referendum, the relationship between monarchy and national identities, and the *Queen of Scots* photograph. The remainder is split into three sections, each unpacking one of the three titles attributed to the Queen in the photograph: 'Queen of Scots', 'Sovereign of the Most Ancient and Most Noble Order of the Thistle' and 'Chief of Chiefs'. I analyse these to expose what they reveal about the complex intersections between monarchy, power (geo)politics, symbolism, sovereignty, national identities and landscape in the UK. When (right-wing) media are increasingly influencing and boosting political agendas,[16] this particularly striking image offers one way to understand the importance of media representations in defining the terms of political debate.

The 2014 Scottish Independence Referendum

On 18 September 2014, Scotland's electorate voted on independence from the United Kingdom, a parliamentary union spanning 307 years following the Union of Parliaments in 1707, whereby the majority of laws and policies were decided by Westminster. The referendum climaxed Scotland's gradual distancing from the union over several decades, including creating a Scottish Parliament with devolved powers in 1999.[17] In 2014, 55 per cent of the electorate voted against independence. Despite this, the referendum captured the (inter)national imagination: 84.6 per cent of Scots voted (the highest turnout in UK electoral and referenda history), and it initiated the rise of the Scottish National Party (SNP), which became the third-largest political party in Britain in the 2015 General Election.[18]

Whilst all newspaper headlines aim to attract readers, the journalism scholar Marina Dekavalla's research demonstrates the media's importance in outlining the terms of a referendum.[19] UK newspapers were overwhelmingly pro-union, and only the *Sunday Herald* (a Scottish publication) campaigned for independence.[20] As the geographers Charles Pattie and Ron Johnston argued, the factors influencing people's support for independence were complex, and included nationalism, inequality and partisanship.[21] But most UK newspapers (and other national media texts) simplified these debates to frame the referendum as a 'crisis of nationalism'. The *Daily Telegraph*, for instance, voiced pro-union sentiment throughout September 2014 by constructing a national 'crisis' through headlines sensationalising economic disaster and national decline: 'Money floods out of UK over Yes vote fears'; 'Stay with us: Cameron's desperate plea to Scots'; 'PM begs Scots not to leave the UK'; and 'Ten days to save the union'.[22]

This framing emerges from a complex history of Scottish national identity. The United Kingdom of Great Britain and Northern Ireland (hereafter the UK) is the 'official umbrella designation' for an assemblage of previously independent countries (England, Scotland, Wales) and Northern Ireland.[23] England and Scotland's unification occurred firstly under the union of the English and Scottish Crowns in 1603, upon the succession of James VI of Scotland who also became James I of England after Elizabeth I died childless and he was the next heir as the progeny of intermarried Scottish and English kings. The Act of Union 1707 then merged Scotland and England into a single state of the United Kingdom of Great Britain,[24] with one parliament at Westminster.[25] Hence, the UK is a collection of nations, and 'Britishness' has been 'superimposed over an array of internal differences',[26] with the state-nations positioned as 'sub-nationalist' to England, as evidenced in the centrality of Westminster party politics.[27] This results in some so-called 'sub-nations' maintaining local national identity through histories and mythologies, such as appropriating Highlanders' kilts and tartan as a Scottish tradition.[28]

Crucially, the 'crisis of nationalism' ignores alternative factors in the independence campaigns. As the sociologist Lindsay Paterson describes, politically Scotland is more left-wing than England, and there was (and remains, even more so after the referendum to leave the European Union) widespread dissatisfaction among Scots with Westminster politics.[29] The Conservative government in power then had no Scottish MPs, and there were significant divergences in political agendas, such as neoliberal privatisation versus social democracy.[30] 'Britishness' was 'seen as itself a conservative identity, associated with a dead empire and a decrepit ruling class' and a 'dominant English tradition of monarchical power'.[31] These competing discourses suggest that one understanding of the referendum 'crisis' is as a struggle over its *meaning* and representation in British media. Rather than a 'crisis of nationalism', the referendum could be considered a 'crisis of representation': *political* representation through electoral geographies; and *cultural* representation, when over one-fifth of Scots feel unfairly portrayed in UK media.[32]

The *Daily Telegraph*'s (re)framing of the debates as nationalist is unsurprising given its editorial demographic and history, supportive of neoliberal policies. Indeed, it was nicknamed the *Torygraph* due to its right-wing leanings, and it supports the Conservative party.[33] The Telegraph Group is owned by David and Frederick Barclay, (in)famously reclusive multi-billionaires who, during the referendum, were the sixteenth richest people in the world.[34] Two years after the Independence Referendum, the *Daily Telegraph* endorsed the Leave campaign in the European Union referendum.[35] Its combination of pro-union and pro-Brexit embeds a (right-wing) UK nationalism for the one per cent and, again, ignores structural factors of global inequalities that underpinned both votes.[36] In October 2019, the Barclay brothers put the *Daily* and *Sunday Telegraph* up for sale for £200 million.[37]

Representing monarchy, representing Britain

In Michael Billig's interviews with British families on their feelings towards monarchy, one respondent noted, 'if you've not got the Royal Family there, then you'll not have the British Isles as we know it'.[38] This exemplifies how the monarchy 'somehow embodies national identity [in a way that is] more or less ubiquitous … self-evident, unproblematic and "eternal"'.[39] Tom Nairn describes how this ubiquity is purposeful:

> [a] personalized and totemic symbolism was needed to maintain the a-national nationalism of a multi-national (and for long imperial) entity; and the Crown could effectively translate identity on to that 'higher plane' required by a country (heartland England) which has since the 17th century existed out of itself as much as in [itself].[40]

Nairn describes how national identities experienced by each UK 'sub-nation' required cohesion using a 'personalized and totemic symbol', the monarchy, acting as a 'national spirit essence' that he terms 'Ukania'.[41] 'Ukania' defines national identity as Crown loyalism, facilitating a 'metaphorical family unity': the royal *family*.[42] As the anthropologist Ernest Gellner notes, there is no 'original' national identity, rather discourses of national identity and/or nationalism produce nations through representations that make it possible to imagine unity; representations of monarchy being one example.[43]

Monarchy's influence on national identity is more than cultural. Monarchy is part of Britain's geopolitical map: the United *Kingdom*. As described in Chapter 1, Britain's political and constitutional structure stems from the transference of power from monarch to Parliament, thus endowing the British government with greater authority than other contemporary political bodies.[44] Until the Nationality Act 1948, UK inhabitants were not 'citizens' but 'subjects', with their existence defined by allegiance to the Crown.[45] Monarchy and nation are thus connected through political and geographical structures, cultural symbols and histories of citizenship. In analysing representations of monarchy, we can analyse representations of nation.

Keepers: The Ancient Offices of Britain

The photograph *Queen of Scots* was taken in 2010 by Julian Calder, for the book *Keepers: The Ancient Offices of Britain* (hereafter *Keepers*), commissioned for the Queen's Diamond Jubilee.[46] Written by the royal commentator Alastair Bruce, *Keepers* explores the 'collection of odd appointments, names and titles that were established hundreds of years ago'.[47] These titles range from the Lord Archbishop of Canterbury, the senior Bishop of the Church of England; to the Bearer of the Dog Whipper's Rod, who cleared cathedrals of wild dogs during church services in the Middle Ages, and is now a ceremonial role. The book aims to celebrate Britain's heritage, claiming that the titles illustrate 'the story of *our* past',[48] and must be 'preserved'.[49] However, the heritage commemorated is exclusively aristocratic: many of the titles are hereditary, and most are tied to family estates. The name 'Keepers' presents the titled as 'wardens' of British culture, suggesting that Britain is 'kept' under hierarchical class systems, not shared between the citizenry. Including the Queen in the book demonstrates the monarchy's attempts to 'keep' power and privilege, or, as Calder and Bruce's dedication to her suggests, how she 'keeps' her Kingdom.[50]

Queen of Scots features on the front cover of *Keepers* and as a two-page spread within. The accompanying text recounts a version of the monarchy's history with Scotland, from the King of Picts in the eighth century, through the Act of Union 1707, Queen Victoria's purchase of Balmoral in the nineteenth century, and the Queen's embracement of Scotland. Calder described how the photograph was carefully constructed to reflect the Queen's three titles in *Keepers*: 'Queen of Scots', 'Sovereign of the Most Ancient and Most Noble Order of the Thistle' and 'Chief of Chiefs', which all have histories in Scotland.[51] This chapter now explores each one in turn to unpack their meaning, their history and how their use in the *Daily Telegraph* as pro-union propaganda constructs belonging through language of bodies, territory and kinship.

'Queen of Scots': the monarch's body politic

'Queen of Scots' is the most perplexing title of the trio considering its abolishment upon the Union of Crowns 1603. It now appears to be an affectionate nickname bestowed by Scottish royalists, implying that Scotland embraces the Queen as *personal* monarch, rather than her official title 'Elizabeth the Second, by the Grace of God, of the United Kingdom of Great Britain and Northern Ireland, and of her other Realms and Territories Queen, Head of the Commonwealth, Defender of the Faith'.

The monarch's symbolic claim to sovereignty over realms has historical context. The Union of Crowns 1603 was a source of contempt for James I who faced widespread disapproval over his crowning, and he sought (unsuccessfully) throughout his reign to consolidate the union and form a single state. This was partly attempted through visual materials, such as the portrait *James I* by John de Critz the Elder, which aimed to legitimate his claim over both thrones through his symbolic body.[52] Painted in around 1605, James I wears a fur cape alongside the accessories of the Order of the Garter, the highest order of chivalry in England.[53] His hat displays a Crown Jewel named 'Mirror of Great Britain', designed in 1604 to commemorate the union by 'dismembering' other royal jewels, such as Elizabethan diamonds from England and a gem from the Crown of Scotland.[54] In this way, English and Scottish history is materially united. Like *Queen of Scots*, *James I* appears at a moment of political crisis, and the monarchs display union on their symbolic bodies: they *are* the United Kingdom.

Describing the monarch's body as symbolic of the nation has a complex history, one account of which is the 'body politic'. This can be etymologised in two 'related but distinct' ways: as the monarch's 'two bodies', and as the citizens of the state becoming a body.[55] The former separates the monarch's body natural (a mortal, human body) and the body politic (a symbolic body constituted by the totality of their subjects).[56] As a mortal body natural, the monarch may die. But they never truly die, rather there is a 'Separation of the two Bodies', and 'the Body politic is transferred and conveyed over from the Body natural now dead ... to another Body natural' – the next monarch.[57] Thus, the *symbolic function* (body politic) of the monarch as Head of State is considered separate from their *human state* (body natural).

The second, more common, understanding of the body politic refers to the collective citizens as a metaphorical human body. The *Head* of State, the sovereign, is considered both the literal and figurative 'head' of the citizens, who constitute the body.[58] This analogy implies order and hierarchy through the mind/body dichotomy.[59] Thomas Hobbes, a figure of European liberal thought, uses this second understanding in his book *Leviathan*.[60] Written during the English Civil War, *Leviathan* argues that political turmoil would be assuaged by a strong government, led by an absolute sovereign as the people's representative. The sovereign becomes an 'artificial person' called the Leviathan, representing not themselves but the 'words and actions of another'.[61] This artificial person is represented through visual metaphor on the cover of Hobbes's book (Figure 3.2).[62] Here, Leviathan emerges from his realm's landscape, his

3.2 Thomas Hobbes, *Leviathan*, 1651

body composed of his subjects who, in this case literally, are incorporated into the body politic. Although the subjects are faceless, they all peer upwards towards their ruler, who towers over all. As the scholar Bernd Herzogenrath writes:

> [the body] visualizes the strengthening armor of scales as the united multiplicity of the consenting individuals, which creates the *person* of the state, the identity of the Body|Politic, the unity of which is achieved only *in/by* representation[63]

The consenting subjects unite for protection, and thus 'strengthen the armour' of the sovereign. In a complex visual depiction of representative politics, the people's subjection feeds the ruler's power, and he is strengthened by their obedience.

The sovereign and/or government as representative of the citizens is a common understanding of democratic contemporary rule.[64] The use of *Queen of Scots* by the pro-union *Daily Telegraph* presents the Queen as the unifying Head of State, and visualises an apparent democratic desire of the UK body politic to remain united. This is signified in the tagline, a quotation from the Queen's press release: 'we have in common an enduring love of Scotland, which is one of the things that helps unite us all'.[65] The collective pronoun 'we' presents her statement as representing the nation, and readers are invited to recognise themselves in that 'we' and, thus, as part of the (re)United Kingdom. As Leviathan's subjects gathered in obedience of their ruler, the newspaper's use of *Queen of Scots* calls for the British public's obedience in (re)affirming their allegiance to the British monarch(y) and concomitant conservative political values, whether the Scottish citizens voted for or against independence.

James I uses the body politic, combined with a marriage metaphor, to claim his right to rule during his first speech to the English Parliament in 1604:

> I am the Husband, and all the whole Isle is my lawful Wife; I am the Head, and it is my Body ... I hope therefore that no man will be so unreasonable as to think that I that am Christian King under

the Gospel, should be a Polygamist and husband to two wives; that
I being the Head, should have a divided and monstrous Body.[66]

He suggests that separating England and Scotland will also separate
him, leaving a 'divided and monstrous Body'. In Christian marriages
at that time, husband and wife became 'one flesh', with marriages
indissoluble except by Act of Parliament or annulment.[67] In describing himself as husband to 'the whole isle', James I unites the two
nations under marital contract. Unlawful polygamy symbolises the
difficulty of ruling over two kingdoms, and the purity of a united
realm versus the monstrosity of separation. The body politic must
remain united. If nations result from our imagined relationships
to one another, then contesting these representations is as much
denying our relationship to each other as it is querying the terms
of our relationship, in whose favour it works, and what privileges
it establishes.

'Sovereign of the Most Ancient and Most Noble Order of the Thistle': Landscape and the body geographic

The second title, 'Sovereign of the Most Ancient and Most Noble
Order of the Thistle', refers to Scotland's equivalent to England's
Order of the Garter, the highest order of chivalry from the
monarch.[68] James II established the Order of the Thistle in the
seventeenth century as a statutory foundation to reward loyalty in
Scotland during a period of political unrest.[69] In *Queen of Scots*, it
is signified by the mantle: the insignia worn by Order members at
ceremonial occasions. The Queen's shoulders are draped in the
Collar of the Order, from which hangs the Jewel depicting Scotland's
patron saint, St Andrew. The Collar is a chain of golden thistles
and rue sprigs, which originate in the Scottish Highlands.

This symbolic detail compares to the Leviathan frontispiece,
which is intricately composed to reflect Hobbes's argument. The

Leviathan figure grasps a sword in his right hand, and a bishop's crozier in his left. The sword depicts the sovereign's temporal power, 'which in the last resort he must use for the preserving of Peace and Security'.[70] The crozier symbolises Leviathan's ecclesiastical power and rule over the whole realm, including the church.[71] The bottom section of the etching features compartments with individual symbols: those under the sword depict temporal power through war (e.g. a cannon), and those under the crozier symbolise ecclesiastical power through religion (e.g. a lightning bolt to signify excommunication).[72] A Latin inscription from the Book of Job frames the top, reading 'there is no power on earth which can be compared to him'.[73] Indeed, the name 'Leviathan' originates in the Book of Job, denoting 'a mighty and terrific beast, usually thought of as a monstrous sea-dweller such as a sea-dragon or serpent' and used in the text to demonstrate God's forceful rule over Job.[74] Hobbes's use of this term for his 'mortal God' highlights the sovereign's monstrosity, towering over the nation like an omnipotent giant, his sword and crozier extending beyond the etching.[75] This frightening embodiment of the state demonstrates Hobbes's own strange positionality somewhere between liberal democracy and absolute monarchy. Leviathan is theoretically representative of 'the people', yet the etching clearly advocates his indissoluble power. The monstrosity of monarchy is visible in his allegorical form.

In both Leviathan and *Queen of Scots*, the sovereign's crown symbolises monarchical rule. Whilst Leviathan's body is constituted by his subjects, the Queen's body is adorned with Scottish cultural markers, connoting Scottish national identity. Both figures are situated in the landscape of their realm. Leviathan physically emerges from the land as though grown from it, the 'natural' leader, whilst the Queen stands upon her 50,000-acre Balmoral Estate. She too appears to emerge from the land, the thistle and sprig collar around her neck and the rich green robe melting into the Scottish countryside, and the stream's curve blending into her robe. Like Leviathan, her presence in/on the Scottish land reaffirms her territorial power and authority, and this power is naturalised through depicting her 'at one' with the landscape.

The art historian W.J.T. Mitchell argues that landscape is not fixed, but a cultural process that structures the formation of national identities.[76] The geographer Kenneth Robert Olwig uses the Leviathan frontispiece to demonstrate how the now-commonsense relationship between a country, the body politic and landscape scenery is actually a historical development rooted in James I's rule.[77] James I's request for the political union of Scotland and England was refused by Parliament because

> the country of England ... was manifested as a polity through its representation by parliament ... Parliament would not have the same legitimacy with regard to the amalgamated body politic of Britain since there was no precedent by which the English parliament could claim a customary right to represent a country such as Scotland.[78]

James I countered this by invoking cultural representations of 'Great Britain' (then a figment of his imagination) not as a country in historical or legal terms but in terms of its landscape.[79] That is, he used court masques to represent the united landscape of his imaginary country. This brought the new nation into being, and facilitated the now-commonsense understanding of the British state as a body politic *within* a body geographic, organised by a central state.

Likewise, in *Queen of Scots*, the UK's body politic is united under a shared body geographic, in this case the recognisable countryside landscape surrounding the Queen. Citizens are 'bound by mystical bonds of soil and blood', as the landscape becomes symbolic of a mutual 'love' – as the headline suggests – of shared national history.[80] Moreover, the Queen's authority transcends her physical body, and becomes embedded in the landscape. The monarch's power is *in* the UK, and its potential break is symbolically damaging to monarchy. *Queen of Scots* demonstrates how sensationalist myth-making about the role of monarchy in an independent Scotland is used to produce fear, specifically here by the *Daily Telegraph* but also in wider discourses. As the Scottish government's White Paper on an independent Scotland explicitly states, the Union of Crowns 1603 means that the Queen would remain Queen unless a separate referendum on republicanism was held.[81] Hence, the *Daily Telegraph's* invocation of losing the Queen merely dissuades pro-monarchy electorates from voting for independence, and models many contemporary media texts by stoking emotion and fear in voters as opposed to documenting knowledge and facts.[82]

'Chief of Chiefs': Extraction, exploitation and enclosure

Whilst we are invited to read *Queen of Scots* through a 'tourist gaze' as a natural landscape, this 'naturalness' is worth investigating.[83] *Queen of Scots* uses key symbols of visual representations of the Scottish Highlands, namely heather, mountains, water and rich foliage. In a special edition of BBC's *Countryfile*, the photographer Julian Calder describes the labour of precisely framing the shot,[84] revealing that it was chosen because it had 'all the ingredients' for an aesthetically pleasing composition.[85] A behind-the-scenes photograph of the photoshoot reveals a different surrounding landscape: punctuated by large boulders, no luscious purple heather, workers disrupting the quiet and powerful solitude and a man-made wooden track for vehicle access.[86]

When placed in historical context, the Queen's presence in the landscape stems from the political terror of the Highland Clearances. As the sociologist Ben Pitcher argues, 'nationalized landscapes have an astonishing capacity to absorb ongoing histories of conflict and struggle over access and ownership',[87] where these struggles are gradually erased from historical memories. In the eighteenth century, the Highlands were inhabited mostly by crofters: communities where each crofter (farmer) tenured individual arable crofts for small-scale food production, while poorer-quality hill ground was shared as common grazing land for animals.[88] By the late eighteenth to early nineteenth century, the Scottish and English aristocracy sought to import mass agricultural production into the region for commercialisation.[89] They enclosed this land through the destruction and mass displacement of crofting communities, where some were forced to emigrate while many others died after their townships were set alight.[90] By 1802, most of the Highlands were 'under sheep'.[91] The 'natural' landscape of *Queen of Scots*, then, has been shaped by the grazing sheep introduced by wealthy landlords for profit, and by the terror wreaked on sustainable crofting communities. *Queen of Scots* actually represents an industrial landscape; a commercial space enclosed for the extraction of marketable resources.

The title 'Chief of Chiefs' stems from a parallel history, referring to ancient Scottish clan systems: extended networks of Highlanders from the same region who adopted the same surname.[92] Clan Chiefs were the regional leaders. In the eighteenth century, many Clan Chiefs supported the Jacobite movement to restore the exiled Stuart king James II to the British throne.[93] The rebellion resulted in the prohibition of traditional dress (predominantly tartan) and Gaelic speech, the confiscation of many Clan Chief estates – leading to the abolishment of the clan system – and the composition of an extra verse of the British national anthem 'God Save the Queen' to generate English patriotic fervour. Specifically, this encouraged the British army officer Marshal Wade to 'crush' and colonise the 'Rebellious Scots':[94]

> Lord grant that Marshal Wade
> May by thy mighty aid
> Victory bring.
> May he sedition hush,
> And lie a torrent rush,
> Rebellious Scots to crush.
> God save the Queen!

Whilst it is debated if this verse was ever popularly sung, it illustrates the Scottish struggle for cultural representation later highlighted in the Independence Referendum.[95] Political disputes continue over replacing the British national anthem,[96] and at the 2012 Olympic Games some Scottish members of Team Great Britain refused to sing 'God Save the Queen' in protest.[97]

Queen of Scots can be compared to Clan Chief portraiture, such as the eighteenth- to nineteenth-century artist Sir Henry Raeburn's portrait *The MacNab*, and indeed *Queen of Scots* is displayed in the Scottish National Portrait Gallery alongside Raeburn's work.[98] Painted in 1810, *The MacNab* depicts the elderly Francis MacNab, chief of Clan MacNab. MacNab wears a military green coat over a red and green tartan kilt, and carries guns and a broadsword to connote power. Despite his dominating stance, and the implicit suggestion of MacNab's wealth given that portraiture was costly,[99] the curator Robin Nicholson describes MacNab as tarnished by debt, and his estates were sold after his death in 1816.[100] Furthermore, the wild Highland landscape of the portrait's background is merely a stage set in Raeburn's studio. As such, Nicholson calls MacNab's outfit a 'fancy dress … a façade of prestige and authority'.[101]

Likewise, *Queen of Scots* appropriates Scottish cultural symbols to establish nationalist ideology. Comparing it to Raeburn's work exposes the Queen's monstrosity, robed in her own 'fancy dress' to perform 'Scottishness'. Julian Calder describes how the Queen's upward gaze presents her as 'looking up at the clans who have amassed on the hillside to come to see her' as their leader.[102] Given the bloodied history of the clan systems, where the British monarchy was one institution destroying the Chiefs' legacies in the Highland Clearances, this is remarkable. The curatorial decision to place *Queen of Scots* alongside Raeburn's portraits further depoliticises the violent history between the monarchy and Scottish clans. When the Queen stakes out her ownership of Scottish land, she symbolically erases the crofters and clans, and – through her hereditary ownership of Balmoral – aligns herself with the aristocrats who initiated the clearances. Indeed, Balmoral was originally owned by the Chief of the Farquharson Clan before Prince Albert persuaded them to sell it to Queen Victoria in 1847,[103] and the estate was demolished and rebuilt.[104] As the journalist George Monbiot suggests, 'this balmorality is equivalent to Marie Antoinette dressing up as a milkmaid while the people of France starved'.[105] As Highlanders were cleared, Victoria and Albert appropriated their dress and customs as costumes, and expounded their emotional attachments to the region in journals.[106] *Queen of Scots* is sited at Balmoral only because of the destruction of indigenous[107] Scottish communities.

Victoria's ownership of Balmoral was one of around 130–150 sporting estates covering 2.5 million acres of Highland land in the late nineteenth century.[108] While roaming in exclusive private playgrounds, many landowning elites designed tartans for their families and staff to appropriate clan traditions.[109] This 'Balmorality'[110] or 'Highland landlordism'[111] was led by the royal family, who have become so affiliated with the region that the area surrounding Balmoral is colloquially renamed 'Royal Deeside'.[112] Other pastiches include Highland Games events, key events in the aristocratic social calendar since the late nineteenth century, with the monarch acting as patron of the Braemar event as the 'Chief of Chiefs'.[113] The royal family's attendance at (and patronage of) the Braemar Highland Games continues.[114]

Conclusion

Representations of the Queen continue to symbolise national unity. In April 2020 during the global COVID-19 pandemic, the Queen gave a short speech to the nation (broadcast simultaneously on BBC One, ITV, Channel 4 and Channel 5) and the Commonwealth, encouraging citizens to draw on traits of 'self-discipline' and 'quiet, good-humoured resolve', and unite to cope with the crisis. Quotations from the speech, alongside an image of the Queen, were later displayed on London's Piccadilly Lights in Piccadilly Circus. This merges 'new' technologies – television – with more traditional forms of sovereign power. With echoes of Leviathan towering over his subjects, the Queen's recognisable face towers over the London skyline as a beacon of national unity. Her message attempts to bring together all British and Commonwealth citizens, yet COVID-19 revealed expansive global inequalities, from disparate healthcare practices, unemployment, homelessness, poverty and lack of government accountability.[115] Just as *Queen of Scots* obscured the referendum's meaning under representations of national identity, the Queen's image dominating London obscures COVID-19's discriminatory consequences and again places responsibility with 'the people' to unite.

This chapter has fractured typical representations of the Queen. In *Queen of Scots*, the *Daily Telegraph* celebrates the culmination of a long-drawn battle for union, using the monarch's symbolic body as representing the (re)United Kingdom. If, as I argue, the Independence Referendum was (partly) concerned with political and cultural representation, then the comparison between *Queen of Scots* and *Leviathan* is extremely ironic. In response to crying for independence, the *Daily Telegraph* presents Scots with a figuration of Hobbes's treatise on absolute monarchy. The referendum is comparable to Hobbes's unstable 'state of nature', where Scots attempted to fracture political hegemony.[116] The 'no' vote is the solution, and the Queen represents the 'stable state' that the British government seeks to provide. The pro-independence campaigners are comparable to Leviathan's subjects, incorporated in the British body politic and forced to 'look up' at the Queen's monstrous figure, as she simultaneously erases and appropriates Scottish cultural motifs, history, ancestry and land. Hobbes's theory may emphasise political representation, but pro-independence Scots have not consented to this particular vision of the United Kingdom. Indeed, in 2017, 44 per cent of 169 Scots surveyed agreed with the statement 'the monarchy is a meaningless institution', a significantly higher percentage than other UK regions (30 per cent of 96 people in Wales, an average of 28 per cent across nine English regions).[117] *Queen of Scots*, then, does not represent Scots. Rather, as William Davies argues, it models contemporary media texts by privileging emotion – here fear, anxiety and nostalgia – over expertise and knowledge to stoke a fractious political environment.[118] This is particularly so at a time of growing global right-wing populism, which, like *Queen of Scots*, hinges on ideologies of nationalism and (non-)belonging.

For *Running the Family Firm*, *Queen of Scots* demonstrates how staging the monarch's body remains a powerful 'mechanism of consent' for political and national ideologies.[119] The political and constitutional uncertainties of the referendum meant that the Queen operated as a symbol of authority and historical legitimacy to contain narratives of crisis. A few years later during the Brexit debate, some anti-Brexit people read the Queen's outfit at the State Opening of Parliament 2017 (the first since the Brexit vote) as symbolising her support of the EU. Her papal purple hat was decorated with yellow flowers, mirroring the yellow stars on the blue EU flag.[120] That this was interpreted as a meaningful statement from the Queen – who cannot offer personal political opinions due to constitutional obligations to remain politically neutral – demonstrates her body's power to absorb political meaning. Only because the Queen *means something* is her hat notable, said to visualise the wishes of the UK body politic to remain united. The Queen's monstrous body continues to offer a symbolic battleground on which to wage debates about national identities and belonging.

4

Let them have Poundbury!
Land, property and pastoralism

In his book on British architecture, *A Vision of Britain*, Prince Charles included enclosure as one of his 'Ten Principles' for the built environment, claiming that it produces 'privacy, beauty, and a feeling of total safety' and 'a recognisable community'.[1] *A Vision of Britain* is formed around Charles's self-positioning as advocating history and rejecting modernist urban architectural style. Yet, his comments on enclosure demonstrate that he knows little history about British agricultural life and the devastating impact of the enclosure system, which removed rights to the commons and drove people from their homes, often into slum dwellings in towns and cities. In fact, Charles's suggestion that enclosure creates 'a feeling of total safety' entirely erases the symbolic and physical violence involved in the process.[2]

Charles's appreciation of enclosure reveals the specificities of his *vision* of Britain: it is an aristocratic version of the pastoral emphasising class hierarchy and land ownership, contextualised in his own position as England's largest private landowner through the Duchy of Cornwall. For the aristocracy, enclosure meant benefiting economically from privatisation: profiting from renting land back to the lower classes, farming arable lands and erasing the surplus population by forcing them into urban areas. Although *A Vision of Britain* is positioned as commentary on architecture, implicit in Charles's vision is a return to the class hierarchy of aristocratic landowner, farm managers and peasant workers. The phrase 'let them eat cake!' is commonly attributed to Marie Antoinette during the French Revolution in response to her subjects having no bread to eat; her privilege meaning she misunderstood their poverty. This can be paraphrased as 'let them have Poundbury!' to illustrate Charles's version of this incomprehensibility. Poundbury also simulates royal attempts to imitate 'ordinary' life, as part of negotiating distance between them and their subjects. Indeed, Marie Antoinette's *Hameau* at the Palace of Versailles is a rustic model village of cottages, a mill and an ornamental dairy.[3] She populated this spectacle with workers, whom she occasionally joined to simulate peasant life before returning to the palace. Similarly, George IV commissioned the 1812 construction of Royal Lodge at Windsor Castle as an imitation rustic country cottage.[4]

The architectural principles Charles documents in *A Vision of Britain* were literalised in his creation of Poundbury, working with the Luxembourgish architect Léon Krier. Poundbury is a 400-acre urban extension to Dorchester in Dorset, England, built on Duchy of Cornwall land and named after nearby Poundbury Hill which hosts a hill fort, the site of a Middle Bronze Age enclosure.[5] Poundbury regenerates a conservative, anti-modernist, neoclassical blend of what Charles calls 'familiar, traditional, well-tried and beautiful' architectural styles.[6] Yet, it is controversial: Poundbury has been described as a 'toytown', and in 2013 the Poundbury road sign was vandalised to read 'Ugly Buildings'.[7]

Charles appears to envisage himself as a social, cultural and/ or political commentator, and uses his public role to broadcast concerns about architecture, agriculture, science, healthcare, ecology, religion and horticulture. His interventions appear in cultural texts such as his Duchy Originals organic food range, a Labybird book on climate change and the infamous 'black spider' memos lobbying government ministers and politicians on his pet themes.[8] These have led to Charles's reputation as 'meddling'. Many commentators criticise him for threatening constitutional conventions for monarchs to be politically neutral; a concern inspiring the BBC drama *King*

Charles III which depicted constitutional breakdown upon his succession.[9] Public polling has consistently found that many Britons surveyed would prefer William to be crowned in Charles's place.[10]

Although Poundbury is a political statement against prevailing architectural trends (urbanisation and postmodernism in particular), Charles links these to social and cultural organisation. Indeed, as this chapter demonstrates, his vision of Britain seems to also be concerned with managing the citizens populating it: arguably an attempt to reclaim a form of sovereign power. Poundbury is an experimental place where all of Charles's concerns play out in material form. His interventions yearn for a past lost to urban modernity, best summarised in a grandiose speech he made in 2002:

> I have come to realize that my entire life has been so far motivated by a desire to heal – to heal the dismembered landscape and the poisoned soul; the cruelly shattered townscape, where harmony has been replaced by cacophony ... so that the temple of our humanity can once again be lit by a sacred flame.[11]

His appropriation of religious discourse reignites a sacrosanct understanding of royalty through the 'royal touch' and 'divine right', where the monarch was positioned as 'God's agent on earth' by healing illness and disease.[12] There is also an assumption that there is *something* to heal by returning to a pastoral past, and that Charles himself has been granted the role of shepherding this process of return. In a more recent book, *Harmony: A New Way of Looking at the World*, Charles channels the romantic poets to describe nature's harmony versus the chaos of man-made industry, claiming that the ancient world had a 'grammar' matching nature's patterns, and modern advancements have lost this synchrony.[13] Only by re-establishing people's relationship with nature can 'harmony' be restored, and Charles maintains that classical architecture, organic farming, alternative medicine and spirituality (amongst others) will achieve this.

In 1993 Charles said he wants to 'put the "Great" back into Great Britain', apparently foreshadowing the former US President

Donald Trump's controversial campaign slogan 'make America great again'.[14] Indeed, I argue that Charles's visions reveal him as a reactionary figure with conservative political inflections (many regressive political movements, such as Brexit, use similar language of 'chaos' versus 'order'). Charles's ideologies reflect traditionalist, neo-feudalist, High Toryism (or traditionalist conservatism), concerned with maintaining a traditional, landed society by privileging lower taxation, social hierarchies, environmental concerns, agrarianism, ruralism, localism and strong community ties.[15] The political commentator George Walden revealingly referred to contemporary versions of High Toryism from Conservative politicians such as Jacob Rees-Mogg as 'Poundbury Toryism'.[16] This conservative imagination opposes neoliberal emphasis on global, technological-connected, mobile cities, preferring provincial, local landscapes.[17] Likewise, Charles's assumptions about nature's harmony reflects politically conservative myths about the countryside as 'a stable, ordered, virtually apolitical society'.[18] As the geographer Michael Woods argues, this erases radical political histories in rural Britain, such as the Peasants' Revolt. Yet, simultaneously, the Duchy of Cornwall was described in the 2019 documentary *Prince Charles: Inside the Duchy of Cornwall*, commissioned by Buckingham Palace and aired on ITV, as a multi-million-pound 'business empire'.[19] Landownership, property investment and developing infrastructure are central facets of neoliberalism under rentier capitalism.[20] This chapter argues that Poundbury illustrates the consolidation of heritage and enterprise under conservative governance.[21]

Charles situates the 'destruction' of social harmony as a postwar phenomenon because of modernist rebuilding projects.[22] However, this period also saw postwar economic migration into Britain from former colonies, the decline of Empire and the crafting of the welfare state. Indeed, this chapter argues that Charles's vision is less concerned with 1950s and 1960s architecture, and more concerned with the social, cultural, political and economic changes that dismantled traditional class and racial hierarchies. The tensions in Charles's investments, sitting between a feudal provincialism and financial neoliberalism, are drawn out throughout this chapter.

Building Poundbury: A history

The Duchy of Cornwall (hereafter the Duchy) owns around 135,000 acres of land across 23 counties. This makes Charles, the Duke of Cornwall, England's largest private landowner.[23] In 2019, the Duchy reported net assets of £931 million, and its holdings included £53 million in development sites and £291 million in commercial property.[24] The Duchy was created by Edward III in 1337 for his son the Black Prince, and is hereditarily owned by male[25] heirs to the throne as Dukes of Cornwall, who are entitled to the annual net revenue surplus of the Duchy to fund their private and public duties. In 2018–19, Charles received £21.6 million.[26]

Like the Firm itself, the Duchy's organisation incorporates private, public and commercial management. The Duchy's annual reports describe it as a 'private estate', allowing it to avoid requests for information made under the Freedom of Information Act.[27] Yet, in *Prince Charles: Inside the Duchy of Cornwall*, the introductory voiceover claimed that 'the Duke has turned an ancient institution into a business empire that last year made over £21 million in profit'.[28] The legal scholar John Kirkhope argues that the Duchy was created by, and is subject to, statute, has its accounts scrutinised by Parliament, and uses its income for public purposes; making it a public company.[29] The Duchy also has unique privileges vested in Crown exemption: it is not legally liable for capital gains tax, corporation tax, inheritance tax or income tax, although Charles 'voluntarily' pays income tax on personal expenses.[30] In 2019, the Duchy had 148 employees working in the head office in London and regional offices across the South-West.[31] Although Poundbury remains its most famous project, the Duchy manages various development schemes including a similar urban extension to Newquay, called Nansledan (nicknamed 'Surfbury') which will

comprise four thousand homes; a sustainable commercial development called Truro Eastern District Centre; and Highgrove Estate
in Gloucestershire, where Charles built an organic farming system,
Duchy Home Farm.[32] Despite describing it as a 'business empire'
and highlighting its commercial enterprising, *Prince Charles: Inside
the Duchy of Cornwall* codes the Duchy through ideologies of family
and morality.[33] All Duchy tenants receive Christmas presents from
Charles, and he describes his protection of rural land – which
he claims is unprofitable – as a gift 'from my family to theirs' to
maintain community businesses.[34] When he visits Duchy property,
towns throw mass celebrations for a royal visit.

Charles is, essentially, their landlord. The etymology of 'landlord'
stems from early fifteenth-century feudalism, an 'owner of a tene-
ment, one who rents land or property': the *lord* of the *land*.[35] For
Karl Marx, rent was a principle of capitalist production whereby
landowners extract profit from land.[36] The campaigner Guy
Shrubsole argues that landownership remains central to inequality,
whilst the scholars Brett Christophers, Guy Standing and Beverley
Skeggs suggest that late capitalism has turned (back) to rent,
expropriation and enclosure to extract profit and value.[37] Like the
Firm itself, the Duchy is invested in aristocratic forms of hereditary
ownership, yet operates as a 'business empire' with corporate strategy.
A 2020 documentary by Republic, *The Man Who Shouldn't Be King*,
documents alleged cases where the Duchy exploited its legal status
for profit.[38] For example, on the Isles of Scilly, investors letting their
second homes out as holiday homes must allegedly give the Duchy
some of the income. Other residents were apparently banned from
buying their homes' freehold, currently owned by the Duchy, despite
the Leasehold Reform Act 1967 that states that leaseholders can
purchase the freehold if they meet particular criteria.[39] In 2021,
the *Guardian* revealed that this Act was subject to the parliamentary
procedure the 'Queen's consent', whereby government ministers
must seek the Queen's permission before debating laws which will
affect her. Under this procedure, the *Guardian* claimed that Charles

screened laws which would affect the Duchy of Cornwall, and the Duchy was given special exemptions to deny residents the legal right to buy their homes outright.[40] Bert Biscoe, a local councillor in Truro, Cornwall, who was campaigning against a new Duchy development project, claimed that 'Charles does not accept his constitutional responsibilities to Cornwall, he just wants the money. He says "stand up for rural life and the farmer", and then builds a supermarket and a hundred houses on good quality farmland.'[41] The Duchy's murky legal status arguably allows it to circumvent laws and policies designed to govern landlords, while simultaneously reaping the profits of rentier capitalism.

Poundbury is a riposte to modernist architecture, which Charles first attacked in 1984. While presenting an award at the Royal Institution of British Architects, he criticised the proposed modernist extension to London's National Gallery as a 'monstrous carbuncle', claiming to be airing the views of 'ordinary people' whose opposition to modernist style is consistently ignored.[42] Charles simultaneously positions himself as a spokesperson for the masses, and claims expert knowledge by suggesting his intimate familiarity of architectural theory.[43] In 1986, Charles ventured beyond verbal interventions to establish the Prince of Wales's Institute of Architecture (now the Prince's Foundation for Building Community), an educational charity to teach urban design principles.[44] This work was continued in 1988 with BBC documentary *HRH The Prince of Wales: A Vision of Britain*, the partner book *A Vision of Britain* and an accompanying exhibition at the Victoria and Albert Museum, all of which evoked landscape painting to demonstrate the 'harmony' of historical architecture versus the 'chaos' of modernism.[45]

Charles's interventions were (and remain) controversial, sparking what the sociologist Dick Hebdige called 'the Great Architectural Debate'.[46] In November 1989, architects attended a sold-out event debating Charles's critiques.[47] Many ripostes or defences of Charles's views were aired in publications like the *Architectural Review*, and the then President of the Royal Institution of British Architects

Maxwell Hutchinson published *The Prince of Wales: Right or Wrong?* in which he argued that Charles abused his royal position.[48] Critics have suggested that he 'exercis[es] benevolent totalitarianism over the mini-kingdom of architecture'. [49] Of course, historically architecture was symbolic of royal power, from palaces and statues to geographical links between royal residences, and religious or political buildings. Charles's direct interventions in an age of constitutional monarchy represent a different form of power.

Poundbury was conceived in 1987, when 400 acres of Duchy land to the west of Dorchester was selected by local government for urban expansion following an affordable housing crisis. The Duchy released the land on the proviso that Charles could manage the design, and Charles hired the architect Léon Krier to design Poundbury on the basis of 'New Urbanist' principles.[50] In *The Architecture of Community*, Krier outlines 'New Urbanist' principles as favouring, amongst other things: mixed-use buildings, limitations to car access and the expansion of public transport, traditional street patterns, local building materials, distinctive civil buildings and no zoning or segregation.[51] These features reflect Charles's 'Ten Principles' outlined in *A Vision of Britain*: respecting the landscape, hierarchy of buildings, scale of buildings, aesthetic harmony, community enclosure, use of local materials, use of decoration, contribution of artists, limiting signs and street lights, and facilitating community spirit.[52] All of these appear in Poundbury. Upon completion in 2025, Poundbury will house around five thousand people.[53]

I visited Poundbury in July 2017. I boarded the train from London to Dorchester, before taking a twenty-minute bus ride from Dorchester to Poundbury's Mansell Square. I employed walking methodology to 'spatio-analyse' Poundbury, photography, field note-taking and collected publicity materials to document my experiences.[54] Poundbury was just over half-way to completion then, with four 'Phases' of development scheduled between 1999 and 2025. The quarters are designed to facilitate walking between home, shopping and work: Phase One centres on Pummery Square with Poundbury Village Stores, The Poet Laureate pub and Brownsword Hall (a community hall). Phases Two, Three and Four take as their centre Queen Mother's Square, which includes a Waitrose and Damer's First School. I began my walk through 'Phase One' and Pummery Square, before travelling the perimeter of 'Phase Two' via Middle Farm Way to Queen Mother's Square, then exploring the 'central' streets of Phase Two. Poundbury's purposefully chaotic design of high-density, mixed-use street patterns made it difficult to achieve this walk methodically, and I frequently became lost, but this contributed to experiencing the space dynamically.[55] I visited Poundbury Village Stores, Mayfair Estate Agents, Waitrose and Poundbury Garden Centre. My field-based reflections and photographs feature throughout this chapter.

At the time of writing, CG Fry and Sons Ltd, Morrish Builders of Poole and Westbury Homes Plc undertake construction of Poundbury; social houses are rented through the Guinness Partnership (see below); architects such as Ben Pentreath, Ken Morgan and Andy Kunz have designed individual buildings or streets; Zero C Holdings and Woodpecker Properties develop commercial buildings; the Duchy employee Ben Murphy acts as Estate Director; Simon Conibear is Development Consultant; and Peter James the Project Manager.[56] Daily management is undertaken by multiple bodies: the Duchy of Cornwall, Dorset County Council, West Dorset District Council, Dorchester Town Council, the Poundbury Residents' Association (see below) and Manco 1 and Manco 2 (see below). Multiple contracts ensure the implementation of Krier's design principles: the Poundbury Building Code offers detailed guidance on building materials and roof heights; the Building Agreement controls building design; and all residents receive a Poundbury Design Guidance to manage alterations, and must sign the Poundbury Code upon moving in.[57] This reflects how the Poundbury community is controlled and manufactured, as I now explore.

#lovepoundbury: Manufacturing a model village

#lovepoundbury is a hashtag and/or group on Facebook, Twitter and Instagram to share local news and events, facilitate discussion between residents and promote the Poundbury community. This is, as I demonstrate, a specifically white, middle-class and middle-aged community, drawing upon markers of middle-class taste. For instance, the Instagram feed consists primarily of lifestyle images to promote Poundbury businesses, such as antiques shop Romans VIII and artisan pizzas from the Engine Room.[58]

#lovepoundbury reflects how Charles's vision is not merely architectural but concerned also with manufacturing the citizens. *A Vision of Britain* describes Poundbury as a 'model village'.[59] This partly evokes the miniature villages displayed as tourist attractions, usually featuring model people in fantasy scenarios. This conjures images of Charles 'playing' with the Poundbury community, using real people to simulate a fantasy society. 'Model village' also describes self-contained communities built by eighteenth- or nineteenth-century landowners and industrialists to house their workers. This began with model cottages built by landlords of large estates, through to the creations of liberal industrialists such as Saltaire in Yorkshire built by the woollen manufacturer Titus Salt, Port Sunlight in Merseyside built by the soap-maker William Lever and Bournville near Birmingham built by the chocolate proprietor George Cadbury. These philanthropic developments aimed to improve working-class living, but also re-established class hierarchies between owner and worker, giving wealthy elites control over workers' lifestyles from their homes to their exercise regimes.[60] The scholar Frank Schaffer describes this as a form of social engineering.[61]

In Poundbury, social engineering is exercised through the Poundbury Code: covenants and stipulations regulating residents' use of the built environment.[62] This demands no exterior property alteration, no caravan parking, no visible repairing of motor vehicles, no removal of pre-planted shrubbery, no displaying of advertisements or placards, no visible television aerials, clothes driers or dustbins, and Charles's unobstructed access to any property. All commercial buildings are subject to strict guidelines on style and size of shop signage, giving them all uniform branding.[63]

Social engineering is evidenced structurally through design decisions that privilege older or middle-aged, middle-class or upper-class residents. Most of the shops are independent boutiques rather than chain stores, which does foster the idea of a unique community but compounds class relations by neglecting those requiring cheaper, own-brand goods. The only supermarket is Waitrose, an upmarket food store in receipt of two Royal Warrants. My field notes remark upon multiple wealth-management offices providing financial services to individuals, small businesses and families, suggesting clientele of at least moderate wealth. Retired people and young families are facilitated for with appropriate shops and events, such as Active Mobility for older customers' living aids, and baby shop Magpie, whilst older children, teenagers and young adults were absent. After visiting, I discovered that a 'youth shelter' named the Belvedere *has* been constructed in a field on the southern perimeter (Figure 4.1), but the stone pavilion was so underwhelming that I did not recognise its use, and residents have reported it is rarely used.[64] The geographer Michelle Thompson-Fawcett's Poundbury resident survey found the lack of child-friendly facilities an ongoing complaint.[65]

These management and design decisions evidence how pre-industrial aesthetics are frequently prioritised over a modern, functional environment. Walkways lined with gravel obstruct prams and wheelchairs, parks lack dog waste bins, few road markings mean that parked cars clog the streets and the decorative pillars outside buildings have allegedly caused accidents (Figure 4.2). Mixed-use neighbourhoods are meant to prioritise walkability between home, shopping and work, but car use is actually higher than the UK average.[66] Stipulations on shop signage have displeased companies, with one owner complaining that 'he relies on custom

4.1 The Belvedere, a youth shelter in Poundbury, depicted in the far distance across the field

from visitors to survive, but with the ban on signs people often fail to find him'.[67] Indeed, many businesses erect signs 'illegally' and remove them when Charles visits.[68]

Façade is central to Poundbury, and the appearance of historical simplicity often merely masks messier realities. The nostalgic peristyle of Poundbury Village Stores actually houses a branch of food store Budgens (Figure 4.3); the pillars on Strathmore House are painted on;[69] gas pipes and ventilation are concealed with gargoyles or intricate designs; and an electricity substation is disguised as a Greek temple (Figure 4.4). History is simulated through Roman numeral construction dates on buildings, which actually translate as '2015'.

Poundbury's imitative quality has led to its comparison to Disneyland: a faux theme-park simulating history.[70] Indeed, it mirrors the neo-urbanist Celebration in Florida, a 'futuristic' model town

SAFETY NOTICE

DUE TO RECENT INCIDENTS
PLEASE BE AWARE OF
THE COLUMNS OUTSIDE
THE MAIN DOOR.

4.2 A safety notice in Poundbury

built by Walt Disney that actually recreates the past. Theatrical associations reveal how it commands aesthetics over functionality: it bears resemblance to the Universal Studios backlot in Hollywood, and in 2017 Poundbury was used as an alternative reality for the sci-fi television drama *Electric Dreams*.[71] Poundbury's New Urbanist influence, the town of Seaside in Florida, was used as the simulated world in the sci-fi film *The Truman Show*.[72] In the satirical Channel 4 sitcom *The Windsors*, which caricatures key royal figures, Poundbury is depicted as a fake, backwards-looking 'vanity project' for Charles's ego.[73] For example, Charles unveils the eighth statue of himself that Poundbury residents must pay weekly homage to for the fictional 'Prince Charles Day', and he evinces horror about a resident installing a boiler, asking 'what's wrong with a bit of elbow grease and a mangle?' Lamp posts and other features are made from polystyrene to symbolise simulation.

4.3 Poundbury Village Stores and its interior Budgens

4.4 An electricity substation disguised as a Greek temple, Poundbury

The 1795 political cartoon 'Affability' by James Gillray satirises George III's nickname 'Farmer George': an informal referent to his agricultural interests and paternal style of rule.[74] In the cartoon, a farmer is bemused by the monarch's incessant interrogation about his life, of which 'Farmer George' has little concept, despite his supposed 'ordinariness'. Similarly, in 2018 photographs by Chris Jackson, commissioned by Clarence House for Charles's seventieth birthday, captured Charles feeding chickens at Highgrove House, dressed in informal boots and trousers like 'Farmer George'.[75] This was part of a set of photographs, including Charles playing with his grandchildren and reading in the garden, and seemed to demonstrate attempts to represent Charles in similarly 'ordinary', upper-middle-class domesticity as William and Kate (see Chapter 6).

Poundbury is designed as Charles's utopia: a perfect community untainted by modernism's 'horrors'. However, as the journalist

Owen Hatherley argues, rather than forward-thinking progress, Charles 'abolish[es] the future in simulation of a fantasy past'.[76] His history misrepresents the reality of experiences structured by intersectional inequalities, and reflects his privilege of never having to suffer the 'gruel, death and cellars' which prompted the 'diverse cheap foodstuffs, antibiotics, and good modern housing' he opposes.[77] The subsequent sections of this chapter explore what Charles's 'fantasy past' resembles, and how Poundbury simulates this, using the architectural principles from *A Vision of Britain*.[78]

'This creeping cancer': Anti-modernism, heritage cultures and factories of production

Charles's *vision* disapproves of modernist architecture: 'our own heritage of regional styles and individual characteristics has been eaten away by this creeping cancer'.[79] Such diagnosis relies on reactionary understandings of 'Britishness' (or 'Englishness') rooted in pastoral nostalgia of the 'green and pleasant land'.[80] *A Vision of Britain* commences with a full-page aerial landscape of the British countryside, featuring characteristic rolling country lanes and lush green fields bordered by hedges and trees. This is contrasted, two pages later, with an industrial London dominated by cranes and scaffolding, its implied drabness consolidated by the grainy, black-and-white focus. Such a picturesque depiction is a common representational technique, from early Stuart monarchs fetishising country houses to encourage the gentry to abandon court interests in London and return to the countryside to slow rural decay; sixteenth-century literature contrasting the pastoral to the greed and corruption of cities; and the 1960s–1970s 'hippy' movement, which emphasised a back-to-the-land mentality through clothing, craft work and vegetarianism.[81]

Although Charles came of age during the latter period, and has been described as 'a hippy' for his alternative ecological and horticultural practices, his version of the pastoral is not the 'free love' iconography of the 1960s.[82] Rather, *A Vision of Britain* references nineteenth-century pastoral writers John Ruskin and William Wordsworth, who although radical in their day now evoke a conservative rurality. This is further consolidated in Charles's association with nineteenth-century institutions the National Trust and *Country Life* magazine. These institutions connect the pastoral and the national, and call for environmental sustainability through protecting country estates (including hunting and shooting) and encouraging heritage tourism.

The 'British heritage industry', which peaked during Poundbury's conception in the 1980s with heritage films and heritage tourism, has a similar ethos.[83] This accompanied Margaret Thatcher's ideology of national identity, which evoked nostalgia through fetishising the country estate and Victorian social values as part of the Conservative party's capitalising upon narratives of history, heritage and tradition.[84] In aligning the country estate with environmental sustainability, heritage culture overlooks disastrous environmental effects wrought by landownership, for example enclosures destroying common land, and hunting depleting wildlife. Despite Britain being 'the first industrial nation', pastoralism and rurality are central to 'Britishness'. The writer Patrick Wright's term 'Deep England' to describe the rural, for example, suggests an inherent connection between the countryside and national identity, whereby the pastoral represents 'true' Britain and industrial urbanisation is a manmade veneer.[85]

Charles's idealisation of the pastoral is not only pre-industrial but varies between a feudal and an agrarian capitalist understanding. *A Vision of Britain* uses N.M. Lund's painting *Heart of Empire* (see below for more detail) to illustrate how the Lord Mayor's Mansion House is given 'appropriate prominence' in relation to its neighbours.[86] This draws on feudal manorial systems of landownership and class stratification. The enclosures he celebrates were key consequences of agrarian capitalism and the 'formal declaration' of land as a capital commodity (see Chapter 3).[87] Enclosure also features in contemporary systems of neoliberalism and financial capital, with public spaces reshaped as commercial to maximise profit.[88] This contradicts community spirit by privatising common land for private interest, as illustrated succinctly in a 'no ball games' sign attached to the Brownsword Hall in Poundbury, dictating what individuals can do in public spaces.

One understanding of Charles's comparison between 'Aerial landscape of the British countryside' and 'Industrial London' is that he considers the countryside more 'natural' than the city. This is intimated in Charles's text, which describes the first image as 'part of an extraordinarily rich tradition which we've inherited from our forebears', and the second as evidence of the 'terrible damage [we have] … inflicted on parts of this country's unique landscape'.[89] In fact, both images indicate the exploitation of nature for economic profit. The hedgerows and fences in the countryside image result from enclosures that imposed capitalism upon the countryside, and undermined people's common access by turning it into private land. As such, these machine-made sectors of arable farming land are actually factories of production in the same way as the industrial buildings in the second image. Many hedgerows and fences are part of the aristocracy's cultivation of the countryside for their aesthetic pleasure. Charles's vision of pastoralism does not exist independently from the capitalism he claims to oppose, nor does it conform to the natural 'harmony' he promotes. In fact, it can be interpreted as what the film scholar Andrew Higson calls a 'flat, depthless pastiche' in heritage culture's reproduction of the past.[90]

How can we interpret Charles's aversion to modernist urban architectural style? Modernism counters hereditary, hierarchical privilege: privileges Charles relies on. It evokes socialist sensibilities, and reveals industries of production. This means making relations of production visible: no hidden vestibules or staircases for servants, as were popular in Victorian architecture, or gargoyles covering gas flues as are popular in Poundbury.[91] Architecture also facilitates social developments; for example gas installation eased domestic labour for the working classes (particularly women). This threatens Charles's investment in maintaining a traditional class system. Or, as the architectural critic Herbert Muschamp suggests, reflecting the framework in this book of the Firm as a theatrical and heavily mediated performance:

> He's like someone ... who has grown up in the midst of an elaborate stage set, and he's furious that there's been a tear in the backdrop, that you can see the pulleys, that the stagehands have walked off the job.[92]

If modernist architecture makes relations of production visible, Poundbury attempts to re-erect the stage set, props and actors of the 'upstairs, downstairs' theatre of historical class hierarchies.

Charles periodises modernist architecture as a postwar phenomenon, underlining his supposition that the 1950s and 1960s are when 'something went wrong'.[93] In fact, modernism has existed since at least the early twentieth century.[94] It is true, however, that postwar housing regeneration triggered modernist building projects as part of the postwar welfare state. The journalist John Grindrod argues against demonising the concrete tower blocks characterising this period, as for many people they symbolised escaping the damp and dysentery of inner-city slums.[95] Likewise, the suburban zoning that Charles despises established the interwar and postwar middle classes, who benefited from affordable housing within commuting distance to work.[96] Charles's rejection of suburbia in favour of mixed-use neighbourhoods could be because suburbia threatened the landlord/serf model of pastoralism.

As the sociologist Nathan Glazer remarks, it is ironic that an architecture concerned with social progress is being condemned as heartless by Charles.[97] Charles entirely overlooks the possibility that the working or middle classes might welcome modernism, and his anti-modernist regeneration is presented as philanthropic without ever consulting the inhabitants. Poundbury is a gentrification project that wilfully erases working- and middle-class history and uses architecture to impose particular social, cultural, political and economic ideals on citizens.

'We raise to heaven that which is valuable to us': Hierarchy, segregation and social housing

One of *A Vision of Britain*'s principal concerns is the hierarchy of buildings in terms of height and embellishment. For Charles, architecture is the physical representation of 'our values as well as our social organisations'.[98] He uses anti-vernacular language to position religion and state at society's centre: 'we raise to heaven that which is valuable to us: emblems of faith, enlightenment or government'.[99] He approves of, for example, churches (particularly St Paul's Cathedral, see below) and the Tower of London dominating the skyline, but disproves of high-rise social housing, office blocks or corporate skyscrapers. This positions secular, aristocratic or royal figures as class dominators. If the corporate skyscraper represents the capitalist white male ego,[100] Charles's concerns about dwarfing the church, the Tower of London and government buildings can be interpreted as insecurities about the destruction of his own royal or aristocratic ego under modernism.

This is visualised in Queen Mother's Square, the primary centre of Poundbury, which is dominated by royal references. Kingspoint House, the largest building in Poundbury, houses a Waitrose, a classed statement due to Waitrose's luxury status. This sits next to the Royal Pavilion, which comprises luxury apartments. Strathmore House – more luxury flats and named after the Queen Mother's father, the Earl of Strathmore – is the most visually imposing building on the square, modelled on Buckingham Palace (Figure 4.5). My field notes describe the yellow panels, grand pillars and lookalike balcony as erroneous in rural Dorset. Next is the Duchess of Cornwall Inn, modelled on London's luxurious Ritz Hotel (Figure 4.6), and finally a statue of the Queen Mother.

4.5 Strathmore House, Poundbury

4.6 The Duchess of Cornwall Inn, Poundbury

Spatial referents to past and present royals is commonplace (in road or building names, for example), but their meanings become more obvious in Poundbury's context. Royalty's position at the centre of Poundbury can be interpreted as Charles considering royalty as the centre of Britain, whereas it is politically marginal in real terms. It also symbolises the upper classes' dominance. All housing in the Square is luxury apartments, with those in Strathmore House selling for £750,000.[101] The Royal Pavilion website suggests that the development brings 'to Dorchester design standards normally associated with Knightsbridge in London', but overlooks the demographic disparity between rural Dorchester and metropolitan London.[102] This is especially ironic considering that Poundbury was originally commissioned to address affordable housing shortages in Dorchester.[103]

Poundbury has failed to address affordable housing.[104] Charles advocates 'pepper-potting': dispersing social housing throughout housing developments rather than segregating them in outer estates, which he disparagingly claims creates 'ghettos of crime and deprivation'.[105] Again, he pinpoints the postwar period, and the mass production of state-funded, local-authority-run housing estates, as when this segregation issue began – once more overlooking the freedom and safety that these housing estates afforded the working classes. In contrast, Charles claims that pepper-potting facilitates more 'inclusive' living[106] and a 'sense of genuine civic life'[107] because the social housing is, in theory, visually indistinguishable from its neighbours.

The author Lynsey Hanley argues against pepper-potting because social housing is often still emphasised as different.[108] Although smart in appearance, Poundbury's social housing lacks the intricate architectural detail of non-social housing. Much of the social housing is in less desirable vistas, such as on the main highway, and the social scientist Dennis Hardy found that the gardens' lack of decoration drew attention to the occupants' lack of disposable income.[109] Repeated references to Poundbury's social housing, such as an article in *Celebrating Poundbury* magazine on 'afford-able housing', also highlight its presence.[110] Thompson-Fawcett's Poundbury resident observation survey found that class divisions were an ongoing concern. Social-housing residents claimed that 'private dwellings do not care for us mere mortals who have to rent our properties', whilst non-social-housing inhabitants said that 'people living in … social housing, do not interact wholeheartedly within the community', suggesting resentment fostering on both sides of the class divide.[111]

Little attention is given to how Poundbury's pepper-potting scheme works in relation to earlier, neighbouring social-housing estates. To the east of Poundbury Village Stores, Cambridge Road is adjoined to Poundbury via Cambridge Walk. However, rather than a through-road to encourage multi-community cohesion, bollards limit access (Figure 4.7). This creates a tangible hierarchy

4.7 Cambridge Walk linking Poundbury to Cambridge Road

between Poundbury and nearby communities. Pepper-potting does not, then, equate to a classless society. Rather, Charles's utopia merely rewrites classed inequalities in an early twentieth-century hierarchical model of the pastoral, where everyone 'knows their place'.

The political alignment of this vision is complex. In theory, Poundbury rejects neoliberal individualism for community (although this community does not extend beyond Poundbury's boundaries). But Charles's demonisation of postwar housing reflects Thatcher's flagship 'Right to Buy' policy, which gave social-housing tenants opportunities to purchase their properties at reduced rates.[112] Poundbury also advocates transferring social-housing stock to independent housing associations. Two hundred and fifty Poundbury homes are owned by the Guinness Partnership, one of the largest housing associations in England, which Charles has been Patron of since 1997.[113] In 2015, Guinness Partnership was accused of social cleansing after displacing tenants on Loughborough Park Estate in London for a £100 million regeneration project, demonstrating a motivation for profit over people.[114] This illustrates Charles's incorporation of neoliberal models where they are profitable.

Alongside the other largest UK landowners – the Duchy of Lancaster, the Crown Estate, the church and the Duke of Westminster – the Duchy of Cornwall consistently fails to meet affordable-housing targets.[115] The journalist Nick Mathiason argues that royal landholders, supposedly acting in benefit of the nation, *should* have a moral obligation to be socially responsible landlords.[116] But Poundbury has always been a commercial venture. Four-hundred-acre plots were originally sold to developers for £40,000 but are now worth twelve times that, and the *Guardian* unearthed a unique arrangement whereby the Duchy extracts 10 per cent of profits from the Poet Laureate pub.[117] Like the Firm itself, capitalist profit is clearly central to Charles's vision, even if it contradicts many of his principles of rural simplicity. These neoliberal values are often masked under veneers of tradition and heritage. Visual signifiers of hierarchy and privilege make visible the classed conflict in Poundbury, and how it recreates Charles's ideal of the aristocrat and the serf.

'A city built on the water like the centre of another great trading empire, Venice': Little England, imperial nostalgia and whiteness

A Vision of Britain's centrepiece is a double-page reproduction of the eighteenth-century Italian artist Canaletto's painting *The Thames from the Terrace of Somerset House*. Here, Venetian iconography depicts the importance of maritime trade in imperial London, with St Paul's Cathedral dominating the skyline. The book overlays this painting with a photograph of contemporary London from the same vantage point: the busy shipyards have disappeared and St Paul's Cathedral is dwarfed by City skyscrapers and industrial cranes. Charles uses this comparison to illustrate the so-called 'destruction' of the 'beautiful' imperial city vista.[118]

Although its vision is primarily rural, nostalgic appraisal of London as a mercantile centre is a recurring theme in *A Vision of Britain* using reproductions of eighteenth- to nineteenth-century oil paintings.[119] The picturesque typically emphasises aesthetic ideals over lived experience, and *A Vision of Britain* embodies this sensibility by failing to reflect on the potential historical inaccuracy, artistic licence or situated viewpoint of the paintings it reproduces. Rather, they operate as de-facto illustrations of London 'as it was', which for Charles was a harmonious centre untouched by modernity's chaos.

St Paul's Cathedral operates throughout *A Vision of Britain* as a key motif to articulate 'the harmony and scale' of London, where its subordination is interpreted as symbolising the displacement of the imperial trading empire by corporate commerce.[120] The book reproduces N.M Lund's 1904 painting *Heart of Empire* to illustrate St Paul's as the hub of empire, while city traders bustle below. As the geographer Stephen Daniels describes, the trade's centrality in this image demonstrates that Charles is not opposed to enterprise, rather commerce becomes associated with civic virtue and responsibility.[121] The sociologists John Corner and Sylvia Harvey's work on *Enterprise and Heritage* demonstrates that these two concepts are not distinct; and heritage is increasingly subject to market values through its commercialisation for profit.[122] They tie this to Thatcherism, and Thatcher's attempt to merge 'old' and 'new' wealth while retaining ideologies of some wealth as more superior.[123] Charles's own so-called 'business empire' – the Duchy – demonstrates that he is not opposed to commercial enterprise.[124] Rather, he moralises this through heritage. Indeed, the name of his organic food company, Duchy Originals, codes the business through language of authenticity, tradition and history. Similarly, Poundbury is coded by Charles not as a town built for profit but as an ideological project seeking to regenerate 'familiar, traditional, well-tried and beautiful' architectural styles, and 'heal the dismembered landscape and the poisoned soul'.[125] The capital profit is merely an additional bonus to more 'noble' ambitions.

St Paul's Cathedral is symbolic of nationalism and Empire. As a location for Queen Victoria's Diamond Jubilee, for example, it represented the 'mother country'.[126] Charles's fear about its dwarfing by surrounding skyscrapers could partly, then, be insecurities about decreasing global royal power after Empire. In celebrating London as a mercantile centre, Charles recreates what the English literature scholar Rob Nixon has called the 'postimperial picturesque'.[127] Charles's claim that 'we should have architecture that celebrates London's mercantile success, and then *humanises* it' clearly demonstrates imperial amnesia in erasing Empire's violence, particularly the slave trade on which London was built (in terms of both labour and financing).[128] The cultural theorist Paul Gilroy's term 'postcolonial melancholia' is useful here.[129] Gilroy describes how Britain mourns its imperial power by using selective and nostalgic accounts of its imperial past, for instance by remembering its role in ending slavery and 'gifting' independence to former colonies, but forgetting centuries of violence. Charles's insecurities about losing power manifest through glamorising imperial dominance.

Imperialist iconography also features in pastoralism. Empire's global expansion was represented alongside traditional English scenery of thatched cottages and gardens, drawing on romanticised conceptions of 'Little England'.[130] This Great Britain / Little England binary established a *national* identity as separate from, and culturally superior to, the *global* Empire. This is racialised: as the sociologist Sarah Neal writes, there is a 'collapsing of rurality into whiteness'.[131] The countryside becomes 'a place of white safety' where racialised groups are excluded from national landscapes.[132] This remains in Poundbury, where Thompson-Fawcett's 2003 demographic survey found that 97 per cent of Poundbury residents were white.[133] The assumed racial homogeny of rural areas was visible in popular analysis of the 2016 Brexit vote, whereby the working-class rural vote was *assumed* as white, hence erasing racialised rural groups.[134] Additionally, the Leave campaign of the UK Independence Party (UKIP) used a nostalgic sense of Englishness with rural landscapes as the 'ethnic homelands of the English'.[135] This partly constructed British citizenship along racialised lines. As Corner and Harvey argue, in periods of globalisation, pastoralism is driven by notions of 'salvage centered, bounded, and coherent identities – placed identities for placeless times'.[136] The sociologist Sivamohan Valluvan suggests this is tied with popular conservatism, and mourning over the 'putative unity, stability, and public morality ascribed to pre-war national whiteness', used in right-wing nationalist rhetoric.[137] Such rhetoric posits close, and closed, community ties.

The separation of rurality and Empire, and the conflation of whiteness and rurality, are false dichotomies. The historian David Olusoga documents Black Britons' role in shaping the landscape, from the Roman period to aristocratic families keeping Black children as slaves, to the postwar *Windrush*, one ship on which British citizens from global colonies arrived in Britain.[138] Many country houses were built using profits from colonialism and the slave trade, as the British aristocracy invested their wealth in expansionism and extraction.[139] Likewise, as this book describes, the British monarchy was built on imperial power. The 'postcolonial melancholia' of *A Vision of Britain*, as embodied in Poundbury, plays out in the Firm by erasing, masking and/or misrepresenting these histories. In Chapter 7, I argue that the Firm uses representations of Meghan Markle as a bi-racial American to attempt to resolve its problematic histories of racism and colonialism. Charles's embracement, and indeed romanticisation, of these histories illustrates that the monarchy has a long way to go.

Conclusion

> I have spent most of my life trying to propose and initiate things that very few people could see the point of or, frankly, thought were plain bonkers at the time, perhaps some of them are now beginning to recognise a spot of pioneering in all this apparent madness. (Prince Charles accepting the 'Londoner of the Decade' award in 2016)[140]

In September 2016, the local newspaper *London Evening Standard* named Charles 'Londoner of the Decade', an award Charles seemingly interpreted as validation of his beliefs. In his acceptance speech, he contrasted critical tabloid headlines with views from 'the public' to demonstrate his apparent populist understanding of 'their values', a sentiment echoing his self-imposed role in *A Vision of Britain* as public spokesman. The award's aim to recognise the 'most influential people' seems to endorse Charles's 'meddling' reputation, and directly opposes the monarchy's purported political 'neutrality'.

This future-looking orientation is especially ironic when, as this chapter has described, Charles's views are underpinned by a reactionary, conservative privileging of the pastoral. Poundbury may be framed as a futuristic eco-town, but the reality is anything but.[141] It is a 'simulation of a fantasy past'.[142] Simulation and pastiche have been recurring themes of this chapter, and describing Pound-bury as 'Disneyland' is perhaps the most analytically poignant.[143] In Poundbury, feudalist, imperialist, hierarchical, C/conservative, nostalgic conceptions of 'Little England' play out in a picturesque setting. It seems to be a space where Charles can 'play' with residents; his imaginary utopia brought to life, purely by fortune of his royal privilege and wealth.

If Poundbury stages monarchy, it is a riposte to the contemporary television and digital culture monarchy. It is perhaps no coincidence that it is the postwar period, which as Chapter 2 demonstrated has seen substantial shifts in the Firm's engagement with media texts, that Charles demonises. He privileges a more traditional version of monarchy. Queen Mother's Square can be read as a microcosm of Charles's *vision*, whereby monarchy is the centre. Poundbury takes the naturalisation of royal power to nature itself. Furthermore, Charles's rejection of suburban housing estates that were central to the composition of the middle classes throughout the twentieth century could suggest a concomitant rejection of the middle classes *as a class*, as they countered the landlord/serf model that he appears to champion.

Charles is not entirely unaware of contemporary media cultures. The BBC documentary *Reinventing the Royals* analysed Buckingham Palace's attempts to sanitise negative public reaction to Charles following Princess Diana's death by hiring the public relations executive Mark Bolland as Charles's Deputy Private Secretary.[144] In 2015, the *Independent* uncovered a fifteen-page contract that obligated broadcast journalists to ask only pre-agreed questions when interviewing Charles. This was believed to breach Ofcom rules of independence and transparency.[145] One interpretation of the meaning of Charles as a royal figure, then, could be that he is contradictory. He is delighted to accept a 'Londoner of the Decade' award yet despises contemporary London; resolutely anti-modernist yet partakes in capitalist wealth creation; espouses housing equality yet facilitates class hierarchies and misses affordable-housing targets;

privileges environmentalism yet builds homes on pastured land;[146] promotes sustainable futures yet only re-creates the past. Indeed, Charles could be interpreted as the living embodiment of the Firm as told in *Running the Family Firm*: an anachronistic institution utilising contemporary media technologies, socio-political shifts and forms of capital accumulation; yet not willing to forgo historical privileges.

5

'I am Invictus': Masculinities, 'philanthrocapitalism' and the military-industrial complex

After his second tour of duty serving with the Army Air Corps in Afghanistan in late 2012 as part of the 'War on Terror', in March 2014 Prince Harry launched the Invictus Games: an annual, international, multi-sport event featuring wounded armed services veterans. Pitched as demonstrating 'the power of sport to inspire recovery, support rehabilitation and demonstrate life beyond disability', the Invictus Games (hereafter Invictus) promote competitive spirit to deal with the physical and mental injuries of contemporary warfare.[1] Competing under the motto 'I am Invictus', Latin for 'unconquered, unsubdued, invincible', the veterans are encouraged to 'rise above' injury, in an individualistic framing which configures rehabilitation as a solo sporting pursuit of 'mind over body'. This self-determining ethos reflects not only the abdication of state responsibility for injured soldiers but also the functioning of 'corporate warfare' in the Middle East.

Photographs of Harry visiting the Invictus competitors are key representations of the Games. These visits are apparently intimate and informal, from Harry partaking in training exercises to giving hugs and personal encouragement, hence contributing to representations of Harry as an 'ordinary', accessible and liberal royal figure. His affable persona and philanthropic work act not only as redemption for his so-called past 'transgressions' but also reveal an attempt to produce consent for the 'War on Terror' in the public imagination. The 'War on Terror' refers to the US military response to the 11 September 2001 attacks, a co-ordinated terrorist attack led by the Islamist terrorist group Al-Qaeda. Supported by the UK, the USA targeted Sunni Islamic fundamentalist groups, initially in Afghanistan and Iraq. As I explore, the 'War on Terror' is subject to a legitimation crisis considering it is not a 'traditional war'. The scholars Callie Batts and David L. Andrews write that 'the disabled body of the Paralympic soldier/athlete holds the potential for *nationalistic representation* and political manipulation'.[2] That is, the soldiers' integration into a 'national sporting team' transforms them into representatives of the nation. Harry's functions in two key national institutions – the monarchy and the army – play an important role in transforming soldiers' bodies through national discourses and through Harry's own redemptive philanthropic and therapeutic military masculinity.

This chapter analyses Invictus to consider the relationship between the Firm and 'philanthrocapitalism': a term describing the use of philanthropy as a form of capital that makes corporations and/or wealthy individuals 'look good' and hence generates profit.[3] Specifically, the chapter argues that representations of Harry articulate narratives of redemption *through* philanthropy, both in the redemptive masculinities of his royal figure and in the redemption of the 'good soldier' from a 'bad war' in producing consent for the 'War on Terror'. I do not aim to present soldiers as victims, or to simplify the positive work Invictus does in helping veteran recovery. Rather, I aim to document the corporate function of contemporary warfare. Invictus, which is anchored to representations of Harry's philanthropic and liberal persona, condenses and disguises a set of contradictions around global conflicts in the twenty-first century, ambiguities in ideas around state responsibility and accountability and the role of corporate capital in these wars. The redemption of Harry as a royal figure, from 'playboy prince' to 'philanthropic prince' via 'soldier prince' maps on to the military-industrial complex, the production of consent for the 'War on Terror' at home, the role of philanthropy in mitigating the effects of warfare and shifting contemporary masculinities.

This chapter was written prior to Harry and his wife Meghan Markle's decision to leave the monarchy. I discuss briefly how this implicates this chapter's argument in the Conclusion section, and the couple's decision will be explored further in Chapter 7 and the Postscript. In fact, their departure represents the next stage in what I describe as Harry's 'redemption'.

The 'War on Terror' and the Invictus Games

Britain's role in the 'War on Terror' has faced widespread public opposition. The 2012 British Social Attitudes survey revealed that 48 per cent of people opposed sending the Armed Forces to Afghanistan (and 58 per cent opposed Iraq).[4] In 2016, a public inquiry established that the UK's legal basis for declaring war on Iraq was 'far from satisfactory'.[5] The British government, then, faced an ongoing crisis in producing public consent for a war that was later deemed illegitimate. However, in contrast, the same 2012 British Social Attitudes survey found that 91 per cent of Britons supported army *personnel* serving in Afghanistan (94 per cent for Iraq), with respect for army personnel's work even increasing post-Afghanistan and Iraq.[6] These statistics demonstrate a detachment between military *operations* and military *personnel*, with the soldier figure appearing to operate separately to unpopular deployments. As the sociologist Sivamohan Valluvan writes, if the soldier becomes a point of celebration, this potentially silences anti-war discourse.[7]

This suggests that the soldier figure could be used to reorient responses in the aftermath of the 'War on Terror'.[8] Such potential is evidenced in representations focusing on soldiers' personal narratives, including the charities Help for Heroes which raises money for injured troops and Tickets for Troops which gifts soldiers free tickets to cultural events; songs from ITV talent show the *X Factor* contestants who released 'Hero' in 2010, and The Choir: Military

Wives, a choir of wives and girlfriends of serving military personnel, who released singles in 2011, 2012 and 2016 and a BBC documentary; the increasing mediatisation of military remembrance; and the launch of the Invictus Games.[9]

Invictus was launched in March 2014 in London as part of Harry's royal patronages (see Chapter 1). Subsequent events were in Florida in 2016, Toronto in 2017 and Sydney in 2018 (2020 was planned for the Netherlands but postponed due to the COVID-19 pandemic). Injured veterans from eighteen countries, including the USA, Canada, New Zealand, Poland and Afghanistan, compete in sports such as wheelchair basketball, indoor rowing and sitting volleyball to receive gold, silver and bronze medals. £1 million was provided by the Royal Foundation to launch Invictus, whilst Jaguar Land Rover provides further sponsorship.[10] Harry is Patron of the Invictus Foundation, and the Chairman is Sir Keith Mills, a multi-millionaire businessman and deputy chairman of the London Olympic and Paralympic Games.[11] The concept was inspired by the US Warrior Games: a multi-sport event for US veterans organised by the United States Department of Defense. The Defence Studies scholar Helen McCartney describes how the USA is a model for Britain's public–military relations because it celebrates army veterans nationally.[12] Indeed, Invictus states an objective to 'generate a wider understanding and respect for those who serve their country'.[13] This chapter examines this statement when the 'War on Terror' is not a 'traditional' national war.

The playboy prince

Representations of Harry have shifted substantially over the years. As this chapter shows, common across these representations is Harry's construction as an 'ordinary', accessible, liberal royal figure who transgresses royal 'tradition', conservatism and class boundaries. Indeed, Harry's tension with his role has often figured him as anti-monarchy (a framing enhanced by his resignation). In 2018, Ipsos

Mori research found that Harry and his brother William are 'the most liked royals since records began', with journalists attributing this to 'a triumph for the modern approach' to monarchy after they 'swept away stuffy manners to bare their emotions in public'.[14] The BBC3 documentary *Prince Harry: Frontline Afghanistan*, chronicling Harry's time in Afghanistan, features his comrades asserting his 'ordinariness': 'it's easy to put aside the fact he's third in line to the throne ... he's a normal guy'.[15] It is the various permutations of this 'ordinariness' through redemptive masculinities, from 'ordinary lad' to a more liberal, emotionally literate masculinity, which this chapter maps.

Harry's representation as a 'playboy' party animal played out across tabloid and celebrity media throughout the early 2000s. In 2002 he admitted smoking cannabis, in 2004 he allegedly punched a paparazzi photographer in a nightclub, in 2005 the *Sun* published photographs of him in fancy dress as a Nazi, in 2006 he was recorded using the racist slur 'p***' to an Asian army colleague and in 2012 he was photographed drunk and playing strip poker in Las Vegas.[16] These representations have led to the popular construction of him as a 'lad'. The 'new lad' figure emerged in the 1990s, and encompasses a white, working-class, youthful masculinity organised around loutish, hedonistic pleasures such as beer, football and sex.[17] This pivots on cultures of sexism repackaged as ironic, postfeminist 'banter'.[18] Harry's interactions with comrades in *Prince Harry: Frontline Afghanistan* draw on 'lad' conventions. They mock each other throughout a console football game, and Harry announces that whoever loses each game 'becomes the brew bitch' and must make hot drinks. Upon introducing his comrades to the camera, Harry refers to them as his 'friends' in a mocking, sarcastic voice, mimicking a scene from the 'lad culture' television sitcom *The Inbetweeners*.[19]

Lad culture also reflects an exploitation of class signifiers, which is condensed into Harry's 'transgressive' cross-class identity. The 'new lad' debuted in men's lifestyle magazines *GQ* and *Loaded* in the early 1990s to subvert the 'new man' of the 1980s: a liberal, middle-class figure performing masculinities associated with aristocratic Englishness.[20] As the scholar John Beynon describes, while the 'new man' reflects the conspicuous consumption of the 1980s, the 'new lad' maps on to the de-industrialisation produced by Thatcherism.[21] While the 'new man' was based upon work roles, 'new lad' divisions were organised around appearance, and performances of 'authentic', jocular working-class masculinity.[22] But both *GQ* (standing for *Gentleman's Quarterly*) and *Loaded* are firmly entrenched in the middle-class market, and hence appropriated working-class identity.[23] When figures such as Prince William dress as a 'chav' (a pejorative stereotype for the British working-class) for a party at the military training centre Sandhurst, it reflects not only the contemporary aversion to working-class culture but also a symbolic classed violence through cultural appropriation.[24] There is a symbiosis here with the spectacularisation of the working classes in entertainment media, which reproduces pejorative class stereotypes.[25] Some key iconography of lad culture is also visible in the so-called Old Boys Networks of public schools, such as excessive drinking, uninhibited heterosex and casual misogyny.[26] The resurgence of Eton College graduates among the elites, particularly within Parliament, or the popularisation of upper-class celebrities such as Bear Grylls, demonstrate the currency of this version of masculinity.[27] Grylls, an ex-Etonian, plays on working-class versions of soldiering, survivalism, and adventuring in performances of 'primitive' masculinity.[28] Indeed, Harry taps into outdoor, reactionary masculine values through his soldiering, charity treks across the South Pole, and conservation work in Africa (leading to the *Daily Mail*'s appellation 'Harry the Lionheart').[29] In embodying these contradictions, Harry appears to transgress class boundaries, where he is somehow every class – aristocrat, middle class and working class – at once.

Although somewhat useful for reinforcing notions of a (royal) family with a difficult, unruly child, representations of Harry's 'laddish' antics were described by the journalist Antony Barnett as 'highly embarrassing for the royal family', and his behaviour is constructed as countering the 'moral and respectable' Family Firm. For example, after he smoked cannabis, one national tabloid columnist branded Harry a 'thoroughly horrible young man' and a 'national disgrace'.[30] The royal biographer Andrew Morton suggests that Prince Charles's then Communications Director, Paddy Harverson, designed a public relations plan for redemption: refigure Harry as a soldier, playing on the historical idea of military service as royal civic duty.[31]

The soldier prince

The institutions of monarchy and army have a relationship spanning thousands of years, from the Middle Ages when the warrior king ruled to today's symbolic relationship in the Trooping the Colour military parade to celebrate the monarch's birthday, and the Queen's Guard protecting the UK's official royal residences in their distinctive red uniform and bearskin caps.[32] Royal family members often wear military uniform for ceremonial events, and various royals have trained, been commissioned or served for military services: the Queen (Auxiliary Territorial Service), Prince Philip (Royal Navy), Prince Charles (Royal Air Force and Royal Navy), Prince Andrew (Royal Navy), Prince Edward (Royal Marines), Prince William (Royal Air Force) and Prince Harry (the Army).[33] Military is, in sum, an acceptable form of 'royal work'.

After graduating from the Royal Military Academy Sandhurst – the two-hundred-year-old army officer training centre – in 2005, Harry joined the Household Cavalry regiment as Second Lieutenant.[34] On 7 January 2008, the Australian women's magazine *New Idea* revealed that Harry had been 'secretly' serving in Afghanistan for ten weeks as a Forward Air Controller, breaking a media blackout imposed by the Ministry of Defence, and prompting his immediate withdrawal from Afghanistan due to security concerns.[35] Harry's second tour of Afghanistan commenced on 7 September 2012 and lasted four months, this time with Harry acting as 'Captain Wales', an Apache Pilot with the Army Air Corps.[36]

British news and entertainment media accounts of Harry's deployment were overwhelmingly positive. These texts typically overlooked the politics of warfare itself, focusing instead on personal narratives of Harry as a heroic figure serving his country. For example, the *Daily Express* refers to 'hero Harry' in a story which seemingly describes him as a hero in equal parts for the 'dangerous missions' he undertakes and for sleeping 'in a shipping container' in the army camp.[37] YouGov found that 82 per cent of Britons approved of Harry's posting.[38]

Among typical representations of Harry's deployment was an associative link between his 'laddish' playboy behaviour and the soldier figure. The *Telegraph*, for instance, ran the headline 'Prince Harry's Afghanistan deployment should lay "Las Vegas fling" to rest, says Gen Sir Richard Dannatt', explicitly evoking Harry's 'transgressions' in narratives of his deployment to establish a linear timeline (or, perhaps, a cause and effect).[39] Associations between masculinity and war have long histories. Hegemonic masculine values are constructed through deliberate social practice, such as identical military uniforms and systematic training in values of aggression, courage, rationality, self-control and physical endurance (values also seen in competitive sports like Invictus, see below).[40]

'Laddism' is further conflated with 'squaddie' subcultures.[41] 'Squaddie' refers to lower-ranked soldiers and their embodiment of crass, brash masculinity dependent on humour, aggression and fraternal ritual.[42] Photographs from Harry's Afghanistan tours saw him riding a motorbike, playing football topless to display a muscular torso, reading '"lads" mag' *Zoo*, carrying a machine gun and wearing an unofficial US Army Special Forces baseball cap reading 'we do bad things to bad people', reinforcing representations of the 'good' soldier fighting a 'bad' enemy.[43] These representations overlook that Harry is not a 'squaddie' but a senior officer, therefore distancing him from hierarchical privilege and making him appear 'ordinary'. It also realigns his 'laddish' behaviour within the codes of war culture, where it can be resituated as 'good boys in difficult situations'. Harry's 'bad behaviour' is redeemed.

As the Human Geographer Rachel Woodward and others state, 'the photograph of the soldier is never just a photograph of a soldier'.[44] Rather, it is a symbolic site upon which cultural and political meanings are inscribed, and these meanings are mediated through Harry's affable figure.

'War on Terror, Inc.'

We can read representations of 'Hero Harry' and his 'laddish' masculinity as attempts to produce consent for the 'War on Terror', whereby the 'good' British or American national soldier fights a 'bad' enemy. This is evidenced further in the *Sun* on 24 February 2011, with a front-page photograph of Harry in camouflage gear grasping a machine gun, with the headline 'one of our boys'.[45] The byline employs a celebratory tone to describe the '30 Taliban' – who signify the 'bad people' – he had killed, and the newspaper promises 'unrivalled coverage including poster' to celebrate Harry's deployment.

Such discourses describe a 'traditional' national soldier in a 'traditional' war, waged by nations with clear, strategic aims.[46] This is given further bolstering through Harry: the monarchy is symbolic of national identity, and the name 'Harry' is loaded with historical associations with Shakespeare's *Henry V* and the warrior king. Historically, national armies developed alongside nation states to replace mismatched feudal mercenaries.[47] Following the 1688 Glorious Revolution, the government established the Bill of Rights 1698 and the Act of Settlement 1701 to prevent subsequent monarchs using the army for personal use. The government took 'de facto control' of the army, but the Crown retained 'government and command'.[48] Soldiers still swear allegiance to the Queen as their Commander-in-Chief, and soldier discourses pivot on patriotism and national identity.[49]

However, the 'War on Terror' is not a 'traditional' war, and representations of soldier Harry act as dissimulations, disguising corporate relations. The 'War on Terror' was not democratic, and indeed it cannot even be claimed that the war was waged against a common enemy, considering that 'terror' is intangible. Unlike the First and Second World Wars, it cannot be represented as a 'just war' fought for 'king and country'. War critics suggest that 'terror' is merely an excuse for the US government to pursue longstanding military objectives, and impose upon civil liberties and human rights while boosting surveillance capitalism.[50] Multiple scholars and activists argue that the 'War on Terror' is a corporate war, fought for private enterprise and profit.[51] The geographer Philippe Le Billon suggested that the 'War on Terror' is primarily a resource war, for colonial acquisition of oil and land.[52] The journalist and writer Solomon Hughes argued that the private sector was so crucial to the campaigns that it influenced government policies.[53] The author and activist Naomi Klein describes this as part of 'disaster capitalism': the extension of capital accumulation into global warfare and catastrophe.[54] This is the military-industrial complex, or what Hughes termed 'War on Terror, Inc.'.[55]

In distinction to representations of the national soldier, many soldiers in Afghanistan and Iraq were outsourced from private military and security companies (PMSCs).[56] Whilst the government's Strategic Defence and Security Review in 2010 recommended that twenty thousand army personnel should be cut, companies such as G4S and Aegis Defence Services made millions of pounds every year by signing contracts with the UK government to deploy contractors to undertake security operations.[57] PMSCs self-regulate under a voluntary code of conduct and are not subject to military codes and honour. The risks of this were demonstrated when the

US corporation Blackwater's employees killed 17 Iraqi civilians in 2007.[58] These companies abdicate nation states' responsibility for human rights violations, war profiteering or any other crimes. The military-industrial complex goes beyond outsourcing soldiers. By the 1980s, private corporations were providing transport, bombs, guns and bullets to the Armed Forces as part of the arms trade.[59] The irony is that UK and US corporations are selling arms to the very countries that the UK and USA are declaring war on. The 'War on Terror' has also seen the privatisation of prisons, detention centres, soldier housing and military bases; new privatised surveillance methods (such as identity cards in the USA); and corporatised intelligence gathering.[60] Corporations underpinned the new Iraqi economy, with the fast-food outlet McDonald's and bank HSBC opening nationwide, and the oil companies Shell and BP receiving shares of Iraq's oil profits.[61]

Public relations companies are also central to the military-industrial complex. Although news reporting during wartime is not new – the nineteenth-century Crimean War was the first reported in real time using the electric telegraph – the expansion of media platforms since means that the 'War on Terror' is a conflict dominated by images.[62] From 24/7 live news reporting to productions of the war as entertainment spectacle on television, film and video games, contemporary warfare can be described as what the Communications Studies scholar Roger Stahl calls 'militainment'.[63] Or, as the sociologist Jean Baudrillard terms it, 'war porn'.[64]

Harry's deployment is contextualised in these issues. On his second tour of duty, rather than enforcing another blackout on reporting, the Ministry of Defence requested that media 'act responsibly' and ask its permission before publishing stories about Harry, effectively giving it control over coverage.[65] In return, reporters from the Press Association were allowed direct access to Harry. This model follows the 'embedded journalism' agreement established during the Vietnam War, where the US Ministry of Defense worried that critical coverage would erode public support.[66] 'Embedded journalism' sees reporters deployed to war zones alongside an attached military unit, which raises ethical issues around impartiality and objectivity.[67]

The few mainstream media accounts critical of Harry's deployment focused on this 'impartiality' angle. The *Independent* referred to Harry as a 'propaganda tool' who is putting 'Afghanistan's future, and the lives of British soldiers, at risk'.[68] The *Guardian* claimed that Harry was the Ministry of Defence's 'chief asset' and is 'gold dust in PR terms'.[69] Such accounts demonstrate how representations of 'hero Harry' are potentially serving the bigger purpose of reframing the 'War on Terror' in the public imagination.

Comparisons can be drawn here between war as a staged photograph opportunity and the choreographing of royal representations. The careful management of war zones does not wholly differ from the other stages Harry moves between. He 'performs' as a solider and 'performs' as a prince. Moreover, the 'embedded journalism' agreement is replicated in Royal Rota journalists accompanying the royals on international tours (see Chapter 1) and in staged royal photographs (see Chapters 2 and 6). Both the Ministry of Defence and the Firm are concerned with carefully managing their mediated image.

The philanthropic prince

Harry's soldiering worked to produce consent for a war happening 'out there', as well as reworking his 'laddism' into a more acceptable hegemonic soldier masculinity. However, after his return this required new framing: philanthropy. The historian Frank Prochaska mapped the historical relationship between monarchy and philanthropy.[70] When ideas of 'divine right' waned, it was increasingly important for the monarch(y) to engage productively with public needs, and appear respectable. Queen Victoria enacted values of social responsibility, supporting the voluntary institutions of Victorian society which compensated for lacking state provisions. After the

Second World War, the welfare state displaced the philanthropic and voluntaristic model of civil society. The monarchy developed a new approach, supporting the government's welfare institutions: NHS hospitals were a key focus of royal visits throughout the mid-twentieth century. Thatcher's privatisation of the welfare state in the 1980s, and her advocacy of Victorian values, saw the re-establishment of civil society, or a 'half-way house between state and society'. Jo Littler's reference to contemporary celebrities doing philanthropy as 'the new Victorians' demonstrates how the Victorian model of civil society has been re-popularised under neoliberalism.[71] This worked in the monarchy's favour, and indeed Prochaska argues that 'the monarchy now needs the voluntary sector more than the voluntary sector needs the monarchy'.[72]

Likewise, framing the 'War on Terror' as a humanitarian mission is one way through which it is moralised in the public imagination, such as narratives that it will 'liberate' Afghan and Iraqi citizens, and the USA's co-option of feminist rhetoric about the oppression of Afghan and Iraqi women.[73] This philanthropic framing of warfare constitutes another pillar of the military-industrial complex, as privatised humanitarian projects abdicate the state of responsibility for recovery schemes both domestically and internationally.

Invictus can be analysed through these concomitant histories. Whilst Harry is presented as socially responsible by caring for veterans, he is also producing consent for the state refusing responsibility for these soldiers. Invictus states that its aim is to 'generate a wider understanding and respect for those who serve their country', and, as described above, the soldier figure is often detached from the politics of warfare.[74] Invictus makes connections between the value systems of military and sport through ideas of combat and heroic warrior identities. This is illustrated in Invictus's claim of 'the power of sport to inspire recovery, support rehabilitation and demonstrate life beyond disability', promoting an individualistic solution to the physical and mental injuries of warfare by redisciplining the body.[75]

Invictus is named after the poem 'Invictus' (1888) by William Ernest Henley.[76] An amputee himself, Henley narrates his battle with illness through unrelenting human spirit, unbeaten despite life's challenges. The poem ends with the words used in Invictus promotional material: 'I am the master of my fate: I am the captain of my soul'. 'I am' is emphasised in the Invictus logo through coloured highlighting. By positioning the rehabilitation process as a solo sporting pursuit of 'mind over body', Invictus distances the injured veteran both from the specificity (and legality) of particular conflicts and from broader social and political meanings of warfare in global contexts. Of course, sometimes this works positively: individual soldiers did not declare war, nor did they necessarily design combat strategy. However, these representations obscure the state's responsibility for sending the soldiers to war, and for providing adequate professional healthcare for those injured. For instance, the work that Invictus does in rehabilitating veterans contrasts with reports that around four hundred serving soldiers committed suicide between 1995 and 2014 (not including those who have left), after mental health conditions were routinely overlooked and untreated by the state.[77] Rather than demanding appropriate state support, the soldiers are figured as 'the masters of their own fates' buttressed by private philanthropic schemes. This is a form of 'philanthrocapitalism', which does the work of the state under ideologies of neoliberal individualism.[78] This is, crucially, in direct contradiction to how soldiers are represented as *doing the work of the state.*

The Politics scholar Joanna Tidy argues that, through competitive sport, the invisible, unruly, damaged soldier body is made visible only once 'they have completed their transformatory "becoming"' and conquered their injuries, thus transforming their plight into personal struggle.[79] This reflects contemporary 'supercrip' figurations, defined as representations of individuals with inspirational stories of 'defying the odds'.[80] The scholar and athlete P. David Howe queries whether these narratives empower disabled athletes, given their tendency to dehumanise and glorify disabled bodies by celebrating the technology that aided them.[81] For Invictus, such a narrative proposes that these heroes have triumphed despite difficulty. The state is absolved of accountability.

Who is benefiting from philanthropic initiatives? The sociologist Andrew Sayer suggests that philanthropy by the rich differs from charity from 'the public' because philanthropists want to be publicly acknowledged.[82] The main sponsor of Invictus is Jaguar Land Rover. This manifested in 2017 not only in advertisements around the games complex, but also in Invictus participants competing in a driving race in Land Rovers around Toronto's Distillery District.[83] This sponsorship is especially notable considering that Land Rovers are manufactured as military vehicles for armies, including for the 'War on Terror'. In associating with Invictus, Land Rover could be enacting its own redemption by trading military violence for philanthropic recovery. Writing about the mental health charity Heads Together, a multi-charity initiative fronted by William and Kate (this included Harry before he left the Firm), Imogen Tyler and Tom Slater note it is 'bankrolled by some of the very corporate and financial organisations who are the beneficiaries of neoliberal economic policies … [which] are exacerbating mental distress among the … most vulnerable'.[84] Likewise, as a luxury, elite brand Jaguar Land Rover has benefited from a culture predicated on neoliberal inequalities. The company documented record sales in 2017 and a tripling of sales since 2009, which coincides with widening wealth inequalities across industrialised countries.[85] By aligning itself with Invictus, Jaguar Land Rover enhances its reputation, and develops customer and employee loyalty. These corporate philanthropic initiatives obscure that it is the very existence of social elites and corporate greed that causes the social and economic inequalities that mean that charity is required in the first place. That is, celebrity charity initiatives like Invictus promulgate the 'fantasy

that these things [social elites and inequality] are *not* connected'.[86]
They produce consent for inequality through ideas of social
responsibility.

Harry's role in Invictus, as representative of the monarchy, is
key to resituating these corporate structures as problems of nation
or nationhood. Injured soldiers symbolise the nation because of
the (bodily) sacrifices they make for the nation's protection, and,
through Harry's support, the soldiers are (re)incorporated into
national ideology. Invictus focuses on the damaged soldier body,
both physically and mentally. Likewise, Harry is represented as
having his own 'problems' through his past behaviour, and he has
now dealt with these and is helping others to do the same. His
interactions with Invictus competitors play on his performance of
a liberal, therapeutic, emotionally literate masculinity.

The spectre of Diana

Representations of masculinities are always in flux.[87] After the
'new lad' of the 2000s, contemporary culture evidences two
new 'figures': one developing 'new lad' reactionary masculinity
into toxic masculinity and misogyny (as embodied by Donald
Trump), and more fluid representations of gender that challenge
heteronormative masculinity.[88] 'Hybrid masculinity' describes
how masculinity routinely absorbs and rejects various identities
usually associated with marginalised masculinities or femininities.[89]
Grayson Perry's *The Descent of Man* and Robert Webb's *How Not
to Be a Boy* both use biographical memoir to narrate how hegemonic masculinities limit their ways of experiencing maleness.[90]
Contemporary paternity, from the 'Instagram Dad' to 'celebrity
postfeminist fatherhood' has also emphasised 'softer', liberal
masculinity and 'hands on' fathering – traits performed by Prince
William.[91]

The former US President Barack Obama is particularly interesting
for this phenomenon, and reflects Harry's shift from 'soldier prince'

to 'philanthropic prince'. Obama continued to pursue neocolonial and capitalist wars in Afghanistan and Iraq, yet, as the scholar John Landreau argues, Obama's approach emphasises 'soft power' and a liberal, emotionally literate masculinity as opposed to George W. Bush's combative rhetoric.[92] Harry and Obama are routinely represented across inter/national news media as friends, depicted as a 'bromance', a portmanteau of 'brother' and 'romance' to describe interpersonal male relationships.[93] In 2016, the Kensington Palace Twitter account (at the time representing Harry, William and Kate) engaged in 'banter' with the Obamas' account over whether Team UK or Team USA would win that year's Invictus Games. After the Obamas uploaded a viral video, Kensington Palace posted a tweet signed by Harry reading, 'you can dish it out, but can you take it?' Following this, Kensington Palace uploaded a video of Harry and the Queen watching the Obama video on an iPhone. In response, the Queen scoffs 'oh really', and Harry looks to camera and says 'boom' while making a 'mic drop'[94] gesture.[95] Jo Littler argues that the video 'builds its comedy by juxtaposing a degree of American black cool with uptight white aristocratic chintz-laden tradition'.[96] It also invests chintz-laden tradition with values of 'cool' through its proximity to the Obamas' culturally accepted scripts of popularity.

For Harry, 'softer' masculinities are represented in his philanthropic initiatives and a new mediated intimacy where he undertakes emotional labour, such as supporting Invictus competitors or discussing mental health issues. For example, in July 2017, ITV aired the documentary *Diana, Our Mother: Her Life and Legacy*, for the twentieth anniversary of Diana's death.[97] The documentary featured William and Harry speaking candidly for the first time about their grief. In various media interviews during Britain's Mental Health Awareness Week in 2017, Harry elaborated on the mental health issues caused by his mother's death, saying he was 'very close to a complete breakdown'.[98] He received counselling and therapy, where he opened up after previously 'shut[ting] down all his emotions', which also acts as an explanatory tool for the 'harder' masculinities he performed earlier in life.[99]

Harry's disclosures were applauded by mental health professionals for contributing towards ending mental health stigma.[100] Indeed, a public figure speaking openly about mental health is a valuable intervention, especially from one typically associated with hegemonic forms of 'laddish' masculinity. This talking ethos is further promoted in Heads Together, which encourages 'chang[ing] the conversation' around mental health to remove the stigma.[101] This emphasis on 'talking' as a cure, and the importance of recognising and embracing emotions, is relatively new, rising in the 1980s when counselling industries expanded, self-help books gained popularity and the language of therapy was used in everyday discourse.[102] This is contextualised in neoliberalism's emphasis on the managed, reflexive self, or as what the sociologist Eva Illouz calls 'emotional capitalism' whereby emotions are increasingly mapped and calculated.[103] Emotional labour operates as a moralising judgement: discerning the 'good' citizens who enact self-care and the 'bad' who do not.[104] In taking responsibility for his emotions, Harry enacts 'good' neoliberal personhood.

Emotional labour features in celebrity cultures to manufacture intimacies with audiences, particularly in reality television.[105] Tabloid talk shows such as *The Oprah Winfrey Show* use 'the confessional': where participants reveal something personal and, in so doing, reveal their 'authentic' selves.[106] However, these confessions are staged and often give participants esteem. This is also a moralised classed, gendered and racialised phenomenon, dependent on one's access to psychological and emotional capital.[107] Whilst the lower classes are 'pathologised' for their admissions, the confessions of the wealthy and/or famous are 'invested with great ritual weight'.[108] For Harry, his confessions of mental health trauma are central to his redemption as the 'philanthropic prince', resolving the 'scandals' of his past. In a 2017 article about Harry, for example, the *Sun* narrated a story of damage and recovery: from young Harry with his mother in the 1980s, his solemn face at her funeral in the 1990s, his falling over outside a nightclub in the 2000s and finally an official photograph for Heads Together where he smiles alongside William and Kate in branded Heads Together headbands.[109]

Princess Diana is a key representational resource in Harry's remaking. She performed a new level of intimacy and engagement for the royals, distancing herself from institutional formality and embodying values of compassion and approachability. Her own emotional openness is well documented, and indeed the documentary *Diana, Our Mother: Her Life and Legacy* was reminiscent of another (in)famous royal documentary over twenty years earlier: Diana's *Panorama* interview.[110] In November 1995, three years after separating from Prince Charles, Diana was interviewed for the BBC's *Panorama* programme, where she openly criticised the treatment she had received from the monarchy. Later, Diana's death prompted widespread criticism of the Firm – particularly the Queen – as cold and inhuman because they did not demonstrate appropriate emotional distress. If one of the biggest royal crises of Elizabeth II's reign was because the royals were not appropriately emotional, this is now being reclaimed and resolved through Diana's son(s) and their ambivalent, shape-shifting masculinities. It is interesting, that twenty-two years after *Panorama*, a similar representation featuring Diana's sons would form part of the carefully constructed tributes to her life, this time sanctioned by Buckingham Palace. The two documentaries are filmed using similar camera angles and close-up shots, and both Diana (Figure 5.1) and Harry (Figure 5.2) look slightly past the camera at an interviewer, drawing on the recognisable codes of the confessional television genre. *Diana, Our Mother: Her Life and Legacy* can be understood as the Firm harnessing emotional labour, mediated intimacies and therapeutic cultures, influenced by the popularity of Diana, whose life and death provide scripts for the younger royals to perform 'modern' monarchy and stage an alternative royal lineage through her (although this is more controlled than Diana, see Chapter 6).

5.1 Still from Diana's *Panorama* interview, BBC, 1995

5.2 Still of Prince Harry on *Diana, Our Mother: Her Life and Legacy*, ITV, 2017

Harry's 'ordinariness' also plays out in his attitude towards the monarchical institution, which he – like Diana – often positions himself in tension with. As the Media scholar Arvind Rajagopal writes, Diana's emotional openness situated her as both inside and outside the establishment.[111] Likewise, even prior to resignation, Harry was positioned as simultaneously inside and outside the Firm. In *Diana, Our Mother: Her Life and Legacy*, Harry criticises outright the decision for him to march behind his mother's coffin in the funeral procession, aged 12, in front of millions of global television viewers, saying 'no child should be asked to do that under any circumstances'.[112] Later in 2017, Harry told *Newsweek* magazine:

> We are involved in modernising the British monarchy. We are not doing this for ourselves but for the greater good of the people … Is there any one of the royal family who wants to be king or queen? I don't think so, but we will carry out our duties at the right time[113]

Harry described the monarchy as undesirable, a duty and burden, again positioning himself as a socially responsible, but alienated, subject. Harry's criticism of the funeral can be understood as royal populism: an attack on an emotionless and 'out-of-touch' Establishment by a member of that Establishment, with authority to criticise it from the inside. But although Harry positions himself in tension with the institution, he makes clear he will not dismantle it. Rather, he will continue taking responsibility for his 'duties' for the sake of 'the greater good of the people', for whom the monarchy is positioned as a valuable symbol. As I explore in the Postscript, even Harry and Meghan's resignation statement still promised to 'continu[e] to fully support Her Majesty'.[114]

In speaking about royal duty, Harry describes the monarchy as 'work', as labour to be undertaken. This is not a new conceptualisation: in 1966 Princess Alice (Queen Victoria's last surviving granddaughter) described the monarchy in her book *Reminiscences* as:

> an arduous profession whose members are seldom granted an opportunity of opting in or out of their predestined fate … The royal motto 'Ich Dien' is no empty phrase. It means what it says – I serve.[115]

This almost directly reflects Harry's rhetoric. Alice bemoans her 'predestined fate', refers to her royalty as a 'profession' and suggests that royals 'serve'. By positioning their roles as work, these royal figures demonstrate that they consider themselves *hard working*, productive and 'doing good'. Michael Billig argues that the notion of royal work 'invites demystification for it implies that an ordinary human being stands behind the extraordinary role'.[116] Hence, Harry constructs a 'real' him, existing in tension with his 'job' as a royal. But, of course, all representations of royal figures contribute towards producing consent for the monarchy.

Conclusion

Since I originally researched this chapter, Harry's story continues to develop. On 8 January 2020, Harry and his wife Meghan Markle announced their intention to 'step back as "senior" members of the Royal Family'.[117] In February 2020, Harry undertook his final royal public engagements, including launching a new eco-friendly travel firm. Upon introducing Harry's speech at this event, the host Ayesha Hazarika said, 'he's made it clear that we are all *just to call him Harry*. So ladies and gentlemen, please give a big, warm, Scottish welcome to Harry' (emphasis added).[118]

The *Daily Mail* claimed this illustrated how Harry has 'drop[ped] his royal title'.[119] But in fact, the couple are retaining their official titles 'The Duke and Duchess of Sussex', while losing HRH (His/ Her Royal Highness). I argue that his request to 'just call me Harry' illustrates a new permutation of the story in this chapter of the redemption from 'playboy prince' to 'philanthropic prince' via 'soldier prince', using discourses of royal 'ordinariness' and shifting masculinities. Such informality evidences Harry's flexible classed identity. The former UK Prime Minister David Cameron, who attended the public school Eton College and whose family are multi-millionaires of inherited wealth, is (in)famous for saying 'just call me Dave': a request obscuring his upper-class background through the codes of working-class authenticity, and populist political styles.[120] The Education scholar Angela Smith suggests that 'just call me Dave' is a performance of liberal masculinity, vested in forms of social progression.[121] This is especially problematic, Smith notes, considering that Cameron's government was towards the political right, promoting austerity and cuts to welfare. Similarly, Harry's request to 'just call me Harry' obscures his class privilege, his inherited wealth and the monarchy's conservative values. Criticism of Harry and Meghan's decision to resign also illustrates the problems with representing Harry as in tension with the Establishment. Whilst it was acceptable for Harry to be 'anti-monarchy' when *within* the institution, after resigning he and Meghan became 'outsiders', tainting royalty with commercial investments (see Postscript). Harry's journey to 'just Harry' evidences the next stage of his redemption story, and the limits of this narrative.

By exploring the Invictus Games, I have argued that Harry has undergone redemption through philanthropy, whereby his past 'transgressions' are resolved through a liberal, 'ordinary', emotionally literate masculinity articulated through rehabilitating the damaged soldier body. Princess Diana is a key representational resource for this remaking, and Harry's mediated intimacies are staged in and through her memory. By positioning his royal life as 'work', and charity as part of his emotional labour, Harry produces consent for the monarchy through ideas of social and civic responsibility. However, this chapter demonstrated a simultaneous process of absolving responsibility. It argued that Harry's role in Invictus condenses and disguises a set of contradictions around twenty-first-century global conflicts, ambiguities in ideas around state responsibility and accountability, and the role of corporate capital in the 'War on Terror'. Representations of Harry remake the 'War on Terror' as a national war, where 'our boys' are fighting a 'bad enemy' for the 'greater good'. The 'war arm' of the Firm and the 'charity arm' of the Firm are directly connected as both are processes of capital accumulation, both produce consent for the Firm in the public imagination, and both are key representational tools to stage monarchy.

6

The heteromonarchy: Kate *Middleton*, '*middle*-classness' and family values

Since the birth of Prince George in 2013, Princess Charlotte in 2015 and Prince Louis in 2018, the Cambridge children's childhoods have been documented through official portraits on notable occasions, such as birthdays, first days at school or family holidays (Figure 6.1). These are released on Kate and William's Instagram account @kensingtonroyal (named for Kensington Palace, the family's official home and the name of their Communications Offices, which runs the account), which as of 2020 has 12 million followers. The photographs *appear* natural, impromptu and informal, and the Instagram is framed as 'the Cambridge family photo album', allowing 'intimate' glimpses into Cambridge family life. The captions often reveal that Kate Middleton takes some photographs herself, enhancing their connotations of familiarity and sharing a private family album.

Instagram is bound with notions of intimacy and authenticity, as people share representations of their everyday lives.[1] For celebrities, and indeed royals, this means giving glimpses into their 'private' lives. As I discussed in Chapter 2, the challenge for the Firm on social media is that it is a form of 'context collapse', whereby institutions and celebrities co-exist on the same platform as their fans and the public, reproducing notions of intimacy and blurring hierarchical boundaries, which the Firm also needs to maintain its monarchical mystique.[2]

6.1 The Cambridge family on holiday, 2016

Although 'the Cambridge family photo album' connotes intimacy, these photographs, as with every official monarchical press release, are precisely choreographed to foreground particular meaning. In comparison to portraiture of historical monarchies depicting royal children as inheritors of political dynasty,[3] these photographs present the Cambridges as a nuclear, heteronormative and (upper-)middle-class family. The historian Patricia Holland suggests that these portraits are often idealised, ensuring that the middle-class family is coded as aspirational and desirable.[4] But considering that traditional family photograph albums have been displaced by digital cultures, their evocation on Instagram by the Cambridges is bound up with nostalgia for traditional family values. It appeals to the nuclear, middle-class family when families and class identifications in Britain are becoming more complex, and, indeed, when the Cambridges are far from middle class.

We have seen that the Firm performs middle-class family values as initially modelled by Queen Victoria to disguise its capitalist and corporate relations, producing the Family Firm. I proposed that, in the nineteenth and twentieth centuries, aristocracy and royalty embraced 'middle-classness' to distance themselves from associations with greed, profligacy and moral 'lack'. We now consider what kind of middle-class family the Firm simulates by examining the figure of Kate Middleton. Kate is primarily represented as middle-class due to her non-aristocratic background, and the news and entertainment media have crafted a 'rags to riches' story of aspirational classed mobility, using the recognisable tropes of classic fairy tales.[5] This is most clearly illustrated in how she is still commonly referred to as 'Kate Middleton'; a middle-class stage name as opposed to the aristocratic 'Catherine, Duchess of Cambridge'. In fact, Kate occupies a complex class position in that her family could be classified as middle-class when she was born (on the basis of occupation: her mother and father were a flight attendant and a flight dispatcher, respectively), but rose to the upper- or upper-middle-class after starting their own 'family firm', the party supplies business Party Pieces in 1987. As of 2019, Party Pieces has an estimated worth of £40 million.[6] I suggest that foregrounding Kate's supposed 'middle classness' is a strategic move for the Firm to mask its hereditary privilege, and *appear* to open aristocratic cultures to the middle classes. However, this openness is merely a gesture. In fact, representations of Kate and the Cambridges illustrate how the Firm is becoming even more remote through Kate's indeterminate persona and staged photoshoots.

Sexual politics and gender roles are also narrated through Kate's middle-class background. Like Princess Diana before her, and Meghan Markle after her, Kate has received sustained media coverage from popular celebrity publications, frequently topping 'best celebrity role model' opinion polls, and voted a 'fashion icon'.[7] She has also featured in academic analysis to exemplify 'postfeminism' and contemporary motherhood.[8] In contrast, I suggest that postfeminism is being developed under new forms of authoritarian neoliberalism, dynastic wealth and patrimonial forms of capitalism, which facilitate more conservative gender roles. Women are increasingly encouraged to embrace traditional femininities and undertake 'dynasty-making' practices to reproduce elite family's wealth and privilege. The feminist scholar Beatrix Campbell uses the term 'neoliberal neopatriarchy' to demonstrate how gendered divisions are not just a by-product of neoliberalism, rather it is 'cause and effect'.[9] That is, under neoliberalism, women (alongside racially minoritised groups, the lower classes, people with disabilities, queer people) are structurally disadvantaged and bear the brunt of inequalities and systemic misogyny.[10]

The feminist scholar Anne McClintock describes how white, heterosexual, upper-/middle-class women have longer histories as standard bearers of the nation, as nations are constructed through domestic spaces.[11] This takes on particular purchase in the monarchy. Whilst *Running the Family Firm* has argued that the Firm is reproduced through media cultures, this chapter extends this to consider how the Firm is also dependent upon the *biological reproduction* of an heir. To maintain power, the monarchy must both reproduce its lineage *and* reproduce itself in the public imagination (and, as photographs of the Cambridges demonstrate, these processes are interlinked). Kate's body is fetishised as reproductive of the citizenry, reproducing the nation's 'First Family'. Kate is a contemporary configuration of the centrality of nostalgic heteronormativity and traditional gender roles to the reproduction of monarchical power, and indeed heterosexual reproduction is key to its 'frontstage'. This is the heteromonarchy.

The happy housewife to the #tradwife

The idealisation of domesticity has a long history interwoven with (conservative) political imagination. In the Victorian era, the 'separate spheres' of work and home were represented through fantasies of the wife or mother as the 'Angel in the House'.[12] After the Second World War, the figure of 'the happy housewife' arose in second-wave feminist critiques of domesticity and motherhood, the best known of which is Betty Friedan's *The Feminine Mystique*.[13] Friedan describes 'the happy housewife myth' in the 1960s USA: poster and advertisement representations of young, conventionally attractive, middle-class women content with their domestic roles due to suburban consumer cultures, used to persuade women (back) into the private sphere after undertaking war work.[14] In the late 1980s and early 1990s, the American feminist Susan Faludi identified similar representations of 'the New Traditionalist' as middle-class stay-at-home mothers who had chosen to return to domestic roles.[15] As the feminist theorist Sara Ahmed writes, 'the happy housewife is a fantasy figure that erases the signs of labour under the sign of happiness ... How better to justify an unequal distribution of labour than to say such labour makes people happy?'[16]

The 'happy housewife' re-emerged again in contemporary British austerity cultures as a moral imperative to encourage domestic restraint as a solution to hardship.[17] This makes specific references to the context of postfeminism: a neoliberal 'sensibility'[18] variously incorporating a 'repudiation' of feminist politics;[19] an emphasis on individualism, choice and agency;[20] and an idealised 'married heterosexual monogamy'.[21] A 'retreatist' narrative in contemporary media culture encourages women to 'choose' to reclaim the domestic space and retreat from work, which feminist scholars have critiqued given the limitations to 'choice' within the context of capitalist patriarchy.[22] Simultaneously, the reproductive female body is increasingly represented as aspirational. Jo Littler's work on the 'yummy mummy', for example, identified 'a type of mother who is sexually attractive and well-groomed',[23] and the pregnant female body is increasingly visible in media culture.[24]

The 'yummy mummy' is distinctly (middle-)classed, revolving around conspicuous consumption and leisure practices. The cultural theorist Angela McRobbie identifies this as 'mediated maternalism', which she argues is used by the political right to reproduce middle-class norms and denigrate working-class single mothers reliant on state benefits.[25] This updates ideas of family values for the neoliberal regime.[26] Marxist feminist work draws attention to women's invisible labour in capital accumulation, with domestic work and child rearing functioning as social reproduction to support the labour market.[27] In this new realm of 'mediated maternalism', the family 'is managed along the lines of a small business or enterprise' whereby motherhood is 'a mode of investment in the human capital of infants and children'.[28] It is, fittingly, a *family firm*.

Representations of the mother as the household's CEO are explicitly present in contemporary #tradwife discourses. This is a hashtag emerging on YouTube and social media in the mid- to late 2010s from women exalting the virtues of staying at home, illustrating the reorientation of 'happy housewife' discourses around social media.[29] The tradwife – traditional wife – describes women who 'choose' to stay at home and care for their husbands and children.[30] In the contemporary equivalent of postwar 'happy housewife' posters, tradwives use photographs, blogs and videos on social media to document their idealised domestic lives. The #tradwife movement is situated in the contemporary (inter)national socio-political context and the rise of nostalgia, of which – as I have described throughout this book – some of the Brexit vote is emblematic, drawing on traditional, middle- or upper-class, right-wing 'British values' to reject freedom of movement, immigration, globalisation and multiculturalism.

One particularly visible tradwife in Britain is Alena Pettitt, who runs the blog and Instagram 'The Darling Academy' with over twenty thousand followers. Pettitt – and those like her – draw on upper-class nationalist iconography. She describes her lifestyle as returning to 'traditional British values', her Instagram has a red, blue and white colour palette which reflects the Union Jack flag, her book *Ladies Like Us* teaches lessons in upper-class British etiquette, and in one Instagram post she hailed Queen Elizabeth II as 'the ultimate Trad Wife' because she supports 'duty, nation and family'.[31] In a blog post, Pettitt celebrates Kate as 'the English Rose personified, charming, intelligent, elegant ... [and] conservative'.[32]

The #tradwife illustrates how the contemporary right-wing movement is gendered. Conservative, heteronormative family values and the re-traditionalisation of gender politics have been re-popularised under political ideologies variously termed authoritarian neoliberalism,[33] libertarian authoritarianism[34] and/or neoconservatism.[35] These values are perhaps best visualised within the 'new elites', where oligarchic and patriarchal families such as the Trumps openly use nepotism to reproduce dynastic power.[36] In their study of 'family offices', the sociologists Luna Glucksberg and Roger Burrows found that 'the link between kinship, property rights and wealth was key. It was about the social reproduction of a particular group' through human capital.[37] The sociologist Melinda Cooper found that ideologies of 'family values' united neoliberals and social neo-conservatives in the USA, with both groups moralising traditional ideas of the family as portals to wealth and status.[38] The anthropologist Sylvia Yanagisako similarly argued that ideologies of 'family values' reflect how kinship, economy and politics increasingly intersect amongst the elites through, for example, inheritance practices.[39] The feminist scholar Laura Briggs argues similarly that gendered issues such as family values, surrogacy, abortions and welfare reform are politicised to emphasise the normalisation of heteronormativity, nuclear familialism and middle-classness (see also Lisa Duggan's work on queer families framed through discourses of 'homonormativity').[40] It is female bodies, and their reproductive capacities, that are the subjects of authoritarian neoliberal regimes. Women become standard-bearers for the reproduction of nation(alism).

It is in this context that the figure of Kate Middleton emerges. Alena Pettitt's celebration of Kate, alongside Pettitt's repeated royalist statements, demonstrate Kate's usefulness for representations of 'happy housewife' or tradwife cultures.

'The Kate effect'

In the 1910s, the Soviet film-maker Lev Kuleshov demonstrated what he called 'the Kuleshov effect': a film-editing phenomenon where viewers receive meaning from the sequential editing of shots rather than each shot on its own. Kuleshov created a short film featuring the expressionless face of the actor Ivan Mosjoukine, which were interspersed with various other, entirely disparate, shots (for example, a girl in a coffin, a bowl of soup). He found that the cumulative effect meant that audiences believed that Mosjoukine's expression changed each time he appeared, depending on which object he appeared to be 'looking at' (grief or hunger, respectively). The experiment demonstrates that cinema's meaning 'exists in the mind of the spectator rather than the celluloid itself', because Mosjoukine's face was the expressionless receptacle on to which audiences projected meaning.[41]

I argue here for the relevance of what I call 'the Kate effect', whereby the meaning of Kate is constructed by virtue of the clothing – the costume – she wears in particular representations, and the cumulative effect of these. Her unchanging smiling face (the *happy* housewife) in all representations can be read in conjunction with Mosjoukine's expressionless one: it relies on the context of Kate's surroundings to give it meaning. Unlike Meghan Markle, who was an established celebrity upon joining the Firm, Kate has been made by the monarchy. Very little is known about Kate and she gives few public speeches. The few times her voice *has* been heard it is directly connected to the Firm, tied to either heterosexual family life (an interview for her and William's engagement), feminised charitable interests (children's and mother's mental health issues, art gallery patronages) or rare feminised television appearances (*A Berry Royal Christmas*, featuring Kate baking with the British chef Mary Berry).[42] Like Mosjoukine's face, in film theory terms Kate is a non-specific sign, with meaning projected on to her depending on her costumes. Art historians have used clothing to unearth the

6.2 Princess Charlotte's christening, 2015

details and significance of portraiture, and Hilary Mantel drew on
this work to describe Kate as 'a jointed doll in which certain rags
are hung … she was a shop-window mannequin … entirely defined
by what she wore'.[43] Kate's image is multiple as she moves between
costumes to present different personas – the housewife, the celebrity,
the middle-Englander and the aristocrat.

In July 2015, the newborn Princess Charlotte's christening was
held at the Sandringham Estate in Norfolk. Here, the Cambridge
family displayed traditional 1950s styling, drawing on royal moments
past (Figure 6.2). George was dressed in an embroidered smock
top with formal red shorts and traditional buckle shoes, an almost
exact copy of an outfit his father had worn as a toddler in 1984.[44]
Charlotte was wrapped in the traditional royal christening gown,
and put in an antique pram used at Prince Charles's christening
in 1948 – not a pushchair designed to fit in a car for the 'mum on
the go', but a retro carriage for the camera.[45] Kate wore a demure
white coatdress with fascinator and low-heeled court shoes. The
image of Kate pushing the pram is an astonishingly retrogressive

representation of contemporary conservative femininity. She is perfectly coiffed yet demonstrably unsexy, fashionable yet twee, and firmly upper- or upper-middle class. The comments on this photograph on the Kensington Palace Instagram demonstrate its power. One user, @robertoalexavillegas, comments to a fellow user 'Babe omfg goals!!!!!!', suggesting that the Cambridges are their life 'goal' (albeit, perhaps, with ironic overstatement).[46] The christening photographs resonate with Sara Ahmed's description of heterosexuality: 'heterosexual love becomes about the possibility of a happy ending; about what life is aimed toward, as being what gives life direction or purpose'.[47] The Cambridges' broad smiles presents their nuclear family unit as fulfilling. The scholar Lauren Berlant argues that people develop 'optimistic attachment[s]' to fantasies of happiness, or 'the good life'.[48] She suggests these fantasies become cruel – what she calls 'cruel optimism' – when these fantasies are unachievable or unsustainable. For user @robertoalexavillegas, the Cambridge family fantasy is unattainable: the monarchy is a hereditary institution, and it is extremely unlikely audiences can marry into it despite the myths of meritocracy that Kate consolidates (see below). Rather, representations of the Cambridges normalise heterosexuality and conservative versions of femininity and family life.

Kate is often described in media culture as a 'fashion icon'. The fansite 'What Would Kate Do?' includes a section called 'repliKate', which advises readers on buying 'lookalike' clothes.[49] The *Daily Mail*'s *Femail* section published an article two days after Kate announced her pregnancy with George entitled 'Queen of the Yummy Mummies and her tiny trendsetter'.[50] The list of products includes a £148 soft toy, and a £1,450 pram. While the happy housewife of the 1950s was targeted by advertisements for domestic technologies,[51] the contemporary mother is targeted by images showing elite mothers and their luxury lifestyles. Diane Negra has described a 'culture of aspirational elitism', where luxury commodities are represented as essential to the middle classes under neoliberal capitalism.[52] Of course, at those prices, these fantasies of 'the good life' and of 'repliKating' are once again 'cruel' for many.[53]

If Kate is a 'fashion icon', this is a particularly conservative version of contemporary fashion trends. Jo Littler describes the 'yummy mummy', as the name implies, as a mother who is sexually appealing.[54] Whilst Kate is conventionally attractive, she is never publicly sexually objectified. Her potential, well-narrated faux pas at university, when she wore a sheer dress for a charity catwalk, has been co-opted by the news and entertainment media as part of a transformation narrative after William fell in love with her, thus lending the occasion a level of respectability because her (temporary) sexualisation led to heterosexual, monogamous marriage.[55] Before her marriage, some tabloid newspapers and entertainment magazines dubbed her 'Waity Katie' because they dated for nine years before engagement, suggesting that she was desperate to be married.[56] At her wedding, any sexual attention was redirected towards her sister, Pippa Middleton, whose bum became the focus of media commentary in a figure-hugging gown.[57] Paparazzi images that do capture Kate's unclothed body – when her skirt blew up, or in a bikini, for example – have been quickly concealed by the British press, despite the usual willingness of tabloid newspapers to reproduce such photographs of female celebrities. When the French edition of the celebrity magazine *Closer* published long-lens photographs of Kate sunbathing topless on private property, Kensington Palace sought an injunction and eventually won €100,000 in damages.[58] In comparison to the invasive coverage of Meghan Markle (see Chapter 7), Kate remains remarkably protected. As I argue below, this is perhaps attributable to connections between the white, middle-class mother and the reproduction of nationhood – particularly one responsible for birthing the heir to the throne.

Kate's fashion style reflects this conservatism, usually incorporating mid-length skirts and high necklines. This suggests a classed and gendered respectability, which the sociologist Beverley Skeggs associates with 'restraint, repression, reasonableness, modesty and denial'.[59] Kate's outfits (or costumes) exemplify the fusing of celebrity, middle-Englander, heritage and aristocratic cultures. At informal occasions, her style evokes countryside rurality and heritage cultures – Barbour jackets, quasi-riding boots and tweed jackets. But as opposed to the Sloane-esque traditionalism of Diana, Kate combines this aesthetic with 'celebrity style' long blow-dried hair, neat make-up and manicured nails. This is alongside a middle-Englander embracement of high-street stores, which the news and entertainment media use to narrate her 'ordinariness'. *Cosmopolitan* magazine, for example, announced 'Kate Middleton just wore a £40 Zara summer dress to the polo', assimilating classed cultures.[60] The fusion of costumes and cultures is best exemplified in Kate's 2016 front cover for *Vogue*. Posing in a Norfolk field, Kate combines a Burberry suede coat (a brand also subject to shifting classed connotations) with a high-street Beyond Retro fedora and trademark long, wavy hair.[61] Inside the magazine, she poses in a Breton-style top leaning against a gatepost; stroking her dog Lupo in a long denim jumpsuit; and pushing an antique bicycle. The blurring classed cultures are further signified in the photograph's display in the National Portrait Gallery to celebrate *Vogue*'s centenary issue, connoting it with artistic and historic value.

If Kate's indeterminate persona make her a non-specific sign, she is useful for the Firm. She simultaneously connotes conservative, upper-class femininity, celebrity style and middle-classness, appealing to multiple audiences, which are mobilised by the Firm.

The 'Middletonization' of the Firm

The first official photograph following George's birth in 2013 was taken by Kate's father, Michael Middleton, in the Middleton family garden. Although it predates the Kensington Palace Instagram, it draws on similar notions of familial intimacy. Kate, William ('Kate and Wills'), George and their spaniel Lupo relax on the grass in casual (yet conservative) clothing, described by Jo Littler as

'Bodenesque' after the upper-middle-class clothing brand.[62] Here, the 'Cambridge family photo album' appeals to a heteronormative, nostalgic 'middle-classness'.

The photograph reflects both the variations and the consistencies in representations of the Family Firm over time. The Cambridges draw on similar values to the intimate, domestic portraits of Queen Victoria and her young family (see Chapter 1), yet Victoria poses in an opulent palace interior, whilst the Cambridges sit in the Middleton family garden, distanced from signifiers of aristocratic privilege. The historian Florence Sutcliffe-Braithwaite argues that in the twentieth-century middle and upper classes blurred due to a cross-class claim to 'ordinariness', which was a 'contested and shifting' term.[63] Likewise, Jo Littler suggests that the royal family are represented as 'normcore aristocrats': ultra-wealthy aristocrats who appear 'ordinary' and 'just like us'.[64]

Indeed, drawing on the signifiers of Kate's family – the *Middle*tons – as 'middle-class', the Firm (re)brands itself through what the journalist Tom Sykes has termed the 'Middletonization' of the royal family.[65] Kate's supposed middle-class background often features in media representations. The ITV documentary *When Kate Met William: A Tale of Two Lives*, released for the Cambridges' wedding, narrates her 'humble beginnings' in contrast to William, and visualises this through symbols of classed hierarchy.[66] Footage of Kensington Palace splices into an image of a suburban house, and the voiceover narrates, 'while Prince William grew up in the grandeur of Kensington Palace, Kate's childhood home was this Victorian semi[67] … bought for £35,000'. The *Daily Mail* used genealogies of Kate's family tree to give 'scientific' evidence of her 'dirt-poor family past' and descent from coal miners.[68] Narratives of upward social mobility featured on the *Daily Telegraph*'s front page on her wedding day, in the headline 'Kate waves farewell to her life as a commoner'.[69] Such discourses use notions of meritocracy to smooth out, and erase, more complex issues of classification and widening inequalities.

A 'middle-class' woman marrying into the monarchy is, indeed, notable. The Royal Marriages Act 1772, which dictated that the first six people in the line of succession need permission from the monarch to marry, was written after George III's anger that his brother Prince Henry had wed the 'commoner' Anne Horton in 1771, and aimed to prevent future marriages deemed inappropriate to the dynasty.[70] William would require such permission to marry Kate, suggesting that opening up aristocratic culture to the lower classes was approved. In so doing, the Firm can draw on the 'myth of meritocracy' to position itself as socially mobile, and overlook the inaccessibility of the inherited classes.[71] In Kate's supposed social mobility, the Firm appears attainable and aspirational. On the other hand, such language reasserts a distinction between 'us' and 'them': Kate is 'waving farewell' to her 'ordinary' life because she moves into something decidedly *extra*ordinary. Michael Billig argues that this contradiction between ordinary and extraordinary is a negotiation strategy, whereby audiences position the royals as simultaneously ordinary and extraordinary to make sense of, and produce consent for, their privilege.[72]

The version of 'middle-classness' that the Cambridges evoke is nostalgic, proposing continuity between the twenty-first-century middle classes and those of the Victorian age. For example, the narration in *When Kate Met William: A Tale of Two Lives* that situates the Middletons in their 'Victorian semi' and the royals in Kensington Palace suggests there is nothing between the two extremities.[73] In fact, the distinct categories of working, middle and upper class that emerged during the Industrial Revolution have shifted under widening inequalities that polarise the top and bottom of society.[74] The Victorian middle classes as a stable, respectable, bourgeois family defined by the 'separate spheres' of work and home is a retrogressive notion of social organisation. As the English scholars Rosalía Baena and Christa Byker argue of the television period drama *Downton Abbey*, 'collective nostalgia can promote a feeling of community that works to downplay or deflect potentially divisive social differences (class, race, gender and so on)'.[75] Likewise, the Cambridges' nostalgic middle-classness deflects widening inequalities.

The attempted 'Middletonization' of the Firm could be interpreted as a strategic antidote to the damaging royal representations of the 1990s. In the Introduction, we saw that the Queen's so-called 'annus horribilis' in 1992 was partly characterised by anger at public funds being used to restore Windsor Castle after a fire.[76] It was also partly characterised by publicised 'sexual transgressions' by the (then) younger royals, after intimate disputes, 'sexual scandals' and divorce were documented by the news and entertainment media and shook 'the patriarchal foundations of the monarchy'.[77] The year 1992 saw Prince Andrew separate from Sarah Ferguson, Princess Anne divorce Captain Mark Phillips, Charles separate from Diana, Diana publish the tell-all book *Diana: Her True Story*, Sarah Ferguson photographed having her toes sucked by the American financer John Bryan, and recordings of Diana's intimate conversations with James Gilbey leaked.[78]

Such publicised 'scandals' were historically commonplace among aristocrats and royalty.[79] The historian Anna Clark argues that they often arose because reproducing monarchical power depends upon a legitimate heir, and challenging this legitimacy could contest power. For example, in the early modern period, James II's controversial Catholic heir was rumoured to be an imposter smuggled into the birthing room, and Henry VIII is best known for his multiple marriages in search of a legitimate heir.[80] The upper classes typically married strategically to foster alliances with powerful inter/national families, rather than for love.[81]

In contrast, 'Wills and Kate' are depicted as living their 'happy ever after'. The sociologists Jemima Repo and Riina Yrjölä analysed UK tabloid coverage of Kate between 2010 and 2012, and found that Kate's ordinary family life was often contrasted with Diana's and the royals' aristocratic upbringing, drawing on the cultural tropes of the respectable, nuclear middle-class family versus the dysfunctional aristocrats.[82] William's relationship with the Middleton family was interpreted by some as a 'positive and healing influence' on his well-being, resolving histories of broken royal marriages through his absorption into middle-class respectability.[83] Distinguishing 'Wills and Kate' from historical narratives of 'scandal' appears to be something the Firm is keen to uphold. In 2019, the US magazine *In Touch* reported that William had had an affair.[84] This was publicly discussed on Twitter, including by *The Times* journalist Giles Coren, who quickly deleted his tweet. [85] However, at the time of writing no mainstream British news publications have published the rumours. The online publication the *Daily Beast* reported that the Firm's lawyers allegedly served legal warnings to British publications banning them from publishing the reports.[86] These alleged reports raise important questions about the Firm's apparent influence over journalistic reporting. I argue that Instagram gives the Firm the opportunity to curate such images without interventions from critical news media.

Representations of the Cambridges do not entirely erase historical 'sexual transgressions'. Rather, past royal representations are incorporated, developed and resolved. The pantomime of 'scandal', criticism and resolution is a recurring trope of royal representations, as I demonstrate for the redemption of Prince Harry in Chapter 5. As for Harry, for William and Kate this pantomime often evokes the spectre of Diana. Kate wears Diana's engagement ring, an object that the media scholar Margaret Schwartz identifies as a 'fetish object ... for an imagined body that has been lost'.[87] William and Kate also restaged Diana's (in)famous Taj Mahal photograph. The photograph of Diana alone on a bench outside the Taj Mahal, taken in 1992 during an official visit to India, was used repeatedly by the news and entertainment media to capture her isolation amidst her and Charles's impending separation considering the Taj Mahal's symbolic meaning as the monument of love. During their own official trip to India in 2016, William and Kate posed in the same spot with identical framing, but presented a united image of happy domesticity, both smiling widely with Kate's body pointing towards William.[88] I argue that this symbolically resolves Charles and Diana's divorce through the respectable Cambridges and their heteronormative, nuclear, middle-class family values. In 2019, the *Daily Mail* used similar language to suggest that representations of 'Brand Cambridge' as 'solid, relatable, [and] reliable' were a counterpoint to a year of negative royal stories, from reports of Prince Andrew's involvement with the sex trafficker Jeffrey Epstein to rising criticism of Harry and Meghan.[89]

However, the 'Middletonization' of the Firm is fractured by both William's and Kate's class privilege. Kate is called 'Catherine, Duchess of Cambridge' in all official royal communications, despite the media continuing to use 'Kate', demonstrating the Firm absorbing her into respectable upper-middle-class circles. William and Kate are represented as 'liberal', 'hands-on' parents, from William driving Kate and newborn George home from the hospital, to the couple taking George and Charlotte to school, which are all documented on the Kensington Palace Instagram. This, of course, erases the labour of domestic staff in Kensington Palace, including nannies, chefs and cleaners, who absorb some responsibilities of social reproduction and caregiving.[90]

Similarly, descriptions of pre-royal Kate as a 'commoner' take extreme liberties with her privileged, bourgeois background. The Middleton family business Party Pieces is a multi-million-pound enterprise, Kate attended two private boarding schools and the Middleton family home is now the 18-acre Bucklebury Manor.[91] As their own family firm, the Middletons went from middle class to successful 'new money', giving them access to upper-middle-class and/or aristocratic circles and institutions of class privilege (the elite University of St Andrews, where Kate met William). However, it remains important that the Middletons' wealth is perceived as largely self-made to align them with respectable narratives of meritocracy and neoliberal 'hard work'. Kate's brother James, for example, retaliated to claims he had used his royal connections for publicity by saying 'nothing is handed to anyone on a plate. There are possibilities for everyone.'[92] The Middletons offer a respectable permutation of 'new money'.

There is constant threat of the Middletons' classed respectability rupturing. The sociologist Steph Lawler's analysis of media representations of Kate and William's brief split in 2008 found that the unsuitability of Kate's family was repeatedly referenced, as they were 'simply too déclassé'.[93] Likewise, accusations of class snobbery and antipathy have endured: from her sister Pippa Middleton marrying the brother of the reality television star Spencer Matthews; royal staff muttering 'doors to manual' behind Kate's back in reference to Carole Middleton's former job as a flight attendant; and Carole Middleton being photographed chewing gum at William's graduating parade from Sandhurst.[94] Kate's class mobility is always already at risk.

'The Great Kate Wait'

On 22 July 2013, hundreds of journalists gathered outside the private maternity Lindo Wing of St Mary's Hospital, London, to await Prince George's birth. The frantic media attention – which included BBC News regularly cutting to Royal Correspondent Peter Hunt, who reported 'no news', and Sky News's Kay Burley asking how many centimetres Kate was dilated, to be told by palace officials it's 'not the kind of information they give out' – has been dubbed in the media and public commentary as 'the Great Kate Wait'.[95]

At 8.30pm, a Kensington Palace press release announced George's birth. At 8.40pm, the Queen's then Press Secretary Ailsa Anderson and palace footman Badar Azim erected a centuries-old ornate gold easel behind Buckingham Palace gates, displaying an announcement signed by Kate's doctors:

> Her Royal Highness The Duchess of Cambridge was safely delivered of a son at 4.24pm today.
>
> Her Royal Highness and her child are both doing well.

6.3 The Cambridges leave the hospital with their newborn son, Prince George, to a crowd of journalists, photographers and fans, 2013

The passive tense of 'was safely delivered' erases Kate's agency. The next morning, William, Kate and George left the hospital to pose for hundreds of photographers and royal fans and gave a brief interview (Figure 6.3). This performance was repeated for Princess Charlotte's birth in May 2015, and Prince Louis's in April 2018.

The reproduction of the (Family) Firm has multiple meanings: its *representational* reproduction through the media industries, and its *biological* reproduction through the female body, as royal birth becomes public spectacle. Like other royal wives before (and after) her, Kate is prized on her ability to give birth and reproduce the dynasty. As Mantel suggested in relation to Henry VIII's reign, 'women, their bodies, their reproductive capacities ... are central to the story.'[96] This reflects Kay Burley's fascination with how many centimetres Kate was dilated, reorienting royal gynaecology for the global media age. Indeed, the dramaturgy of royal births that led Henry VIII to host a jousting tournament to celebrate

Katherine of Aragon birthing a son in 1511 (the baby later died), which was immortalised in a scroll, seems not to have abated, but is now rather mediated through live news bulletins and social media.[97]

Following successful birthing of an heir (and spares), Kate's royal purpose is to successfully raise respectable royal children. Indeed, her royal identity is constructed almost entirely around her identity as a mother. On the official royal website, the 'featured quote' from Kate on her biography page, designed to document the 'individual interests' of royal figures, reads: 'it is our duty, as parents and as teachers, to give all children the space to build their emotional strength and provide a strong foundation for their future'.[98] Likewise, her key patronages are themed around early years support, including mother's and children's mental health and children's hospitals. On an official tour of New Zealand in 2014, Kate and George (notably, without William) visited a local playgroup, where they were photographed playing with other children and Kate chatting casually to other parents.[99] The event was coded through middle-class leisure practices typical of McRobbie's 'mediated maternalism'.[100] Visits to, or interviews about, Kate's patronages are often mediated through her own reflections of motherhood. In 2020, she featured on the podcast series *Happy Mum, Happy Baby*, where the writer and celebrity mother Giovanna Fletcher interviews celebrity mothers on their experiences. Kate shared stories on hypnobirthing and morning sickness to demonstrate that, as she claims, 'no matter what walk of life you've come from, there's so many things that really unify parents and families in their struggles', again positioning the Cambridges as 'ordinary'.[101] If royal patronage is understood in this book as royal 'work', Kate's use of her mothering experiences can be read as a 'professionalisation of motherhood' similar to that of so-called 'mummy bloggers', who use their motherhood and children as a form of capital online.[102] Kate's job is (royal) motherhood, used to produce capital (economic, social, symbolic) for the Firm.

Royal brides are most symbolically effective when they produce royal offspring. Whilst Henry VIII hosted the jousting tournament to celebrate his son's birth – wearing a letter 'K' on his coat to celebrate Katherine of Aragon and laying the trophies at her feet as gratitude for her fertility – after the baby's death six weeks later and a further six unviable pregnancies, Henry VIII annulled the marriage and wed another woman.[103] Indeed, he would famously marry six women in search of an heir. In more recent history, royal women who fail to be *contained* as wives and mothers have lost favour in the monarchy, and sometimes hence in public opinion. Diana was vocal about her unhappy marriage, leading to her distancing from the Firm. Likewise, in Chapter 7 I argue that Meghan's departure from the Firm was in part because she was too 'symbolically loaded' to be contained as Harry's wife and Archie's mother.

The dramaturgy of royal birth also reflects its symbolism as reproducing the nation state. The feminist scholar Anne McClintock describes how 'nations are frequently figured through the iconography of the familial and domestic space', for example, the USA's First *Family*, the UK *Home* Office or the royal *family*.[104] Media descriptions of the 2011 Royal Wedding as 'the people's wedding', or George's gestation as 'the people's pregnancy', fetishise Kate's body as reproducing the citizenry: her reproductive capacities are representative of (and belong to) the wider public imagination.[105] This assumes that a white, heterosexual, cis-gendered, upper-class wedding and subsequent nuclear family *are* representative of citizens, which erases alternative identities from ideas of nationhood. Writing about Diana, the media scholar Raka Shome argues that white, heterosexual, upper-/middle-class women become 'biological and social reproducer[s] of the nation's future'.[106] Of course, for Kate in the monarchy, this plays out in specific ways. Upon birth, George became third in line to the throne. At the age of two, he featured on a set of postage stamps alongside the Queen, Charles and William: four generations of (future) monarchs acting as signifiers of British national identity.[107] Kate is tasked with reproducing this genealogy.

On a broader socio-political scale, nationalism and the family are interconnected under authoritarian neoliberalism, which attempts to maintain national cultures through the re-establishment of patriarchal power and traditional gender norms.[108] As described earlier, the #tradwife movement as an alt-right project illustrates the re-emergence of conservative, heteronormative family values vested in women's domestic subservience. As the sociologist Miranda Christou posits, the #tradwife embodies the intersections between toxic masculinity and white supremacy, where women are encouraged to 'save the nation by helping the (white race) become great again'.[109] The women are tasked with reproducing future white supremacists and misogynists, securing the future of the alt-right movement. #Tradwife Alena Pettitt's claim that she wants to 'submit to her husband like it's 1959' and serve him is suggestive of restoring 'traditional English manners, lifestyle and values', visualised in her Union Jack paraphernalia.[110] The scholars Agnieszka Graff and others argue that right-wing nationalist slogans like Trump's 'America First' appeal to 'traditional family values'.[111] These values are imposed through the retrenchment of women's sexual/reproductive agency, and the stigmatisation of women who transgress social norms (for example, single women depicted as responsible for facilitating national 'family breakdown').[112]

In Britain, family values are coded through Second World War nostalgia of familial sacrifice and responsibility. Indeed, the sociologists Kim Allen and others have argued that representations of Kate embody precisely these values.[113] Second World War fantasies of Britain as a wartime hero have since been co-opted into the Brexit movement, informing far-right ideologies of social exclusion, anti-welfarism and white British superiority.[114] During the COVID-19 pandemic in 2020, the Queen compared experiences of COVID-19 to wartime in her televised speech, with both articulated through discourses of national restraint and sacrifice.[115] During the pandemic, the Cambridges were represented as part of the country's collective caring efforts. Kate, William and their children partook in the national 'Clap for our Carers' movement, where citizens stood outside their homes each week to applaud NHS and other care workers for their sacrifices. In the video, produced for a BBC fundraiser programme and uploaded to the Kensington Palace Instagram, the Cambridges emerge from a traditional wooden front door framed by retro lamps and neatly trimmed foliage, meant to signify their home, wearing co-ordinating blue outfits and clapping.

Applauding doctors, nurses and other NHS staff as heroes of the crisis erases the government's accountability for failing to provide the NHS with appropriate safety equipment to deal with the outbreak.[116] Kate and William's family, shored up against the virus in their 'family home' and applauding key workers, depicts them as the idealised, responsible middle-class citizens for the wider public to emulate in response to the pandemic. Such response overlooks institutionalised inequalities, such as the Cambridges' access to elite medical care, their lack of concerns about job security and their ability to self-isolate in any one of their palaces. It also reproduces conservative ideologies of individualism, and legitimises the destruction of health and social care provision under successive Conservative governments.[117]

In an interview between Rosalind Brunt and Michael Billig about Diana's submission to royal patriarchy, Billig says, 'it wasn't just the position of a woman *vis-à-vis* a man or men. It was also a class position. Patriarchy *within* a class position. And a *national* position.'[118] Royal brides occupy a unique position, where their submission to patriarchy is inseparable from their reproduction of a class system and their connection to the nation. This is, perhaps, why Kate is a useful signifier for the #tradwife movement, which also connects reproductive bodies to class, race and nation. 'The Great Kate Wait' illustrates the ongoing interest in the wombs of royal brides, and indeed, of women around the world who find their reproductive rights being eroded by alt-right governments.

Conclusion

On 2 May 2020, Princess Charlotte's fifth birthday, Kensington Palace Instagram published four new photographs of Charlotte, taken by Kate.[119] Published during the COVID-19 pandemic lockdown in the UK, the photographs depicted Charlotte clutching a gift bag filled with homemade pasta, knocking on a turquoise front door with a heart-patterned doormat. The caption says the images were taken 'as the family helped to pack up and deliver food packages for isolated pensioners in the local area', implying that Charlotte is knocking on neighbouring front doors. The front door is noticeably less austere than the one pictured for the Cambridges' aforementioned 'Clap for your Carers' appearance a week earlier.

The photographs capture the relations described in this chapter. The Cambridges are depicted as liberal: a respectable, middle-class family assisting the community effort to support the vulnerable. Yet, these 'philanthropic' actions erase the government's accountability for supporting those vulnerable in the first place. The emphasis on Kate taking the photographs depicts her as teaching her children values of care and personal responsibility. The photographs also connote intimacy and access, documenting a private moment in Charlotte's, and the Cambridges', life. There remains a contradiction in representations of the Cambridges, in that they connote openness through apparently 'intimate' photographs, yet these representations are precisely choreographed. Although 'the Cambridge family photo album' stages royal domesticity, for example, this is not in the same way as the 1969 *Royal Family* fly-on-the-wall documentary (see Chapter 2). If the Firm was still modelled on this documentary, each royal figure might have a personal Instagram or Twitter account like celebrities. Rather, the Firm appears to be tightly restricting and managing access through its official channels, which is unusual in contemporary celebrity culture.

Kate is a PR coup for a Firm recovering from 'scandals' throughout the 1990s: a nice, middle-class woman from a respectable, nuclear, heteronormative family. If she is respectable, paparazzi cannot take photographs of her naked; if she is middle-class, she takes photographs of her own children. And so, royal representations are carefully contained. Likewise, if Diana caused a crisis in 'the patriarchal foundations of the monarchy', Kate has successfully re-established them.[120] Indeed, representations of the Cambridges illustrate how the British monarchy acts as the ultimate bastion of heteronormativity: the *heteromonarchy*, which performs heterosexuality and nuclear familialism as its 'frontstage'. The continued centrality of heteronormativity demonstrates that the sexual politics of monarchy have never changed. Despite the publicised 'sexual scandals' throughout the 1990s, the real 'scandal' would be a senior royal figure defying heteronormativity and having a royal baby out of wedlock or being homosexual. In 2018, the Queen's cousin Lord Ivar Mountbatten married his partner James Coyle and it made headlines for being the first same-sex royal wedding; yet Mountbatten remains a distant relative to the monarchy *and* it took until 2018 for this marriage to happen.[121] Royal homosexuality would also be a 'scandal' because of the multiple meanings of reproduction described in this chapter. The Firm is dependent upon both biological reproduction *and* its reproduction in the public imagination to maintain its power, privilege and wealth. However unusual Kate's non-aristocratic marriage into the monarchy might be, her traditional sexuality and femininity merely reproduces royal gender politics, and the publicised royal 'transgressions' are limited in scope as part of the royal pantomime of 'scandal', criticism and resolution.

'The Kate effect', a phrase adapted from Kuleshov's film theory, works cumulatively. That is, because we know little about Kate as an individual person, it is only through representations produced by the Firm that Kate's meaning is constructed. She has been carefully contained in the image of the heteromonarchy: the idealised standard-bearer of the nation, the idealised mother of authoritarian neoliberalism, the idealised wife of a future king. In the next chapter, I use the figure of Meghan Markle to explore the consequences when royal wifedom and motherhood are not, and cannot be, 'contained'. In opposition to 'the Kate effect', Meghan's identity and background (a celebrity, a woman with an established career, a racialised body and a feminist) mean she is *too* animated for containment. Whilst Kate's indeterminate persona reproduces the Family Firm, Meghan's intersectional symbolism threatens to rupture the norms it relies upon.

7

Megxitting the Firm: Race, postcolonialism and diversity capital

On 19 May 2018, Prince Harry married Meghan Markle, a bi-racial (her mother is African American, her father white American), divorced, self-identified feminist American actor with a working-class background. Unlike Kate Middleton before her, who is publicly known only through her royal role, Meghan entered the royal family with an already-established media persona. She played the lawyer Rachel Zane in the American cable TV drama *Suits* between 2011 and 2018, and had small roles in Hollywood films *Get Him to the Greek* and *Remember Me*.[1] She undertook international charity initiatives, such as an Advocate for the United Nations Entity for Gender Equality and the Empowerment of Women; and ran a lifestyle blog, *The Tig*, and social media accounts on Facebook, Twitter and Instagram, giving her a public voice.[2]

Media and public commentary of Harry and Meghan's wedding seemed to position it as a feminist, post-racial, meritocratic utopia.[3] For example, the American civil rights activist Al Sharpton claimed that the wedding showed that white supremacy 'is on its last breath',[4] and BBC coverage of the wedding ceremony repeatedly referenced a progressive future, as the presenter Richard Bacon claimed, 'this marriage is going to change the world'.[5] Hannah Yelin and I have argued elsewhere that these headlines 'co-opted' the Firm into a narrative of progress through Meghan.[6] The *Sun*'s headline, for example, read 'Kisstory: Harry and Meg's historic change for monarchy', as Meghan's identity was seen to diversify the monarchy and illustrate its progressive values.[7] I argued in Chapter 5 that the younger generation of royals have staged a break from the older generation and remodelled themselves as liberal and cosmopolitan, and Harry and Meghan's wedding reflects this process. Indeed, Meghan illustrates how this book has come full circle, and the modernisation of the media monarchy described in Chapter 2 was arguably given new life through Meghan as a royal figure. Her pre-royal career was used in her official biography on the official royal website upon her marriage: for instance her 'featured quote' on the website was 'I am proud to be a woman and a feminist', and elsewhere it linked to her 2017 opinion piece in *Time* magazine about the stigmatisation of menstruation and period poverty.[8] This language of activism seems to contrast directly with Kate Middleton's 'featured quote' about our 'duty' to care for children (see Chapter 6), which invests Kate with more traditional feminine values.[9] The official royal website highlights what each royal does, and, in including Meghan's pre-royal work on women's issues, I argue that the Firm made its own claim about its investment in these issues. Meghan's pre-royal individual voice is 'co-opted' by the Firm for the larger purpose of reproducing the institution.[10]

Under two years after the wedding, on 8 January 2020, Harry and Meghan announced their intention to 'step back as "senior" members of the Royal Family'.[11] Media and public commentary colloquially referred to this as 'Megxit', a portmanteau of Meghan and exit, and a play on 'Brexit', referring to Britain's exit from the European Union.[12] As I argue, 'Megxit' exposes the racialised discourses surrounding Meghan and the Firm, given that Brexit was waged in part through racialised and xenophobic ideologies.[13] Indeed, the couple's decision to leave the monarchy was largely blamed on critical, sexist and racist media coverage of Meghan. In the *Guardian*, the writer Amna Saleem wrote, 'it didn't take long … for Markle's mere existence to become a tokenistic rhetorical device for those who claimed our country didn't have a problem with race'.[14] The writer Afua Hirsch wrote in the *New York Times* that 'Black Britons know why Meghan Markle wants out', citing a universal experience of racism and injustice.[15] Despite the suppositions of progress described above, Meghan had been subject to racist media and public commentary since her relationship with Harry was announced in 2016. The right-wing US politician Paul Nehlen tweeted an image of Meghan with the face of the 'Cheddar Man' – Britain's oldest complete skeleton discovered to have had Black skin – superimposed on it;[16] the right-wing political party UKIP leader Henry Bolton's girlfriend claimed that 'Meghan's seed will taint our Royal Family';[17] and the Scottish schoolgirl @Hollyynaylorr tweeted 'unpopular opinion but a black American should not be allowed to marry into a white British royal family', sparking a backlash culminating in far-right extremist protesters hashtagging #IStandWithHolly.[18]

The Firm's responses again opened up opportunities for it to appear progressive. In November 2016, Kensington Palace released a statement on behalf of Harry, reading:

> The past week has seen a line crossed. His girlfriend, Meghan Markle, has been subject to a wave of abuse and harassment. Some of this has been very public – the smear on the front page of a national newspaper; the racial undertones of comment pieces; and the outright sexism and racism of social media trolls and web article comments.[19]

I do not dispute Harry's statement. But I argue that, by identifying the media coverage as racist and sexist (what Black feminists would term 'misogynoir' to describe the particular intersections of sexism and racism), the monarchy attaches itself to narratives of racial progress.[20] This is useful for its image, given the Firm's regressive values on both individual and structural levels: this book has demonstrated the idealisation of bounded national identities (Chapter 3), nostalgia for the landlord/serf model of social order and the romanticisation of imperialism (Chapter 4) and retrogressive gender traditionalism (Chapter 6). The redemption of Prince Harry that I described in Chapter 5 comes full circle in his statement above: a 'lad' famous for hedonistic drinking and sex, dressing as a Nazi and using racist slurs, is now calling out the British media and public for racism and sexism. Crucially, the monarchy's historical relationship with racism and sexism goes beyond isolated incidents like Harry's behaviour, or Prince Philip's so-called 'gaffes' (see below). I argue it is an institution built on subordinating women's bodies, and systems of slavery, exploitation, extraction, enclosure, colonialism and imperialism. In blaming the media for racist and sexist coverage, and in 'co-opting' Meghan's identity to claim its diversity, multiculturalism and relevance, the Firm's own role in reproducing racial, gendered and classed inequalities is obscured.

Harry and Meghan's wedding and subsequent departure from the Firm highlight a series of issues related to this book. I have told a story of radical contextualisation: the Firm is constantly reimagined in relation to socio-political shifts, from changes in capital accumulation to the expansion of media technologies, to varying gender roles. I have argued that representations of the royal *family* are central to obscuring the Firm's power.

But what happens when an heir to the throne marries a Black celebrity? Representations of Meghan confront the Firm with longer, complex, intersectional histories of racism (post-)colonialism, voice(lessness), servitude, media and celebrity, genealogy, gender, feminism, capital accumulation, social injustice and inequalities. Like 'Wills and Kate's' fairy-tale romance as resolution to royal sexual 'scandals', I suggest that Harry and Meghan's marriage provides a narrative of resolution to these histories, as the Firm was represented as progressive and inclusive. I argue that the couple's resignation demonstrates that this narrative was too much for the Firm to contain, and representations of Meghan carried *too much* symbolic weight to resolve those histories. As the critical race scholar Kehinde Andrews argues of the royals, 'their Whiteness is not a coincidence, it is the point. ... Far from Markle's inclusion changing the symbol, she is the exception that proves the rule.'[21] Similarly, the cultural scholar Sara Ahmed writes, 'bodies stick out when they are out of place ... sticking out from whiteness can thus reconfirm the whiteness of the space'.[22] Rather than resolving royal histories, then, representations of Meghan seem to have merely pulled these inequalities into view.

I visited Windsor Park for Harry and Meghan's wedding in May 2018. During the ceremony, I stood amongst the crowd on the Long Walk – which had been decorated with flags and bunting, and included multiple temporary toilets, snack bars, drink bars and ice cream vans – watching one of the large television screens that had been erected for the crowd to view the wedding. I used photography and field-notes to document my experiences, and some of these observations inform the analysis in this chapter.

It is worth reiterating here that I analyse *representations of royal figures*. Meghan's 'real' personality, or her 'real' beliefs, are unknown by the media culture representing her and by myself. There are serious issues of voice(lessness) in Meghan's presence in the Firm, and how she seems to have been silenced by the institution itself and in media culture; issues which are especially poignant considering the broader social silencing of women of colour. But my point here is that royal figures serve larger purposes to stage the monarchy. I am interested in how representations of royal figures work alongside, through and in service of the broader structural relations that keep monarchy in place. Or, in Meghan's case, how representations of her may threaten to disturb these structural relations.

'Megxit is the New Brexit'

On 15 January 2020, a week after Harry and Meghan's resignation announcement, the *New York Times* published a commentary article by the journalist Mark Landler entitled '"Megxit" is the New Brexit in a Britain Split by Age and Politics'.[23] Comparisons between the couple's resignation and Britain's exit from the EU had been made throughout the week, with the talks between the Firm and the couple nicknamed the 'Megxit summit', like the 'EU summit'.[24] Landler argued that Megxit was 'resurfacing the same questions that animated the Brexit debate. What kind of society do the British want: open or closed, cosmopolitan or nationalist, progressive or traditional?' Both debates, he wrote, were waged 'along political and generational fault lines': 'young people and liberals' more likely to have voted 'remain' in the Brexit referendum and more likely to support Harry and Meghan, and 'older, more conservative people', who likely voted 'leave' and likely supported the Queen.[25]

Whilst this analysis simplifies Brexit statistics, it neatly exposes the context of Meghan's introduction to the Firm. Meghan appeared as a royal figure at a particularly pertinent time in British history, and responses to her are entangled in wider socio-political debates about race, nation, imperialism and nostalgia. The couple's engagement announcement came eighteen months after Brexit, and their time in the Firm matched Britain's withdrawal period from the European Union: the UK left the European Union on 31 January 2020, and Harry and Meghan left the monarchy on 31 March 2020. Harry and Meghan's UK–US relationship also echoes the UK strengthening its 'special relationship' with the US as a potential post-Brexit trading partner. The media scholar Nathalie Weidhase argues that Harry and Meghan's union represents 'bringing two nations together', particularly pertinent considering the Firm's role as nationally symbolic.[26] At Windsor Park during the wedding, I witnessed multiple references to a UK–US union, from two friends dressed in complementary Union Jack and US flag-patterned suits to multiple US television broadcasters and a contingent of students or alumni from Meghan's former university, Northwestern University, Illinois. BBC coverage stationed one reporter, Richard Bacon, in Meghan's 'hometown' of Los Angeles to offer live commentary alongside celebrity guests and people from Meghan's past, such as the principal of her former school.[27]

Brexit is partly invested in lingering nostalgia for the British Empire, or what the cultural theorist Paul Gilroy calls 'postcolonial

melancholia'.[28] The debate to 'leave' was waged through a racialised lens, as Sivamohan Valluvan summarises: 'issues relating to
immigration, refugees, Muslims, the spectre of Turkey, the Roma,
and the tyranny of political correctness'.[29] This occurred alongside
increasingly negative media coverage of immigrants and refugees;
then Home Secretary Theresa May's promise to 'create, here in
Britain, a really hostile environment for illegal immigrants'; the
'Windrush scandal' where people were wrongly deported from
Britain for not meeting citizenship requirements; rising numbers of
racist hate crimes; and the election of right-wing, populist governments across the globe, supporting racist and anti-gender policies.[30]
These growing global far-right movements have prompted expanding
social justice protests, seen in Black Lives Matter and #MeToo, and
more radical left-wing political organisations, such as Momentum
supporting Jeremy Corbyn's leadership of the UK Labour party. In
this factional context, left-wing views of, for example, anti-racism
and feminism are attacked in right-wing rhetoric for being too
'politically correct', or for championing 'identity politics', a term
that was originally coined by the radical Combahee River Collective
to describe intersecting oppression, but which has since become a
pejorative term to dismiss social justice movements.[31]

Meghan quickly became associated with 'identity politics' in the
British right-wing press. The right-wing populist journalist and
commentator Piers Morgan repeatedly attacked Meghan via his
Daily Mail column. He used stereotypes associated with the contemporary political factions, including accusing her of 'playing
[the] race card' (a dismissive term implying that people of colour
abuse their oppression to win arguments) and being a 'whiny spoiled
brat', and referring to 'Me-Me-Meghan Markle's shamelessly
hypocritical super-woke Vogue stunt' ('woke' is a slang term, now
used pejoratively, for social justice awareness).[32] In the *Daily Telegraph*,
the journalist Sherelle Jacobs referred to Meghan's guest editorship
of *Vogue* magazine (see below) as showcasing the '"woke" liberal
elite', a disparaging phrase used to describe left-wingers who are

highly educated and affluent.[33] Meghan was used as the prototypical 'leftist', open to attack – by virtue of her visibility – by racist, xenophobic and anti-gender ideologists. The anti-racist advocacy group Hope Not Hate analysed over five thousand tweets using anti-Meghan hashtags, and found many of these users were also tweeting right-wing, pro-Brexit and pro-Donald Trump hashtags, suggesting an overlapping of concerns.[34] Indeed, #Megxit was being used by these accounts to forge connections between Meghan and populist politics long before the couple's announcement to leave the Firm. The language of 'Megxit', therefore, is indissoluble from racism, xenophobia and misogyny.

To report the exit agreement between the Firm and the couple, the *Sunday Mirror* used the headline 'Queen Orders a Hard Megxit'.[35] This plays on language of a 'hard Brexit', referring to the plan of some Conservative party MPs (such as the now Prime Minister Boris Johnson) for the UK to leave the EU, the EU's single market and the EU Customs Union. In a 'hard Brexit', it is reactionary, populist figures like Johnson who are shoring up the country against 'unwanted' immigration and the 'woke liberal elites'. According to that logic, in a 'hard Megxit', it is the Queen shoring up our country against Meghan as an 'unwanted immigrant' and a 'woke liberal elite'. That is, if the Queen represents the conservative ideal, Meghan is the antithesis. The multiple media reports claiming that Meghan had disagreed with Kate arguably play on similar oppositions. The journalist Helen Lewis identifies the Kate versus Meghan reports as a 'culture war', where 'women's lives provide a particularly vivid arena for the clash between traditionalism and modernity' because they are seen to represent *all* women.[36] If I argue that Kate is seen as representing the right-wing #tradwife (Chapter 6), then Meghan is seen as signifying social progression and 'wokeness'.

Understanding this context is necessary to understanding responses to Meghan. Her gendered, classed and racialised identity are given meaning through the socio-political context of Britain and beyond, and she came to act as a shorthand for broader political factions. I argue that Meghan was subject to symbolic overload, unable to embody the representational demands put upon her, and instead merely emphasising the inequalities her image supposedly resolved.

Diversity capitalism in the Firm

Two days after Harry and Meghan's son, Archie, was born in May 2019, their Instagram account @sussexroyal published an official photograph of the Queen meeting her great-grandson.[37] The photograph, taken at Windsor Castle, features Meghan cradling baby Archie surrounded by Harry, the Queen, Philip and Meghan's mother Doria Ragland. Like other official royal photographs (see Chapter 6), the image blends 'traditional' and modern, ordinary and extraordinary. The men wear grey suits, Meghan wears a formal white shirt-dress, Doria a cream dress and gold scarf, and the Queen a casual blue cardigan and skirt. Most notable in this family portrait are markers of racial identity. Doria, Meghan and Archie's presence in official royal portraiture represents a shift from generations of British royal portraits, which have been almost exclusively white. Indeed, the composition of this photograph as an 'ordinary', multigenerational and *multicultural* family arguably invests the Firm with progressive, inclusive and future-oriented values.

This reflects narratives told during Harry and Meghan's wedding. In addition to the media commentary described above, many mixed-race and Black commentators or publics celebrated Harry and Meghan's wedding as representative of inclusivity and progress. Colleen Harris, a former royal aide and one of the first women of colour working in the Firm, wrote that the wedding was 'the day the monarchy embraced multicultural Britain's future'.[38] The broadcaster Afua Hirsch, whose book *Brit(ish)* critiqued the history of British racism, lauded the wedding as a 'rousing celebration of blackness'.[39] On social media, @MsJillMJones tweeted 'that was probably, the most diverse ... event in the history of The Royals' and @yemsxo tweeted 'WHAT A TIME TO BE ALIVE! IM SO HAPPY!'.[40]

My analysis is not disputing that the wedding was an important symbolic and iconographical moment. Although some historians suggest that Charlotte of Mecklenburg-Strelitz, who married George III in 1761, was Black, having a woman of colour at the centre of British hereditary power is still something rarely represented.[41] Fantasies of the Firm as meritocratic, beginning with Diana and then intensifying with 'commoner' Kate's class mobility, were invested with new meaning under Meghan. Now, even a Black American with a working-class background can enter the elite British establishment (of course, since then, some media have exposed the limitations of this narrative, as she may *enter* the establishment but they make clear she is not *welcomed*, nor does she apparently *fit*).

If we understand the Firm as a corporation, Meghan's entrance takes on new significance. I have argued in *Running the Family Firm* how royal figures serve particular purposes to reproduce the institution. Representations of Harry's affable persona makes the Firm appear 'ordinary' and distracts from the military-industrial complex, Kate's investment in being a wife and mother reproduce ideologies of conservative, 'middle-class', nuclear 'family values'. Similarly, representations of Meghan can be seen as a form of diversity capitalism, used to extend the Firm's markets through notions of diversity, post-imperialism and post-racialism. The sociologists Celia Lury, Henry Giroux, and Les Back and Vibeke Quaade have each analysed the global clothing retailer Benetton's 1990 campaign 'The United Colors of Benetton', which comprised advertisements featuring people from various racial and ethnic backgrounds wearing signifiers of US national identity (for example, stars and stripes to represent the flag) to promote the 'diversity' of both the products and the customers.[42] Their analyses argued that Benetton tried to produce a new corporate image as a company of diversity and inclusivity, to attract customers with vested interests in social change.

That is, racial politics were used to expand Benetton's markets, or what the authors refer to as 'diversity capitalism'. Similarly, the marketing scholar David Crockett proposes that US advertisers have 'marketed Blackness' to make claims about the companies' progressive values and appeal to broader consumers.[43] The media scholar Jennifer Fuller argues that US television cable channels use Blackness as a marketing tool to differentiate themselves from growing competitors.[44]

There is an important distinction here between notions of 'diversity' and notions of 'difference'. Scholars argue that 'diversity' suggests a dilution of identity, where 'we are all different' and therefore 'we are all the same in our difference'.[45] There are no dominating groups because we are all equal in our diversity. Diversity is a 'respectable' and 'more palatable' way to mark identity because it refuses to engage with structural inequalities.[46] A politics of 'difference', meanwhile, recognises structural inequalities and marks out points of disparity between groups; for example speaking as a woman of colour draws attention to the specific, embodied experiences of being part of this identity group. 'Difference' is marked to acknowledge the politics of this difference. Sara Ahmed's work on institutional diversity notes that these definitions mean that 'diversity', *not* 'difference', acts as a useful image-maker for organisations wishing to appear as if they are doing 'good work'.[47] Vague references to 'diversity' offer a veneer of repairing racialised histories, because they suggest progress without actually attending to the structural inequalities arising from these histories.[48] One way to resolve the histories of an institution that has an image problem around race is to co-opt an image of diversity.

'Diversity capitalism' builds on ideas of 'racial capitalism', which the critical race theorist Cedric Robinson describes as how 'the development, organization and expansion of capitalist society pursued essentially racial directions'.[49] That is, capital is extracted from processes of invasion, expropriation and hierarchy – all of which are racialised – and classification and racial hierarchy were used to justify colonial pillages, theft and dispossession.[50] 'Diversity capital' describes how racialisation is used as a tool of differentiation under a guise of progress, but without structural or institutional changes to systems of inequality. The business scholars Janet L. Borgerson and others found that Benetton's 'operational identity' failed to live up to its diversity-focused brand identity, whereby its fashion shows and promotional materials had few ethical values beyond casting multicultural models.[51] They argue that this created a '"hollow" visual identity', where symbolism outranked deeper meaning.[52] The language of diversity is depoliticised, and the inherent whiteness of institutional power remains.

Likewise, the image of the Queen and Philip meeting Archie does little to alter inequalities in the Firm beyond casting a new set of more diverse royal figures. Even the setting of the photograph reproduces the structural inequalities of monarchy. The town of Windsor is home to the prestigious Eton College, an all-boys public boarding school enshrined in systems of class and racial inequality in the UK.[53] Windsor Castle was originally built in the eleventh century by William the Conqueror as a motte-and-bailey castle to fortify the building against invasion by other monarchs or overthrow by the public, and hence preserve hereditary royal power. It is now the Queen's 'weekend home' – a surplus palace in the monarch's property portfolio. The pastel painting in the background of the photograph of Archie meeting the Queen is *Landscape with a Groom and two Horses, and two Peasant Women* by the eighteenth-century Italian artist Francesco Zuccarelli. The image depicts inequality and servitude. The term 'peasant' refers to a pre-industrial agricultural labourer, and 'Groom' is an alternative for 'stable boy' – both workers would have typically been very poor and served the wealthy. More broadly, Doria, Meghan and Archie's family history intersects with the monarchy's colonial voyages. According to the journalist Andrew Morton, Doria's first identifiable African American ancestor was Richard Ragland, born in Georgia in 1830.[54] The state of Georgia was founded as a British colony in 1733, named after King

George II as a symbol of monarchical power. Meghan, Archie and Doria's presence in the Firm does not alter or absolve these histories of inequality and white supremacy. Rather, the group is absorbed into the Firm's narrative of progress.

If we understand representations of Meghan as a form of diversity capital, her royal 'work' also gives the Firm access to more diverse markets. In 2019, before 'stepping back' from the monarchy, Meghan guest-edited the September edition of *British Vogue*, a glossy, high-profile, British fashion magazine.[55] The edition was headlined 'Forces for Change', and Buckingham Palace's press release claimed that it highlights 'trailblazing change makers, united by their fearlessness in breaking barriers'.[56] The cover featured 15 women, including the teenage climate activist Greta Thunberg and the author Chimamanda Ngozi Adichie, as part of what Meghan called 'the strength of the collective in the diverse selection of women chosen for the cover'.[57] She continued in her introduction, 'I hope readers feel as inspired as I do, by the forces of change they'll find within these pages'.[58] *Vogue*'s editor-in-chief Edward Enninful said of her, 'to have the county's most influential beacon of change guest edit British *Vogue* at this time has been an honour', hence incorporating Meghan into this narrative of activism and transformation.[59]

Whilst royals have guest-edited magazines before (for example Charles and *Country Life*) and appeared on *Vogue*'s cover (for example Kate, see Chapter 6), Meghan's edition has a markedly different tone from the conservative, aristocratic versions preceding her. She writes that the cover women were chosen for 'their commitment to a cause, their fearlessness in breaking barriers'.[60] Celebrating women who have a voice and enact change is the opposite of the retrogressive, traditional royal femininities we saw in Chapter 6. And, indeed, it ignores the fact that Meghan's individual voice, previously heard in her blog and social media accounts, has been silenced. The *Vogue* editorship is part of Meghan's philanthropic 'work', undertaken by royal figures to reproduce, and produce consent for, the Firm. The very purpose of this work is to maintain hegemonic norms of monarchical power through ideologies of social responsibility and value. The language of diversity in *Vogue* is 'co-opted' by the Firm to remake itself in a new model of liberal, cosmopolitan and multicultural Britishness, and ensure its survival in a changing socio-political context.[61] Ideas of diversity are used here as a form of capital – both symbolic and economic – to serve the Firm. As I have demonstrated throughout *Running the Family Firm*, the monarchy is always changing in order to stay the same, and representations of Meghan are the latest iteration of this process.

Meghan also gives the Firm access to patronages focusing on women's rights. During her time as a royal, she worked with Smart Works, an organisation providing clothing for unemployed women to attend job interviews, and visited the charity One25, which provides food packages to sex workers in Bristol.[62] She published the charity cookery book *Together*, which featured recipes from the women displaced in the Grenfell Tower fire, who created a temporary communal kitchen to cook for other survivors.[63] In her introduction to *Together*, Meghan repeatedly references the importance of unity and collectivity in responding to the crisis: 'this is a tale of friendship, and a story of togetherness'.[64] As I argue elsewhere, while this may describe the displaced women cooking for their community, when written in an introduction by Meghan who is operating on behalf of the Firm this incorporates the monarchy 'into narratives of tragedy and resilience', 'eras[ing] the realities of inequality, and classed and racialised violence' in Kensington and Chelsea, and obscuring the monarchy's role in creating the structural conditions of inequality that caused the Grenfell fire in the first place.[65]

During an official royal visit to South Africa, Harry and Meghan visited the Mbokodo Girls' Empowerment Program, which provides self-defence training to young girls who have suffered trauma. Meghan spoke to the community, saying:

> May I just say that while I am here with my husband as a member
> of the royal family, I want you to know that for me, I am here as

a mother, as a wife, as a woman, as a woman of colour and as
your sister.[66]

In this quotation, which received cheers from the audience, Meghan
plays with notions of authenticity. On one hand, she separates
herself as an individual 'mother … wife … woman … woman of
colour and … sister' from the monarchy, laying bare the institutional
power of the royal family in her 'official visit' role. On the other
hand, her authenticity as 'a mother … a wife … a woman [and]
… a woman of colour' invests the Firm itself with new authenticity.
Royal visits have historically had colonialist implications, or, as the
Indigenous Australian Studies scholar Holly Randell-Moon argues,
'perpetuate colonial "ways of seeing"', through invocations of the
white (royal) saviour.[67] Raka Shome discusses how Diana became
a symbol of white virtue in photographs of, for instance, Diana
playing with and caring for Black children in Africa.[68] She argues
such images construct children of the Global South as unhealthy
or deprived, legitimising the white saviour 'rescuing' them.[69] In
comparison, Meghan's reference to herself as a 'woman of colour'
suggests that she identifies with the women she visits, and can
position herself as their 'sister'. Considering she is 'working' for
the Firm on this visit, this could in turn make the Firm more
able to identify with the women, and works to obscure colonialist
tensions.

Meghan's speech in South Africa gestures towards conflicts
between her assimilation as a royal and a continued process of
'othering'. She suggests that there is her role in the royal family,
and then there is her role as woman of colour. This reproduces the
Firm's whiteness. It also speaks to the politics of diversity capitalism.
For institutions to claim diversity, those identified as 'diverse' 'must
stay in place as "other"' so they offer a comparison, and can be celebrated as the 'diverse' face (for example, university prospectuses
that use images of students of colour to do what Ahmed calls
'diversity work').[70]

There are, however, limitations to what 'diversity work' is allowed to look like. People of colour must continue to represent diversity symbolically, Ahmed argues, but also not disrupt the status quo and not address the institutionalisation of whiteness.[71] That is, they must *appear* diverse but their values must *assimilate* with existing institutional values (see below for how this connects to racialised 'respectability politics'). Meghan has been accused of not appropriately assimilating into the Firm. Critical commentary of Meghan has used language of 'othering' to suggest her presence disturbs traditional monarchical norms; traditions which, through their symbolic importance, are vested in imaginaries of British national identity.[72] The *Sun*, for example, has variously accused her of 'American Wife Syndrome' for renovating Frogmore Cottage, said that 'her extravagant spending' has offended 'our frugal Queen', and called her 'difficult and demanding'.[73] These descriptors draw on stereotypes of the 'angry Black woman', which displace and dehumanise in comparison to white 'normative' respectability.[74] This is a form of 'misogynoir'.[75] The claim that her actions have offended 'our frugal Queen' is particularly loaded. In her apparently offending 'our' Queen, the *Sun* makes associated claims that Meghan's actions offend Britain as a whole. She is portrayed as the alien 'other', becoming what the sociologist Nirmal Puwar refers to as a 'space invader'.[76] Meghan disrupts the status quo.

This all came to a head upon Meghan and Harry's resignation from the Firm. Much of the commentary blamed Britain's tabloid press for Meghan's desire to leave: the activist Aaron Bastani claimed that the 'royal couple can't challenge Britain's sick press', and the journalist Sean O'Grady wrote 'Meghan and Harry are stepping back because of the press', reflecting the couple's own statements about press criticism and abuse (see Postscript).[77] These discourses depict the British news media as racist (which they are), whilst in turn the Firm looked progressive in comparison. Harry's statements against the media's racism, as described above, were laudable, but arguably gave the Firm a veneer of liberal, tolerant values standing up against traditionalist institutions. Sara Ahmed writes that 'institutions can "keep their racism" by eliminating those whom they identify as racists'.[78] Likewise, the Firm can 'keep its racism' by scapegoating other institutions in their place and co-opting an image of diversity. This is not to deny that the British media *have* been racist towards Meghan. But as the journalist Zoe Williams writes in the *Guardian*, 'the royals haven't moved, but the political context in which they are now operating has shifted so far that merely through anti-racist advocacy ... they've fetched up on the same team as the socialists'.[79] Meghan offered the Firm an opportunity to diversify at a time of global political upheaval, and global elites increasingly invested in far-right political projects (such as the Trumps), with which the Firm risks being associated. Meghan offered the Firm a chance to promote itself to new markets, and tap into new sources of (diversity) capital. Her resignation perhaps demonstrates that this was a marketing ploy too far. It is notable that only since her resignation have we seen more meaningful anti-racist statements and engagement with contemporary anti-racist movements from Meghan, such as a speech in support of Black Lives Matter.[80] In contrast, despite there being 450 global Black Lives Matter protests in May–June 2020 to demand justice for George Floyd, a Black American man murdered by a white police officer, the Firm has yet to offer any concrete, visible gestures of support. The Firm's apparent refusal to engage with a politics of 'difference' in favour of a more palatable 'diversity', reveals the limits to the institution's progressive values.

Post-racial imaginaries

The MP David Lammy hailed Harry and Meghan's wedding as 'Britain's Obama moment' because he believed it symbolised racial progress.[81] An alternative interpretation of it being 'Britain's Obama moment' is that it has comparable representations of post-racialism.[82] The royal wedding was not automatically progressive because a white, elite man married a woman of colour (nor, indeed, was it automatically feminist because Meghan self-identifies as one). As Raka Shome writes, 'cosmopolitanism is not colourful global identity politics'.[83] What matters is the social, political and cultural context of the wedding, and how the marriage prompts, or does not prompt, structural social change.

The sentiment of those commentators celebrating Harry and Meghan as changing UK race relations reflects the 'post-racial'. The critical race scholar David Theo Goldberg defines post-raciality as 'the claim that we are, or are close to, or ought to be living outside of debilitating racial reference', whereby 'key conditions of social life are less and less now predicated on racial preferences, choices and resources'.[84] That is, race is no longer a deciding factor in people's life trajectory because we have overcome such inequalities. Goldberg identifies Barack Obama's election as the first Black US president as central to the emergence of post-racial ideologies. It was seen to represent the breaking-down of racial barriers, yet, despite these suppositions, structural racism continues to underpin US society. Similarly, the sociologist Remi Joseph-Salisbury discusses post-race as the individualisation of race, whereby structural and historical racism is overlooked in favour of individual achievements (again, Obama is a good example).[85] The critical race scholar Alana Lentin compares the post-racial to the politics of 'diversity' as I described above, where both homogenise difference and obscure structural inequalities and intersectional experiences of difference.[86]

Meghan's individual presence as a woman of colour in an institution that has been almost exclusively white is symbolically and representationally notable. For people of colour to see themselves represented in an elite institution, particularly one symbolic of national identity, is extremely valuable. But this assumes that visibility equals power. Meghan's presence does not erase histories of racism in Britain, nor does it absolve the ongoing racial inequalities in the present. Rather, in the spirit of the post-racial, her *individual* progress as a visibly racialised person in an elite position is celebrated at the expense of structural changes. Both Britain and the monarchy are seen as 'post-race' because they have co-opted an image of diversity. Yet, to describe either as 'post-racial' is absurd. Indeed, I have contextualised Harry and Meghan's wedding in a period of xenophobic messages on which part of the Brexit vote was waged, and other racialised injustices such as the 'Windrush scandal' and the Grenfell Tower fire, all of which demonstrate how institutionalised racism continues to structure British society.

Likewise, reactions to Meghan from the Firm and the British media demonstrate that representations of progress do not necessarily correspond to their values. The plethora of media commentary focusing on Meghan's ancestry and genealogy, usually written as pieces about 'diversity' in the monarchy, evidences an ongoing racialised concern with royal blood purity. As the sociologist Ben Carrington points out, notions of the royals having a distinct blood category – 'blue blood' – are classed and racialised metaphors referring to someone with such pale skin that blood vessels were visible underneath, and therefore they did not work in the fields where the sun would darken skin.[87] Prior to Harry and Meghan's engagement, the *Daily Mail* reported that 'Harry's girl is (almost) Straight Outta Compton', drawing on racist stereotypes of Black urban poverty.[88] A few weeks later, an article entitled 'How in 150 years, Meghan Markle's family went from cotton slaves to royalty via freedom in the US Civil War', detailed a family tree to 'track' Meghan's family history.[89] Although they created a similar family tree for Kate (see Chapter 6), for Meghan it was her relatives' racial profiles that were emphasised, and many included descriptors of her relatives' race, such as 'recorded as "coloured"', which essentialises race.[90] Royal family trees are recreated over time to illustrate dynasty and legitimacy to rule. The *Daily Mail*'s version of Meghan's 'alternative' family tree reasserts the white royal bloodline by marking Meghan through her race. It seeks to illustrate not the *continuation* of the dynasty like the royal version does but rather a classed and racialised meritocracy of 'rising above' her history. For example, referring to Meghan's great-great-great-grandmother Mattie Turnipseed, they assert there is a 'colossal gulf separating the most powerful woman in the world from a young, uneducated, "coloured" woman without a vote'.[91] It is Meghan's *distance* from, and ability to overcome, these histories that is celebrated. The journalist Rachel Johnson (sister of the UK Prime Minister Boris Johnson) used colonialist language in the *Daily Mail* to suggest that 'the Windsors will thicken their watery, thin blue blood and Spencer pale skin and ginger hair with some rich and exotic DNA', but added 'genetically, she [Meghan] is blessed', perhaps because her lighter skin and physical appearance meets white, Western beauty standards.[92] This makes Meghan an 'acceptable' face of diversity.[93] She is 'just exotic enough'. The sociologist Maxine Leeds Craig calls this 'pigmentocracy', whereby racial hierarchies favour people of colour with lighter skin.[94] I argue that Johnson's mixing of the language of 'pigmentocracy' with discussions about DNA creates a hierarchical genealogy, where Meghan is seemingly accepted because she is light-skinned and has moved beyond her family's 'difficult' history.

Harry and Meghan's wedding ceremony was understood by some as anti-racist, or, as Afua Hirsch called it, a 'rousing celebration of Blackness'.[95] The African American bishop Michael Curry referenced Martin Luther King and slavery, the ceremony included a gospel choir singing 'Stand by Me' which is an anthem from the Black Civil Rights movement and the Black British cellist Sheku Kanneh-Mason performed. Again, these are important representational moments. To highlight Black culture at a royal ceremony, which is steeped in histories of British national identity, is remarkable. Yet, as the sociologist Stefanie Boulila argues, the sermon referenced only American anti-racism, and so 'race and racism were mobilised solely in relation to a past or with reference to an "elsewhere"', ignoring (not resolving) the specificities of structural racisms in Britain.[96] Public responses to the ceremony also demonstrate varying engagement with Black culture. At Windsor

Park, I observed people who had previously demanded fellow viewers be quiet as Harry and Meghan declared their vows actively ignoring Curry's address and commenting 'he goes on a bit', 'who invited him?' and, towards the end, beginning to boo. Later, a man told his companion, 'I didn't like that Muslim preacher', conflating two religions and incorrectly identifying Islam as a race. He essentialised and conflated skin colour and religion, where whiteness equals Christianity and people of colour equal Muslim, which reflects the essentialised, racist rhetoric of the Brexit vote. These responses demonstrate that, although the *symbol* of a multicultural monarchy appeals to some viewers, the reality of this experience provokes criticism (and, indeed, confusion for those who essentialise identity along racialised lines).

Figures in the Firm have also been publicly racist. Prince Philip was infamous for making racist comments during royal tours and visits.[97] These comments were widely reported in the British media, yet, as the scholar Hamid Dabashi argues, were often described as 'gaffes', which trivialises and dismisses racism.[98] The BBC, for example, recounted Philip's 'memorable one-liners that can make some people chuckle and others cringe'.[99] By the BBC not identifying and critiquing racism, the potential harm he caused is dismissed. Other royals have been more explicitly criticised for racism, including Harry as described above. Princess Michael of Kent wore a blackamoor brooch to the Queen's Christmas lunch at Buckingham Palace, the first time she met Meghan. She apologised for 'causing offence' after media and public critique.[100]

There are issues here in individualising racism in the Firm. By making racism the problem of individual royals, the monarchy's history as a racist, patriarchal, imperial institution is masked, as is the effect of this institutional whiteness on British citizens, who are meant to be represented by the monarch(y). In Michael Billig's interviews with British families about the royals in the late 1980s, he describes one incident where a white family were discussing Prince Charles's choice of brides: 'the younger son then raised the issue of race. [They said that] Prince Charles would not have been free to marry a black girl. In the exchange which followed, there was ... joking and ... laughter.'[101] As he outlines, the family's 'humorous' exchange made clear that they thought the idea of Charles marrying a woman of colour, and more specifically someone Black, was ludicrous. As with Philip's comments, the joke format here is key. The family police the boundaries of whiteness in the monarchy (although the word 'white' was never explicitly mentioned), while denying their own racism through humour.

This family also repeatedly referred to a mystical 'they': 'they don't allow them [the royals] to marry into different religions'.[102] 'They' are unidentifiable, yet they are attributed power. If the Firm is understood as an institution – or a corporation – the 'they' referenced here could refer to the institution as a whole. Sara Ahmed argues that 'it is important that we do not reify institutions by presuming they are simply given ... rather, institutions *become* given, as an effect of the repetition of the decisions made over time'.[103] The cryptic 'they' obscures the responsibility of the institution, and those working for it, for shaping the institution's values. The Firm's shaping as a white racial institution has 'become given' through much broader histories of empire, colonialism and imperialism. The monarchy supported colonisation projects across the British Empire by granting Royal Charters, funding trade voyages and signifying their ownership of slaves with branding. They continue to extract value from goods stolen during colonisation, such as the Koh-i-Noor diamond.[104] The British monarchy as we know it would not exist without histories of extraction and exploitation. The monarchy also operated symbolically as Empire's figurehead. This is, as the English Literature scholar Diane Roberts argues, vested in politicised notions of the royals as idealised white subjects. During the period of Britain's initial colonial voyages and increasingly multicultural population, Elizabeth I emphasised her white skin by painting it lighter to 'underscore ... her difference, her elevation, in whiteness'.[105] Victoria was described as 'the whitest woman in the world' due to her 'pale-skinned, white-haired, pearl-draped' image featuring on stamps, money, memorabilia and portraiture across the Empire.[106] Royals have served as symbols of institution-alised whiteness for hundreds of years, used as 'evidence' of white superiority and right to rule.

Those discourses claiming that Meghan's introduction to the Firm 'will change the world' were tasking one woman with restructur-ing centuries' worth of exploitation and violence.[107] Stuart Hall identifies this as the 'burden of representation', whereby Black people, for example, are expected to speak for the entire Black race because they are seen to represent the communities' views.[108] This homogenises diverse groups on account of their racial identity, and fails to recognise politics of difference. Critical race theory describes whiteness as 'unmarked', because it is expected and assumed.[109] Meghan stood out as visibly raced in a white, unmarked institution. Her body did not 'fit' alongside those white royal figures in the Firm, nor, indeed, in the nation state imagined as white. As such, Meghan was marked from the beginning. Whilst her identity may have been intended to resolve the royals' problematic histories of race, her marked status meant it was difficult to absorb her into the institutional narrative. Rather than smoothing over stories of Princess Michael of Kent wearing a blackamoor brooch, for example, Meghan's presence (rightly) emphasised the racism. Remarks previ-ously dismissed as 'gaffes' were invested with more urgency. The symbolism of Meghan, as a woman of colour confronting the Firm with its racist histories, was too much to contain.

Class, race and respectability politics

At the time of Harry and Meghan's wedding, media representations of Meghan's family had resonances with those of the Middleton family during Kate and William's wedding, and Kate's classed ascent into the royal family (see Chapter 6). The aforementioned interest in Meghan's family tree, for example, used terms of classed and racialised meritocracy. Many of these pieces entirely erased Meghan's self-made wealth and high-profile career. Headlines such as 'How in 150 years, Meghan Markle's family went from cotton slaves to royalty' jump 150 years to create a binary of slavery to royalty, ignoring everything between.[110] Whilst Kate's classed ascent was complicated by her parent's wealth, Meghan was a multi-millionaire of her own making, yet this narrative was rewritten to emphasise her as meritocratic by marriage, hence erasing her previous achievements and reinscribing traditional femininities.[111]

At the same time, and again resonating with Kate, some media texts continued to emphasise and disparage Meghan's working-class background. The *Daily Mail*, in particular, represented her family in ways reminiscent of 'white trash' discourses – an American slur, equivalent to the UK's 'chav', for an abject working-class figure.[112] As the sociologist Matt Wray writes, intersectionality means that whiteness is coded differently according to other identity markers, such as class, gender and sexuality, which creates hierarchies of whiteness.[113] Meghan's father, Thomas Markle, was persistently featured in the British tabloid media, culminating in an exposé in the *Mail on Sunday* about how 'Meghan's Dad staged photos with the paparazzi' for profit while the 'Palace pleaded for privacy'.[114] Meghan's nephew owns a cannabis farm in Oregon, USA, and sold the product under the name 'Markle's Sparkle', but has denied any association with Meghan.[115] The *Daily Mail* reported on Meghan's aunt and cousin, who had spent the royal wedding in a Burger King in Florida wearing the cardboard crowns produced by the food chain as promotion. The *Daily Mail* wrote, 'at exactly the time the Markles hit Burger King in Sanford, 4,300 miles away in Windsor the new Duke and Duchess of Sussex and their 600 guests were being hosted by the Queen in St George's Hall, Windsor'.[116] This creates clear class distinctions between Meghan's 'past' and 'future', positioning her family as objects of mockery and disparagement. The fast-food chain Burger King, associated with working-class stereotypes, provides contrast through its monarchical-themed name to the meal at Windsor, which is coded as upper-class and aspirational. As with her ancestors, it is Meghan's *distance* from these relations that is celebrated.

The only close relation of Meghan's to attend the wedding was her mother, Doria, and Doria has since been visible at some royal events. The film scholar Fiona Handyside has discussed how representations of Doria reflect the post-racial, whereby she was frequently described in terms such as 'elegance; glow; grace; poise', usually associated with white motherhood.[117] Doria's coding as white, and Meghan's working-class family's coding as outside the boundaries of whiteness, demonstrate that what is actually being lauded here is individualised behaviour, and how this behaviour adheres to white, upper- or middle-class (and cis-gender) norms.

This individualisation has been referred to as a politics of 'respectability'. Beverley Skeggs described how white working-class women are subjected to intense surveillance according to codes of 'respectability', usually organised around feminised markers of taste and propriety.[118] Meanwhile, Black studies scholars such as Brittney Cooper have referred to the proscription of the actions of people of colour as 'respectability politics'.[119] Racial uplift is undertaken through observing white, middle-class norms, including being 'mainstream, articulate, and clean-cut, black but not too black, friendly, upbeat, and accommodating'.[120] This creates a hierarchy of 'good blacks' and 'more problematic black others', designated along intersectional lines of race, class, gender and sexuality.[121]

Meghan's classed respectability (because she differs from her working-class family) and investment in structures of neoliberal ideology (for example, her language of 'empowerment' for women) ensures that she adheres to ideals of respectable Black femininity.[122] The sociologist Enid Logan writes about categories of the 'model minority, racialised in contradistinction to both the black poor and to traditional civil rights leaders and organisations'.[123] Likewise, in research on race and class in Brazil, the sociologist Luisa Farah Schwartzman interrogates the phrase 'money whitens' to consider how socio-economic status intersects with the construction of racial identity, speaking similarly to how respectability politics structures access and inclusion.[124]

The intersections of class, race, gender and sexuality mean that some individuals experience 'racial transcendence', and are no longer shaped by their racial profile. Discussing Oprah Winfrey's 'racial transcendence', Harwood K. McClerking and others argue that Winfrey *had* transcended Blackness by minimising her race and rejecting Black activism, becoming equally popular amongst Black and white viewers (we could read this as Winfrey being 'post-racial').[125] But when she publicly endorsed Obama as presidential candidate, her popularity weakened. This, they argue, demonstrates how racial transcendence is 'fleeting and fragile' when 'popular figures enter a realm far different than the realm where the aura of transcendence was generated' (in Winfrey's case, entertainment to politics).[126] For Meghan, as a celebrity she could be racially mobile. Yet, as the Firm is an institution invested in, and indeed built on, the reproduction of whiteness, this was much more difficult. Money did not 'whiten', and Meghan's body remained 'out of place' and marked.[127]

Conclusion

On her first post-wedding royal engagement in May 2018 at Prince Charles's seventieth birthday party, Meghan wore a mid-length beige dress with chiffon sleeves, formal beige hat, mid-heel beige heels and beige 'nude' tights (Figure 7.1). This marked a shift from her pre-royal styling, which often included bolder colours, shorter hemlines and short sleeves. The 'nude' tights, in particular, drew attention on social media. The garment made her, as Tweeter @HannahFlint claims, 'officially a Royal' as they are typical of royal women's styling of modest, conservative, 'respectable' femininity.[128]

7.1 Meghan Markle, with her husband Prince Harry, at Prince Charles's birthday party, 2019

Meghan wearing them on her first post-wedding engagement indicates an attempt to remodel Meghan as an idealised royal bride. However, this ideal royal bride is white. As multiple social media commenters pointed out, the tights were 'paler than her own skin tone'.[129] While this illustrates the inherent white privilege in the available shades of 'skin-coloured' clothing and accessories, it also demonstrates how Meghan did not 'fit' the descriptor of the royal bride.[130] Whilst Kate could be contained as a British, 'middle-class', white woman with little background, Meghan cannot be contained in the same way. If Kate is a static 'mannequin' royal bride, as Hilary Mantel claimed, Meghan is too animated – by virtue of her identity – to be moulded in the same way.[131] She cannot be 'beiged' with nude-coloured tights, or absorbed into developed histories of institutional power, because her very identity draws attention to the beige tights and to the inequalities in the Firm. As Sara Ahmed writes, 'adding color to the white face of the organization *confirms the whiteness of that face*'.[132] Meghan is too symbolically loaded to do the work of obscuring unequal histories – work that is required by the Firm's members to ensure the institution's reproduction.

Despite suppositions of Meghan representing progress, we have seen how Meghan's classed and racialised meritocracy does not equal equality or social justice. Rather, the politics of 'difference' are obscured under vague, depoliticised notions of 'diversity'. Moreover, attempts to absorb Meghan into the Firm are attempts to tap into new markets and appear progressive, diverse and liberal; all of which are part of producing consent for the reproduction of monarchical power in a period punctuated by factional political ideologies and growing global inequalities. As *Running the Family Firm* has, I hope, demonstrated, any form of feminist, anti-racist agenda Meghan is represented as promoting can be fulfilled only through abolishing the British monarchy and the class system it upholds, and reparations to those countries affected by colonialism, imperialism and enslavement. Even in their resignation letter, Harry and Meghan promised to 'continu[e] to fully support Her Majesty'.[133] They might have left, but (at the time of writing) they have made no attempts to dismantle the institution. Indeed, they continue to benefit from the systems of inequality and privilege that monarchy affords them.

Postscript: The post-royals

As this research comes to an end, new royal representations continue to emerge. In their statement on 8 January 2020 announcing they were 'stepping back' from the Firm, Harry and Meghan said they wanted to 'carve out a progressive new role within this institution' and 'work to become financially independent, while continuing to fully support Her Majesty The Queen'.[1] In so doing, they proposed a new model for 'working' royals, simultaneously inside and outside of the institution. In the *Guardian*, the historian Kate Williams called it a 'flexi-royal plan', reflecting the model of the so-called 'bicycle' monarchies in Europe (named due to their performances of 'ordinariness', such as riding bicycles), such as Prince Constantijn, the King of the Netherlands' brother, who is a lawyer.[2]

According to the media, after multiple negotiations with the Firm, many of Harry and Meghan's proposals for this new 'working model' were rejected.[3] Before their resignation, trademark applications were filed for the brand 'Sussex Royal', including branded goods such as toiletries, sporting goods and alcohol. Post-resignation, Harry and Meghan were allegedly banned from using 'Sussex Royal', with the *Express* reporting that 'the Queen's most senior officials say it is no longer tenable to use the term Royal as a money-making machine'.[4] Later in 2020, the couple trademarked a new name, Archewell, named after their son Archie. At the time of writing, Harry and Meghan's 'post-royal' life saw them move first to Vancouver Island, Canada, and then to Los Angeles, USA. The global outbreak of COVID-19 has presumably delayed their plans to fully launch Archewell, but they have undertaken some activities, including Meghan's narration of the Disney documentary *Elephant* and a new podcast series, Archewell Audio, and in February 2020 the couple completed their first paid event speaking at a summit for the investment bank J.P. Morgan, which was fined £7 billion in 2013 and 2014 for manipulating foreign exchange markets.[5] In June 2020, *Tatler* revealed that the couple have signed with Harry Walker, a high-profile agency in the USA for speaking engagements.[6] Their official website retains a section called 'serving the monarchy', where they state 'The Duke and Duchess of Sussex deeply believe in the role of The Monarchy, and their commitment to Her Majesty The Queen is unwavering'.[7] This draws on discourses of royal servitude, duty and 'work' (see Chapter 5).

Harry and Meghan's emerging roles as 'post-royals' reveals ongoing tensions in the Firm. I argued in Chapter 2 that the balance between visibility and invisibility is carefully choreographed, across a now more diffuse media system, to reproduce monarchy's power. Harry and Meghan's resignation temporarily disturbed this balance. Indeed, I argue that it temporarily made visible those institutional infrastructures and relations that are usually kept invisible. Such visibility makes their resignation useful for us to draw together the various threads of this book.

Commercialisation and corporate capital

Harry and Meghan's resignation prompted a series of media and public debates about the commercialisation of the British monarchy. In the majority, it seems to be Meghan who is blamed (couched in racist and sexist language, see Chapter 7) for exposing the Firm to the 'vulgar world' of corporate capitalism. In the *Daily Mail*, the commentator Max Hastings criticised the 'vulgar Hollywoodising of the young royals' due to Meghan's introduction, and the media consultant Sara Flanagan said in the *Guardian* 'before Meghan was a royal, she was an influencer … what will be new is these hurdles they're going to have to get over as far as being royal, and not being seen to cheapen the royal brand' ('influencers' are popular social media users who undertake paid sponsorship deals with companies to advertise products to their followers). [8] The commentator Rob Shuter told the *Express*:

> You cannot forget that Meghan is not new to this, she has been working in Hollywood for years and she understands the power of the press and photography particularly. While other members of the Royal Family are happy to let their PR people make all these decisions, Meghan is not.[9]

Likewise, in the *Sun*, the journalist Emily Andrews claimed that 'Maverick Meghan Markle is the "new Diana" with PR tactics … defying stuffy palace bigwigs', directly contrasting the 'stuffy' Buckingham Palace staff with Meghan's celebrity credence.[10]

These discourses seem to assume that the Firm is inexperienced in media relations, and Meghan is 'outwitting' them. In fact, *Running the Family Firm* has argued that the Firm has adapted to changing media landscapes (Chapter 2), and has staff highly experienced in media production and distribution (Chapter 1). The royals and their staff know precisely 'the power of the press and photography', and have made full use of it. I have foregrounded the role of media representations in constructing the British monarchy, and I used the classic work of Stuart Hall to argue that media culture is a key site through which class power is exercised under growing conditions of social inequality. I proposed that media culture produces consent for monarchical power, through both spectacular visibility at state occasions and more everyday representations of the Firm as a successful family, constituted by royal figures who each contribute characteristics to appropriately stage the royal story. The media are central to monarchy's survival. The supposition that Meghan is 'outwitting' them ultimately helps to conceal the stage production, because it obscures the Firm's backstage relations and makes royal representations appear happenstance, authentic and natural, in comparison to Meghan's strategy.

Similarly, discussions of Meghan 'cheapen[ing] the royal brand' seem to assume that the Firm is not otherwise 'commercial' or involved in corporate capital reproduction. Indeed, the *Guardian* noted 'the gulf between regal precedent and the current influencer economy'.[11] Like reality television stars, 'influencers' are associated with taxonomies of low-level celebrity – popularly known as the 'Z-list'.[12] The very point of influencers is that they reveal the transactional commodification relations in celebrity cultures: they *are* branding. Associating the Firm with such an explicit form of self-promotion and commodification precisely counteracts the careful balance of visibility and invisibility. But in light of the argument in *Running the Family Firm*, we might ask, is the Firm ultimately involved in the same process? As I demonstrated in Chapter 6, the @kensingtonroyal Instagram account is run as 'the Cambridge family photo album', and the content does not hugely differ from typical influencers in its aesthetic (although royal posts are not sponsored). Equally, I revealed in Chapter 1 that the Firm has many corporate investments, interests and contacts, from produce brands such as Duchy Originals, and sponsorship deals for its charitable initiatives with corporations such as HSBC, BAE Systems and Aston Martin Lagonda Ltd. Individual royals have even been involved in sponsorship deals, such as Zara Phillips for Rolex, and Peter Phillips for Jersey Milk. Historically, the Firm has connections with corporations such as the East India Company, involved in global colonisation projects. To single out Harry and Meghan for commercialising the Firm is to conceal a whole set of corporate connections that contribute towards reproducing the British monarchy.

Critique of royal commercial activities seems to depend on the *type* of activity, and how this is culturally considered. Whilst Duchy Originals is veiled in a veneer of heritage culture and authenticity, other deals are depicted as unsolicited. In 1950, Marion Crawford, who was the Queen and Princess Margaret's former nanny, published a book entitled *The Little Princesses* about her time with the royals. According to Pimlott, she was ostracised from the Firm and left her grace-and-favour home in Nottingham Cottage at Kensington Palace because they allegedly disproved of her capitalising on her royal connections.[13] In 2020, the Crown launched a legal case against Prince Charles's former butler Grant Harrold, who had trademarked the business name 'The Royal Butler'. The Crown's lawyers claimed that the name was 'misleading' people into believing he was 'a representative' of the monarchy.[14] Elsewhere, Prince Andrew's ex-wife Sarah Ferguson has been consistently mocked for her corporate deals since leaving the Firm. The *Guardian* published a ridiculing piece about her 'flogging blenders on QVC' and 'doing ghastly, vulgar things that are causing silent conniptions in private corners of Buck House'.[15] The slang 'flogging' connotes cheapness and dishonesty, loading Fergie with classed connotations as she is depicted *outside of* the more respectable Firm.

Likewise, Harry and Meghan are depicted as capitalising on their royal connection for personal profit. In the *Daily Mail*, the journalist Robert Hardman contrasted the Queen's values with Harry and Meghan's attempt to trademark Sussex Royal:

> It might have sounded just fine and dandy to the team of super-slick US rights agents, intellectual property lawyers and digital marketing experts flocking to advise the couple on their new modus operandi. But it was never going to meet with the approval of the ultimate arbiter on all things royal – the Queen. ... So they [Harry and Meghan] can hardly object when the Queen and her officials, representing an institution which has been protecting its own brand for centuries, lay down what is very well-established law to protect their own 'intellectual property'.[16]

Although Hardman recognises the monarchy as a 'brand', it is juxtaposed with 'US-based' corporate marketing experts. The implication is that monarchy is superior to such institutions, and that to suggest otherwise is to fundamentally misunderstand this hierarchy. It also situates corporate capital as 'out there' in the USA, while Britain remains steeped in tradition and 'respectable' forms of 'old wealth'. Like the 'nabobs' of the British Empire tainting the 'respectable' British economy with their global 'new money' (see Chapter 1), Harry and Meghan are seen as the vulgar 'others' tainting a stately institution (and, by extension, Britain) with their international, corporate connections. In so doing, the idea that there *is* some superior sort of monarchical capital is being maintained.

To describe Harry and Meghan as significantly moving away from the 'working model' of the Firm is to misunderstand what the Firm is. *Running the Family Firm* argues that the Firm operates precisely through capitalist logics, invested in reproducing its own wealth and power, using many of the same tactics as global corporations. Even reports of Harry and Meghan receiving payment for speaking engagements does not wholly differ from speeches they gave in the Firm, except the 'payment' received in the monarchy is not directly monetary but acts as a tool to produce consent for monarchical power – and hence, indirectly, reproduces wealth. This is a form of what Annette Weiner terms 'keeping-while-giving', where monarchy's wealth is hoarded and symbolic gestures are offered as replacements.[17] Now Harry and Meghan are outside of this royal moral economy, I suggest they are just seen as 'keeping'.

I use the term 'post-royals' in the title of this chapter to draw attention to these contradictions. Semantically, 'post' is 'used to signal a "breaking with" the past' or 'a linear time progression'.[18] Scholars of post-feminism and post-racialism have argued that a linear timeline is false, and in fact the terms hold together the past and the present.[19] Likewise, Harry and Meghan are not straightforwardly 'post-royal'. They continue to benefit from the capital – economic, cultural, social, symbolic – that royalty provides. Their attempt to trademark 'Sussex Royal' demonstrates this explicitly, but the global media interest in the couple stems from their position as former royals. Moreover, they cannot be described as post-royal because the Firm relies on almost identical logics. The couple's attempts to capitalise on their brand continues attempts to (re)produce wealth and power using discourses of royalty. The publicising of Harry and Meghan's commercial endeavours merely *draws attention to them*, in a way that the Firm has, for the most part, seemed to avoid. Rather than being straightforwardly commercial, I have argued that the Firm's wealth is mediated through a series of moralising economies. Royal wealth accumulation is moralised through ideas of philanthropy, social responsibility and value (Chapter 1); the Firm's investment in territory, enclosure and kinship is moralised through the monarch as symbolising national identity and belonging (Chapter 3); Charles's property empire, the Duchy of Cornwall, is moralised through narratives of history and heritage (Chapter 4); Harry's contribution to the military-industrial complex is moralised through representations of the national soldier (Chapter 5); the monarchy's reliance on traditional gendered roles is moralised through idealised representations of the heterosexual, nuclear family (Chapter 6); and histories of colonialist exploitation are moralised through notions of post-racialism and diversity (Chapter 7). Likewise, logics of exchange mean the royals appear to 'give back' through social responsibility and public service. Any payments Harry and Meghan receive for philanthropic speeches are more tangible than the Firm's indirect profiting, making this logic harder to maintain.

More broadly, I argue that the monarchy's corporate connections are moralised through representations of the family: the Family Firm. In Harry and Meghan stepping away from 'the family', their part in the Firm seemed to be exposed, because it lost those moralising relations. In representations of Meghan as a so-called 'bad influence', attention is deflected on to the couple who become the scapegoats for royal wealth accumulation and capital profit. Again, the Firm as an institution seems to evade responsibility.

The media–monarchy relationship

Following their resignation announcement in January 2020, Harry and Meghan detailed a new 'media relations policy' on their website sussexroyal.com, aiming to encourage 'diverse and open access to their work'.[20] They intimate dissatisfaction with how the media–monarchy relationship has historically run. Their statements repeatedly imply tradition: they say they will prioritise 'young, up-and-coming journalists', presumably instead of more established ones who would traditionally cover royal events; 'give greater access to their cause-driven activities, widening the spectrum of news coverage', suggesting that current royal news production is narrow; prioritise 'credible media outlets', implying that some are not; and 'no longer participate in the Royal Rota system', which is the main organisational structure for mediating royal events (see Chapter 2). They detail specific problems with Royal Correspondents, a key gatekeeper for royal news, by claiming that 'Britain's Royal Correspondents are regarded internationally as credible sources … this misconception propels coverage that is often carried by other outlets around the world, amplifying frequent misreporting'.[21]

Running the Family Firm has detailed the changing nature of the media–monarchy relationship. It has found mutual agreements in place between the Firm's Communications Offices and the British media. From co-organising the mediation of royal events (Chapter 2) to 'pressure cooker agreements' for images of royal children (Chapter 2), banning publications from publishing unsolicited paparazzi photographs (Chapter 5 and 6), using an 'embedded journalism' model on royal tours and activities (Chapters 1 and 5) and limiting interviews with key royal figures (Chapters 3 and 6), there are both tacit and official protocols in place to dictate when, how, who and how much access the British media get. Releasing strategic and choreographed representations means that, to some extent, the Firm has control over its public image (even if it cannot control how audiences respond to those representations).

Harry and Meghan seem to criticise the very system that has developed to uphold the monarchy. Their statement says they 'believe in a free, strong, and open media industry', but then claim that *all* Royal Rota journalists are portraying them unfairly, and that *all* Royal Correspondents lack credibility. In April 2020, they wrote another letter to the editors of four UK tabloids, the *Sun*, the *Daily Mirror*, the *Daily Mail* and the *Daily Express*, to say they would stop engaging with them, following Meghan's ongoing legal case against the *Daily Mail* for publishing her letter to her father.[22] Whilst, as we have seen, a lot of royal media coverage has been racist and sexist towards Meghan (Chapter 7), homogenising media outlets works to shut down legitimate criticism which holds the couple to account over issues of, for example, using private jets to travel to climate-change summits.[23] Being inside the Firm offers the couple a level of control: there are existing agreements in place about access and privacy. Being outside of the Firm, as they are now, means this protection no longer exists.

In vocalising their issues with media coverage, Harry and Meghan draw attention to the agreements in place between the media and the monarchy. *Running the Family Firm* has argued how royal representations are regularly concealed and/or limited in circulation if they do not work in favour of the Firm, from the 1969 *Royal Family* documentary deemed 'too intimate' (Chapter 2) to unsolicited photographs of Harry in Afghanistan (Chapter 5) and paparazzi photographs of the Cambridges (Chapter 6). Indeed, despite criticising the media–monarchy system, Harry and Meghan's use of social media (primarily Instagram) to make announcements does not wholly differ from other royal uses of social media to release strategic mediations (Chapter 6). Attempts to close down royal representations are well worn. Yet, Harry and Meghan make these battles visible because they have resigned. Similarly, Diana's media 'transgressions', from setting up paparazzi photographs of herself and her children to undertaking a celebrity 'confessional' on *Panorama*, were seen to taint the monarchy's majesty, even though contemporary royals have done similar posed photoshoots (Chapter 6) and 'confessional' interviews (Chapter 5). The aforementioned quotation from the *Sun* describing Meghan as the 'new Diana' because of her media work repurposes those same narratives which ensured Diana's estrangement from the Firm, but with added stereotypes of the 'angry Black woman' (Chapter 7).[24]

Rather than the popular response which seems to scapegoat Harry and Meghan for making 'controversial' decisions about media access, this book proposes that their exit can throw a more critical spotlight on the invisible (media) relations that secure monarchy's economic power, and the extent to which the monarchy is held appropriately to account in the British media.

The elites and value

Aforementioned commentary accusing Meghan of triggering the 'vulgar Hollywoodising of the young royals' speaks to the merging of royal and celebrity cultures.[25] *Running the Family Firm* describes how some royals have been represented as celebrities, from Princess Margaret in gossip magazines and Diana as a paparazzi favourite (Chapter 2) to Harry's affable media persona (Chapter 5) and Kate as a 'fashion icon' (Chapter 6). However, Meghan is the first major royal with a high-profile media career prior to joining the Firm. Her established celebrity persona made visible the relations of royalty and celebrity. Celebrity Studies scholars have described various taxonomies of celebrity, whereby they are classified on the basis of what made them famous, the work they do, their gender, race or sexuality and so on.[26] As I will show, Meghan's previous celebrity career is classified very differently from that of the royals.

Running the Family Firm has told a story about access versus closure: a balance the Firm has been seeking to strike for hundreds of years. In Meghan, these struggles take another turn, as her previous celebrity status draws attention to the differences and similarities between royal news coverage and celebrity news coverage in terms of how these are staged, produced and disseminated. Upon joining the Firm, Meghan's personal social media accounts and her lifestyle blog, *The Tig*, were all closed down, and her social media presence was run by a communications team, initially that of Kensington Palace.[27] This is a curtailing of freedoms and individual voice that I argue makes visible how the royal figures are small parts of a much larger operation – and how they serve the institution. Although each is an individual – and indeed I have demonstrated how they each offer a different moral narrative for the royal stage – their 'real' personalities are entirely irrelevant. Part of the appeal of celebrity cultures is the possibility of gaining access to an 'authentic', 'real' celebrity self, and how authenticity and media representation are held in tension.[28] For the Firm, access to the 'authentic' royals is both impossible and irrelevant. For example, royal trips abroad do not promote individual royals, rather they 'work' for the Firm, and indeed often on behalf of Britain itself as ambassadors.

A Marxist reading of the Firm is that it is a production company, where what the Firm produces is representations. Thousands of people work for the Firm, but where do royal figures sit in this infrastructure? In work on the Hollywood star system, the film scholar Richard Dyer argues that 'stars are involved in making themselves into commodities; they are both labour and the thing that labour produces'.[29] That is, the representations they produce of themselves *are* the value of their commodity: they are the labour force and the capital to be bought and sold.[30] Royal figures could be described similarly for the work they do to reproduce the Firm. But there is a form of servitude at the core of monarchy, in that royal figures are *born into* their royal role. They are again both similar to, and much more than, their celebrity counterparts. These relations indicate why it is problematic to represent the Firm as a 'family'. A 'family' implies a private space. The Firm is a public operation, and its members' activities are of public interest because they are invested in conceptions of the British state. The closure of royal media representations is, then, problematic because it closes down the possibility of public critique and institutional responsibility. Invisibility works to the Firm's advantage.

On the other hand, Meghan's celebrity status makes visible the similarities between royal and celebrity cultures. As a trained actor Meghan draws attention to how *all* royal figures are acting, whether 'trained' or otherwise. The Duchess of Sussex is merely another 'role', even though Meghan's former acting career is disparaged in some media and public commentary. Her role as a 'suitcase girl' on the gameshow *Deal or No Deal* in 2006 has been subjected to particular ridicule. The *Daily Mail*'s article entitled 'From Cases to Castles' referred to her 'thigh-skimming mini dresses' and 'rather tacky diamante embellishments' on *Deal or No Deal*, with the implication being this was inappropriate for a royal.[31] This is a classed judgement resting on the monarchy being hierarchically superior. It also threatens the distance the monarchy needs to maintain between itself and its public – it is what I described in Chapter 2 as 'context collapse'.[32] Meghan challenges the careful balance of in/visibility precisely through the mechanisms that the Firm uses to preserve it. Media and public commentary tries to downgrade Meghan's celebrity, and she is constantly made too accessible, from her father revealing their personal correspondence to her body being exposed in televised sex scenes, which were then uploaded to the pornographic website Pornhub by users.[33] Such accessibility to Meghan is so stark against the Firm's staged version of media representation. I argue that Meghan is 'othered' in these discourses, and positioned outside of the more 'respectable' Firm.

Meghan's former career also reveals the Firm's connections to global elites. Harry and Meghan's wedding guest list included people from a variety of elite professions, including the tennis player Serena Williams, human rights lawyer Amal Clooney, actor George Clooney, activist and presenter Oprah Winfrey, former Prime Minister Sir John Major and Prince Seeiso of Lesotho.[34] The couple have a well-documented friendship with Barack and Michelle Obama (Chapter 5), and upon moving to Los Angeles lived in the mansion of Tyler Perry, an American actor and producer.[35] I have argued that the Firm has a variety of connections to international elites that are largely secret (Chapter 1), yet Harry and Meghan make these relationships visible. Their lifestyle has also been described as lavish and ostentatious.[36] Their use of private jets, in particular, attracted public and media criticism for being hypocritical when they do philanthropic work around climate change.[37] Yet, royal travel arrangements have long been expensive and extravagant (see Chapter 1), and Charles has long lectured on climate change (see Chapter 4).

Similarly, Harry and Meghan's claim that their post-royal life would see them 'become financially independent' drew rare media attention to monarchy's funding. Following media and public criticism, the couple agreed to pay back the £2.4 million spent on renovating Frogmore Cottage, which was adapted as their official royal residence using public funds from the Sovereign Grant.[38] Yet, it was only because they left the monarchy that their receipt of public funding generated more widespread attention, because they were no longer offering royal 'value'. *Running the Family Firm* has aimed to demonstrate that much broader questions should be asked about monarchical wealth and the cultural relations that sustain it. I have complicated the concept of 'value', particularly capitalist logics of 'value for money', because monarchy is not a process of exchange among equals. Rather, I propose that monarchical privileges are entrenched in past actions informing present propriety, whereby the Firm continues to benefit from histories of constitutional development, class privilege and colonialism. For example, Charles built his 'model village' Poundbury because he owns the Duchy of Cornwall, land passed down for nearly seven hundred years (Chapter 4). As the documentary *Prince Charles: Inside the Duchy of Cornwall* exclaimed, 'the Duke has turned an ancient institution into a business empire that last year made over £21 million in profit'.[39] We can see similar issues at play in the *Guardian*'s discovery that the parliamentary procedure of the 'Queen's consent' had been used for the monarchy to lobby the government to alter bills and laws which will affect their private and personal assets or interests.[40] The Firm puts 'old' forms of capital to work, and exploits its historical privileges at the same time as concealing them, in the age of financial capital.

Why does monarchy matter?

Running the Family Firm has told a story of capital in the Firm, and how the Firm adapts itself to shifting socio-political periods. Analysing the British monarchy requires radical contextualisation. Whilst at the height of the British Empire the monarchy made use of imperialist forms of capital, in the 2010s–2020s it merges with forms of neoliberal and financial capital. From adapting feudal forms of rentier capitalism into property empires, to disaster capital and the military-industrial complex, 'philanthrocapitalism', promotion on social media and diversity capital, the Firm is constantly changing in order to stay the same. New royal figures in the form of spouses and children offer new spaces for capital reproduction, devising new characters and new styles of symbolic power for the royal stage. Across historical periods the Firm puts on a new costume or erects a new stage set to continue with wealth and power accumulation. The Firm excels at incorporating new representations into its corporate body, and the royal *family* continually absorbs new figures to take on new forms. Indeed, *Running the Family Firm* is a complex and continual process.

There is not a singular royal narrative, and the analysis in this book demonstrates that sometimes each new form is merely reactive: a response to crisis, or a shift in socio-political context. Sometimes, this shape-shifting is achieved to various degrees of success. The fly-on-the-wall documentary *Royal Family* proved a step too far in royal visibility, and was quickly redacted. Meghan's racialised, gendered and classed body meant that she was too symbolically loaded to be 'fully absorbed' as a royal figure. Other shapes have been more successful, for example the rehabilitation of Harry's 'laddism' into a 'soldier masculinity' and later an emotionally literature masculinity, or the problematic royal 'sexual scandals' of the 1990s resolved through Kate and William's heteronormative, nuclear familialism. Responsive shape shifting partly explains why representations of the Firm are so contradictory, and indeed the contradictions of royal representations are as revealing as the repetitions. Harry and Meghan may have resigned from the Firm and noted the Commonwealth's imperialist origins, yet they still proclaim to serve the monarchy and (at the time of writing) Harry remains President of the Queen's Commonwealth Trust.[41] Kensington Palace might use its Instagram account as a 'family photo album', yet the intimacy of royal representations is closely monitored. The Queen might be represented as an elderly grandmother, yet her position upholds the British constitution. It might be a Family Firm, yet the Firm is invested in international wealth accumulation. It is the act of exposing the contradictions that reveals the power held therein.

One key conclusion of *Running the Family Firm* is that the very invisibility of the Firm's social and economic power *is* its power, and invisibility, visibility and power intersect. As Walter Bagehot argued, 'we must not let in daylight upon magic'.[42] The relations between the corporate, economic, state and symbolic power of monarchy described in this book are not widely known to the British public, despite most people recognising individual royal figures; the Queen's image is the most reproduced in the world.[43] Spectacular royal events provide a theatrical masquerade, whereby they are so visible they disguise what is invisible. This is partly why finding a language for the analysis in *Running the Family Firm* – of revealing versus concealing, visibility versus invisibility, access versus closure – has been so difficult. It is a complex process of cultural politics that unpacks the representations of monarchy *we normally see*, to reveal what these representations are doing to *maintain the things we do not see*. I have not claimed that every representation of the royal family is 'true', but that does not matter, as the *effect* of these representations on the public imagination has already taken place. The royal figures chosen for analysis in *Running the Family Firm* are also notable. Why is there no chapter on William, the future king? William has always operated under a veil of secrecy: we know very little about him, and he has been sheltered from the 'scandals' of his younger brother. This is perhaps the very point. As the future king, it is more powerful for him to be invisible. Harry does the 'celebrity work', while William preserves his sovereign power. The fact that there are limited stories on William *is* the analysis.

Whilst *Running the Family Firm* has illustrated how extensive media representations of the British monarchy are, these representations are largely ubiquitous, woven into the very fabric of Britain with a global reach, and seem to be mostly taken for granted. In the Preface, I described how responses to critical analysis of monarchy have claimed that society has 'more important problems' to worry about. I rebutted this by saying that these so-called 'more important problems' are not detached from the institution of monarchy. In an analysis of the French Empire, the anthropologist Ann Laura Stoler uses the term 'aphasia' to describe how problematic histories are often collectively forgotten through purposeful action: 'it is not a matter of ignorance or absence. Aphasia is a dismembering, a difficulty speaking, a difficulty generating a vocabulary that associates appropriate words and concepts with appropriate things.'[44] There is a targeted effort to disassociate France's history from histories of colonial conquest and profit. Likewise, aphasia is at work in media representations depicting the British monarchy as ubiquitous (as a family, or as an emblem of national identity, for example), because it draws attention away from issues of inequality and power and produces consent for its continuation. *Running the Family Firm* has drawn out the cultural, social, political and economic functions of monarchy in relation to these representations, to expose what is being taken for granted.

The central story of *Running the Family Firm* is inequality. The British monarchy invites us to think about wider issues of class, power, inequality, media culture, wealth, capital(ism), ideology, democracy, warfare, national identity, citizenship, belonging, land, gender, race, (post)colonialism and (post)imperialism. After completing this research, I am left wondering where it ends. My intention was for you, the reader, to finish with a deeper understanding of the 'backstage' of monarchical power, where the stage curtain of the 'frontstage' representations has been lifted. I have mapped out the strands through which we see monarchy connected to infrastructures which perpetuate inequalities. Yet, *Running the Family Firm* has (purposefully) barely touched on Prince Andrew, a man visibly connected to global elites known to exploit their wealth and privilege by trafficking and abusing young women, and then offer little remorse for the victims on the BBC, a public-funded media institution.[45] Likewise, it has not detailed the monarchy's relationship to other aristocratic families, and how other forms of 'old wealth' support and uphold each other in their adaptation to financial capital (through, for example, personal relationships, business deals, in/direct marketing). I aim to explore some of these in future research, but the point here is that it is impossible to provide a comprehensive account of monarchy, media and capital, simply because its reach is so extensive. And, indeed, this is exactly why monarchy is an extremely 'important problem' in Britain.

I have argued that we cannot talk about inequalities in Britain, historically and in the present, without talking about the monarchy. If we are ever to resist the global forces of inequality and dismantle the systems perpetuating them, we must address monarchical power. Global inequalities will never be addressed while monarchy exists.

Notes

Introduction: Why does monarchy matter?

1 Hilary Osborne, 'Revealed: Queen's Private Estate Invested Millions of Pounds Offshore', Guardian, 5 November 2017, www.theguardian.com/news/2017/nov/05/revealed-queen-private-estate-invested-offshore-paradise-papers [Accessed 06/11/2017].

2 Ibid.

3 Paradise Papers Reporting Team, 'Queen's Private Estate Invested Offshore', BBC News, 6 November 2017, www.bbc.com/news/uk-41878305 [Accessed 19/07/2018].

4 Charlie Proctor, 'The Chair of the Duchy of Lancaster Is Knighted at Buckingham Palace by The Queen', Royal Central, 7 November 2017, http://royalcentral.co.uk/uk/thequeen/the-chair-of-the-duchy-of-lancaster-is-knighted-at-buckingham-palace-by-the-queen-91226 [Accessed 19/07/2018].

5 Hilary Osborne, 'Prince Charles's Estate Made Big Profit on Stake in Friend's Offshore Firm', Guardian, 7 November 2017, www.theguardian.com/news/2017/nov/07/prince-charles-profit-best-friend-hugh-van-cutsem-offshore-firm-paradise-papers [Accessed 10/11/2017].

6 Ibid.

7 Ibid.

8 Ashley Cowburn, 'John McDonnell Calls on Queen to Release Financial Records amid Paradise Papers Leak', Independent, 10 November 2017, www.independent.co.uk/news/uk/politics/john-mcdonnell-queen-labour-paradise-papers-tax-return-monarchy-brexit-a8048916.html [Accessed 13/11/2017].

9 Duchy of Lancaster, 'Duchy of Lancaster Annual Report – Year Ended 31st March 2018', July 2018, www.duchyoflancaster.co.uk/wp-content/uploads/2018/07/2018-DoL-Annual-Report-and-Accounts.pdf [Accessed 01/08/2018].

10 Patrick Greenfield, 'UK Tax Avoiders Face Being Blocked from Honours List', Guardian, 1 September 2018, www.theguardian.com/politics/2018/sep/01/uk-tax-avoiders-face-being-blocked-from-honours-list [Accessed 26/09/2018].

11 Hilary Osborne and Nick Hopkins, 'Queen's Cash Invested in Controversial Retailer Accused of Exploiting the Poor', Guardian, 6 November 2017.

12 Google Trends, '"British Royal Family"', 2017, https://trends.google.com/trends/explore?date=2017–11–01%202017–11–30&geo=GB&q=british%20royal%20family [Accessed 12/08/2020].

13 Richard Palmer, 'The Look of Love', Daily Express, 28 November 2018, www.pressreader.com/uk/daily-express/20171128/281479276730000 [Accessed 12/08/2020]; 'She's The One!', Sun, 28 November 2018.

14 Marshall Sahlins and David Graeber, On Kings (Chicago: University of Chicago Press, 2017).

15 Stuart Hall, Chas Critcher, Tony Jefferson, John Clarke and Brian Roberts, Policing the Crisis: Mugging, the State, and Law and Order, 2nd ed. (London: Macmillan, 2013).

16 Oxfam, '5 Shocking Facts about Extreme Global Inequality and How to Even It Up', Oxfam International, 4 October 2019, www.oxfam.org/en/5-shocking-facts-about-extreme-global-inequality-and-how-even-it [Accessed 08/01/2020]; The Equality Trust, 'The Equality Trust Wealth Tracker 2017', 2017, www.equalitytrust.org.uk/sites/default/files/WealthTracker2017.docx.pdf] [Accessed 19/07/2018].

17 The Trussell Trust, 'End of Year Stats', The Trussell Trust, 2020, www.trusselltrust.org/news-and-blog/latest-stats/end-year-stats/ [Accessed 31/07/2020]; Joseph O'Leary, 'Poverty in the UK: A Guide to the Facts and Figures', Full Fact, 27 September 2019, https://fullfact.org/economy/poverty-uk-guide-facts-and-figures/ [Accessed 31/07/2020].

18 Imogen Tyler, Revolting Subjects: Social Abjection and Resistance in Neoliberal Britain (London: Zed Books, 2013); Kayleigh Garthwaite, Hunger Pains: Life inside Foodbank Britain (Bristol: Bristol University Press, 2016); Vickie Cooper and David Whyte, eds, The Violence of Austerity (London: Pluto Press, 2017); Tracey Jensen, Parenting the Crisis: The Cultural Politics of Parent-Blame (Bristol: Policy Press, 2018).

19 Mike Savage and Karel Williams, Remembering Elites (Oxford: Blackwell Publishing, 2008), 2.

20 Thomas Piketty, Capital in the Twenty-First Century (Cambridge, MA: Harvard University Press, 2014); Danny Dorling, Inequality and the 1% (London: Verso, 2014).

21 Andrew Sayer, Why We Can't Afford the Rich (London: Policy Press, 2015); Roger Burrows, Richard Webber and Rowland Atkinson, 'Welcome to "Pikettyville"? Mapping London's Alpha Territories', The Sociological Review,

Notes

65, no. 2 (2017): 184–201; Aeron Davis, *Reckless Opportunists: Elites at the End of the Establishment* (Manchester: Manchester University Press, 2018); Sam Friedman and Daniel Laurison, *The Class Ceiling* (Bristol: Policy Press, 2019); Daniel R. Smith, *Elites, Race and Nationhood: The Branded Gentry* (London: Palgrave, 2016); Jo Littler, *Against Meritocracy: Culture, Power and Myths of Mobility* (London: Routledge, 2017); Ashley Mears, *Very Important People: Status and Beauty in the Global Party Circuit* (Princeton: Princeton University Press, 2020); Karen Ho, *Liquidated: An Ethnography of Wall Street* (Durham, NC: Duke University Press, 2009); Sylvia Yanagisako, *Producing Culture and Capital: Family Firms in Italy* (Princeton, NJ, Princeton University Press, 2002).

22 David Cannadine, *The Decline and Fall of the British Aristocracy* (New Haven and London: Yale University Press, 1990).

23 Guy Shrubsole, *Who Owns England?* (London: William Collins, 2019).

24 Kevin Cahill, *Who Owns Britain and Ireland* (London: Canongate Books, 2002).

25 Inequality Briefing, 'Almost One Third of Wealth in the UK Is Inherited, Not Earned', Inequality Briefing, 2014, http://inequalitybriefing.org/brief/briefing-26-almost-one-third-of-wealth-in-the-uk-is-inherited-not-earned [Accessed 22/01/2015]; Gregory Clark and Neil Cummins, 'Intergenerational Wealth Mobility in England, 1858–2012: Surnames and Social Mobility', *The Economic Journal*, 125, no. 582 (2014): 61–85.

26 Rowland Atkinson, Simon Parker, and Roger Burrows, 'Elite Formation, Power and Space in Contemporary London', *Theory, Culture and Society*, 34, nos 5–6 (2017): 179–200.

27 Grosvenor, 'Our Properties and Places', 2020, www.grosvenor.com/our-properties-and-places [Accessed 23/07/2020].

28 Anita Biressi and Heather Nunn, *Class and Contemporary British Culture* (Basingstoke: Palgrave Macmillan, 2013); Smith, *Elites, Race and Nationhood: The Branded Gentry*; David Edgerton, *The Rise and Fall of the British Nation: A Twentieth-Century History* (London: Allen Lane, 2018); Sayer, *Why We Can't Afford the Rich*; Littler, *Against Meritocracy: Culture, Power and Myths of Mobility*.

29 'Life Is Toff' (producer: James Quinn and Nicholas Kent, BBC Three, 28 October 2014); Sylvia Yanagisako, 'Kinship: Still at the Core', *Hau: Journal of Ethnographic Theory*, 5, no.1 (2015): 489–494.

30 Michel Foucault, *Power/Knowledge: Selected Interviews and Other Writings 1972–1977*, ed. Colin Gordon (New York: Vintage, 1980); Christopher Pye, *The Regal Phantasm: Shakespeare and the Politics of Spectacle* (London: Routledge, 1990).

31 Biressi and Nunn, *Class and Contemporary British Culture*.

32 Meg Russell, *The Contemporary House of Lords: Westminster Bicameralism Revived* (Oxford: Open University Press, 2013).

Notes

33 Nadine El-Enany, 'The Colonial Logic of Grenfell', Versobooks.com, 3 July 2017, www.versobooks.com/blogs/3306-the-colonial-logic-of-grenfell [Accessed 11/02/2020].

34 Tracy Shildrick, 'Lessons from Grenfell: Poverty Propaganda, Stigma and Class Power', *The Sociological Review*, 66, no. 4 (2018): 785; see also Ida Danewid, 'The Fire This Time: Grenfell, Racial Capitalism and the Urbanisation of Empire', European Journal of International Relations, Online first (2019), https://doi.org/10.1177/1354066119858388; Remi Joseph-Salisbury and Laura Connelly, 'Grenfell Was the Result of a Campaign of Racial Terror', Novara Media, 17 June 2018, https://novaramedia.com/2018/06/17/grenfell-one-year-on-an-unatoned-act-of-racial-terror/ [Accessed 10/02/2020].

35 Laura Clancy, '"This Is a Tale of Friendship, a Story of Togetherness": The British Monarchy, Grenfell Tower, and Inequalities in The Royal Borough of Kensington and Chelsea', Cultural Studies, Online first (2020), https://doi.org/10.1080/09502386.2020.1863997.

36 Shildrick, 'Lessons from Grenfell', 784.

37 Caroline Mortimer, 'Paradise Papers: Queen Faces Backlash after News Duchy of Lancaster Invests Millions Offshore', Independent, 6 November 2017, www.independent.co.uk/news/uk/politics/paradise-papers-queen-offshore-investments-royal-family-duchy-lancaster-estate-millions-tax-a8039636.html [Accessed 19/07/2018]; Nicholas Cecil, 'Jeremy Corbyn in Tax Jibe at Queen over "Paradise Papers"', Evening Standard, 6 November 2017, www.standard.co.uk/news/uk/jeremy-corbyn-in-tax-jibe-at-queen-over-paradise-papers-labour-leader-says-palace-must-say-sorry-to-a3677531.html [Accessed 19/07/2018].

38 Mortimer, 'Paradise Papers: Queen Faces Backlash'.

39 Conor Lynch, 'Bono, the Queen and Many More: Paradise Papers Reveal the Rise of The Global Oligarchy', AlterNet, 12 November 2017, www.alternet.org/economy/paradise-papers-reveal-rise-new-class-global-oligarchy?akid=16345.2691576.wHm-mi&rd=1&src=newsletter1085105&t=16 [Accessed 19/07/2018].

40 Sayer, *Why We Can't Afford the Rich*; Edgerton, *The Rise and Fall of the British Nation*.

41 Silvia Federici, *Caliban and the Witch: Women, the Body, and Primitive Accumulation* (New York: Autonomedia, 2004); Ellen Meiksins Wood, *The Pristine Culture of Capitalism* (London: Verso, 1991); Ellen Meiksins Wood, *The Origin of Capitalism* (London: Monthly Review Press, 1999).

42 Meiksins Wood, *The Pristine Culture of Capitalism*, 19.

43 Annette B. Weiner, *Inalienable Possessions: The Paradox of Keeping-While-Giving* (Berkeley and Los Angeles: University of California Press, 1992).

44 David Graeber, *Debt: The First 5,000 Years* (New York: Melville House Publishing, 2013).

45 Frank Prochaska, *Royal Bounty: The Making of a Welfare Monarchy* (New Haven and London: Yale University Press, 1995), 8.

46 Jo Littler, 'The New Victorians? Celebrity Charity and the Demise of the Welfare State', *Celebrity Studies*, 6, no. 4 (2015): 471–485; Jon Dean, *The Good Glow: Charity and the Symbolic Power of Doing Good* (Bristol: Policy Press, 2020); Samantha King, *Pink Ribbons, Inc.: Breast Cancer and the Politics of Philanthropy* (Minneapolis: University of Minnesota Press, 2006); Linsey McGoey, *No Such Thing as a Free Gift: The Gates Foundation and the Price of Philanthropy* (London: Verso, 2015).

47 Clancy, '"This Is a Tale of Friendship, a Story of Togetherness"'.

48 Ben Pimlott, *The Queen: Elizabeth II and the Monarchy*, 2nd ed. (London: Harper Press, 2012).

49 Tom Nairn, *The Enchanted Glass: Britain and Its Monarchy*, updated ed. (London: Vintage, 1994); A.N. Wilson, *The Rise and Fall of the House of Windsor* (London: W.W. Norton & Co., 1993).

50 Andrew Marr, *The Diamond Queen: Elizabeth II and Her People* (London: Macmillan, 2011).

51 Simon Neville and Jill Treanor, 'Starbucks to Pay £20m in Tax over Next Two Years after Customer Revolt', Guardian, 6 December 2012, www.theguardian.com/business/2012/dec/06/starbucks-to-pay-10m-corporation-tax [Accessed 03/08/2018].

52 Ibid.

53 Ibid.

54 Nicholas Shaxson, *Treasure Islands: Tax Havens and the Men Who Stole the World* (London: The Bodley Head, 2011), 8–9.

55 El-Enany, 'The Colonial Logic of Grenfell'; Danewid, 'The Fire This Time'.

56 Ko Unoki, *Mergers, Acquisitions and Global Empires: Tolerance, Diversity, and the Success of M&A* (London: Routledge, 2012), 3–4.

57 Shrubsole, *Who Owns England?*

58 Guy Standing, *The Corruption of Capitalism* (London: Biteback Publishing Ltd, 2016).

59 Catherine Casson and Mark Casson, *Compassionate Capitalism: Business and Community in Medieval England* (Bristol: Policy Press, 2020), 7.

60 Ibid., 8.

61 Walter Bagehot, *The English Constitution* (Oxford: Oxford University Press, 2001).

62 David Pegg, Rob Evans and Michael Barton, 'Royals Vetted More than 1,000 Laws via Queen's Consent', Guardian, 8 February 2021, www.theguardian.com/uk-news/2021/feb/08/royals-vetted-more-than-1000-laws-via-queens-consent [Accessed 09/02/2021].

63 David Pegg and Rob Evans, 'Revealed: Queen Lobbied for Change in Law to Hide Her Private Wealth' Guardian, 7 February 2021,

Notes

www.theguardian.com/uk-news/2021/feb/07/revealed-queen-lobbied-for-change-in-law-to-hide-her-private-wealth [Accessed 09/02/2021].

64 Nairn, *The Enchanted Glass*, 102.

65 Michael Billig, *Talking of the Royal Family* (London: Routledge, 1992).

66 Littler, *Against Meritocracy*.

67 Stuart Hall, ed., *Representation: Cultural Representations and Signifying Practices* (London: SAGE Publications, 1997); Hall et al., *Policing the Crisis*.

68 Hall et al., *Policing the Crisis*, 207.

69 Ibid.

70 Ibid.

71 Stephen Orgel, *The Illusion of Power: Political Theater in the English Renaissance* (Berkeley and Los Angeles: University of California Press, 1975); Kenneth Robert Olwig, *Landscape, Nature and the Body Politic* (Madison: University of Wisconsin Press, 2002); Norbert Elias, *The Court Society*, trans. Edmund Jephcott (New York: Pantheon Books, 1983); Anna Keay, *The Magnificent Monarch: Charles II and the Ceremonies of Power* (London: Continuum, 2008); Edward Shils and Michael Young, 'The Meaning of the Coronation', *The Sociological Review*, 1, no. 2 (1953): 63–81.

72 Kevin Sharpe, *Selling the Tudor Monarchy: Authority and Image in Sixteenth-Century England* (London: Yale University Press, 2009); Kevin Sharpe, *Image Wars: Promoting Kings and Commonwealths in England 1603–1660* (New Haven: Yale University Press, 2010); Louis Montrose, *The Subject of Elizabeth: Authority, Gender and Representation* (Chicago: University of Chicago Press, 2006); Peter Burke, *The Fabrication of Louis XIV* (London: Yale University Press, 1992).

73 John Plunkett, *Queen Victoria: First Media Monarch* (Oxford: Oxford University Press, 2003); Jeffrey Richards 'The Monarchy and Film 1900–2006', in *The Monarchy and the British Nation, 1780 to the Present*, ed. Andrzej Olechnowicz (Cambridge: Cambridge University Press, 2007), 258–279.

74 Richard Dyer, *Stars* (London: British Film Institute, 1979), 38.

75 Donna J. Haraway, *Modest_Witness@Second_Millenium. FemaleMan_Meets_Onco-Mouse* (London: Routledge, 1997); Claudia Castañeda, *Figurations: Child, Bodies, Worlds* (Durham, NC: Duke University Press, 2002); Imogen Tyler, '"Chav Mum, Chav Scum": Class Disgust in Contemporary Britain', *Feminist Media Studies*, 8, no. 1 (2008): 17–34; Lucy Suchman, 'Configuration', in *Inventive Methods: The Happening of the Social*, ed. Celia Lury and Nina Wakeford (London: Routledge, 2012); Sara Ahmed, *The Promise of Happiness* (Durham, NC: Duke University Press, 2010).

76 Castañeda, *Figurations*, 3.

77 Ibid.

78 Hall et al., *Policing the Crisis*.

79 David Cannadine and Simon Price, *Rituals of Royalty: Power and Ceremonials in Traditional Societies* (Cambridge: Cambridge University Press, 1987); David

Cannadine, 'From Biography to History: Writing the Modern British Monarchy', *Historical Research*, 77, no. 197 (2004): 289–312; Sharpe, *Selling the Tudor Monarchy*; Sharpe, *Image Wars*; Montrose, *The Subject of Elizabeth*; John Plunkett, *Queen Victoria: First Media Monarch* (Oxford: Oxford University Press, 2003) Margaret Homans, *Royal Representations: Queen Victoria and British Culture, 1837–1876* (Chicago: University of Chicago Press, 1998); Dorothy Thompson, *Queen Victoria: Gender and Power* (London: Virago, 1990); Irene Morra and Rob Gossedge, eds, *The New Elizabethan Age: Culture, Society and National Identity after World War II* (London: I.B. Tauris, 2016); Matthew Glencross, Judith Rowbotham and Michael D. Kandiah, eds, *The Windsor Dynasty 1910 to the Present* (London: Palgrave Macmillan, 2016); Edward Owens, *The Family Firm: Monarchy, Mass Media and the British Public, 1932–53* (London: Institute of Historical Research, 2019); Wilson, *The Rise and Fall of the House of Windsor*.

80 Mandy Merck, ed., *The British Monarchy on Screen* (Manchester: Manchester University Press, 2016); Jeffrey Richards, *Films and British National Identity: From Dickens to Dad's Army* (Manchester: Manchester University Press, 1997); Giselle Bastin, 'Filming the Ineffable: Biopics of the British Royal Family', *Auto/Biography Studies*, 24, no. 1 (2009): 34–52.

81 Cele C. Otnes and Pauline Maclaran, *Royal Fever: The British Monarchy in Consumer Culture* (Oakland: University of California Press, 2015); Neil Blain and Hugh O'Donnell, *Media, Monarchy and Power* (Bristol: Intellect, 2003); David Morley and Kevin Robins, eds, *British Cultural Studies* (Oxford: Oxford University Press, 2001); Nicola J. Palmer and Philip Long, eds, *Royal Tourism: Excursions around Monarchy* (Clevedon: Channel View Publications, 2008).

82 Billig, *Talking of the Royal Family*; Heather Mendick, Kim Allen, Laura Harvey and Aisha Ahmed, *Celebrity, Aspiration and Contemporary Youth: Education and Inequality in an Era of Austerity* (London: Bloomsbury, 2018); Hannah Yelin and Michele Paule, '"The Best Thing about Meghan Markle Is She's Got a Bit of Black in Her": Girls Making Meaning around Meghan Markle, the Monarchy, and Meritocracy', *Women's Studies International Forum*, 86 (May–June 2021), Online first, https://doi.org/10.1016/j.wsif.2021.102456; Anne Rowbottom, '"The Real Royalists": Folk Performance and Civil Religion at Royal Visits', *Folklore*, 109 (1998): 77–88.

83 Rosi Braidiotti, 'In the Sign of the Feminine: Reading Diana', *Theory and Event*, 1, no. 4 (1997); Helen Bramley, 'Diana, Princess of Wales: The Contemporary Goddess', Sociological Research Online, 7, no. 1 (2002), www.socresonline.org.uk/7/1/bramley.html [Accessed 14/01/2015]; Beatrix Campbell, *Diana, Princess of Wales: How Sexual Politics Shook the Monarchy* (London: The Women's Press Ltd, 1988); Nick Couldry, 'Remembering Diana: The Geography of Celebrity and the Politics of Lack', *New Formations*, 36 (1999): 77–91; Jude Davies, *Diana, A Cultural History: Gender, Race and Nation and the People's Princess* (London: Palgrave, 2001); Jeffrey

Notes

Richards, Scott Wilson and Linda Woodhead, eds, *Diana: The Making of a Media Saint* (London: I.B. Tauris, 1999); Jemima Repo and Riina Yrjölä, "'We're All Princesses Now": Sex, Class and Neoliberal Governmentality in the Rise of the Middle-Class Monarchy', *European Journal of Cultural Studies*, 18, no. 6 (2 March 2015); Kim Allen, Heather Mendick, Laura Harvey and Aisha Ahmed, 'Welfare Queens, Thrifty Housewives, and Do-It-All Mums', *Feminist Media Studies*, 30 July 2015, 1–19; Laura Clancy and Hannah Yelin, "'Meghan's Manifesto": Meghan Markle and the Co-Option of Feminism', *Celebrity Studies*, 2018, https://doi.org/10.1080/19392397.2018.1541541.

84 Littler, *Against Meritocracy*; Biressi and Nunn, *Class and Contemporary British Culture*.

85 Raka Shome, *Diana and Beyond: White Femininity, National Identity and Contemporary Media Culture* (Chicago: University of Illinois Press, 2014); Nairn, *The Enchanted Glass*; Rosalind Brunt, "'A Divine Gift to Inspire"? Popular Cultural Representation, Nationhood and the British Monarchy', in *'Come on Down'? Popular Media Culture in Postwar Britain*, ed. D.. Strinati and S. Wagg (London: Routledge, 1992).

86 David McClure, *Royal Legacy: How the Royal Family Have Made, Spent and Passed on Their Wealth* (London: Thistle Publishing, 2014).

87 Philip Murphy, *Monarchy and the End of Empire: The House of Windsor, the British Government, and the Postwar Commonwealth* (Oxford: Oxford University Press, 2013); Philip Murphy, *The Empire's New Clothes: The Myth of the Commonwealth* (London: C. Hurst & Co. Publishers Ltd, 2018).

88 Vernon Bogdanor, *The Monarchy and the Constitution* (Oxford: Oxford University Press, 1995).

89 Shils and Young, 'The Meaning of the Coronation'; Rob Turnock, *Interpreting Diana: Television Audiences and the Death of a Princess* (London: BFI, 2000); C.W. Watson, "'Born a Lady, Became a Princess, Died a Saint": The Reaction to the Death of Diana, Princess of Wales', *Anthropology Today*, 13, no. 6 (1997): 3–7; Adrian Kear and Deborah Lynn Steinberg, eds, *Mourning Diana: Nation, Culture and the Performance of Grief* (London: Routledge, 1999); Claire Wardle and Emily West, 'The Press as Agents of Nationalism in the Queen's Golden Jubilee: How British Newspapers Celebrated a Media Event', *European Journal of Communication*, 19, no. 2 (2004): 195–214; Paul Barker, Elaine Bauer, Belinda Brown, Geoff Dench, Nick Green and Peter Hall, 'The Meaning of the Jubilee' (Institute of Community Studies, Working Paper No. 1, 2002); James Bennett, 'Celebrity Forum Introduction: The Royal Wedding', *Celebrity Studies*, 2, no. 3 (2011): 353–354; Beth Mudford, 'Royal Celebrations in the Twenty-First Century: "Cool Britannia" versus "Britannia Ruled the Waves"', in *Identity Discourses and Communities in International Events, Festivals and Spectacles*, ed. Udo Merkel (London: Palgrave Macmillan, 2015).

90 Joan Smith, *Down with the Royals* (London: Biteback Publishing Ltd, 2015); Anthony Taylor, *Down with the Crown: British Anti-Monarchism and Debates about Royalty Since 1790* (London: Reaktion Books, 1999); Nairn, *The Enchanted Glass*; Les Back, 'God Save the Queen: The Pistols' Jubilee', Sociological Research Online, 7, no. 1 (2002), www.socresonline.org.uk/7/1/back.html [Accessed 14/01/2015].

91 Penny Junor, *The Firm: The Troubled Life of the House of Windsor* (London: Harper Collins, 2006); Andrew Duncan, *The Reality of Monarchy* (London: Pan Books Ltd, 1970); Robert Lacey, *Majesty: Elizabeth II and the House of Windsor* (New York: Avon, 1977); Catherine Mayer, *Charles: The Heart of a King* (London: Penguin, 2015); Paul Burrell, *A Royal Duty* (London: Penguin, 2004); Marr, *The Diamond Queen*; Ben Pimlott, *The Queen: Elizabeth II and the Monarchy*, 2nd ed. (London: Harper Press, 2012); Stephen Bates, *Royalty Inc.: Britain's Best Known Brand* (London: Aurum Press Ltd, 2015); John Pearson, *The Ultimate Family: The Making of the Royal House of Windsor* (London: Michael Joseph Ltd, 1986); David Rogers, *By Royal Appointment* (London: Biteback Publishing Ltd, 2015); Dickie Arbiter, *On Duty with The Queen: My Time as a Buckingham Palace Press Secretary* (Dorking: Blink Publishing, 2014); Stephen P. Barry, *Royal Service: My Twelve Years as Valet to Prince Charles* (New York: Macmillan Publishing Co., 1983); Stephen P. Barry, *Royal Secrets: The View from Downstairs* (New York: Villard Books, 1985); Lacey, *Majesty: Elizabeth II and the House of Windsor*.

92 Billig, *Talking of the Royal Family*, 1.

93 The Prince of Wales, *A Vision of Britain* (London: Doubleday, 1989).

94 Ibid., 12.

Chapter 1: The (Family) Firm: Labour, capital and corporate power

1 Otnes and Maclaran, *Royal Fever*.

2 Elizabeth Jane Timms, 'A History of the Royal Balcony at Buckingham Palace', Royal Central, 29 March 2018, http://royalcentral.co.uk/blogs/a-history-of-the-royal-balcony-at-buckingham-palace-99137 [Accessed 10/07/2018].

3 Denis Judd, *George VI* (London: I.B. Tauris, 2012), 40.

4 *The King's Speech* (dir. Tom Hooper, Momentum Pictures, 2010).

5 Brunt, '"A Divine Gift to Inspire"? Popular Cultural Representation, Nationhood and the British Monarchy', 292.

6 Pimlott, *The Queen*.

7 Robert Shrimsley, 'Royals to Royalties: The Firm Is in Business', Financial Times, 30 June 2011, www.ft.com/cms/s/0/e31c28ac-a341-11e0-8d6 d-00144feabdc0.html#axzz4HU4im7FV [Accessed 16/08/2016].

8   'Serving the Royals: Inside the Firm' (dir. John Curtin, CBC, 17 January 2013).

9   Owens, *The Family Firm*.

10 Michèle Barrett and Mary McIntosh, *The Anti-Social Family* (London: Verso, 1991) 32.

11 Helen Dunne, 'Communications Professional of the Year 2018', Corp-Comms Magazine, 3 December 2018, www.corpcommsmagazine.co.uk/features-and-analysis/view/communications-professional-of-the-year-2018 [Accessed 07/12/2018].

12 Pearson, *The Ultimate Family*; Lacey, *Royal*.

13 Ros Coward, *Female Desire* (London, Paladin, 1984); Judith Williamson, *Consuming Passions* (London: Marion Boyars, 1986); Brunt, '"A Divine Gift to Inspire"?'; Biressi and Nunn, *Class and Contemporary British Culture*; Littler, *Against Meritocracy*.

14 Otnes and Maclaran, *Royal Fever*, 10.

15 Andrea Coli and Mary B. Rose, 'Families and Firms: The Culture and Evolution of Family Firms in Britain and Italy in the Nineteenth and Twentieth Centuries', *Scandinavian Economic History Review*, 47, no.1 (1999): 24–47, 24.

16 Stana Nenadic, 'The Small Family Firm in Victorian Britain', in *Family Capitalism*, ed. G. Jones and M. Rose (London: Frank Cass and Company Limited, 1993), 86–114.

17 Edgerton, *The Rise and Fall of the British Nation*, 103.

18 Nicholas B. Dirks, *The Scandal of Empire: India and the Creation of Imperial Britain* (Cambridge, MA: Harvard University Press, 2008).

19 Nenadic, 'The Small Family Firm'.

20 Ibid., 87.

21 Ibid.

22 Ibid.; Sylvia Yanagisako, 'Accumulating Family Values', Goody Lecture 2018, Marl Planck Institute for Social Anthropology, www.eth.mpg.de/5317376/Goody_Lecture_2018.pdf [Accessed 31/01/2021].

23 In Joel Bakan, *The Corporation: The Pathological Pursuit of Profit and Power* (London: Constable, 2004), 18.

24 Stephan Shakespeare, 'Public Opinion on Business and Business Attitudes to Public Opinion'. YouGov, 22 October 2014, https://yougov.co.uk/topics/politics/articles-reports/2014/10/22/public-opinion-business-and-business-attitudes-pub [Accessed 01/02/2017].

25 Yanagisako, 'Accumulating Family Values'; Maria Pramaggiore and Diane Negra, 'Keeping Up with the Aspirations: Commercial Family Values and the Kardashian Family Brand', in *Reality Gendervision: Sexuality and Gender on Transatlantic Reality Television*, ed. B.R. Weber (Durham, NC: Duke University Press, 2014), 76–96

26 Alan Kidd and David Nicholls, *The Making of the British Middle Class?* (Stroud: Sutton Publishing, 1998).

27 Simon Gunn and Rachel Bell, *Middle Classes: Their Rise and Sprawl* (London: Cassell & Co., 2002).

28 Steph Lawler, '"Normal People": Recognition and the Middle Classes', in *Contesting Recognition*, ed. S. Lawler, J. McLaughlin, P. Phillimore and D. Richardson (London, Palgrave, 2011), 53–73, 56.

29 Ibid.

30 Jose Harris, *Private Lives, Public Spirit: A Social History of Britain 1870–1914* (Oxford: Oxford University Press, 1993); Leonore Davidoff and Catherine Hall, *Family Fortunes: Men and Women of the English Middle Class 1780–1850* (London: Routledge, 2002); Eleanor Gordon and Gwyneth Nair, *Public Lives: Women, Family and Society in Victorian Britain* (London: Yale University Press, 2003); Carolyn Steedman, *Labours Lost: Domestic Service and the Making of Modern England* (Cambridge: Cambridge University Press, 2009).

31 Linda Colley, *Britons: Forging the Nation 1707–1837* (London: Pimlico, 1992); Florence Sutcliffe-Braithwaite, *Class, Politics, and the Decline of Deference in England, 1968–2000* (Oxford: Oxford University Press, 2018).

32 Margaret Homans, '"To the Queen's Private Apartments": Royal Family Portraiture and the Construction of Victoria's Sovereign Obedience', *Victorian Studies*, 37, no. 1 (1993), 1–41, 4.

33 Dorothy Thompson, *Queen Victoria: Gender and Power* (London: Virago, 1990).

34 Ira Nadel, 'Portraits of the Queen'. *Victorian Poetry*, 25, nos 3–4 (1987): 169–191

35 Merck, *The British Monarchy on Screen.*

36 Margaret Homans, *Royal Representations: Queen Victoria and British Culture, 1837–1876* (Chicago: University of Chicago Press, 1998).

37 Monika Wienfort, 'Dynastic Heritage and Bourgeois Morals', in *Royal Heirs and the Uses of Soft Power in Nineteenth-Century Europe* F.L. Muller and H. Mehrkens (London: Palgrave, 2016), 163–179.

38 David Bain, 'A Royal Family Office', 16 February 2016, www.famcap.com/articles/2016/2/10/a-royal-family-office [Accessed 27/03/2017].

39 Ibid.

40 LGT, 'Living Our Values', 2017, www.lgt.com/en/about-us/tradition-and-values/values/ [Accessed 27/03/2017].

41 Adam Hanieh, *Money, Markets and Monarchy* (Cambridge: Cambridge University Press, 2018).

42 Puangchon Unchanam, *Royal Capitalism: Wealth, Class and Monarchy in Thailand.* (Madison: University of Wisconsin Press, 2020).

43 John Balmer, 'Corporate Heritage Brands and the Precepts of Corporate Heritage Brand Management', *Journal of Brand Management*, 18 (2011):

Notes

517–544; John Balmer, 'Scrutinising the British Monarchy: The Corporate Brand that was Shaken, Stirred and Survived', *Management Decision*, 47 no. 4 (2009): 639–675; 'Understanding the Value of the British Monarchy as a Brand', *Brand Finance Journal*, June 2012; Otnes and Maclaran, *Royal Fever*.

44 Philip Kotler, Kevin Lane Keller, Mairead Brady, Malcolm Goodman and Torben Hansen, *Marketing Management* (Harlow: Pearson Education Ltd, 2009), 425.

45 Otnes and Maclaran, *Royal Fever*

46 Gordon Rayner, 'Duke and Duchess of Cambridge Set up Companies to Protect Their "Brand"', Telegraph, 18 January 2014, www.telegraph.co.uk/news/10581090/Duke-and-Duchess-of-Cambridge-set-up-companies-to-protect-their-brand.html [Accessed 24/01/2017].

47 Otnes and Maclaran, *Royal Fever*.

48 Bakan, *The Corporation*; 'Corporation'. *Oxford Dictionaries*, 2017, https://en.oxforddictionaries.com/definition/corporation [Accessed 24/01/2017].

49 Bakan, *The Corporation*, 16.

50 Martin Loughlin, 'The State, the Crown and the Law', in *The Nature of the Crown: A Legal and Political Analysis*, ed. Maurice Sunkin and Sebastian Payne (Oxford: Oxford University Press, 1999), 53.

51 Nick Robins, *The Corporation that Changed the World: How the East India Company Shaped the Modern Multinational* (London: Pluto Press, 2012).

52 John Micklethwait and Adrian Wooldridge, *The Company: A Short History of a Revolutionary Idea* (London: Weidenfeld & Nicolson, 2003).

53 Ibid.

54 Ibid.

55 David Harvey, *A Brief History of Neoliberalism* (Oxford: Oxford University Press, 2005).

56 Naomi Klein, *The Shock Doctrine* (London: Penguin, 2007).

57 Zala Volcic and Mark Andrejevic, *Commercial Nationalism: Selling the Nation and Nationalizing the Sell* (London: Palgrave, 2016); Diane Negra and Anthony McIntyre, 'Ireland Inc.', International Journal of Cultural Studies, 2019, Online first, https://doi.org/10.1177/1367877919882437.

58 Beverley Skeggs, 'The Forces that Shape Us', *The Sociological Review*, 67, no. 1 (2019): 28–35.

59 Bogdanor, *The Monarchy and the Constitution*; Peter Hennessy, *The Hidden Wiring: Unearthing the British Constitution* (London: Indigo, 1996); Ivor Jennings, *The Queen's Government* (West Drayton: Penguin, 1954).

60 Michael Everett, 'The Privy Council', Briefing Paper CBP7460, House of Commons Library, 8 February 2016; Sunkin and Payne, *The Nature of the Crown*; Bogdanor, *The Monarchy and the Constitution*.

61 Pegg, Evans and Barton, 'Royals Vetted More than 1,000 Laws'

62 David Ciepley, 'Beyond Public and Private: Toward a Political Theory of the Corporation', *American Political Science Review*, 107, no. 1 (2013): 139–158.

Notes

63 Robert Wyatt, 'The Crown and Its Employees', in *The Nature of the Crown: A Legal and Political Analysis*, ed. Maurice Sunkin and Sebastian Payne (New York: Oxford University Press, 1999), 293–314.

64 Cindy Stockman, 'The Royal Household'. Royal Central, 28 October 2014, http://royalcentral.co.uk/blogs/the-royal-household-38785 [Accessed 06/10/2016].

65 Brian Hoey, *At Home with the Queen* (London: Harper Collins, 2003); Burrell, *A Royal Duty*.

66 Barry, *Royal Service*.

67 Burrell, *A Royal Duty*.

68 Anne Somerset, *Ladies in Waiting: From the Tudors to the Present Day* (London: Phoenix Press, 1984); Hoey, *At Home*; Arbiter, *On Duty with the Queen*.

69 James Brookes, 'Upstairs and Downstairs: A Job Interview at Buckingham Palace', Royal Central, 6 January 2015, http://royalcentral.co.uk/blogs/upstairs-and-downstairs-a-job-interview-at-buckingham-palace-42653 [Accessed 23/09/2016].

70 Barry, *Royal Service*, 21.

71 The Royal Household, 'Job Vacancies: Housekeeping Assistant', The Royal Household, 17 April 2015, https://theroyalhousehold.tal.net/vx/mobile-0/appcentre-1/brand-0/candidate/so/pm/1/pl/4/opp/844-Housekeeping-Assistant/en-GB [Accessed 12/10/2016].

72 Ibid.

73 Since this was written, the official royal website has removed salary information from many of the job advertisements.

74 Brian Hoey, *Not in Front of the Corgis: Secrets of Life Behind the Royal Curtains* (London: The Robson Press, 2011).

75 National Audit Office, *The Royal Household: The Sovereign Grant* (London: House of Commons, 10 October 2013).

76 Press Association, 'Royal Household Slated on Top Pay', AOL Money UK, 15 October 2013, money.aol.co.uk/2013/10/15/royal-household-slated-on-top-pay/ [Accessed 07/10/2016]; David McClure, *Royal Legacy: How the Royal Family Have Made, Spent and Passed on Their Wealth* (London: Thistle Publishing, 2014).

77 Larry Elliott, 'Household Income Falling at Fastest Rate since 1976 as UK Savings Rates Crash', Guardian, 30 June 2017, www.theguardian.com/business/2017/jun/30/britons-savings-at-record-low-as-household-incomes-drop-says-ons [Accessed 07/12/2018].

78 Sebastian Shakespeare, 'Queen to Pay the Living Wage to Servants', Daily Mail Online, 18 May 2015, www.dailymail.co.uk/news/article-3085742/SEBASTIAN-SHAKESPEARE-Queen-pay-Living-Wage-servants.html [Accessed 22/08/2016]; Hoey, *At Home*; Simon Neville, Matthew Taylor, and Phillip Inman, 'Buckingham Palace Uses Zero-Hours Contracts for Summer Staff', Guardian, 30 July 2013, www.theguardian.com/

money/2013/jul/30/buckingham-palace-zero-hours-contracts [Accessed 07/03/2016].

79 Gordon Rayner, 'Queen's Staff Could "Strike" for the First Time', Telegraph, 30 March 2015, www.telegraph.co.uk/news/uknews/ queen-elizabeth-II/11503795/Queens-staff-could-strike-for-the-first-time-as-Windsor-Castle-workers-vote-on-action-over-appalling-low-pay.html [Accessed 31/03/2015].

80 Hoey, *Not in Front of the Corgis*; Hoey, *At Home*; Burrell, *A Royal Duty*.

81 Robert Verkaik, 'Queen's Finances: Crisis Facing the Monarch Revealed in Secret Documents', *Belfast Telegraph*, 31 March 2010, www.belfasttelegraph.co.uk/news/queens-finances-crisis-facing-the-monarch-revealed-in-secret-documents-28527628.html [Accessed 07/10/2016].

82 Hoey, *At Home*.

83 Hugh Dougherty and Robert Jobson, '"I Served the Queen Breakfast"', Evening Standard, 19 November 2003, www.standard.co.uk/news/ i-served-the-queen-breakfast-6943358.html [Accessed 10/10/2016]; Ciar Byrne, 'Mirror Reporter "Breached Palace Contract"', Guardian, 20 November 2003, www.theguardian.com/media/2003/nov/20/ pressandpublishing.mirror [Accessed 10/10/2016].

84 Richard Palmer, 'Gender Pay Gap Row: Buckingham Palace's Female Staff Paid 12% LESS than Men', Daily Express, 29 March 2018, www.express.co.uk/news/royal/939107/Buckingham-Palace-gender-pay-gap-Queen-Elizabeth-female-staff-paid-less [Accessed 11/07/2018].

85 Rachael Pells, 'The Queen Has Hired Her First Ever Black Assistant', Independent, 9 July 2017, www.independent.co.uk/news/people/ queen-elizabeth-hires-first-ever-black-assistant-royal-major-nana-kofi-twunmasi-ankrah-a7831596.html [Accessed 14/08/2017].

86 Official Website of the British Monarchy, 'Diversity and Inclusion', The Royal Family, 2016, www.royal.uk/diversity-and-inclusion-0 [Accessed 08/01/2020].

87 Anthony Bevins, 'The Queen Fails in Duty to Minorities', Independent, 7 July 1997, www.independent.co.uk/news/the-queen-fails-in-duty-to-minorities-1249486.html [Accessed 18/08/2016].

88 Ibid.

89 Ibid.

90 Pells, 'The Queen Has Hired Her First Ever Black Assistant'.

91 This information is correct to my best knowledge as of December 2020, compiled from information on the internet and in media publications.

92 The Peerage, 'William James Robert Peel, 3rd Earl Peel', 5 November 2015, www.thepeerage.com/p10629.htm#i106285 [Accessed 05/11/2015].

93 The Official Website of the British Monarchy, 'The Private Secretary to The Queen', 26 October 2017, www.royal.uk/private-secretary-queen [Accessed 10/07/2018].

94 George Pascoe-Watson, 'Queen of the Spinners', New Statesman, 30 May 2012, www.newstatesman.com/politics/politics/2012/05/queen-spinners [Accessed 24/10/2016]; LinkedIn Profile, 'Edward Young', 2016, www.linkedin.com/in/edward-young-3b238ab [Accessed 24/10/2016].

95 George Kerevan, 'A Mere Royal Messenger, or a Key Political Player?', The National, 23 March 2015, www.thenational.scot/comment/a-mere-royal-messenger-or-a-key-political-player.1294 [Accessed 26/08/2016].

96 The Peerage, 'Rt. Hon. Sir Christopher Geidt', 9 March 2014, http://thepeerage.com/p34796.htm [Accessed 24/10/2016].

97 Great Britain Rifle Team, 'Tom Laing-Baker', Canada 2017, 2017, www.gbrt.org.uk/canada2017/tour-information/team-list/tom-laing-baker/ [Accessed 03/08/2020].

98 Jack Royston, 'The 5ft 3in Queen Appoints a 7ft 2in Giant to Be One of Her Key Aides', The Sun, 11 March 2018, www.thesun.co.uk/news/5777676/queens-giant-matthew-magee-7ft-2in-aide/ [Accessed 10/07/2018].

99 Hola Connect, 'Matt Magee', 2020, https://holaconnect.com/profile/matt-magee-1b400a7d [Accessed 03/08/2020].

100 Kristin Contino, 'The Queen Appoints Donal McCabe as Communications Secretary', Royal Central, 21 February 2019, https://royalcentral.co.uk/uk/the-queen-appoints-donal-mccabe-as-communications-secretary-116385/ [Accessed 26/02/2020].

101 Gordon Rayner, 'Former BBC PR Boss Sally Osman Becomes Prince of Wales's New Communications Chief', Telegraph, 18 April 2013, www.telegraph.co.uk/news/uknews/prince-charles/10003570/Former-BBC-PR-boss-Sally-Osman-becomes-Prince-of-Waless-new-communications-chief.html [Accessed 26/08/2016].

102 John Owens, 'Burberry Hands BBC's Julian Payne Top PR Job', PR Week, 9 April 2014, www.prweek.com/article/1289564/burberry-hands-bbcs-julian-payne-top-pr-job [Accessed 24/10/2016]; Charlie Proctor, 'New Communications Secretary Appointed for Charles and Camilla', Royal Central, 10 May 2016, http://royalcentral.co.uk/uk/charlesandcamilla/new-communications-secretary-appointed-for-charles-and-camilla-60033 [Accessed 24/10/2016].

103 LinkedIn Profile, 'Christian Jones', 2020, www.linkedin.com/in/christian-jones-57142341/?originalSubdomain=uk [Accessed 03/08/2020].

104 Gordon Rayner, 'An American at the Palace: Duke and Duchess of Cambridge Hire RBS Spin Doctor Jason Knauf', 21 November 2014, www.telegraph.co.uk/news/uknews/kate-middleton/11245163/An-American-at-the-Palace-Duke-and-Duchess-of-Cambridge-hire-RBS-spin-doctor-Jason-Knauf.html [Accessed 16/06/2015].

105 Victoria Ward, 'Duke and Duchess of Cambridge's Former Press Secretary to Run Their Royal Foundation', Telegraph, 23 July 2019,

www.telegraph.co.uk/news/2019/07/23/duke-duchess-cambridges-former-press-secretary-run-royal-foundation/ [Accessed 03/08/2020].

106 Herald Scotland, 'Sir Alan Reid, the Queen's Money Man, to Hand over Royal Purse Strings next Year', Herald Scotland, 26 July 2016, www.heraldscotland.com/news/14643043.Sir_Alan_Reid__the_Queen_s_money_man__to_hand_over_Royal_purse_strings_next_year/ [Accessed 24/10/2016].

107 Herald Scotland.

108 Royal Parks, 'Who We Are', 2020, www.royalparks.org.uk/about-us/who-we-are [Accessed 03/08/2020].

109 The London Gazette, 'Supplement to The London Gazette', London Gazette, 30 April 1979, www.thegazette.co.uk/London/issue/47830/data.pdf [Accessed 24/10/2016].

110 Merco Press, 'Helicopter Veteran of the Falkland's War Becomes Scotland's New Admiral', Merco Press, 20 December 2006, http://en.mercopress.com/2006/12/20/helicopter-veteran-of-the-falkland-s-war-becomes-scotland-s-new-admiral [Accessed 24/10/2016].

111 NATO, 'Visit of the Chief of Staff of NATO's Allied Command Transformation', NATO, 12 April 2013, www.enseccoe.org/en/news/archive/visit-of-the-r87k.html [Accessed 24/10/2016].

112 The Royal Collection, 'Appointment of New Director of the Royal Collection', 16 July 2009, www.royalcollection.org.uk/press-release/appointment-of-new-director-of-the-royal-collection [Accessed 24/10/2016].

113 Aeron Davis, *Reckless Opportunists*, 126.

114 Andrew Sayer, *Why We Can't Afford the Rich*, 245; see also Edgerton, *The Rise and Fall of the British Nation*.

115 The Telegraph, 'Sir Michael Peat to Step Down as Advisor to Prince of Wales', Telegraph, 24 January 2011, www.telegraph.co.uk/news/uknews/theroyalfamily/8278436/Sir-Michael-Peat-to-step-down-as-advisor-to-Prince-of-Wales.html [Accessed 12/10/2016].

116 Davis, *Reckless Opportunists*, 127.

117 Kate Gerbeau, 'Kate Meets … The Master of the Royal Household', Forces TV, 14 March 2016, http://forces.tv/89905232 [Accessed 26/08/2016].

118 Ministry of Defence, 'Freedom of Information Request', 14 July 2014, www.gov.uk/government/uploads/system/uploads/attachment_data/file/331130/20140714_Annual_Cost_Equerries.pdf [Accessed 12/10/2016].

119 Norbert Elias, *The Court Society*, trans. Edmund Jephcott (New York: Pantheon Books, 1983); R. Malcolm Smuts, *Court Culture and the Origins of a Royalist Tradition in Early Stuart England* (Philadelphia: University of Pennsylvania Press, 1987); Anna Keay, *The Magnificent Monarch: Charles II and the Ceremonies of Power* (London: Continuum, 2008).

Notes

120 Evening Standard, 'Progress 1000: Media', Evening Standard, 19 October 2017, www.standard.co.uk/news/the1000/progress-1000-londons-most-influential-people-2017-communicators-media-a3656386.html [Accessed 13/08/2018].

121 Dunne, 'Communications Professional of the Year 2018'.

122 Owens, *The Family Firm*, 23.

123 Dunne, 'Communications Professional of the Year 2018'.

124 Gordon Rayner, 'Merger of Palace Staff Is Latest Step on Prince of Wales's Journey to Kingship', Telegraph, 18 January 2014, www.telegraph.co.uk/news/uknews/prince-charles/10580812/Merger-of-Palace-staff-is-latest-step-on-Prince-of-Waless-journey-to-kingship.html [Accessed 24/08/2016].

125 Dunne, 'Communications Professional of the Year 2018'.

126 Nicholas Watt, 'How a Hung Parliament Would Put the Queen Centre Stage', Guardian, 14 February 2014, www.theguardian.com/uk/2010/feb/14/queen-power-hung-parliament [Accessed 12/10/2016].

127 Bogdanor, *The Monarchy and the Constitution*.

128 Paul H. Emden, *Behind the Throne* (London: Hodder and Stoughton, 1934), 14.

129 David Cannadine, *Making History Now and Then: Discoveries, Controversies and Explorations* (New York: Springer, 2008), 49.

130 George Kerevan, 'A Mere Royal Messenger, or a Key Political Player?', The National, 23 March 2015, www.thenational.scot/comment/a-mere-royal-messenger-or-a-key-political-player.1294 [Accessed 26/08/2016]; Bogdanor, *The Monarchy and the Constitution*.

131 Hoey, *At Home*.

132 Somerset, *Ladies in Waiting*.

133 The Royal Post, 'What's the Deal with Ladies-in-Waiting?', The Royal Post, 12 November 2013, http://theroyalpost.com/2013/11/12/whats-the-deal-with-ladies-in-waiting/ [Accessed 11/08/2016].

134 Dominic Utton, 'The New Countess Mountbatten: Who Is Penelope Brabourne?', Daily Express, 29 June 2017, www.express.co.uk/news/royal/822613/countess-mountbatten-lady-penelope-brabourne-Norton-Knatchbull [Accessed 11/07/2018].

135 Telegraph Obituaries, 'Hugh van Cutsem', Telegraph, 3 September 2013, www.telegraph.co.uk/news/obituaries/royalty-obituaries/10284814/Hugh-van-Cutsem.html.

136 Aaron Reeves, Sam Friedman, Charles Rahal and Magne Flemmen, 'The Decline and Persistence of the Old Boy: Private Schools and Elite Recruitment 1897 to 2016', American Sociological Review, 2017, https://doi.org/10.1177/0003122417735742 [Accessed 11/07/2018]; Andy Wightman, Peter Higgins, Grant Jarvie and Robbie Nicol, 'The Cultural Politics of Hunting: Sporting Estates and Recreational Land Use in the

Highlands and Islands of Scotland', *Culture, Sport, Society*, 5, no. 1 (2002): 53–70; Friedman and Laurison, *The Class Ceiling*.

137 Barry, *Royal Secrets*, 20.

138 Marion Crain, Winifred Poster and Miriam Cherry, *Invisible Labor: Hidden Work in the Contemporary World* (Oakland: University of California Press, 2016).

139 Lucy Delap, *Knowing Their Place: Domestic Service in Twentieth-Century Britain* (Oxford: Oxford University Press, 2011).

140 Rachel Sherman, *Class Acts: Service and Inequality in Luxury Hotels* (Berkeley: University of California Press, 2007).

141 Ibid., 177; emphasis in original.

142 Ibid.

143 Sutcliffe-Braithwaite, *Class, Politics, and the Decline of Deference.*

144 Davis, *Reckless Opportunists*, 126.

145 Nigel Saul, *A Companion to Medieval England, 1066–1485* (Stroud: Tempus, 2000); Casson and Casson, *Compassionate Capitalism.*

146 Brett Christophers, *The New Enclosure: The Appropriation of Public Land in Neoliberal Britain* (London: Verso, 2018), 77.

147 Sunkin and Payne, eds, *The Nature of the Crow.*

148 National Audit Office, *The Royal Household: The Sovereign Grant* (London: House of Commons, 10 October 2013).

149 Ibid.

150 Ibid.

151 Herald Scotland, 'Royal Train Trip from Scotland to Yorkshire Cost Tax-payers £33,000', HeraldScotland, 28 June 2016, www.heraldscotland.com/news/14584113.Royal_train_trip_from_Scotland_to_Yorkshire_cost_taxpayers___33_000/ [Accessed 16/11/2016].

152 Brand Finance Journal, 'Understanding the Value of the British Monarchy as a Brand', *Brand Finance*, June 2012.

153 Jonathan Prynn, 'Queen's Private Income from Duchy of Lancaster Estate Hits £20m', Evening Standard, 20 July 2017, www.standard.co.uk/news/uk/queens-private-income-from-duchy-of-lancaster-estate-hits-20m-for-first-time-a3892461.html [Accessed 04/07/2019].

154 Ibid.

155 National Audit Office, *The Royal Household: The Sovereign Grant.*

156 Ibid.

157 Republic, 'Royal Expenses: Counting the Cost of the Monarchy', 2015.

158 Shrimsley, 'Royals to Royalties'.

159 Paul Bowers and Richard Cracknell, *Sovereign Grant Bill* (London: House of Commons, 12 July 2011).

160 National Audit Office, *The Royal Household: The Sovereign Grant.*

161 The Royal Household of Queen Elizabeth II, *The Sovereign Grant and Sovereign Grant Reserve Annual Report and Accounts 2018–19* (House of Commons

Notes

Research Paper, 24 June 2019), www.royal.uk/sites/default/files/media/final_sovereign_grant_for_website.pdf [Accessed 03/07/2019].

162 Republic, 'Royal Expenses: Counting the Cost of the Monarchy'.

163 McClure, *Royal Legacy*, 422.

164 The Royal Household of Queen Elizabeth II, *The Sovereign Grant and Sovereign Grant Reserve Annual Report and Accounts 2018–19*.

165 The Royal Household of Queen Elizabeth II, *The Sovereign Grant and Sovereign Grant Reserve, Annual Report and Accounts, 2017–18* (London, 27 June 2018).

166 McClure, *Royal Legacy*, 419.

167 National Audit Office, *The Royal Household: The Sovereign Grant*.

168 Ben Riley-Smith, 'Queen Facing Million-Pound Black Hole in Estate Finances after Brexit', Telegraph, 22 October 2016, www.telegraph.co.uk/news/2016/10/22/queen-facing-million-pound-black-hole-in-estate-finances-after-b/ [Accessed 31/10/2016].

169 Robert Verkaik, 'Queen Tried to Use State Poverty Fund to Heat Buckingham Palace', Independent, 24 September 2010, www.independent.co.uk/news/uk/home-news/queen-tried-to-use-state-poverty-fund-to-heat-buckingham-palace-2088179.html [Accessed 09/09/2015].

170 Republic, 'Royal Expenses: Counting the Cost of the Monarchy'.

171 Littler, *Against Meritocracy*.

172 H. David Sherman and S. David Young, 'Where Financial Reporting Still Falls Short', Harvard Business Review, 2016, https://hbr.org/2016/07/where-financial-reporting-still-falls-short [Accessed 31/10/2019].

173 Michael Moore, 'Fat Cat Monarchy Earns Average UK Salary in One Hour', Republic, 1 January 2018, www.republic.org.uk/what-we-do/news-and-updates/fat-cat-monarchy [Accessed 07/12/2018].

174 Rupert Neate, '"Fat Cat Thursday": Top Bosses Earn Workers' Annual Salary by Lunchtime', Guardian, 4 January 2018, www.theguardian.com/business/2018/jan/04/fat-cat-thursday-top-bosses-earn-workers-annual-salary-by-lunchtime [Accessed 07/12/2018].

175 Sunkin and Payne, *The Nature of the Crown*.

176 HM Government, *Memorandum of Understanding on Royal Taxation* (London: House of Commons, March 2013).

177 The Royal Household of Queen Elizabeth II, *The Sovereign Grant and Sovereign Grant Reserve Annual Report and Accounts 2018–19*, 7.

178 The Prince of Wales and the Duchess of Cornwall Royal Household, 'The Prince of Wales and the Duchess of Cornwall Annual Review', 2016.

179 HM Government, *Memorandum of Understanding on Royal Taxation*.

180 Marr, *The Diamond Queen*, 295.

181 The Royal Household of Queen Elizabeth II, *The Sovereign Grant and Sovereign Grant Reserve Annual Report and Accounts 2018–19*.

182 ITV, 'Lewis Hamilton Races into Rich List … but Super-Wealthy Are Seeing Flatline in Their Fortunes', ITV News, 24 April 2016, www.itv.com/news/2016–04–24/lewis-hamilton-races-into-rich-list-but-super-wealthy-are-seeing-flatline-in-their-fortunes/ [Accessed 04/11/2016].

183 Angus Berwick, 'British Monarchy Richer than Ever as Queen's Reign Reaches Record', Reuters, 7 September 2015, http://uk.reuters.com/article/uk-britain-royals-wealth-idUKKCN0R71ZI20150907 [Accessed 11/04/2016].

184 Brand Finance Journal, 'Understanding the Value of the British Monarchy as a Brand'.

185 McClure, *Royal Legacy*.

186 Pegg and Evans, 'Revealed: Queen Lobbied for Change'.

187 Marr, *The Diamond Queen*; Bates, *Royalty Inc.*

188 Bates, *Royalty Inc.*, estimates this to be approximately 7,000 paintings, 40,000 watercolours and 150,000 prints (from artists such as Rembrandt and da Vinci), plus eighteenth-century French furniture, statues and tapestries.

189 Republic, 'Royal Expenses: Counting the Cost of the Monarchy'.

190 The Crown Estate, 'Another Record Income Return of £304.1 Million to the Public Finances', The Crown Estate, 28 June 2016, www.thecrownestate.co.uk/news-and-media/news/2016/another-record-income-return-of-304–1m-to-the-public-finances/ [Accessed 04/11/2016].

191 The Crown Estate, 'The Crown Estate Announces £329.4m Income Returned for the Public Finances', The Crown Estate, 28 June 2018, www.thecrownestate.co.uk/en-gb/media-and-insights/news/2018-the-crown-estate-announces-3294m-income-returned-for-the-public-finances/ [Accessed 03/07/2019].

192 Jillian Ambrose, 'Queen's Property Manager and Treasury to Get Windfarm Windfall of Nearly £9bn', Guardian, 8 February 2021, www.theguardian.com/business/2021/feb/08/queens-treasury-windfarm-bp-offshore-seabed-rights [Accessed 09/02/2021].

193 The Crown Estate, 'Our People', The Crown Estate, 2016, www.thecrownestate.co.uk/who-we-are/our-people/ [Accessed 04/11/2016].

194 Andrew Duncan, *The Reality of Monarchy* (London: Pan Books Ltd, 1970), 194.

195 Simon Murphy, 'Crown Estate Faces Tenants' Anger over Rent Hikes, Evictions and Repair Delays', Guardian, 30 June 2019, www.theguardian.com/society/2019/jun/30/crown-estate-faces-tenants-anger-over-rent-hikes-evictions-and-repair-delays [Accessed 01/07/2019].

196 Richard Palmer, 'Thank You Ma'am: Royals Earn Britain Nearly £2billion a Year', Express.co.uk, 20 November 2017, www.express.co.uk/news/uk/881710/Royal-Family-monarchy-Queen-Prince-Philip-Prince-William-Prince-Harry [Accessed 31/10/2019].

197 Caroline Davies, 'The Queen Costs Her Subjects 60p Each a Year', The Telegraph, 27 June 2003, www.telegraph.co.uk/news/uknews/1434183/The-Queen-costs-her-subjects-60p-each-a-year.html [Accessed 31/10/2019].

198 Caroline Gammell, 'Monarchy Attracts £500 Million a Year from Overseas Tourists', Telegraph, 28 July 2010, www.telegraph.co.uk/news/uknews/7914479/Monarchy-attracts-500-million-a-year-from-overseas-tourists.html [Accessed 24/05/2015].

199 These calculations are usually based on the annual finance reports, which as described are often inaccurate.

200 Weiner, *Inalienable Possessions*.

201 The Royal Warrant Holders Association, 'Home', The Royal Warrant Holders Association, 2016, www.royalwarrant.org [Accessed 07/11/2016].

202 Ibid.

203 Ibid.

204 Otnes and Maclaran, *Royal Fever*, 165.

205 Melanie Whitehouse, 'Fit for the Queen: The Companies Proud to Be Royal Warrant Holders', Express.co.uk, 10 July 2010, www.express.co.uk/news/royal/413717/Fit-for-the-Queen-The-companies-proud-to-be-Royal-Warrant-holders [Accessed 07/11/2016].

206 GOV.UK, 'The Honours System', GOV.UK, 2016, www.gov.uk/honours/overview [Accessed 14/11/2016].

207 Ibid.

208 Colin Brown, 'Honours Condemned as Outdated, Class-Bound and Mired in Secrecy', Independent, 14 July 2004, www.independent.co.uk/news/uk/politics/honours-condemned-as-outdated-class-bound-and-mired-in-secrecy-553107.html [Accessed 03/03/2020].

209 Ibid.

210 Tobias Harper, 'Voluntary Service and State Honours in Twentieth-Century Britain', *The Historical Journal*, 58, no. 2 (2015), 641–661.

211 Tobias Harper, *From Servants of the Empire to Everyday Heroes: The British Honours System in the Twentieth Century* (Oxford: Oxford University Press, 2020), 4.

212 Stanley Martin, *The Order of Merit: One Hundred Years of Matchless Honour* (London: I.B. Tauris, 2006), 3.

213 The James Dyson Foundation, 'James Dyson Admitted to Order of Merit', The James Dyson Foundation, 2016, www.jamesdysonfoundation.co.uk/news/james-dyson-admitted-to-order-of-merit.html [Accessed 17/08/2020]; Philip Williams, 'Queen Awards Howard Order of Merit', ABC News, 1 June 2012, www.abc.net.au/news/2012-06-01/queen-awards-howard-order-of-merit/4045800 [Accessed 17/08/2020]; Shropshire Star, 'Queen Talks about New Great-Grandson as Philip Joins Her at Order of Merit

Lunch', Shropshire Star, 7 May 2019, www.shropshirestar.com/news/uk-news/2019/05/07/queen-talks-about-new-great-grandson-as-philip-joins-her-at-order-of-merit-lunch/ [Accessed 17/08/2020].

214 Weiner, *Inalienable Possessions*.

215 Kaisha Langton, 'Meghan Markle at Bottom of Royal Family Engagements List for 2020 – Court Circular Reveals', Express, 3 January 2020, www.express.co.uk/news/royal/1222869/meghan-markle-royal-engagements-kate-middleton-maternity-hardest-working-royal-2019 [Accessed 03/03/2020].

216 Anne Rowbottom, '"The Real Royalists"'.

217 Ibid.

218 Ibid.

219 The Official Website of the British Monarchy, 'Charities and Patronages', The Royal Family, 2020, www.royal.uk/charities-and-patronages [Accessed 03/08/2020].

220 The Royal Foundation, 'About', The Royal Foundation, 2020, https://royalfoundation.com/about/ [Accessed 03/08/2020].

221 Ibid.

222 Sayer, *Why We Can't Afford the Rich*, 287.

223 Jessica Sklair and Luna Glucksberg, 'Philanthrocapitalism as Wealth Management Strategy: Philanthropy, Inheritance and Succession Planning among a Global Elite'. *The Sociological Review*, 2020, Online first, https://doi.org/10.1177/0038026120963479.

224 Rowbottom, '"The Real Royalists"'.

225 Bates, *Royalty Inc.*

226 Arbiter, *On Duty with The Queen*.

227 Lucy Bannerman, 'Princess Anne Crowned Busiest Royal', The Times, 29 December 2017, www.thetimes.co.uk/article/princess-anne-crowned-busiest-royal-c5vr5jpm7 [Accessed 06/01/2018]. There is a potentially interesting discussion here about the role of royal 'fans' and audiences in doing the labour to reproduce royal power. I do not have the space to consider this here, but it is worthy of further investigation.

228 Caroline Fiennes, 'Royal Patronages of Charities Don't Seem to Help Charities Much', Giving Evidence, 16 July 2020, https://giving-evidence.com/2020/07/16/royal-findings/ [Accessed 31/07/2020].

229 David Graeber, *Debt*.

230 Weiner, *Inalienable Possessions*.

231 Bev Skeggs, 'Values beyond Value? Is Anything beyond the Logic of Capital?', *The British Journal of Sociology*, 65, no. 1 (2014): 4.

232 Ibid.

233 Graham Smith, 'It's Good for Tourism', Republic, 2012, www.republic.org.uk/what-we-want/monarchy-myth-buster/its-good-tourism [Accessed 17/08/2020].

234 Hall et al., *Policing the Crisis*.

235 Saskia Sassen, *The Global City: New York, London, Tokyo* (Princeton: Princeton University Press, 2001).

236 Eric Williams, *Capitalism and Slavery* (London: André Deutsch Limited, 1964); Federici, *Caliban and the Witch*; Lisa Lowe, *The Intimacies of Four Continents* (Durham, NC: Duke University Press, 2015); Dirks, *The Scandal of Empire*; Ann Laura Stoler and Frederick Cooper, eds, *Tensions of Empire: Colonial Cultures in a Bourgeois World* (Berkeley and Los Angeles: University of California Press, 1997).

237 Hilary McD. Beckles, *Britain's Black Debt: Reparations for Caribbean Slavery and Native Genocide* (Kingston: University of the West Indies Press, 2012).

238 Robins, *The Corporation that Changed the World*.

239 Beckles, *Britain's Black Debt*

240 Ibid.

241 Ibid.

242 William Dalrymple, *Koh-i-Noor: The History of the World's Most Infamous Diamond* (London: Bloomsbury Publishing, 2017).

243 Dirks, *The Scandal of Empire*.

244 Tony Norfield, *The City: London and the Global Power of Finance* (London: Verso, 2016).

245 The Commonwealth, 'Charter of the Commonwealth' (2013), https://thecommonwealth.org/sites/default/files/page/documents/CharteroftheCommonwealth.pdf [Accessed 06/04/21].

246 Murphy, *The Empire's New Clothes*, 156.

247 Ibid., 156.

248 Ibid., 43.

249 David Cannadine, *Ornamentalism* (London: Penguin, 2001).

250 Murphy, *Monarchy and the End of Empire*, 7.

251 Holly Randell-Moon, 'Body, Crown, Territory: Geocorpographies of the British Monarchy and White Settler Sovereignty', in *Security, Race, Biopower*, ed. Holly Randell-Moon and Ryan Tippet (London: Palgrave, 2016), 41.

252 Edward Owens, 'Love, Duty and Diplomacy: The Mixed Response to the 1947 Engagement of Princess Elizabeth', in *Royal Heirs and the Uses of Soft Power in Nineteenth-Century Europe*, ed. Frank Muller and Heidi Mehrkens (Basingstoke: Palgrave Macmillan, 2016), 232.

253 Randell-Moon, 'Body, Crown, Territory', 405.

254 The Commonwealth, 'Charter of the Commonwealth'.

255 Commonwealth Network, 'International NGOs', *Commonwealth of Nations* (blog), 2017, www.commonwealthofnations.org/sectors/civil_society/international_ngos/ [Accessed 10/02/2017]..

256 CWEIC, 'About CWEIC', CWEIC, 2017, www.cweic.org/about/ [Accessed 15/02/2017].

257 Emma Sheppard, 'Lord Marland: "People Are Obsessed with Free Trade Agreements"', Guardian, 13 January 2017, www.theguardian.com/ small-business-network/2017/jan/13/lord-marland-people-are-obsessed-with-free-trade-agreements [Accessed 13/01/2017].

258 Commonwealth Trade Review, 'The Commonwealth in the Unfolding Global Trade Landscape: Prospects, Priorities, Perspectives' (London: Commonwealth Secretariat, 2015), http://thecommonwealth.org/sites/ default/files/inline/Commonwealth%20Trade%20Review%20 2015-Full%20Report.pdf [Accessed 02/10/2017].

259 Ibid.

260 Rieko Karatani, *Defining British Citizenship: Empire, Commonwealth and Modern Britain* (London: Frank Cass Publishers, 2004).

261 Reece Jones, *Violent Borders: Refugees and the Right to Move* (London: Verso, 2016).

262 Karatani, *Defining British Citizenship: Empire, Commonwealth and Modern Britain*.

263 Tyler, *Revolting Subjects*.

264 Robin Cohen, *Frontiers of Identity: The British and the Others* (Harlow: Longman Group Limited, 1994).

265 GOV.UK, 'Types of British Nationality – GOV.UK', GOV.UK, 2015, www.gov.uk/types-of-british-nationality/overview [Accessed 30/07/2015].

266 Pimlott, *The Queen*.

267 Jonathan Ritchie and Don Markwell, 'Australian and Commonwealth Republicanism', *The Round Table*, 95, no. 387 (2006): 727–737.

268 Cris Shore and David V. Williams, *The Shapeshifting Crown: Locating the State in Postcolonial New Zealand, Australia, Canada and the UK* (Cambridge: Cambridge University Press, 2019).

269 David Estep, 'Losing Jewels from the Crown: Considering the Future of the Monarchy in Australia and Canada', *Temple International and Comparative Law Journal*, 7, no. 2 (1993): 225.

270 George Winterton, 'The Evolution of a Separate Australian Crown', *Monash University Law Review*, 19, no. 1 (1993): 4.

271 Peter John Boyce, *The Queen's Other Realms: The Crown and Its Legacy in Australia, Canada and New Zealand* (Sydney: The Federation Press, 2008).

272 Ty Salandy, 'The British Royal Wedding, Empire and Colonialism', CounterPunch, 23 May 2018, www.counterpunch.org/2018/05/23/ the-british-royal-wedding-empire-and-colonialism/ [Accessed 23/05/2018].

273 Australian Electoral Commission, 'Key Results', Australian Electoral Commission, 2017, www.aec.gov.au/Elections/referendums/1999_ Referendum_Reports_Statistics/Key_Results.htm [Accessed 13/02/2017].

274 Mark Kenny, 'Republican Movement Wanes amid Royal Revival', Sydney Morning Herald, 15 April 2014, www.smh.com.au/federal-politics/

republican-movement-wanes-amid-royal-revival-20140415-zqv05.html [Accessed 13/02/2017].

275 David Smith, *The Invisible Crown: The First Principle of Canadian Government* (Toronto: University of Toronto Press, 2013).

276 Murphy, *The Empire's New Clothes*, 95, 96.

277 Shore and Williams, *The Shapeshifting Crown*.

278 Tom Warren and Laura Silver, 'The Queen's Grandson Set Up a Charity that Gave His Own Firm the Contract to Arrange Her Birthday Party', BuzzFeed, 9 February 2016, www.buzzfeed.com/tomwarren/the-queens-grandson-set-up-a-charity-that-gave-his-own-firm [Accessed 09/02/2016].

279 Peter Hunt, 'Peter Phillips' Company Was Paid £750,000 for Queen's Party', *BBC News*, 6 March 2017, www.bbc.co.uk/news/uk-39183622 [Accessed 06/03/2017].

280 Oliver Harvey, 'Peter Phillips' Milk Ad Should Warn Harry & Meg of the Perils of Independence', Sun, 22 January 2020, www.thesun.co.uk/news/10791374/peter-phillips-toe-curling-milk-promo-is-a-stark-warning-to-harry-and-meghan-of-the-perils-of-financial-independence/ [Accessed 13/03/2020].

281 Ibid.

282 Shannon Barbour, 'Prince Harry and Meghan Markle's Netflix Deal Was Apparently Their Backup Plan', Cosmopolitan, 14 September 2020, www.cosmopolitan.com/entertainment/celebs/a34011594/queen-rejected-prince-harry-meghan-markle-netflix-deal-backup-plan/ [Accessed 01/10/2020].

283 Imogen Tyler, *Stigma: The Machinery of Inequality* (London: Zed, 2020).

284 Ibid., 250.

285 The Prince's Trust, 'Regional Prince's Trust Awards 2019 Sponsors', The Prince's Trust, 2020, www.princes-trust.org.uk/about-the-trust/initiatives/regional-princes-trust-awards/regional-princes-trust-awards-sponsors [Accessed 13/03/2020].

286 The Duke of Edinburgh's Award, 'Our Supporters', The Duke of Edinburgh's Award, 2020, www.dofe.org/support/our-supporters/ [Accessed 13/03/2020].

287 The Official Website of the British Monarchy, 'The Queen's Young Leaders', The Official Website of the British Monarchy, 2018, www.royal.uk/queens-young-leaders [Accessed 11/07/2018].

288 The Prince's Trust, 'Youth Can Do It – with Your Help', The Prince's Trust, 2018, www.princes-trust.org.uk/support-our-work/youth-can-do-it [Accessed 11/07/2018].

289 Eva Bendix Petersen and Gabrielle O'Flynn, 'Neoliberal Technologies of Subject Formation: A Case Study of the Duke of Edinburgh's Award Scheme', *Critical Studies in Education*, 48, no. 2 (2007): 197–211.

290 Martha Cliff, 'Prince Andrew Reveals that He Thinks of Himself as an "Ideas Factory"', Daily Mail Online, 3 December 2017, www.dailymail.co.uk/~/article-5141341/index.html [Accessed 11/07/2018].

291 Petersen and O'Flynn, 'Neoliberal Technologies of Subject Formation'.

292 Biressi and Nunn, *Class and Contemporary British Culture*.

293 John Corner and Sylvia Harvey, *Enterprise and Heritage: Crosscurrents of National Culture*. (London, Routledge, 1991).

294 Telegraph Reporters, 'Prince Andrew Facing More Questions about Kazakhstan Links', Telegraph, 23 May 2016, www.telegraph.co.uk/news/2016/05/22/prince-andrew-facing-more-questions-about-kazakhstan-links/ [Accessed 11/07/2018].

295 Ibid.

296 Ibid.

297 Patrick Sawer, '"Prince Andrew Brokered £385m Deal with Kazakh Regime while Working as British Trade Envoy"', Telegraph, 20 May 2016, www.telegraph.co.uk/news/2016/05/20/duke-brokered-385m-for-corrupt-regime-while-working-as-british-t/ [Accessed 11/07/2018].

298 Daniel Margrain, 'The Royal Family: Making a Killing from the Arms Trade', Scisco Media, 6 January 2017, https://sciscomedia.co.uk/royal-family-making-killing/ [Accessed 11/07/2018].

299 Ibid.

300 Richard Norton-Taylor, 'The Future British King, Saudi Princes, and a Secret Arms Deal', Guardian, 24 February 2014, www.theguardian.com/uk-news/defence-and-security-blog/2014/feb/24/arms-gulf-prince-charles [Accessed 11/07/2018].

301 Graeber, *Debt*.

Chapter 2: 'The greatest show on earth': Monarchy and media power

1 Bates, *Royalty Inc*.

2 Pye, *The Regal Phantasm*, 43.

3 Anna Keay, *The Magnificent Monarch: Charles II and the Ceremonies of Power* (London: Continuum, 2008), 8; David Cannadine, 'The Context, Performance and Meaning of Ritual: The British Monarchy and the "Invention of Tradition"', c. 1820–1977', in Eric Hobsbawm and Terence Ranger, eds, *The Invention of Tradition* (Cambridge: Cambridge University Press, 1983), 104–164.

4 David Starkey, *The English Court: From the Wars of the Roses to the Civil War* (London and New York: Longman, 1987).

5 Montrose, *The Subject of Elizabeth*; Professor Keith Jeffery, 'Crown, Communication and the Colonial Post: Stamps, the Monarchy and the British Empire', *The Journal of Imperial and Commonwealth History*, 34, no. 1

Notes

(2006): 45–70; Jan Penrose, 'Designing the Nation. Banknotes, Banal Nationalism and Alternative Conceptions of the State', *Political Geography*, 30, no. 8 (2011): 429–440.

6   Sharpe, *Image Wars*, xiii; Burke, *The Fabrication of Louis XIV*.

7   Plunkett, *Queen Victoria*; Richards, 'The Monarchy and Film'.

8   Owens, *The Family Firm*.

9   Ibid.

10 Jürgen Habermas, *The Structural Transformation of the Public Sphere* (London: Polity Press, 1992).

11 Sharpe, *Selling the Tudor Monarchy*.

12 Ibid.; Sharpe, *Image Wars*; Burke, *The Fabrication of Louis XIV*; David Cannadine and Simon Price, *Rituals of Royalty: Power and Ceremonials in Traditional Societies* (Cambridge: Cambridge University Press, 1987); Jeffery, 'Crown, Communication and the Colonial Post'; Plunkett, *Queen Victoria: First Media Monarch*; Owens, *The Family Firm*.

13 Morley and Robins, eds, *British Cultural Studies*; Blain and O'Donnell, *Media, Monarchy and Power*; Merck, ed., *The British Monarchy on Screen*; Otnes and Maclaran, *Royal Fever*; Cannadine, 'The Context, Performance and Meaning of Ritual'; Brunt, '"A Divine Gift to Inspire"?'; Coward, *Female Desire*; Williamson, *Consuming Passions*.

14 Michel Foucault, *Society Must Be Defended: Lectures at the Collège de France, 1975–6* (New York: Picador, 1997), 26; Michel Foucault, *Power/Knowledge: Selected Interviews and Other Writings 1972–1977*, ed. Colin Gordon (New York: Vintage, 1980), 119.

15 Michel Foucault, *The History of Sexuality Volume 1*, trans. Robert Hurley (New York: Vintage, 1990), 136.

16 Diane Purkiss, *The English Civil War: A People's History* (London: Perennial, 2007).

17 Michel Foucault, *Discipline and Punish: The Birth of the Prison*, trans. Alan Sheridan (London: Penguin, 1977), 170; Foucault, *Power/Knowledge*.

18 Hall et al., *Policing the Crisis*.

19 Bagehot, *The English Constitution*, 59.

20 The Observer, 'Profile: Sir David Eccles', *Observer*, 7 June 1953.

21 David Kynaston, *Family Britain 1951–1957* (New York: Walker Publishing Co., 2009).

22 Su Holmes, *British TV and Film Culture in the 1950s* (Bristol: Intellect, 2012); Our Parliamentary Correspondent, 'Development of Television', *The Times*, 10 June 1953.

23 Raymond Williams, *The Country and the City* (London: Chatto and Windus, 1973).

24 Helen Wood, 'Television – the Housewife's Choice? The 1949 Mass Observation Television Directive, Reluctance and Revision', *Media History*, 21, no. 3 (2015): 342–359.

25 Mark Easton, 'Coronation 1953: Magic Moment the TV Cameras Missed', BBC News, 4 June 2013, www.bbc.co.uk/news/uk-22764987 [Accessed 06/03/2017].

26 'The People's Coronation with David Dimbleby' (dir. John Hayes Fisher, BBC One, 9 June 2013).

27 Paddy Scannell, *Radio, Television and Modern Life* (Oxford: Blackwell Publishing, 1996), 81.

28 Jennifer Clark, 'Queen for a Day: Representation, Materiality, and Gender in Elizabeth II's Televised Coronation', *Journal of E-Media Studies*, 4, no. 1 (2015).

29 Asa Briggs, *The History of Broadcasting in the United Kingdom: Volume IV: Sound and Vision* (Oxford: Oxford University Press, 1979); Peter Hennessy, *Having It So Good: Britain in the Fifties* (London: Penguin Books, 2006); Tony Currie, *A Concise History of British Television 1930–2000*, 2nd ed. (Tiverton: Kelly Publications, 2000); Kynaston, *Family Britain 1951–1957*.

30 Scannell, *Radio, Television and Modern Life*; Peter Ward, 'The 1953 Coronation Ob', Guild of TV Cameramen's Magazine, 1985, www.tech-ops.co.uk/page86.html [Accessed 02/06/2017]; Matt Verrill, 'The Coronation and the BBC', BBC, 28 May 2013, www.bbc.co.uk/blogs/aboutthebbc/entries/6e258b7f-3b29-399e-9356-c538706ff933 [Accessed 02/06/2017].

31 Scannell, *Radio, Television and Modern Life*.

32 Ibid.

33 Briggs, *The History of Broadcasting*.

34 Kynaston, *Family Britain*.

35 Scannell, *Radio, Television and Modern Life*.

36 Briggs, *The History of Broadcasting*; Hennessy, *Having It So Good*.

37 Roy Strong, *Coronation: From the 8th to the 21st Century* (London: Harper Perennial, 2005); Ward, 'The 1953 Coronation Ob'.

38 Verrill, 'The Coronation and the BBC'.

39 Briggs, *The History of Broadcasting*; BBC, 'On This Day: 2nd June 1953', BBC, n.d., http://news.bbc.co.uk/onthisday/hi/dates/stories/june/2/newsid_2654000/2654501.stm [Accessed 03/10/2017].

40 Radio Times, 'Radio Times', 29 May 1953.

41 Thomas Hajkowski, *The BBC and National Identity in Britain, 1922–53* (Manchester: Manchester University Press, 2010).

42 Radio Times, 'Radio Times'.

43 Verrill, 'The Coronation and the BBC'; Clark, 'Queen for a Day'.

44 Daniel Dayan and E. Katz, *Media Events: Live Broadcasting of History* (Cambridge: Cambridge University Press, 1992).

45 Nick Couldry, *Media Rituals: A Critical Approach* (London: Routledge, 2003), 58.

46 Horace Newcomb, *TV: The Most Popular Art* (New York: Anchor Books, 1974); Jonathan Bignell, *An Introduction to Television Studies*, 3rd ed. (London: Routledge, 2013).

47 Scannell, *Radio, Television and Modern Life*, 84; Stephanie Marriott, *Live Television: Time, Space and the Broadcast Event* (Los Angeles: SAGE Publications, 2007), 5.

48 The Observer, 'Television', *Observer*, 7 June 1953, ROYALTY 1942–64 [Topic Collection 69_7034] University of Sussex, www.massobservation. amdigital.co.uk/Documents/Details/TopicCollection-69 [Accessed 31/07/2017].

49 Mass Observation Survey, 'Coronation Day Account' (Mass Observation Survey, 3 June 1953), ROYALTY 1942–64 [Topic Collection 69_3612] University of Sussex, www.massobservation.amdigital.co.uk/Documents/Images/TopicCollection-69/3603#Sections [Accessed 19/02/2019].

50 Shils and Young, 'The Meaning of the Coronation'.

51 Émile Durkheim, *The Elementary Forms of Religious Life*, trans. Joseph Ward Swain (London: Novello and Company Ltd, 1971).

52 Ibid., 427.

53 Shils and Young, 'The Meaning of the Coronation', 139.

54 Tom Nairn, *The Enchanted Glass*, 116; N. Birnbaum, 'Monarchs and Sociologists', *The Sociological Review*, 3, no. 1 (1955): 5.

55 Dayan and Katz, *Media Events*.

56 Ibid., 32.

57 Quoted in Nick Couldry, Andreas Hepp and Friedrich Krotz, *Media Events in a Global Age* (London: Routledge, 2009).

58 Hall, ed., *Representation*.

59 Couldry, *Media Rituals*.

60 Ibid., 2.

61 Ibid., 99.

62 Ibid., 2.

63 Michael Warner, *Publics and Counterpublics* (New York: Zone Books, 2005); Michael Warner, 'Publics and Counterpublics', *Public Culture*, 14, no. 1 (2002): 49–90.

64 Warner, 'Publics and Counterpublics', 50.

65 Warner, *Publics and Counterpublics*, 8; Warner, 'Publics and Counterpublics', 50.

66 Kynaston, *Family Britain*; Pimlott, *The Queen*; Cannadine and Price, *Rituals of Royalty*.

67 Verrill, 'The Coronation and the BBC'; Hajkowski, *The BBC and National Identity*; Science Museum, 'Television Reigns: Broadcasting Queen Elizabeth's Coronation', Science Museum, 28 October 2018,

Notes

www.sciencemuseum.org.uk/objects-and-stories/television-reigns-broadcasting-queen-elizabeths-coronation [Accessed 03/02/2020].

68 Media and Memory in Wales, 'The Coronation of Elizabeth II', Media and Memory in Wales, 2012, www.mediaandmemory.co.uk/themes/coronation.php [Accessed 13/03/2017].

69 Robert Cannell, 'Queen's Day – TV's Day', *Daily Express*, 3 June 1953.

70 Sobell, 'Sobell: The Lowest-Priced Luxury 14" TV', *Daily Mirror*, 18 March 1953.

71 Joe Moran, *Armchair Nation: An Intimate History of Britain in Front of the TV* (London: Profile Books Ltd, 2013).

72 David Chaney, 'The Mediated Monarchy', in *British Cultural Studies*, ed. David Morley and Kevin Robins (Oxford: Oxford University Press, 2001), 221–234).

73 Couldry, *Media Rituals*, 69.

74 Laura Clancy, '"Queen's Day – TV's Day": The British Monarchy and the Media Industries', *Contemporary British History*, 33, no. 3 (2019): 427–450.

75 Billig, *Talking of the Royal Family*, 78.

76 Ibid., 78.

77 Warner, *Publics and Counterpublics*, 8; Warner, 'Publics and Counterpublics', 50.

78 Shils and Young, 'The Meaning of the Coronation', 69.

79 Tom de Castella, 'How the Coronation Kick-Started the Love of Television', *BBC News*, 30 May 2013, www.bbc.com/news/magazine-22688498 [Accessed 03/02/2020].

80 Hugo Vickers, 'Queen's Coronation: You Can't Televise the Coronation – the Queen Licks Her Lips!: Sixty Years Ago Today, the Nation Gathered Round Their TV Sets. But behind the Scenes, Panic Reigned', Daily Mail, 1 June 2013, www.dailymail.co.uk/news/article-2334407/Queens-Coronation-You-televise-Coronation–Queen-licks-lips–Sixty-years-ago-today-nation-gathered-round-TV-sets-But-scenes-panic-reigned.html [Accessed 03/02/2020].

81 Clancy, '"Queen's Day – TV's Day"'.

82 Cannadine 'The Context, Performance and Meaning of Ritual'.

83 Currie, *A Concise History of British Television*.

84 Quoted in Morra and Gossedge, eds, *The New Elizabethan Age*, 270.

85 'Royal Family' (dir. Richard Cawston, BBC/ITV, 21 June 1969).

86 Sophie Gallagher, 'The Crown: "Royal Family" Documentary that the Queen Quietly Banned', Independent, 21 November 2019, www.independent.co.uk/life-style/the-crown-royal-family-documentary-queen-banned-a9212716.html [Accessed 04/02/2020].

87 Nairn, *The Enchanted Glass*.

88 Pearson, *The Ultimate Family*.

89 Bob Crew, *Britain's Television Queen* (London: MX Publishing, 2012), 113.

Notes

90 Alan Rosenthal, *The New Documentary in Action: A Casebook in Film Making* (Los Angeles: University of Los Angeles Press, 1971).

91 Michael Thornton, 'The Home Movie One Doesn't Want You to See: Why Is the Queen STILL Keeping under Wraps the Fly on the Wall Film that Changed Our View of the Royals', Daily Mail Online, 14 January 2014, www.dailymail.co.uk/femail/article-1346984/The-home-movie-doesnt-want-Why-Queen-STILL-keeping-wraps-fly-wall-film-changed-view-Royals.html [Accessed 03/02/2020].

92 In 2021, the documentary briefly appeared on YouTube before being removed again; Kate Nicholson, 'BBC's "Conspiracy Of Silence" Over Leaked Royal Doc Show Its Just 'Accessory to Monarchy'", Express, 29 January 2021, www.express.co.uk/news/royal/1390757/bbc-royal-family-documentary-leak-youtube-silence-queen-elizabeth-ii-spt [Accessed 03/02/2020].

93 Anita Biressi and Heather Nunn, *Reality TV: Realism and Revelation* (New York: Columbia University Press, 2005).

94 Su Holmes and Deborah Jermyn, *Understanding Reality Television* (London: Routledge, 2004), 11.

95 Alice E. Marwick and danah boyd, 'I Tweet Honestly, I Tweet Passionately: Twitter Users, Context Collapse, and the Imagined Audience', *New Media & Society*, 13, no. 1 (2010): 114–133.

96 Holmes and Jermyn, *Understanding Reality Television*; Beverley Skeggs and Helen Wood, *Reacting to Reality Television: Performance, Audience and Value* (London: Routledge, 2012); Helen Wheatley, *Spectacular Television: Exploring Televisual Pleasure* (London: I.B. Tauris, 2016).

97 Skeggs and Wood, *Reacting to Reality Television*.

98 Holmes and Jermyn, *Understanding Reality Television*, 9.

99 Coward, *Female Desire*, 163.

100 Ibid.

101 Ibid., 164.

102 Christine Geraghty, *Women and Soap Opera: A Study of Prime Time Soaps* (Cambridge: Polity Press, 1991), 60.

103 Coward, *Female Desire*, 171.

104 Hall et al., *Policing the Crisis*.

105 Helen Dunne, 'Communications Professional of the Year 2018', Corp-Comms Magazine, 3 December 2018, www.corpcommsmagazine.co.uk/features-and-analysis/view/communications-professional-of-the-year-2018 [Accessed 07/12/2018].

106 Malcolm Muggeridge, 'The Royal Soap Opera', New Statesman, 30 May 2012, www.newstatesman.com/lifestyle/lifestyle/2012/05/royal-soap-opera [Accessed 09/01/2015].

107 Christine Geraghty, 'The Study of Soap Opera', in *A Companion to Television*, ed. Janet Wasko (London: Blackwell Publishing, 2005).

108 Marwick and boyd, 'I Tweet Honestly, I Tweet Passionately'.

109 'It's a Royal Knockout' (dir. Martin Hughes and Geoffrey C.D Wilson, BBC One, 1987).

110 Daniel Roseman, 'Was This the Day When Royalty Lost the Plot?', Independent, 21 April 1996, www.independent.co.uk/news/uk/home-news/was-this-the-day-when-royalty-lost-the-plot-1305932.html [Accessed 07/02/2020].

111 Ibid.

112 Pimlott, *The Queen*, 526.

113 Roseman, 'Was This the Day When Royalty Lost the Plot?'

114 Marwick and boyd, 'I Tweet Honestly, I Tweet Passionately'.

115 *The Crown* (dir. Peter Morgan, Netflix, 2016).

116 The Telegraph, 'The Crown Viewing Figures Revealed: 73 Million Households Watch Royal Drama', Telegraph, 21 January 2020, www.telegraph.co.uk/news/2020/01/21/crown-viewing-figures-revealed-73-million-households-watch-royal/ [Accessed 17/02/2020].

117 ITV, 'Broadcaster John Sergeant Hits out at Royal Drama The Crown', ITV News, 26 November 2019, www.itv.com/news/2019-11-26/broadcaster-john-sergeant-hits-out-at-royal-drama-the-crown/ [Accessed 04/02/2020].

118 Zoe Williams, 'The Crown: Shameless Royal Propaganda – or an Insult to the Monarchy?', Guardian, 26 November 2019, www.theguardian.com/tv-and-radio/shortcuts/2019/nov/26/the-crown-shameless-royal-propaganda-or-an-insult-to-the-monarchy [Accessed 04/02/2020].

119 Sarah Hughes, 'How the Crown Has Changed the World's View of the Royals', BBC, 17 November 2019, www.bbc.com/culture/story/2019111 7-how-the-crown-has-changed-the-worlds-view-of-the-royals [Accessed 04/02/2020].

120 Mandy Merck, 'Melodrama, Celebrity, the Queen', *Women: A Cultural Review*, 24, no. 2–3 (2013): 151.

121 Richards, 'The Monarchy and Film 1900-2006'.

122 *Game of Thrones* (dir. D.B. Weiss and David Benioff, HBO, 2011-2019).

123 *Stranger Things* (The Duffer Brothers, Netflix, 2016-).

124 Lynn Spigel and Jan Olsson, eds, *Television After TV: Essays on a Medium in Transition* (Durham, NC, and London: Duke University Press, 2004).

125 Cannadine, 'From Biography to History'.

126 Andrew Higson, *English Heritage, English Cinema: Costume Drama Since 1980* (Oxford: Oxford University Press, 2003); Claire Monk and Amy Sargeant, eds, *British Historical Cinema* (London: Routledge, 2002).

127 Rosalia Baena and Christa Byker, 'Dialects of Nostalgia: Downton Abbey and English Identity', *National Identities*, 17, no. 3 (2015): 259–269; Katherine Byrne, 'Adapting Heritage: Class and Conservatism in Downton Abbey', *Rethinking History*, 18, no. 3 (2014): 311–327.

128   Ryan Linkof, '"The Photographic Attack on His Royal Highness": The Prince of Wales, Wallis Simpson and the Prehistory of the Paparazzi', *Photography and Culture*, 4, no. 3 (2011): 277–291.

129   Adrian Bingham and Martin Conboy, *Tabloid Century: The Popular Press in Britain, 1896 to the Present* (Oxford: Peter Lang Ltd, 2015).

130   Owens, *The Family Firm*, 15–16.

131   Linkof, '"The Photographic Attack on His Royal Highness"'.

132   Ibid., 282.

133   Rebecca Cope, 'How Princess Margaret Did More to Modernise the Royal Family than the Queen', Grazia, 18 January 2018, https://graziadaily.co.uk/celebrity/news/princess-margaret-modernise-royal-family-queen/ [Accessed 20/02/2020].

134   The Guardian, 'Obituary: Princess Margaret', Guardian, 11 February 2002, www.theguardian.com/news/2002/feb/11/guardianobituaries.princessmargaret [Accessed 20/02/2020].

135   BBC, '1955: Princess Margaret Cancels Wedding', BBC, 31 October 1955, http://news.bbc.co.uk/onthisday/hi/dates/stories/october/31/newsid_3202000/3202307.stm [Accessed 20/02/2020]; Anna Kretschmer, 'How Princess Margaret's Public SLIP Led to a CRISIS', Express, 29 April 2019, www.express.co.uk/news/royal/1120004/royal-news-princess-margaret-peter-townsend-queen-elizabeth-ii-public-slip-crisis-spt [Accessed 20/02/2020].

136   Katie Frost, 'The True Story of Princess Margaret and Antony Armstrong-Jones's Love Affair', Town & Country, 6 November 2019, www.townandcountrymag.com/society/news/a9255/princess-margaret-lord-snowdon-relationship/ [Accessed 20/02/2020].

137   Erin Blakemore, 'When Princess Margaret's Affair Hit the Tabloids – and Torpedoed Her Marriage', History, 21 February 2019, www.history.com/news/princess-margaret-affair-roddy-llewellyn-divorce-antony-armstrong-jones-lord-snowdon [Accessed 20/02/2020].

138   Ibid.

139   Ibid.

140   Lydia Brauer and Vickie Rutledge Shields, 'Princess Diana's Celebrity in Freeze-Frame: Reading the Constructed Image of Diana through Photographs', *European Journal of Cultural Studies*, 2, no. 1 (1999): 5–25; Couldry, 'Remembering Diana'; Geoffrey Craig, 'Princess Diana, Journalism and the Construction of a Public: An Analysis of the Panorama Interview', *Continuum: Journal of Media and Cultural Studies*, 11, no. 3 (1997): 12–22; Kear and Steinberg, eds, *Mourning Diana*; William Merrin, 'Crash, Bang, Wallop! What a Picture! The Death of Diana and the Media', *Mortality*, 4, no. 1 (1999): 41–62; Richards, Wilson and Woodhead, eds, *Diana*; Anne Rowbottom and Gillian Bennett, '"Born a Lady, Married a Prince, Died a Saint": The Deification of Diana in the Press and

Popular Opinion in Britain', *Media and Folklore* Contemporary Folklore IV (2009): 271–287.

141 Craig, 'Princess Diana, Journalism and the Construction of a Public: An Analysis of the Panorama Interview'; Jackie Abell and Elizabeth H. Stokoe, 'Broadcasting the Royal Role: Constructing Culturally Situated Identities in the Princess Diana Panorama Interview', *British Journal of Social Psychology*, 40, no. 3 (2001): 417–435; Jackie Abell and Elizabeth H. Stokoe, '"I Take Full Responsibility, I Take Some Responsibility, I'll Take Half of It But No More Than That": Princess Diana and the Negotiation of Blame in the "Panorama" Interview', *Discourse Studies*, 1, no. 3 (1999): 297–319.

142 Lucy Biddle and Tony Walter, 'The Emotional English and Their Queen of Hearts', *Folklore*, 109, nos 1–2 (1998): 96–99.

143 'Reinventing the Royals' (dir. Steve Hewlett, BBC Two, 19 February 2015).

144 This has now been rebranded as the News Media Association, and is the trade body for UK newspapers.

145 Hewlett, 'Reinventing the Royals'.

146 Ibid.

147 Voice of The Mirror, 'Harry's Had an Accident; But We're Not Allowed to Tell You', Mirror, 19 November 1998, www.thefreelibrary.com/Voice+of+The+Mirror%3A+Harry%27s+had+an+accident%3B+But+we%27re+not+allowed...-a060614370 [Accessed 15/10/2018].

148 Jane Kerr, 'Sorry; ... but We Are Unable to Apologise for a Story We Weren't Allowed to Publish', Mirror, 20 November 1998, www.thefreelibrary.com/Sorry%3b+..but+we+are+unable+to+apologise+for+a+story+we+weren%27t...-a060620424 [Accessed 15/10/2018].

149 News Media Association, 'Royal Rota', News Media Association, 2020, http://www.newsmediauk.org/Industry-Services/Royal-Rota [Accessed 10/08/2020].

150 Richards, Wilson and Woodhead, *Diana*; Shome, *Diana and Beyond*.

151 Chris Rojek, *Celebrity* (London: Reaktion Books, 2001).

152 Bingham and Conboy, *Tabloid Century*.

153 Holmes and Jermyn, *Understanding Reality Television*.

154 Nairn, *The Enchanted Glass*, 27.

155 Mendick et al., *Celebrity, Aspiration and Contemporary Youth*; Yelin and Paule, '"The Best Thing about Meghan Markle"'.

156 Yelin and Paule, '"The Best Thing about Meghan Markle".'

157 Nick Couldry, 'Everyday Royal Celebrity', in *British Cultural Studies*, ed. David Morley and Kevin Robins (Oxford, Oxford University Press, 2001), 224.

158 Brunt, '"A Divine Gift to Inspire"?', 294.

159 Marwick and boyd, 'I Tweet Honestly, I Tweet Passionately'.

160 Warner, *Publics and Counterpublics*, 8; Warner, 'Publics and Counterpublics', 50.

161 Spigel and Olsson, *Television After TV: Essays on a Medium in Transition*.

162 Couldry, Hepp and Krotz, *Media Events in a Global Age*, 12.

163 Espen Ytreberg, 'Towards a Historical Understanding of the Media Event', *Media, Culture & Society*, 39, no. 3 (2017): 321.

164 Couldry, *Media Rituals*.

165 James Pamment, 'Strategic Communication Campaigns at the Foreign and Commonwealth Office: Managing Mediatization During the Papal Visit, the Royal Wedding, and the Queen's Visit to Ireland', *International Journal of Strategic Communication*, 9, no. 2 (2015): 118–133.

166 Rory Cellan-Jones, 'Digital Royal Wedding: Or #rw2011', BBC, 19 April 2011, www.bbc.co.uk/blogs/thereporters/rorycellanjones/2011/04/digital_wedding_or_rw2011.html [Accessed 11/10/2017].

167 Mark Sweney, 'Royal Wedding 2.0: Palace Gears up for Big Day', Guardian, 19 April 2011, www.theguardian.com/media/2011/apr/19/royal-wedding-william-kate-youtube [Accessed 11/10/2017].

168 Cellan-Jones, 'Digital Royal Wedding: Or #rw2011'.

169 Sylvia Barak, 'Royal Wedding: 6.8 Million People Comment on Face-Book', KitGuru, 1 May 2011, www.kitguru.net/channel/event/slyvia/royal-wedding-6-8-million-people-comment-on-facebook/ [Accessed 11/10/2017].

170 Ytreberg, 'Towards a Historical Understanding of the Media Event'.

171 Jim Waterson, 'Royal Wedding Confirmed as Year's Biggest UK TV Event', Guardian, 20 May 2018, www.theguardian.com/uk-news/2018/may/20/royal-wedding-confirmed-as-years-biggest-uk-tv-event [Accessed 11/10/2017]; Michael O'Connell, 'TV Ratings: 22.4 Million U.S. Viewers RSVP to Royal Wedding', Hollywood Reporter, 20 May 2018, www.hollywoodreporter.com/news/tv-ratings-royal-wedding-brings-18-million-viewers-us-broadcast-1113498 [Accessed 11/10/2017]; 'The Royal Wedding: Prince Harry and Meghan Markle' (dir. Helen Scott, BBC One, 19 May 2018).

172 KensingtonRoyal, 'Prince Harry Has Asked His Brother The Duke of Cambridge to Be His Best Man at His Wedding to Ms. Meghan Markle', Twitter, 26 April 2018, https://twitter.com/KensingtonRoyal/status/989436382404849664 [Accessed 17/08/2020].

173 theroyalfamily, 'Instagram Stories', Instagram, 19 May 2018, www.instagram.com/theroyalfamily/?hl=en [Accessed 19/05/2018].

174 Bates, *Royalty Inc.*

175 Sarah Young, 'Prince William and Kate Middleton Play Virtual Bingo with Care Home Residents', Independent, 22 May 2020,

www.independent.co.uk/life-style/royal-family/prince-william-kate-middleton-bingo-callers-care-home-cardiff-video-a9527566.html [Accessed 11/08/2020].

176 Elisa Menendez, 'Princess Anne Teaches the Queen How to Use Zoom for First Time', *Metro*, 29 July 2020, https://metro.co.uk/2020/07/29/princess-anne-teaches-queen-how-use-zoom-first-time-13052718/ [Accessed 11/08/2020].

177 Alice Marwick and danah boyd, 'To See and Be Seen: Celebrity Practice on Twitter', *Convergence*, 17, no. 2 (2011): 144.

178 Marwick and boyd, 'I Tweet Honestly, I Tweet Passionately'.

179 Marwick and boyd, 'To See and Be Seen', 143.

180 Sam Knight, '"London Bridge Is Down": The Secret Plan for the Days after the Queen's Death', Guardian, 17 March 2017, www.theguardian.com/uk-news/2017/mar/16/what-happens-when-queen-elizabeth-dies-london-bridge [Accessed 17/03/2017].

181 Ibid.

182 McClure, *Royal Legacy*.

183 Knight, '"London Bridge Is Down"'.

184 Richards, 'The Monarchy and Film 1900–2006', 258.

185 Bates, *Royalty Inc.*

Chapter 3: 'Queen of Scots': National identities, sovereignty and the body politic

1 Nick Brown, 'Queen's Pledge to Help Reunite the Kingdom', *Daily Telegraph*, 20 September 2014.

2 Elizabeth II quoted in ibid.

3 Hall et al., *Policing the Crisis*.

4 Paul Moorhouse and David Cannadine, *The Queen: Art and Image* (London: National Portrait Gallery Publications, 2012).

5 Michael Billig, *Banal Nationalism* (London: SAGE Publications, 1995).

6 Olechnowicz, *The Monarchy and the British Nation*, 33.

7 Zadie Smith, 'Mrs Windsor', *Vogue*, December 2017.

8 Michael Streeter, 'The Queen Bows to Her Subjects', Independent, 5 September 1997, www.independent.co.uk/news/the-queen-bows-to-her-subjects-1237450.html [Accessed 21/08/2020].

9 BBC, *Queen Broadcasts Live to Nation*, 1997, www.bbc.co.uk/news/special/politics97/diana/queen.html [Accessed 28/06/2018].

10 Richard Hartley-Parkinson, 'Happy Birthday, Gan Gan: Historic Picture of Queen with Her Five Great-Grand Children', Metro, 21

April 2016, https://metro.co.uk/2016/04/21/happy-birthday-gan-gan-historic-picture-of-queen-with-her-five-great-grand-children-5830677/?ito=cbshare [Accessed 28/06/2018].

11 Back, 'God Save the Queen: The Pistols' Jubilee'.

12 chunkymark, Kate Just a Vessel: For the Hairy Goat Legged Queen, 2013, www.youtube.com/watch?v=vg01gPv7hbk [Accessed 29/02/2016].

13 David Icke, *The Biggest Secret: The Book that Will Change the World* (London: Bridge of Love, 1999).

14 escavações sonoras, 'Sons of Kemet – Your Queen Is a Reptile', YouTube, 5 June 2018, www.youtube.com/watch?v=SooQHjIhDfk [Accessed 21/02/2020].

15 Margrit Shildrick, *Embodying the Monster: Encounters with the Vulnerable Self* (London, SAGE, 2002), 16.

16 William Davies, *Nervous States: How Feeling Took Over the World* (London: Jonathan Cape, 2018).

17 James Mitchell, David Denver, Charles Pattie and Hugh Bochel, 'The 1997 Devolution Referendum in Scotland', *Parliamentary Affairs*, 51, no. 2 (1998): 166–181; Tom Devine, *The Scottish Nation: 1700–2000* (London: Penguin Books, 1999); Gerry Hassan and Chris Warhurst, eds, *Anatomy of the New Scotland: Power, Influence and Change* (London and Edinburgh: Mainstream Publishing, 2002).

18 Nicola McEwen, 'The Independence Referendum: Setback or Progress for the National Movement?', Discover Society, 30 September 2014, http://discoversociety.org/2014/09/30/the-independence-referendum-setback-or-progress-for-the-national-movement/ [Accessed 21/10/2015]; James Oliver, 'The Scottish Questions Linger, Forcing a Shift in British Politics', The Conversation, 6 May 2015, http://theconversation.com/the-scottish-questions-linger-forcing-a-shift-in-british-politics-41098 [Accessed 21/10/2015].

19 Marina Dekavalla, 'Issue and Game Frames in the News: Frame-Building Factors in Television Coverage of the 2014 Scottish Independence Referendum', *Journalism*, 19, no. 11 (2018): 1588–1607; see also Marina Dekavalla, *Framing Referendum Campaigns in the News* (Manchester: Manchester University Press, 2018); Marina Dekavalla, 'Framing Referendum Campaigns: The 2014 Scottish Independence Referendum in the Press', *Media, Culture & Society*, 38, no. 6 (2016): 793–810.

20 Alex Law, 'Mediating the Scottish Independence Debate', *Media Education Journal*, no. 56 (2015): 3–7; Dekavalla, 'Issue and Game Frames in the News'.

21 Charles Pattie and Ron Johnston, 'Sticking to the Union? Nationalism, Inequality and Political Disaffection and the Geography of Scotland's 2014 Independence Referendum', *Regional and Federal Studies*, 27, no. 1 (2017): 83–96.

22 Simon Johnson and Matthew Holehouse, 'Money Floods out of UK over Yes Vote Fears', *Daily Telegraph*, 13 September 2014; Peter Dominiczak, Peter Spence and Simon Johnson, 'Stay with Us: David Cameron's Desperate Plea to Scots', *Daily Telegraph*, 9 September 2014; Peter Dominiczak and Simon Johnson, 'PM Begs Scots Not to Leave the UK', *Daily Telegraph*, 16 September 2014; Peter Dominiczak, Simon Johnson and Matthew Holehouse, 'Ten Days to Save the Union', *Daily Telegraph*, 7 September 2014.

23 Linda Colley, *Acts of Union and Disunion* (London: Profile Books Ltd, 2014), 6.

24 England became a single kingdom in the tenth century following years of conquest by different monarchs. Ireland formally joined the UK in 1801, but seceded in 1922 to become a sovereign republic, apart from six counties in the north which became Northern Ireland. Wales is a constituent unit of the United Kingdom, and joined the kingdom of England in 1536. In 1997 the Welsh Assembly took authority for local politics (Linda Colley, *Britons: Forging the Nation 1707-1837* (London, Pimlico, 1992); Colley, *Acts of Union and Disunion*).

25 Colley, *Acts of Union and Disunion*; Colley, *Britons*.

26 Colley, *Britons*, 6.

27 Tom Nairn, *The Break-up of Britain: Crisis and Neo-Nationalism* (Melbourne: Common Ground Publishing, 2003), 156; see also David McCrone, 'Unmasking Britannia: The Rise and Fall of British National Identity', *Nations and Nationalism*, 3, no. 4 (1997): 579–596; John MacInnes and David McCrone, eds, *Stateless Nations in the 21st Century: Scotland, Catalonia and Quebec* (Edinburgh: Unit for the Study of Government in Scotland, 2001); Alex Law and Gerry Mooney, 'Devolution in a "Stateless Nation": Nation-Building and Social Policy in Scotland', *Social Policy and Administration*, 46, no. 2 (2012): 161–177.

28 Hugh Trevor-Roper, 'The Invention of Tradition: The Highland Tradition of Scotland', in *The Invention of Tradition*, ed. Eric Hobsbawm and Terence Ranger (Cambridge: Cambridge University Press, 1983), 15–42.

29 Lindsay Paterson, 'Utopian Pragmatism: Scotland's Choice', *Scottish Affairs*, 24, no. 1 (2015): 22–46.

30 Tom Gallagher, 'Scottish Democracy in a Time of Nationalism', *Journal of Democracy*, 20, no. 3 (2009): 56–70; Chunfang Zhu, 'Discourses and Scottish Nationalist Movement', *Canadian Social Science*, 11, no. 3 (2015): 63–69.

31 Paterson, 'Utopian Pragmatism', 28.

32 Jasper Jackson, 'Broadcasters Failing to Make Minorities Feel Represented on TV, Says Ofcom', Guardian, 2 July 2015, www.theguardian.com/media/2015/jul/02/broadcasters-minorities-tv-ofcom [Accessed 08/12/2015]; George Monbiot, 'How the Media Shafted the

People of Scotland', Guardian, 16 September 2014, www.theguardian.com/ commentisfree/2014/sep/16/media-shafted-people-scotland-journalists [Accessed 08/12/2015].

33 Bryan Curtis, 'Paper Tiger: Strange Days at the Daily Telegraph', *Slate*, 25 October 2006, http://primary.slate.com/articles/news_and_politics/ letter_fromlondon/2006/10/paper_tiger.html [Accessed 15/12/2015].

34 BBC News, '"Rich List" Counts More than 100 UK Billionaires', BBC News, 11 May 2014, www.bbc.co.uk/news/uk-27360032 [Accessed 15/12/2015].

35 Steven Swinford, 'Costs of EU Membership "Outweigh Benefits"', Telegraph, 29 December 2015, www.telegraph.co.uk/news/newstopics/ eureferendum/12072128/Costs-of-EU-membership-outweigh-benefits.html [Accessed 12/11/2019].

36 Zsolt Darvas, 'High Inequality and Poverty Helped Trigger the Brexit Protest Vote', LSE Blogs, 31 August 2016, https://blogs.lse.ac.uk/ brexit/2016/08/31/brexit-should-be-a-wake-up-call-in-the-fight-against-inequality/ [Accessed 12/11/2019].

37 Mark Sweney and Rob Davies, 'Telegraph Sale Could Herald Breakup of Vast Barclays Empire', Guardian, 28 October 2019, www.theguardian.com/ media/2019/oct/28/telegraph-sale-could-herald-breakup-of-vast-barclays-empire [Accessed 12/11/2019].

38 Billig, *Talking of the Royal Family*, 34.

39 Olechnowicz, *The Monarchy and the British Nation*, 34.

40 Tom Nairn, *The Enchanted Glass*, 11.

41 Ibid., 92.

42 Ibid., 90.

43 Quoted in Benedict Anderson, *Imagined Communities: Reflections on the Origin and Spread of Nationalism*, rev. ed. (London: Verso, 2006).

44 Bogdanor, *The Monarchy and the Constitution*; Hennessy, *The Hidden Wiring*.

45 Karatani, *Defining British Citizenship*; Tyler, *Revolting Subjects*.

46 Alastair Bruce, Julian Calder and Mark Cator, *Keepers: The Ancient Offices of Britain* (London: Julian Calder Publishing, 2013).

47 Ibid., 10.

48 Ibid., 2.

49 Ibid., 10.

50 Ibid., 9.

51 'Countryfile:, Royal Special: Balmoral' (dir. William Lyons, BBC One, 3 June 2018).

52 John de Critz, *James I of England*, oil on panel, circa 1605, National Galleries of Scotland.

53 Caroline Rae and Aviva Burnstock, 'A Technical Study of Portraits of King James VI and I Attributed to John de Critz The Elder (d. 1642); Artist, Workshop and Copies', in *European Paintings 15th–18th Century:*

Copying, Replicating and Emulating, ed. Erma Hermens (London: Archetype, 2014).

54 Roy Strong, 'Three Royal Jewels: The Three Brothers, the Mirror of Great Britain and the Feather', *The Burlington Magazine*, 108, no. 760 (1966): 351.

55 Marie Axton, *The Queen's Two Bodies: Drama and the Elizabethan Succession* (London: Royal Historical Society, 1977), 12.

56 Ernst Hartwig Kantorowicz, *The King's Two Bodies: A Study in Medieval Political Theology* (Princeton: Princeton University Press, 1957).

57 Ibid., 7–13.

58 Bernd Herzogenrath, *An American Body-Politic: A Deleuzian Approach* (Lebanon: University Press of New England, 2010).

59 Elizabeth Grosz, *Volatile Bodies: Toward a Corporeal Feminism* (Bloomington: Indiana University Press, 1994).

60 Thomas Hobbes, *Leviathan* [1651] (Oxford: Oxford Paperbacks, 2008).

61 Ibid., 106.

62 Keith Brown, 'The Artist of the "Leviathan" Titlepage', *The British Library Journal*, 4, no. 1 (1978): 24–36; Margery Corbett and R.W. Lightbown, *The Comely Frontispiece: The Emblematic Title-Page in England 1550–1660* (London: Routledge, 1979); Noel Malcolm, 'The Titlepage of Leviathan, Seen in a Curious Perspective', *The Seventeenth Century*, 13, no. 2 (1998): 124–155.

63 Herzogenrath, *An American Body-Politic*, 7; emphasis in original.

64 Joseph Lowndes, 'Barack Obama's Body: The Presidency, the Body Politic, and the Contest over American National Identity', *Polity*, 45, no. 4 (2013): 469–498.

65 Brown, 'Queen's Pledge to Help Reunite the Kingdom'.

66 Steven G. Ellis and Christopher Maginn, *The Making of the British Isles: The State of Britain and Ireland, 1450–1660* (London: Routledge, 2013), 290.

67 Anne McLaren, 'Monogamy, Polygamy and the True State: James I's Rhetoric of Empire', *History of Political Thought*, 25, no. 3 (2004): 446–480.

68 Bruce, Calder and Cator, *Keepers*.

69 The Official Website of the British Monarchy, 'Order of the Thistle', The Official Website of the British Monarchy, 2015, www.royal.gov.uk/MonarchUK/Honours/OrderoftheThistle.aspx [Accessed 11/11/2015].

70 Corbett and Lightbown, *The Comely Frontispiece*, 224.

71 Ibid.

72 Ibid.

73 Ibid., 219.

74 Glen Newey, *Routledge Philosophy Guidebook to Hobbes and Leviathan* (London: Routledge, 2008), 34.

75 Hobbes, *Leviathan*, 114.

76 David Matless, *Landscape and Englishness* (London: Reaktion Books, 2001).

Notes

77 Olwig, *Landscape, Nature and the Body Politic*.

78 Ibid., 44.

79 Ibid.

80 Ibid., 219.

81 APS Group Scotland, 'Scotland's Future: Your Guide to an Independent Scotland' (Scottish Government, November 2013), www.gov.scot/resource/0043/00439021.pdf [Accessed 26/10/2015].

82 Davies, *Nervous States*.

83 John Urry, *The Tourist Gaze: Leisure and Travel in Contemporary Societies* (London: SAGE Publications, 1990).

84 'Countryfile'.

85 Chris Hastings, 'Is This the Most Astonishing Photoshoot of the Queen Ever? Yes, It Really IS Her Majesty as Queen of Scots amid the Heather (Moments before a Midge Invasion)', Daily Mail Online, 25 May 2013, www.dailymail.co.uk/news/article-2330996/Is-astonishing-photoshoot-Queen-Yes-really-IS-Her-Majesty-Queen-Scots-amid-heather-moments-midge-invasion.html [Accessed 07/07/2015].

86 Robert Hardman, 'Monarch of the Glen: This Astonishing Photo of the Queen Was Taken at Her Beloved Balmoral and Marks the 60th Anniversary of Her Coronation. Robert Hardman Tells the behind-the-Scenes Story', Mail Online, 24 May 2015, www.dailymail.co.uk/femail/article-2329591/Photo-Queen-beloved-Balmoral-marks-60th-anniversary-Coronation-Robert-Hardman-tells-the-scenes-story.html [Accessed 30/09/2015].

87 Ben Pitcher, 'Belonging to a Different Landscape: Repurposing Nationalist Affects', *Sociological Research Online*, 21, no. 1 (2016): 1–13.

88 Thomas Martin Devine, *Clanship to Crofter's War: The Social Transformation of the Scottish Highlands* (Manchester: Manchester University Press, 1994).

89 Ibid.

90 Eric Richards, *The Highland Clearances* (Edinburgh: Birlinn Ltd, 2012).

91 Devine, *Clanship to Crofter's War*, 34.

92 John Prebble, *Culloden* (London: Secker and Warburg, 1961).

93 James II was exiled after his son-in-law William of Orange invaded England in 1688, in order to depose the Catholic James II and re-establish the throne as Protestant.

94 David Batty, 'Should We Save God Save the Queen?', Guardian, 3 December 2007, www.theguardian.com/news/blog/2007/dec/03/shouldwesavegodsavethequ1 [Accessed 11/12/2015].

95 Alistair McConnachie, 'The Alleged Rebellious Scots "Verse" Debunked', A Force For Good, 29 May 2013, www.aforceforgood.org.uk/precious/anthem1 [Accessed 11/12/2015].

96 Batty, 'Should We Save God Save the Queen?'; BBC News, 'National Anthem Lyric Questioned', BBC, 4 December 2007, http://news.bbc.

co.uk/1/hi/uk_politics/7126929.stm [Accessed 11/12/2015]; Gary Cleland, 'National Anthem "Could Be Anti-Scots"', 3 December 2007, www.telegraph.co.uk/news/uknews/1571286/National-anthem-could-be-anti-Scots.html [Accessed 11/12/2015].

97 Katherine Faulkner and Gavin Madeley, 'Fury as Welsh and Scots Snub National Anthem: Captain Giggs Stayed Silent for God Save The Queen', Mail Online, 26 July 2012, www.dailymail.co.uk/news/article-2179523/London-2012-Olympics-Fury-Welsh-Scots-snub-National-Anthem.html [Accessed 11/12/2015].

98 Tim Barribeau, 'Scottish National Portrait Gallery Acquires Most Epic Photo of the Queen', Popular Photography, 16 January 2014, www.popphoto.com/news/2014/01/scottish-national-portrait-gallery-acquires-most-epic-photo-queen [Accessed 30/09/2015].

99 Simon Schama, 'Face of Britain: The Face of Power', *Face of Britain* (London: BBC2, 14 October 2015).

100 Nicholson, 'From Ramsay's Flora MacDonald'.

101 Ibid., 164.

102 'Countryfile'.

103 Clan Farquharson, 'Associated History', Clan Farquharson, 2015, www.farquharson-clan.co.uk/content/history/asso_history.htm [Accessed 10/11/2015].

104 Richard W. Butler, 'The History and Development of Royal Tourism in Scotland: Balmoral, the Ultimate Holiday Home?', in *Royal Tourism: Excursions around Monarchy*, ed. Philip Long and Nicola J. Palmer (Clevedon: Channel View Publications, 2008).

105 George Monbiot, 'I'd Vote Yes to Rid Scotland of Its Feudal Landowners', Guardian, 19 May 2015, www.theguardian.com/commentisfree/2014/may/19/vote-yes-rid-scotland-of-feudal-landowners-highlands?CMP=fb_gu [Accessed 19/05/2015].

106 Queen Victoria, *Leaves from the Journal of Our Life in the Highlands* (London: Smith, Elder and Co., 1868).

107 The Scottish Crofting Foundation has been campaigning to have crofters recognised as an indigenous population (Scottish Crofting Foundation, 'Crofters: Indigenous People of the Highlands and Islands', 2008, www.crofting.org/uploads/news/crofters-indigenous-peoples.pdf [Accessed 10/11/2015].

108 P. Higgins, L. Jackson, and G. Jarvie, 'Deer Forests, Sporting Estates and the Aristocracy: Some Preliminary Observations', *Scottish Centre Research Papers in Sport, Leisure and Society*, 2 (1997): 32–52.

109 A. Wightman, Peter Higgins, Grant Jarvie and Robbie Nicol, 'The Cultural Politics of Hunting: Sporting Estates and Recreational Land Use in the Highlands and Islands of Scotland', *Culture, Sport, Society*, 5, no. 1 (2002): 53–70.

Notes

110 Ibid.

111 Ewen A. Cameron, 'The Political Influence of Highland Landowners:
A Reassessment', *Northern Scotland*, 14, no. 1 (1994): 27–46.

112 Butler, 'The History and Development of Royal Tourism in Scotland'.

113 G. Jarvie and I.A. Reid, 'Sport, Nationalism and Culture in Scotland',
The Sports Historian, 19, no. 1 (1999): 97–124; Butler, 'The History and
Development of Royal Tourism in Scotland'.

114 Agency, 'Queen and Prince Philip Brave Cold to Celebrate 200th
Anniversary of Highland Games', Telegraph, 5 September 2015,
www.telegraph.co.uk/news/uknews/queen-elizabeth-II/11846770/
Queen-and-Prince-Philip-brave-cold-to-celebrate-200th-anniversary-
of-Highland-Games.html [Accessed 10/12/2015].

115 Harriet Sherwood, 'Global "Catastrophe" Looms as Covid-19 Fuels
Inequality', Observer, 11 July 2020, www.theguardian.com/world/2020/
jul/11/global-catastrophe-looms-as-covid-19-fuels-inequality [Accessed
11/08/2020].

116 Hobbes, *Leviathan*.

117 James Endersby, 'Paradise Papers Deals a Blow to the Queen's Favourability
Ratings', Opinium, 13 November 2017, www.opinium.co.uk/paradise-
papers-deals-blow-queens-favourability-ratings/ [Accessed 19/07/2018].

118 Davies, *Nervous States*.

119 Hall et al., *Policing the Crisis*, 207.

120 Morwenna Ferrier, 'Hat's That: Did the Queen's Headgear Allude to
Brexit?', Guardian, 21 June 2017, www.theguardian.com/fashion/2017/
jun/21/queens-hat-alludes-to-brexit [Accessed 24/02/2020].

Chapter 4: Let them have Poundbury! Land, property and pastoralism

1 The Prince of Wales, *A Vision of Britain*, 86–87.

2 Ibid., 87.

3 Meredith Martin, *Dairy Queens: The Politics of Pastoral Architecture from
Catherine de Medici to Marie-Antoinette* (Cambridge, MA: Harvard University
Press, 2011).

4 David Watkin, *The English Vision: The Picturesque in Architecture, Landscape
and Garden Design* (London: John Murray, 1982).

5 P.E. Farwell and T.I. Molleson, *Poundbury Volume 2: The Cemeteries* (Dorchester: Dorset Natural History and Archaeological Society, 1993).

6 The Prince of Wales, *A Vision of Britain*, 12.

7 Mark Townsend, 'Trouble in Charles's Toytown', Observer, 4 April
2004, www.theguardian.com/environment/2004/apr/04/urbandesign.
themonarchy [Accessed 01/08/2017]; Hayley Dixon, 'Vandals Turn Prince

Charles's Dream Village of Poundbury into "Ugly Buildings"', *Telegraph*, 10 June 2013, www.telegraph.co.uk/news/uknews/prince-charles/10109894/Vandals-turn-Prince-Charless-dream-village-of-Poundbury-into-Ugly-Buildings.html[Accessed 21/06/2016].

8   HRH The Prince of Wales, Tony Juniper and Emily Shuckburgh, *Climate Change* (London: Penguin, 2017).

9   Nick Cohen, 'Prince Charles, We'll Not Stomach a Meddling Monarch', *Guardian*, 3 January 2015, www.theguardian.com/commentisfree/2015/jan/03/prince-charles-meddling-monarch-royal-neutrality   [Accessed 06/01/2015]; 'King Charles III' (dir. Rupert Goold, BBC Two, 10 May 2017).

10 Ipsos Mori, 'Monarchy / Royal Family Trends – The Next Monarch', Ipsos Mori, 19 July 2013, www.ipsos.com/ipsos-mori/en-uk/monarchyroyal-family-trends-next-monarch [Accessed 16/08/2017].

11 Andreas Whittam Smith, 'A Political Prince Cannot Make a Constitutional King', Independent, 30 May 2004, www.independent.co.uk/voices/commentators/andreas-whittam-smith/a-political-prince-cannot-make-a-constitutional-king-62858.html [Accessed 18/07/2017].

12 Larry Dossey, 'The Royal Touch: A Look at Healing in Times Past', *Explore: The Journal of Science and Healing*, 9, no. 3 (2013): 121–127.

13 The Prince of Wales, Tony Juniper and Ian Skelly, *Harmony: A New Way of Looking at Our World* (London: Blue Door, 2010), 9.

14 Sally Bedell-Smith, *Prince Charles: The Passions and Paradoxes of an Improbable Life* (New York: Random House, 2017), 273.

15 Tim Bale, *The Conservative Party: From Thatcher to Cameron*, 2nd ed. (London: Polity Press, 2016).

16 George Walden, 'The New Feudalism', *New Statesman*, 1 March 2010.

17 Sivamohan Valluvan, *The Clamour of Nationalism: Race and Nation in Twenty-First-Century Britain* (Manchester: Manchester University Press, 2019).

18 Michael Woods, *Contesting Rurality: Politics in the British Countryside* (London: Routledge, 2005), 2.

19 'Prince Charles: Inside the Duchy of Cornwall' (dir. Charlie Clay, ITV One, 24 October 2019).

20 Ibid.; Christophers, *The New Enclosure*; Standing, *The Corruption of Capitalism*.

21 Corner and Harvey, eds, *Enterprise and Heritage*.

22 The Prince of Wales, *A Vision of Britain*.

23 Guy Shrubsole, 'What Land Does the Duchy of Cornwall Own?', Who Owns England?, 15 March 2017, https://whoownsengland.org/2017/03/15/what-land-does-the-duchy-of-cornwall-own/ [Accessed 09/05/2017].

24 Duchy of Cornwall, 'Duchy of Cornwall Integrated Annual Report 2019', Duchy of Cornwall, 31 March 2019, https://duchyofcornwall.org/assets/pdf/DuchyOfCornwallIAR2019.pdf [Accessed 27/03/2020].

25 Should there be a female heir, the Duchy reverts to the monarch.

26 Duchy of Cornwall, 'Duchy of Cornwall Integrated Annual Report 2019'.

27 Ibid.

28 Clay, 'Prince Charles: Inside the Duchy of Cornwall'.

29 John Kirkhope, 'The Duchy of Cornwall and the Principle of Crown Immunity Part II', *Plymouth Law and Criminal Justice Review*, 1 (2016), www.academia.edu/19647163/The_Duchy_of_Cornwall_and_the_Principle_of_Crown_Immunity_Part_II [Accessed 07/01/2016].

30 The Prince of Wales and the Duchess of Cornwall Royal Household, 'The Prince of Wales and the Duchess of Cornwall Annual Review', 2016.

31 Duchy of Cornwall, 'Duchy of Cornwall Integrated Annual Report 2019'.

32 The Duchy of Cornwall, 'People and Places', The Duchy of Cornwall, 2017, http://duchyofcornwall.org/places/ [Accessed 07/08/2017]; Duchy of Cornwall, 'Duchy of Cornwall Integrated Annual Report 2019'; Kim Severson, 'Talk to the Plant: Prince Charles's Organic Revolution', New York Times, 26 April 2007, www.nytimes.com/2007/04/25/travel/25iht-prince.1.5434896.html [Accessed 04/08/2017].

33 Clay, 'Prince Charles: Inside the Duchy of Cornwall'.

34 Ibid.

35 Online Etymology Dictionary, 'Landlord', 2020, www.etymonline.com/word/landlord [Accessed 15/06/2020].

36 Karl Marx, *Das Kapital, Volume III*, 1894, Online version, www.marxists.org/archive/marx/works/1894-c3/ [Accessed 15/06/2020].

37 Shrubsole, *Who Owns England?*; Brett Christophers, 'The Rentierization of the United Kingdom Economy', Environment and Planning A: Economy and Space, 11 September 2019, https://doi.org/10.1177/0308518X19873007; Standing, *The Corruption of Capitalism*; Skeggs, 'The Forces that Shape Us'.

38 Republic, 'The Man Who Shouldn't Be King' (YouTube, 27 March 2020), www.youtube.com/watch?v=TGamLrHlikc&feature=youtu.be [Accessed 31/03/2020].

39 Robert Booth, 'Duchy of Cornwall Residents Fight "Unfair" Freehold Ban', Guardian, 11 September 2017, www.theguardian.com/uk-news/2017/sep/11/duchy-of-cornwall-residents-fight-freehold-ban-prince-charles [Accessed 14/09/2017].

40 Rob Evans, David Pegg and Michael Barton, 'Prince Charles Vetted Laws that Stop His Tenants Buying Their Homes', Guardian, 9 February 2021, www.theguardian.com/uk-news/2021/feb/09/prince-charles-vetted-laws-that-stop-his-tenants-buying-their-homes [Accessed 12/02/2021].

41 Charlie Cooper, 'Give Us Your Duchy: Demand for Charles' £728m Cornish Estate', Independent, 29 September 2012, www.independent.co.uk/news/

uk/home-news/give-us-your-duchy-demand-for-charles-728m-cornish-estate-8190493.html [Accessed 31/03/2020].

42 Jonathan Glancey, 'Life after Carbuncles', Guardian, 17 May 2004, www.theguardian.com/artanddesign/2004/may/17/architecture.regeneration [Accessed 14/07/2017].

43 The Prince of Wales, *A Vision of Britain*.

44 Prince's Foundation, 'Princes Foundation: About Us', 2017, http://princesfoundation.org [Accessed 14/07/2017].

45 'HRH The Prince of Wales: A Vision of Britain' (dir. Nicholas Rossiter, BBC One, 28 October 1988); The Prince of Wales, *A Vision of Britain*.

46 Dick Hebdige, 'Designs for Living', *Marxism Today*, October 1989.

47 Paul Goldberger, 'The Prince, the Architects and a Question of Influence', New York Times, 4 November 1989, www.nytimes.com/1989/11/04/arts/the-prince-the-architects-and-a-question-of-influence.html [Accessed 07/08/2017].

48 Nathan Glazer, 'The Prince, the People, and the Architects', *American Scholar*, 59, no. 4 (1990): 507–519; Maxwell Hutchinson, *The Prince of Wales: Right or Wrong? An Architect Replies* (London: Faber and Faber, 1989).

49 Goldberger, 'The Prince, the Architects and a Question of Influence'.

50 Peter Neal, ed., *Urban Villages and the Making of Communities* (London: Spon Press, 2003).

51 Léon Krier, *The Architecture of Community* (London: Island Press, 2009).

52 The Prince of Wales, *A Vision of Britain*.

53 Dennis Hardy, *Poundbury: The Town that Charles Built* (London: Town and Country Planning Association, 2006).

54 Alasdair J.H. Jones, *On South Bank: The Production of Public Space* (Farnham: Ashgate, 2014), 8.

55 Hardy, *Poundbury: The Town that Charles Built*.

56 Ibid.; Duchy of Cornwall, 'Poundbury Factsheet', 2016, http://duchyofcornwall.org/assets/images/Poundbury_Factsheet_2016.pdf [Accessed 17/07/2017]; Simon Conibear, 'Poundbury' (Poundbury Residents' Association General Meeting, Poundbury, 14 June 2017), www.poundburyresidentsassociation.uk/docs/PRA%20-%20RSC%20 14.06.17.pdf [Accessed 18/07/2017].

57 Hardy, *Poundbury: The Town that Charles Built*.

58 @lovepoundbury, 'Love Poundbury', Instagram, 2020, www.instagram.com/lovepoundbury/ [Accessed 17/06/2020].

59 The Prince of Wales, *A Vision of Britain*, 140.

60 Carol Corden, *Planned Cities: New Towns in Britain and America* (London: SAGE Publications, 1977); John Burnett, *A Social History of Housing 1815–1985*, 2nd ed. (London: Methuen, 1986); Gillian Darley, *Villages of Vision* (London: Paladin, 1978).

61 Frank Schaffer, *The New Town Story* (London: MacGibbon and Kee, 1970).

62 Poundbury Manco 1, 'Covenants and Stipulations', *Poundbury Manco 1 Limited*, 2017, www.poundbury.org/?page_id=2 [Accessed 15/06/2017].

63 Hardy, *Poundbury: The Town that Charles Built*.

64 Poundbury, 'Letting Young People of Poundbury Have Their Say', *Poundbury*, 19 May 2009, http://poundbury.boards.net/thread/212/ letting-young-people-poundbury-say [Accessed 18/07/2017].

65 Michelle Thompson-Fawcett, '"Urbanist" Lived Experience: Resident Observations on Life in Poundbury', *Urban Design International*, 8, nos 1/2 (2003): 67–84.

66 Ibid.

67 Adharanand Finn, 'Poundbury: A Town Fit for a Prince', Independent, 16 July 2008, www.independent.co.uk/property/house-and-home/ poundbury-a-town-fit-for-a-prince-868296.html [Accessed 21/06/2016].

68 Ibid.

69 Oliver Wainwright, 'A Royal Revolution: Is Prince Charles's Model Village Having the Last Laugh?', Guardian, 27 October 2016, www. theguardian.com/artanddesign/2016/oct/27/poundbury-prince-charles-village-dorset-disneyland-growing-community [Accessed 27/10/2016].

70 Ibid.

71 Alexandra Cook, 'Harry Potter Star Timothy Spall Films New Channel 4 Series in Poundbury Based on Philip K. Dick Short Stories', Dorset Echo, 21 March 2017, www.dorsetecho.co.uk/news/15171204.UPDATED__ Pictures_and_video_as_Harry_Potter_star_Timothy_Spall_films_new_ series_in_Poundbury/?ref=mmsp [Accessed 25/07/2017].

72 *The Truman Show* (dir. Peter Weir, Paramount, 1998).

73 'The Windsors' (dir. George Jeffrie and Bert Tyler-Moore, Channel 4, 2016-); Laura Clancy, 'Big Fat Royal Weddings: Kate the "Commoner" Princess and Classed Moral Economies' in *The Wedding Spectacle Across Contemporary Media and Culture*, ed. Helen Wood, Melanie Kennedy and Jilly Kay (London: Routledge, 2019), 81–94.

74 James Fisher, 'George III: Notes on Agriculture', Royal Collection: Georgian Papers Programme, January 2017, www.royalcollection.org.uk/ collection/georgian-papers-programme/george-iii-notes-on-agriculture#/ [Accessed 13/06/2017].

75 Roya Nikkhah, 'Exclusive Photography Special: Charles, the Prince of Wales at 70', The Times, 18 November 2018, www.thetimes.co.uk/article/ exclusive-photography-special-charles-the-prince-of-wales-at-70-vb02gl6lc [Accessed 15/06/2020].

76 Owen Hatherley, *Militant Modernism* (London: Zero Books, 2009), 20.

77 Owen Hatherley, 'Prince Charles Is Not a Dabbler – He's Deeply Committed. But He's Naive', Guardian, 2 May 2013, www.theguardian.com/ commentisfree/2013/may/02/prince-charles-not-a-dabbler [Accessed 18/07/2017].

Notes

78   The Prince of Wales, *A Vision of Britain.*

79   Ibid., 77.

80   Christine Berberich, 'This Green and Pleasant Land: Cultural Constructions of Englishness', in *Landscape and Englishness,* ed. Robert Burden and
Stephan Kohl (Amsterdam: Rodopi, 2006), 207–224.

81   Williams, *The Country and the City.*

82   Severson, 'Talk to the Plant: Prince Charles's Organic Revolution'.

83   Monk and Sargeant, eds, *British Historical Cinema*; Dallen J. Timothy and
Stephen W. Boyd, *Heritage Tourism* (Harlow: Prentice Hall, 2003).

84   Ryan S. Trimm, 'Nation, Heritage and Hospitality in Britain after Thatcher',
CLCWeb: Comparative Literarture and Culture, 7, no. 2 (2005), http://
docs.lib.purdue.edu/cgi/viewcontent.cgi?article=1265&context=clcweb
[Accessed 04/08/2017]; Emily Robinson, *History, Heritage and Tradition
in Contemporary British Politics: Past Politics and Present Histories* (Manchester:
Manchester University Press, 2012); Corner and Harvey, *Enterprise and Heritage.*

85   Patrick Wright, *On Living in an Old Country: The National Past in Contemporary
Britain,* updated edition (Oxford: Oxford University Press, 2009).

86   The Prince of Wales, *A Vision of Britain,* 69.

87   Williams, *The Country and the City,* 107.

88   Standing, *The Corruption of Capitalism.*

89   The Prince of Wales, *A Vision of Britain,* 17, 21.

90   Trimm, 'Nation, Heritage and Hospitality', 2.

91   John Summerson, *Victorian Architecture in England* (London: W.W. Norton
& Co., 1971).

92   Herbert Muschamp, 'The Winds of Windsorism', New Republic, 11
December 1989, https://newrepublic.com/article/71073/the-winds-
windsorism [Accessed 29/06/2017].

93   The Prince of Wales, *A Vision of Britain,* 21.

94   Júrgen Tietz, *The Story of Architecture of the 20th Century* (Rheinbreitbach:
Ullmann Publishing, 1999).

95   John Grindrod, *Concretopia: A Journey around the Rebuilding of Postwar Britain*
(Brecon: Old Street Publishing Ltd. 2013).

96   Gunn and Bell, *Middle Classes.*

97   Glazer, 'The Prince, the People, and the Architects'.

98   The Prince of Wales, *A Vision of Britain,* 81.

99   Ibid., 83.

100 Martin Parker, 'Vertical Capitalism: Skyscrapers and Organization',
Culture and Organization, 21, no. 3 (2015): 217–234.

101 Wainwright, 'A Royal Revolution'.

102 Royal Pavilion, 'An Introduction', Royal Pavilion, 2017, www.
royalpavilionpoundbury.co.uk/ [Accessed 28/07/2017].

103 Neal, *Urban Villages.*

Notes

104 Alex Peace, 'HOUSING CRISIS: Dorset Hard Hit Due to Low Wages, Lack of Affordable Houses and Second Homes', Dorset Echo, 3 August 2016, www.dorsetecho.co.uk/news/14657664.HOUSING_CRISIS__Dorset_hard_hit_due_to_low_wages__lack_of_affordable_houses_and_second_homes/ [Accessed 28/07/2017].

105 The Prince of Wales, Juniper and Skelly, *Harmony*, 172.

106 Hardy, *Poundbury*, 98.

107 Wainwright, 'A Royal Revolution'.

108 Lynsey Hanley, *Estates: An Intimate History* (London: Granta Books, 2007).

109 Hardy, *Poundbury*.

110 Sarah Collins, 'Affordable Housing', *Celebrating Poundbury*, July 2017.

111 Thompson-Fawcett, '"Urbanist" Lived Experience', 7.

112 David Madden and Peter Marcuse, *In Defence of Housing* (London: Verso, 2016).

113 The Guinness Partnership, 'Celebrating 125 Years with the 250th Home in Poundbury', The Guinness Partnership, 23 September 2015, www.guinnesspartnership.com/news/celebrating-125-years-250th-home-poundbury/ [Accessed 31/07/2017].

114 Mark Tran, 'Guinness Partnership Defers Eviction of Brixton Social Housing Tenant', Guardian, 20 February 2015, www.theguardian.com/society/2015/feb/20/brixton-social-housing-tenants-guinness-partnership-defer-eviction [Accessed 15/06/2017].

115 Nick Mathiason and Will Fitzgibbon, 'Get the Data – Royal and Historic Landowners' Housing Developments', The Bureau of Investigative Journalism, 8 February 2014, www.thebureauinvestigates.com/stories/2014–02–08/get-the-data-royal-and-historic-landowners-housing-developments [Accessed 03/07/2017].

116 Ibid.

117 Townsend, 'Trouble in Charles's Toytown'.

118 The Prince of Wales, *A Vision of Britain*, 59, 58.

119 Stephen Daniels, *Fields of Vision: Landscape Imagery and National Identity in England and the United States* (London: Polity Press, 1993), 11.

120 The Prince of Wales, *A Vision of Britain*, 69.

121 Daniels, *Fields of Vision*.

122 Corner and Harvey, *Enterprise and Heritage*.

123 Ibid.

124 Clay, 'Prince Charles: Inside the Duchy of Cornwall'.

125 The Prince of Wales, *A Vision of Britain*, 12; Whittam Smith, 'A Political Prince Cannot Make a Constitutional King'.

126 Daniels, *Fields of Vision*.

127 Quoted in Ian Baucom, *Out of Place: Englishness, Empire, and the Locations of Identity* (Princeton: Princeton University Press, 1999), 175.

Notes

128 The Prince of Wales, *A Vision of Britain*, 63; David Olusoga, *Black and British: A Forgotten History* (London: Macmillan, 2016).

129 Paul Gilroy, *After Empire: Melancholia or Convivial Culture?* (London: Routledge, 2004).

130 Daniels, *Fields of Vision*, 6.

131 Sarah Neal, 'Rural Landscapes, Representations and Racism: Examining Multicultural Citizenship and Policy-Making in the English Countryside', *Ethnic and Racial Studies*, 25, no. 3 (2002): 443.

132 Sarah L. Holloway, 'Burning Issues: Whiteness, Rurality and the Politics of Difference', *Geoforum*, 38, no. 1 (2007): 7–20; Divya P. Tolia-Kelly, *Landscape, Race and Memory: Material Ecologies of Citizenship* (Farnham: Ashgate, 2010).

133 Thompson-Fawcett, '"Urbanist" Lived Experience'.

134 Aurelien Mondon and Aaron Winter, 'Whiteness, Populism and the Racialisation of the Working Class in the United Kingdom and the United States', *Identities*, 26, no. 5 (2019): 510–528.

135 Sally Brooks, 'Brexit and the Politics of the Rural', *Sociologia Ruralis*, 60, no. 4 (2019): 790–809.

136 Corner and Harvey, *Enterprise and Heritage*, 40.

137 Valluvan, *The Clamour of Nationalism*, 94–95.

138 Olusoga, *Black and British*.

139 Williams, *The Country and the City*; Olusoga, *Black and British*; Margot Finn and Kate Smith, eds, *The East India Company at Home 1757–1857* (London: UCL Press Ltd, 2018); Gretchen H. Gerzina, *Britain's Black Past* (Oxford: Oxford University Press, 2020).

140 Robert Jobson, 'Prince Charles Named "Londoner of the Decade" at The Progress 1000', Evening Standard, 7 September 2016, www.standard.co.uk/ news/the1000/the-progress-1000-prince-charles-named-londoner-of-the-decade-at-evening-standard-bash-a3339516.html [Accessed 20/09/2016].

141 Finn, 'Poundbury: A Town Fit for a Prince'.

142 Hatherley, *Militant Modernism*, 20.

143 Wainwright, 'A Royal Revolution'.

144 Hewlett, 'Reinventing the Royals'.

145 Ian Burrell, 'The 15-Page Contract that Reveals How Charles Tries to Control the Media', Independent, 2 December 2015, www.independent.co.uk/news/uk/home-news/prince-charles-the-15-page-contract-that-reveals-how-the-prince-of-wales-tries-to-control-the-media-a6756541.html [Accessed 03/12/2015].

146 Catherine Bennett, 'Back off, Prince Charles … The Countryside Is Too Vital to Leave to Its Grasping Owners', Guardian, 16 November 2014, www.theguardian.com/commentisfree/2014/nov/16/prince-charles-countryside-planning-green-belt [Accessed 03/03/2017].

Notes

Chapter 5: 'I am Invictus': Masculinities, 'philanthrocapitalism' and the military-industrial complex

1 Invictus Games Foundation, 'Invictus Games Foundation', 2018, https:// invictusgamesfoundation.org/ [Accessed 10/01/2018].

2 Callie Batts and David L. Andrews, '"Tactical Athletes": The United States Paralympic Military Program and the Mobilization of the Disabled Soldier/Athlete', *Sport in Society*, 14, no. 5 (2011): 553–568, 555; emphasis added.

3 McGoey, *No Such Thing as a Free Gift*; Dean, *The Good Glow*; King, *Pink Ribbons, Inc*; Jo Littler, 'The New Victorians'.

4 Alison Park, Elizabeth Clery, John Curtice, Miranda Phillips and David Utting, 'British Social Attitudes: The 29th Report' (London: NatCen Social Research, 2012), www.bsa-29.natcen.ac.uk [Accessed 18/07/2016].

5 Committee of Privy Counsellors, 'The Report of the Iraq Inquiry: Executive Summary' (London: House of Commons, 2016).

6 Park et al., 'British Social Attitudes: The 29th Report'. In this chapter I often conflate the wars in Afghanistan and Iraq in line with the public imaginary, where the two have been linked. It is important to note, however, that these are two separate conflicts, although their aims were interlinked, and Prince Harry served only in Afghanistan.

7 Valluvan, *The Clamour of Nationalism*.

8 K. Neil Jenkings, Nick Megoran, Rachel Woodward and Daniel Bos, 'Wootton Bassett and the Political Spaces of Remembrance and Mourning', *Area*, 44, no. 3 (2012): 361; Rachel Woodward, Trish Winter and K. Neil Jenkings, 'Heroic Anxieties: The Figure of the British Soldier in Contemporary Print Media', *Journal of War and Culture Studies*, 2, no. 2 (2009): 211–223; Rachel Woodward and Trish Winter, *Sexing the Soldier: The Politics of Gender and the Contemporary British Army* (London: Routledge, 2007); Nicola Cooper and Martin Hurcombe, 'The Figure of the Soldier', *Journal of War and Culture Studies*, 2, no. 2 (2009): 103–104; Jon Robert Adams, *Male Armor: The Soldier-Hero in Contemporary American Culture* (Charlottesville: University of Virginia Press, 2008); Helen McCartney, 'Hero, Victim or Villain? The Public Image of the British Soldier and Its Implications for Defense Policy', *Defense and Security Analysis*, 27, no. 1 (2011): 43–54.

9 Maggie Andrews, 'Mediating Remembrance: Personalization and Celebrity in Television's Domestic Remembrance', *Journal of War and Culture Studies*, 4, no. 3 (2011): 357–370; Jenkings et al., 'Wootton Bassett'.

10 Invictus Games Foundation, 'Invictus Games Foundation'.

11 Ibid.

Notes

12 Helen McCartney, 'The Military Covenant and the Civil–Military Contract in Britain', *International Affairs (Royal Institute of International Affairs 1944-)*, 86, no. 2 (2010).

13 Invictus Games Foundation, 'Prince Harry Launches a New International Sporting Event for Wounded, Injured and Sick Service Personnel Today', Invictus Games Foundation, 6 March 2014, https://invictusgamesfoundation.org/prince-harry-launches-a-new-international-sporting-event-for-wounded-injured-and-sick-service-personnel-today/ [Accessed 14/09/2018].

14 Joe Murphy, 'William and Harry "Are the Most Liked Royals since Records Began"', Evening Standard, 2 February 2018, www.standard.co.uk/news/uk/william-and-harry-are-the-most-liked-royals-since-records-began-a3756191.html [Accessed 14/05/2018].

15 'Prince Harry: Frontline Afghanistan' (dir. Richard Grange, BBC Three, 28 January 2013), www.youtube.com/watch?v=YmTqwz2wQks. At the time of filming, Harry was third in line to the throne. Since the birth of Prince William and Kate Middleton's children, Harry has moved down the line of succession behind them.

16 Andrew Alderson, 'Prince Harry Sent to Clinic after He Admits Drug Abuse', Telegraph, 13 January 2002, www.telegraph.co.uk/news/uknews/1381285/Prince-Harry-sent-to-clinic-after-he-admits-drug-abuse.html [Accessed 08/04/2016]; Scotsman, 'The Moment Prince Harry's Temper Snapped', Scotsman, 2004, www.scotsman.com/news/uk/the-moment-prince-harry-s-temper-snapped-1-559210 [Accessed 14/09/2018]; Ingrid Seward and Andrew Morton, 'Prince Harry: Royal Experts Give Their Verdicts – Brave as a Lion, but Always the Playboy Prince', 26 August 2012, www.telegraph.co.uk/news/uknews/prince-harry/9500073/Prince-Harry-Royal-experts-give-their-verdicts-brave-as-a-lion-but-always-the-playboy-prince.html [Accessed 14/09/2018]; Teri Finneman and Ryan J. Thomas, 'The British National Press and the 2012 Royal Family Photo Scandals', *Journalism Practice*, 8, no. 4 (2014): 407–420.

17 Rosalind Gill, 'Power and the Production of Subjects: A Genealogy of the New Man and the New Lad', *The Sociological Review*, 51, no. S1 (2003): 34–56.

18 Imelda Whelehan, *Overloaded: Popular Culture and the Future of Feminism* (London: The Women's Press Ltd, 2000).

19 Gordon Anderson, Ben Palmer, Damon Beesley and Iain Morris, 'The Inbetweeners' (London: E4, 2008–2010). *The Inbetweeners* is a British sitcom about four teenage boys in a British high school, mainly focusing on their failed sexual encounters and 'laddish' jokes. The scene referred to in the main text is perhaps one of the most famous, where two of the boys, Simon and Neil, continually mock Jay for making new friends

outside of their group, repeating the word 'friends' in an increasingly high-pitched tone to annoy him. Like Harry's complex class identity, the characters of *The Inbetweeners* live a comfortable, middle-class, suburban life, yet appropriate the signifiers of working-class masculinities.

20 Sean Nixon, 'Resignifying Masculinity: From "New Man" to "New Lad"', in *British Cultural Studies: Geography, Nationality and Identity*, ed. David Morley and Kevin Robins (Oxford: Oxford University Press, 2001), 373–385.

21 John Beynon, 'The Commercialization of Masculinities: From the "New Man" to the "New Lad"', in *Critical Readings: Media and Gender*, ed. Cynthia Carter and Linda Steiner (Maidenhead: Open University Press, 2004), 198–217.

22 Gill, 'Power and the Production of Subjects'.

23 Rhian E. Jones, *Clampdown: Pop-Cultural Wars on Class and Gender* (Alresford: Zero Books, 2013).

24 John Harris, 'Bottom of the Class', *Guardian*, 11 April 2006, www.theguardian.com/stage/2006/apr/11/comedy.pressandpublishing [Accessed 19/04/2016]; Tyler, *Revolting Subjects*; Sam Friedman, Dave O'Brien and Daniel Laurison, '"Like Skydiving without a Parachute": How Class Origin Shapes Occupational Trajectories in British Acting', *Sociology*, Online first (2016): 1–19.

25 Tyler, *Revolting Subjects*; Tracey Jensen, 'Welfare Commonsense, Poverty Porn and Doxosophy', *Sociological Research Online*, 19, no. 3 (2014): 3; Helen Wood, 'The Politics of Hyperbole on Geordie Shore: Class, Gender, Youth and Excess', *European Journal of Cultural Studies*, 20, no. 1 (2017): 39–55; Kim Allen, Imogen Tyler and Sara de Benedictis, 'Thinking with "White Dee": The Sexual Politics of "Austerity Porn"', *Sociological Research Online*, 19, no. 3 (2014): 2.

26 Tatler, 'Inside Oxford University's Secret Drinking Clubs', Tatler, 16 September 2014, www.tatler.com/news/articles/september-2014/inside-oxford-university-secret-drinking-clubs [Accessed 15/04/2016].

27 Andy Beckett, 'Eton: Why the Old Boys' Network Still Flourishes', Guardian, 13 November 2012, www.theguardian.com/education/2012/nov/13/eton-old-boys-network-flourishes [Accessed 25/03/2016].

28 Matthew P. Ferrari, '"Born" Survivors and Their Trickster Cousins: Masculine Primitive Ideals and Manly (Re)Creation on Reality Television', in *Reality Television: Oddities of Culture*, ed. Alison F. Slade, Amber J. Narro and Burton P. Buchanan (Lanham: Lexington Books, 2014), 219.

29 Caroline Davies, 'Prince Harry Reaches South Pole on Walking with the Wounded Expedition', Guardian, 13 December 2013, www.theguardian.com/uk-news/2013/dec/13/prince-harry-reaches-south-pole [Accessed 19/07/2016]; Barbara Jones, 'Harry the Lionheart: Remarkable Images of the Conservationist Prince', Mail Online, 30 August 2015, www.dailymail.co.uk/news/article-3215556/

Harry-Lionheart-Remarkable-images-conservationist-Prince-declares-way-life-want-here.html [Accessed 01/09/2015].

30 Penny Junor, 'Harry Loves Breaking the Rules', Mail Online, 27 November 2017, www.dailymail.co.uk/~/article-5122929/index.html [Accessed 14/09/2018].

31 Seward and Morton, 'Prince Harry'.

32 Charles Carlton, *Royal Warriors: A Military History of the British Monarchy* (Edinburgh: Pearson Education Ltd, 2003); Allan Mallinson, *The Making of the British Army: From the English Civil War to the War on Terror* (London: Bantham Press, 2009).

33 Gordon Rayner, 'Medals, Braid, Sashes: What Exactly Are the Military Uniforms Worn by the Royal Family?', Telegraph, 13 March 2015, www.telegraph.co.uk/news/uknews/theroyalfamily/11471375/Medals-braid-sashes-what-exactly-are-the-military-uniforms-worn-by-the-Royal-family.html [Accessed 08/04/2016].

34 Prince Henry of Wales, 'Prince Henry of Wales: Biography', 2016, www.princehenryofwales.org/prince-harry/biography [Accessed 11/04/2016].

35 Caroline Gammell, 'How the Prince Harry Blackout Was Broken', 28 February 2008, www.telegraph.co.uk/news/uknews/1580111/How-the-Prince-Harry-blackout-was-broken.html [Accessed 28/03/2016].

36 Prince Henry of Wales, 'Prince Henry of Wales: Biography'.

37 Richard Palmer, 'Hero Prince Harry's Back in Afghanistan', Express.co.uk, 8 September 2012, www.express.co.uk/news/uk/344704/Hero-Prince-Harry-s-back-in-Afghanistan [Accessed 19/11/2018].

38 Harris MacLeod, 'Let William Go to Afghanistan', YouGov: What the world thinks, 25 January 2013, https://yougov.co.uk/news/2013/01/25/let-william-go-afghanistan/ [Accessed 19/07/2016].

39 Telegraph, 'Prince Harry's Afghanistan Deployment Should Lay "Las Vegas Fling" to Rest, Says Gen Sir Richard Dannatt', Telegraph, 9 July 2012, News, www.telegraph.co.uk/news/uknews/prince-harry/9528314/Prince-Harrys-Afghanistan-deployment-should-lay-Las-Vegas-fling-to-rest-says-Gen-Sir-Richard-Dannatt.html [Accessed 18/08/2020].

40 Woodward and Winter, *Sexing the Soldier*; Harry Brod and Michael Kaufman, eds, *Theorizing Masculinities* (London: SAGE Publications, 1994).

41 John Hockey, *Squaddies: Portrait of a Subculture* (Liverpool: Liverpool University Press, 2006).

42 Katerina Agostino, 'Masculinity, Sexuality and Life on Board Her Majesty's Royal Australian Ships', *Journal of Interdisciplinary Gender Studies*, 2, no. 1 (1997): 15–30; Paul R. Higate, 'Drinking Vodka from the "Butt Crack": Men, Masculinities and Fratriarchy in the Private Militarized Security Company', *International Feminist Journal of Politics*, 14, no. 4 (2012): 450–469.

43 Sarah Sands, 'Masculinity, Sexuality and Dependency', Financial Times, 8 March 2008, www.ft.com/content/5e27ec86-ebf6-11dc-9493-0000779fd2ac [Accessed 18/08/2020].

44 Woodward, Winter and Jenkings, 'Heroic Anxieties', 222.

45 Sun, 'One of Our Boys', *Sun*, 24 February 2011.

46 Valluvan, *The Clamour of Nationalism*, 117.

47 Solomon Hughes, *War on Terror, Inc.: Corporate Profiteering from the Politics of Fear* (London: Verso, 2007).

48 Mallinson, *The Making of the British Army*, 40.

49 Richard Knight, 'Whose Hand Is on the Button?', BBC, 2 December 2008, http://news.bbc.co.uk/1/hi/uk/7758314.stm [Accessed 08/04/2016].

50 Hughes, *War on Terror, Inc.*

51 Ibid.; P.W. Singer, *Corporate Warriors: The Rise of the Privatized Military Industry* (Ithaca: Cornell University Press, 2007); James Der Derian, *Virtuous War: Mapping the Military-Industrial-Media-Entertainment-Network*, 2nd ed. (London: Routledge, 2009).

52 Philippe Le Billon, 'Corruption, Reconstruction and Oil Governance in Iraq', *Third World Quarterly*, 6, nos 4–5 (2005): 685–703.

53 Hughes, *War on Terror, Inc.*, 3.

54 Naomi Klein, *The Shock Doctrine* (London: Penguin, 2007).

55 Hughes, *War on Terror, Inc.*

56 Ibid.; Singer, *Corporate Warriors*; Jeremy Scahill, *Blackwater: The Rise of the World's Most Powerful Mercenary Army* (London: Serpent's Tail, 2008).

57 Emma Atkinson, 'Armed Forces Job Cuts Reach Target Three Years Early', BBC News, 29 July 2015, www.bbc.co.uk/news/uk-33638492 [Accessed 21/07/2016].

58 Scahill, *Blackwater*.

59 Hughes, *War on Terror, Inc.*

60 Ibid.

61 Klein, *The Shock Doctrine*.

62 Mallinson, *The Making of the British Army*; Der Derian, *Virtuous War.*

63 R. Stahl, *Militainment, Inc.: War, Media and Popular Culture* (New York: Routledge, 2010), 6; Bruce Bennett, 'Framing Terror : Cinema, Docudrama and the War on Terror', *Studies in Documentary Film*, 4, no. 3 (2010): 209–225; Des Freedman and Daya Kishan Thussu, eds, *Media and Terrorism: Global Perspectives* (London: SAGE Publications, 2012).

64 Jean Baudrillard, 'War Porn', trans. Paul Taylor, *Journal of Visual Culture*, 5, no. 1 (2006): 86–88.

65 Nick Hopkins, 'Prince Harry: How the MoD Gambled to Keep Him Safe – from the Media', Guardian, 22 January 2013, www.theguardian.com/uk/2013/jan/21/mod-gamble-prince-harry-afghanistan [Accessed 28/03/2016].

66 Howard Tumber and Jerry Palmer, *Media at War: The Iraq Crisis* (London: SAGE Publications, 2004).

67 Judith Butler, 'Photography, War, Outrage', *PMLA*, 120, no. 3 (2005): 822–827.

68 Tom Latchem, 'Prince Harry Might Think War Is Just a Game, but as a Propaganda Tool', Independent, 22 January 2013, www.independent.co.uk/voices/comment/prince-harry-might-think-war-is-just-a-game-but-as-a-propaganda-tool-he-has-his-safety-afghanistans-8461796.html [Accessed 19/07/2016].

69 Guardian, 'Prince Harry May Be a Captain, but He Is No Marvel', Guardian, 22 January 2013, www.theguardian.com/commentisfree/2013/jan/22/prince-harry-afghanistan-editorial [Accessed 11/04/2016].

70 Prochaska, *Royal Bounty*.

71 Littler, 'The New Victorians?'.

72 Prochaska, *Royal Bounty*, 275.

73 Krista Hunt, '"Embedded Feminism" and the War on Terror', in *(En)gendering the War on Terror: War Stories and Camouflaged Politics*, ed. Krista Hunt and Kim Rygiel (Aldershot: Ashgate, 2006); Jasbir K. Puar, *Terrorist Assemblages: Homonationalism in Queer Times* (Durham, NC, and London: Duke University Press, 2007).

74 Invictus Games Foundation, 'Prince Harry Launches a New International Sporting Event for Wounded, Injured and Sick Service Personnel Today'.

75 Invictus Games Foundation, 'Invictus Games Foundation'.

76 William Ernest Henley, 'Invictus', Poets, unknown, https://poets.org/poem/invictus [Accessed 18/08/2020].

77 Dan Warburton, 'Shocking Truth of an Armed Forces Suicide Every 2 WEEKS', Mirrror, 5 March 2016, www.mirror.co.uk/news/uk-news/armed-forces-suicide-every-2-7503692 [Accessed 21/07/2016].

78 Littler, 'The New Victorians?', 472.

79 Joanna Tidy, 'Forces Sauces and Eggs for Soldiers: Food, Nostalgia, and the Rehabilitation of the British Military'. *Critical Military Studies*, 1, no. 3 (2015): 220–232, 226; Paul Achter, 'Unruly Bodies: The Rhetorical Domestication of Twenty-First-Century Veterans of War', *Quarterly Journal of Speech*, 96, no. 1 (2010): 46–68.

80 R.J. Berger, 'Disability and the Dedicated Wheelchair Athlete: Beyond the "Supercrip" Critique', *Journal of Contemporary Ethnography*, 37, no. 6 (2008): 648.

81 P. David Howe, 'Cyborg and Supercrip: The Paralympics Technology and the (Dis)Empowerment of Disabled Athletes', *Sociology*, 45, no. 5 (2011): 868–882.

82 Sayer, *Why We Can't Afford the Rich*.

83 Invictus Games Foundation, 'Concentrating on the Clock: The Jaguar Land Rover Driving Challenge', Invictus Games Foundation (blog), 2017,

www.invictusgames2017.com/concentrating-on-the-clock-the-jaguar-land-rover-driving-challenge/ [Accessed 01/10/2018].

84 Imogen Tyler and Tom Slater, 'Introduction: Rethinking the Sociology of Stigma', *The Sociological Review Monographs*, 66, no. 4 (2018): 727.

85 BBC, 'Record Annual Sales for Jaguar Land Rover', BBC News, 8 January 2018, www.bbc.co.uk/news/business-42603271 [Accessed 10/01/2018].

86 Littler, 'The New Victorians?', 247.

87 R.W. Connell, *Masculinities* (London: Polity Press, 1995).

88 Sarah Banet-Weiser, *Empowered: Popular Feminism and Popular Misogyny* (Durham, NC, and London: Duke University Press, 2018).

89 T. Bridges and C.J. Pascoe, 'Hybrid Masculinities: New Directions in the Sociology of Men and Masculinities.', *Sociology Compass*, 8 (2014): 246.

90 Grayson Perry, *The Descent of Man* (London: Penguin, 2017); Robert Webb, *How Not to Be a Boy* (Edinburgh: Canongate Books, 2017).

91 Molly Gunn, 'Move over Mumsnet: All Hail the Dad Bloggers of Instagram', Telegraph, 17 June 2016, www.telegraph.co.uk/men/thinking-man/move-over-mumsnet-all-hail-the-dad-bloggers-of-instagram/ [Accessed 17/06/2016]; Hannah Hamad, '"Hollywood's Hot Dads": Tabloid, Reality and Scandal Discourses of Celebrity Post-Feminist Fatherhood', *Celebrity Studies*, 1, no. 2 (2010): 151–169.

92 John C. Landreau, 'Fighting Words: Obama, Masculinity and the Rhetoric of National Security', Thirdspace: A Journal of Feminist Theory & Culture, 10, no. 1 (2011), http://journals.sfu.ca/thirdspace/index.php/journal/article/view/landreau; Carol Johnson, 'From Obama to Abbott', *Australian Feminist Studies*, 28, no. 75 (2013): 14–29.

93 Michael DeAngelis, ed., *Reading the Bromance: Homosocial Relationships in Film and Television* (Detroit: Wayne State University Press, 2014), 2; Hannah Furness, '"How's Meghan?": Prince Harry and Barack Obama Rekindle "bromance" at Invictus Games', Telegraph, 29 September 2017, www.telegraph.co.uk/news/2017/09/29/prince-harry-barack-obama-rekindle-bromance-invictus-games/ [Accessed 18/07/2018].

94 The 'mic drop' is the gesture of intentionally dropping a microphone at the end of a performance to suggest triumph.

95 Dan Roberts, 'Obamas, Prince Harry and the Queen Trade Mic Drops in Comedy Sketch', Guardian, 29 April 2016, www.theguardian.com/us-news/2016/apr/29/obamas-prince-harry-queen-elizabeth-invictus-games-video [Accessed 18/07/2018].

96 Jo Littler, *Against Meritocracy*, 126.

97 'Diana, Our Mother: Her Life and Legacy' (dir. Ashley Gething, ITV One, 24 July 2017).

98 Hannah Furness, 'Prince Harry: I Sought Counselling after 20 Years of Not Thinking about the Death of My Mother, Diana, and Two Years of Total Chaos in My Life', Telegraph, 19 April 2017, www.telegraph.co.uk/

news/2017/04/16/prince-harry-sought-counselling-death-mother-led-two-years-total/ [Accessed 26/05/2017].

99 Ibid.

100 Eva Wiseman, 'It's Good to Talk about Mental Health. But Is It Enough?', *Guardian*, 14 May 2017, www.theguardian.com/lifeandstyle/2017/may/14/mental-health-awareness-prince-harry-william-theresa-may-health-cuts [Accessed 10/01/2018].

101 Heads Together, 'About Heads Together', 2018, www.headstogether.org.uk/about-heads-together/ [Accessed 10/01/2018].

102 Fiona McQueen, 'Male Emotionality: "Boys Don't Cry" versus "It's Good to Talk"', *NORMA: International Journal for Masculinity Studies*, 12, nos 3–4 (2017): 205–219; Frank Furedi, *Therapy Culture: Cultivating Vulnerability in an Uncertain Age* (London: Routledge, 2004), 1.

103 Eva Illouz, *Cold Intimacies: The Making of Emotional Capitalism* (Cambridge: Polity Press, 2007); Arlie Russell Hochschild, *The Managed Heart: Commercialization of Human Feeling*, Updated (Los Angeles: University of California Press, 2012).

104 Eva Illouz, *Saving the Modern Soul: Therapy, Emotions and the Culture of Self-Help* (Berkeley and Los Angeles: University of California Press, 2008).

105 Beverley Skeggs and Helen Wood, 'The Moral Economy of Person Production: The Class Relations of Self-Performance on "Reality" Television', *The Sociological Review*, 57, no. 4 (2009): 626–644; Skeggs and Wood, *Reacting to Reality Television*; Helen Wood, Beverley Skeggs and Nancy Thumim, '"It's Just Sad": Affect, Judgement and Emotional Labour in "Reality" Television Viewing', in *Femininity, Domesticity and Popular Culture*, ed. Joanne Hollows and Stacy Gillis (London: Routledge, 2009), 135–150.

106 Skeggs and Wood, *Reacting to Reality Television*, 220; Minna Aslama and Mervi Pantti, 'Talking Alone: Reality TV, Emotions and Authenticity', *European Journal of Cultural Studies*, 9, no. 2 (2006): 168.

107 Wood, Skeggs and Thumim, '"It's Just Sad"'.

108 Sean Redmond, *The Star and the Celebrity Confessional* (London: Routledge, 2011), 13; Wood, Skeggs and Thumim, '"It's Just Sad"'.

109 Jack Royston, 'MUM'S DEATH LED TO TOTAL CHAOS: Prince Harry Reveals His 20-Year Agony over Princess Diana's Death Which Left Him Close to a Breakdown and in Need of Counselling', Sun, 16 April 2017, www.thesun.co.uk/news/3345565/prince-harry-agony-over-diana-death-almost-breakdown-counselling/ [Accessed 14/09/2018].

110 Gething, 'Diana, Our Mother: Her Life and Legacy'; 'Diana: the Panorama Interview' (producer: Mike Robinson, BBC One, 20 November 1995).

111 Arvind Rajagopal, 'Celebrity and the Politics of Charity: Memories of a Missionary Departed', in *Mourning Diana: Nation, Culture and the Performance of*

Grief, ed. Adrian Kear and Deborah Lynn Steinberg (London: Routledge, 1999): 126–141.

112 Gething, 'Diana, Our Mother'.

113 Angela Levin, 'Exclusive: Prince Harry on Chaos after Diana's Death and Why the World Needs "the Magic" of the Royal Family', Newsweek, 21 June 2017, www.newsweek.com/2017/06/30/prince-harry-depression-diana-death-why-world-needs-magic-627833.html [Accessed 04/01/2018].

114 sussexroyal, 'The Duke and Duchess of Sussex on Instagram'.

115 In Prochaska, *Royal Bounty*, 261–262.

116 Billig, *Talking of the Royal Family*, 69.

117 sussexroyal, 'The Duke and Duchess of Sussex on Instagram'.

118 Rebecca English, 'Harry Drops Royal Name to Launch Eco-Friendly Tourism Firm "Travalyst"', Mail Online, 26 February 2020, www.dailymail.co.uk/news/article-8045921/Prince-Harry-today-launch-eco-friendly-Travalyst-firm.html [Accessed 03/07/2020].

119 Ibid.

120 Angela Smith, 'Just Call Me Dave: David Cameron's Perilous Populist Status', *Journal of Language and Politics*, 19, no. 1 (2020): 10–29.

121 Ibid., 10.

Chapter 6: The heteromonarchy: Kate *Middle*ton, '*middle*-classness' and family values

1 Feona Attwood, Jamie Hakim and Alison Winch, 'Mediated Intimacies: Bodies, Technologies and Relationships', *Journal of Gender Studies*, 26, no. 3 (2017): 249–253.

2 Marwick and boyd, 'I Tweet Honestly, I Tweet Passionately'.

3 Sharpe, *Selling the Tudor Monarchy*; Sharpe, *Image Wars*.

4 Jo Spence and Patricia Holland, eds, *Family Snaps: The Meanings of Domestic Photography* (London: Virago, 1991), 5.

5 Lawler, '"Normal People"', 61; Diane Reay, 'Social Mobility, a Panacea for Austere Times: Tales of Emperors, Frogs, and Tadpoles', *British Journal of Sociology of Education*, 34, nos 5–6 (2013): 660–677.

6 Margaret Abrams, 'From Helicopters to Country Piles, How Much Are the Cambridges Worth?', Evening Standard, 12 April 2019, www.standard.co.uk/insider/royalssociety/prince-william-and-kate-middleton-net-worth-a4066281.html [Accessed 22/04/2020].

7 Maybelle Morgan, 'Parents Rank Miley Cyrus as WORST Celebrity Role Model for Children', Mail Online, 25 August 2015, www.dailymail.co.uk/femail/article-3209970/Parents-rank-Miley-Cyrus-WORST-celebrity-role-model-children.html [Accessed 14/05/2018]; Amber Graafland, '6 Reasons Kate Middleton Has Been Voted the Most Influential Style Icon', Mirror,

15 September 2016, www.mirror.co.uk/3am/style/celebrity-fashion/6-
reasons-duchess-cambridge-been-8841164 [Accessed 14/05/2018].

8 Allen et al., 'Welfare Queens, Thrifty Housewives, and Do-It-All Mums';
Repo and Yrjölä, '"We're All Princesses Now"'; Mendick et al., *Celebrity,
Aspiration and Contemporary Youth*.

9 Beatrix Campbell, 'Neoliberal Neopatriarchy: The Case for Gender Revolution', openDemocracy, 6 January 2014, www.opendemocracy.net/5050/
beatrix-campbell/neoliberal-neopatriarchy-case-for-gender-revolution
[Accessed 08/03/2018].

10 Nancy Fraser, 'Feminism, Capitalism and the Cunning of History', *New
Left Review*, II, no. 56 (2009): 97–117; Alison Phipps, *The Politics of the
Body: Gender in a Neoliberal and Neoconservative Age* (Cambridge: Polity Press,
2014).

11 Anne McClintock, 'Family Feuds: Gender, Nationalism and the Family',
Feminist Review, no. 44 (1993): 61–80.

12 Davidoff and Hall, *Family Fortunes*.

13 Betty Friedan, *The Feminine Mystique* (London: Penguin, 1965); Germaine
Greer, *The Female Eunuch* (London: Paladin, 1971); Ann Oakley, *Housewife*
(London: Penguin, 1974); Simone de Beauvoir, *The Second Sex* (London:
Vintage Classics, 1997).

14 Friedan, *The Feminine Mystique*.

15 Shani Orgad, *Heading Home: Motherhood, Work, and the Failed Promise of
Equality* (New York: Columbia University Press, 2019), 79; Susan Faludi,
Backlash: The Undeclared War Against Women (London: Vintage Classics,
1993).

16 Sara Ahmed, *The Promise of Happiness* (Durham, NC: Duke University
Press, 2010), 50.

17 Rebecca Bramall, *The Cultural Politics of Austerity: Past and Present in Austere
Times* (London: Palgrave Macmillan, 2013); see also Allen et al., 'Welfare
Queens, Thrifty Housewives, and Do-It-All Mums'; Tracey Jensen, *Parenting
the Crisis*.

18 Rosalind Gill, 'Postfeminist Media Culture: Elements of a Sensibility',
European Journal of Cultural Studies, 10, no. 2 (2007): 147–166.

19 Angela McRobbie, 'Post-Feminism and Popular Culture', *Feminist Media
Studies*, 4, no. 3 (2004): 256.

20 Rosalind Gill and Shani Orgad, 'The Confidence Cult(ure)', *Australian
Feminist Studies*, 30, no. 86 (2016): 324–344; Angela McRobbie, *The Aftermath
of Feminism* (London: SAGE, 2008); Angela McRobbie, 'Notes on the
Perfect', *Australian Feminist Studies*, 30, no. 83 (2015): 3–20.

21 Rosalind Gill and Elena Herdieckerhoff, 'Rewriting the Romance: New
Femininities in Chick Lit?', *Feminist Media Studies*, 6, no. 4 (2006): 500.

22 Diane Negra, *What a Girl Wants? Fantasizing the Reclamation of Self in
Postfeminism* (London: Routledge, 2009).

23 Jo Littler, 'The Rise of the "Yummy Mummy": Popular Conservatism and the Neoliberal Maternal in Contemporary British Culture', *Communication, Culture & Critique*, 6, no. 2 (2013): 227.

24 Imogen Tyler, 'Pregnant Beauty: Maternal Femininities under Neoliberalism', in *New Femininities: Postfeminism, Neoliberalism and Subjectivity*, ed. Rosalind Gill and Christina Scharff (Bristol: Palgrave Macmillan, 2013), 21–36.

25 Angela McRobbie, 'Feminism and the New Mediated Maternalism: Human Capital at Home', *Feministische Studien*, 31, no. 1 (2013): 136; Jensen, *Parenting the Crisis*.

26 Angela McRobbie, 'Feminism, the Family and the New "Mediated" Maternalism', *New Formations*, 80 and 81 (2013): 119–137.

27 Zillah R. Eisenstein, ed., *Capitalist Patriarchy and the Case for Socialist Feminism* (London: Monthly Review Press, 1979); Maria Mies, *Patriarchy and Accumulation on a World Scale: Women in the International Division of Labour* (London: Zed Books, 1986); Barrett and McIntosh, *The Anti-Social Family*; Silvia Federici, *Revolution at Point Zero* (Oakland: PM Press, 2012).

28 McRobbie, 'Feminism, the Family and the New "Mediated" Maternalism', 130.

29 Annie Kelly, 'The Housewives of White Supremacy', New York Times, 1 June 2018, www.nytimes.com/2018/06/01/opinion/sunday/tradwives-women-alt-right.html [Accessed 17/06/2020].

30 Hadley Freeman, '"Tradwives": The New Trend for Submissive Women Has a Dark Heart and History', Guardian, 27 January 2020, www.theguardian.com/fashion/2020/jan/27/tradwives-new-trend-submissive-women-dark-heart-history [Accessed 08/03/2018].

31 BBC, 'Why I Submit to My Husband like It's 1959', BBC News, 17 January 2020, www.bbc.com/news/av/stories-51113371/tradwife-submitting-to-my-husband-like-it-s-1959 [Accessed 08/03/2018]; thedarlingacademy, 'Alena Kate Pettitt on Instagram', Instagram, 21 April 2020, www.instagram.com/p/B_PO8_on4qs/ [Accessed 08/03/2018].

32 Alena Pettitt, 'Lessons from a Duchess. How Does Kate Do It?', The Darling Academy etiquette books, n.d., www.thedarlingacademy.com/articles/lessons-from-a-duchess-how-does-kate-do-it/ [Accessed 08/03/2018].

33 Jensen, *Parenting the Crisis*; Ian Bruff, 'The Rise of Authoritarian Neoliberalism', *Rethinking Marxism*, 26, no. 1 (2014): 113–129.

34 Wendy Brown and Jo Littler, 'Interview: Where the Fires Are', *Soundings: A Journal of Politics and Culture*, no. 68 (Spring 2018): 15.

35 Phipps, *The Politics of the Body*.

36 Sylvia Yanagisako, 'Accumulating Family Values'; Jo Littler, 'Normcore Plutocrats in Gold Elevators: Reading the Trump Tower Photographs.', *Cultural Politics*, 15, no. 1 (2019): 15–28; Laura Bear, Karen Ho, Anna Lowenhaupt Tsing and Sylvia Yanagisako, 'Gens: A Feminist Manifesto

Notes

for the Study of Capitalism', Society for Cultural Anthropology, 30 March 2015, https://culanth.org/fieldsights/gens-a-feminist-manifesto-for-the-study-of-capitalism; Luna Glucksberg, 'A Gendered Ethnography of Elites', *Focaal*, no. 18 (2018): 16–28.

37 Luna Glucksberg and Roger Burrows, 'Family Offices and the Contemporary Infrastructures of Dynastic Wealth', *Sociologica*, 2 (2016): 16.

38 Melinda Cooper, *Family Values: Between Neoliberalism and the New Social Conservatism* (New York: Zone Books, 2017), 69.

39 Yanagisako, 'Accumulating Family Values'.

40 Laura Briggs, *How All Politics Became Reproductive Politics: From Welfare Reform to Foreclosure to Trump* (Berkeley: University of California Press, 2017), 17; Lisa Duggan, 'The New Homonormativity: The Sexual Politics of Neoliberalism', in *Materializing Democracy: Toward a Revitalized Cultural Politics*, ed. Russ Castronovo and Dana D. Nelson (Durham, NC: Duke University Press, 2002), 175–194.

41 Michael Russell, 'The Kuleshov Effect and the Death of the Auteur', FORUM: University of Edinburgh Postgraduate Journal of Culture & the Arts, no. 01 (2005): 6, www.forumjournal.org/article/view/547.

42 'A Berry Royal Christmas' (dir. Sarah Myland and Lana Salah, BBC One, 16 October 2019).

43 Mantel, 'Royal Bodies', London Review of Books, 35, no. 4 (21 February 2013) www.lrb.co.uk/the-paper/v35/n04/hilary-mantel/royal-bodies [Accessed 02/12/2014].

44 Gordon Rayner, 'Prince George's £85 Christening Outfit Sells out after His Starring Role on Princess Charlotte's Big Day', Telegraph, 6 July 2015, www.telegraph.co.uk/news/uknews/prince-george/11720815/Prince-Georges-85-christening-outfit-sells-out-after-his-starring-role-on-Princess-Charlottes-big-day.html [Accessed 14/05/2018].

45 Jo Tweedy, 'Princess Charlotte Makes Vintage Prams All the Rage', Mail Online, 6 July 2015, www.dailymail.co.uk/femail/article-3150740/A-regal-carriage-Princess-Charlotte-enjoys-ride-royal-heirloom-christening-Harrods-launches-range-bespoke-5-000-coach-built-prams.html [Accessed 14/05/2018].

46 kensingtonroyal, 'Duke and Duchess of Cambridge on Instagram', Instagram, 5 July 2015, www.instagram.com/p/4wq1vmqZHl/ [Accessed 17/08/2020].

47 Ahmed, *The Promise of Happiness*, 90.

48 Lauren Berlant, *Cruel Optimism* (Durham, NC: Duke University Press, 2011), 2.

49 What Would Kate Do?, 'Goat Washington Coat', repliKate, 6 November 2017, http://replikate.co/product/goat-washington-coat/ [Accessed 26/11/2018].

50 Catherine Ostler, 'Queen of the Yummy Mummies and Her Tiny Trendsetter – Kate's Choice of Pram, Toys and Name Will Set Global

Trends', Mail Online, 5 December 2012, www.dailymail.co.uk/femail/article-2243142/Kate-Middleton-Queen-Yummy-Mummies-choice-pram-toys-set-global-trends.html [Accessed 28/04/2020].

51 Friedan, *The Feminine Mystique*.

52 Negra, *What a Girl Wants?*, 125.

53 Berlant, *Cruel Optimism*.

54 Littler, 'The Rise of the "Yummy Mummy"', 227.

55 C.R. Staff, 'The Dress Kate Middleton Wore that Wooed Prince William', CR Fashion Book, 9 January 2020, www.crfashionbook.com/celebrity/a25804498/kate-middleton-birthday-charity-dress/ [Accessed 28/04/2020].

56 Katie Nicholl, '"Waity Katie" Has a Wobble as Prince William Commits Seven Years to the RAF', Mail Online, 8 November 2008, www.dailymail.co.uk/tvshowbiz/article-1084113/Waity-Katie-wobble-Prince-William-commits-seven-years-RAF.html [Accessed 22/05/2018].

57 Janet McCabe, 'And Bringing up the Rear: Pippa Middleton, Her Derrière and Celebrity as Feminine Ideal', *Celebrity Studies*, 2, no. 3 (2011): 355–357.

58 Kim Willsher, 'Court Awards Duchess of Cambridge Damages over Topless Photos', Guardian, 5 September 2017, www.theguardian.com/uk-news/2017/sep/05/topless-photos-of-duchess-of-cambridge-were-invasion-of-privacy [Accessed 19/04/2018]; Finneman and Thomas, 'The British National Press and the 2012 Royal Family Photo Scandals'.

59 Beverley Skeggs, *Class, Self, Culture* (London: Routledge, 2004), 99.

60 Abigail Malbon, 'Kate Middleton's £40 Zara Dress Is the Look We All Need This Summer', Cosmopolitan, 11 June 2018, www.cosmopolitan.com/uk/fashion/celebrity/a21263730/kate-middleton-zara-dress-polo/ [Accessed 15/10/2018].

61 Lauren Milligan, 'Duchess of Cambridge Vogue Cover', Vogue, 30 April 2016, www.vogue.co.uk/article/duchess-of-cambridge-vogue-cover-catherine-centenary-issue [Accessed 17/06/2020].

62 Littler, *Against Meritocracy*, 124.

63 Sutcliffe-Braithwaite, *Class, Politics, and the Decline of Deference in England*, 6; 7.

64 Littler, *Against Meritocracy*, 115.

65 Sykes, 'The New Royal Baby and the "Middletonization" of the Royal Family'.

66 'When Kate Met William: A Tale of Two Lives' (dir. Stuart Ramsay, ITV One, 26 April 2011).

67 Referring to a semi-detached house.

68 Christopher Wilson, 'Kate, the Coal Miner's Girl', Mail Online, 22 December 2006, www.dailymail.co.uk/femail/article-424446/Kate-coal-miners-girl.html [Accessed 31/08/2016].

69 Gordon Rayner, 'Royal Wedding: Kate Waves Farewell to Her Life as a Commoner', Daily Telegraph, 28 April 2011, www.telegraph.co.uk/news/uknews/royal-wedding/8481716/Royal-wedding-Kate-waves-farewell-to-her-life-as-a-commoner.html [Accessed 12/02/2018].

70 Elizabeth Nix, 'British Royals Have Been Scandalously Marrying Commoners Since 1464', History, 15 June 2017, www.history.com/news/british-royals-have-been-scandalously-marrying-commoners-since-1464 [Accessed 28/08/2018].

71 Littler, Against Meritocracy, 3.

72 Billig, Talking of the Royal Family.

73 Ramsay, 'When Kate Met William: A Tale of Two Lives'.

74 Mike Savage, Social Class in the 21st Century (London: Pelican, 2015), 392.

75 Rosalia Baena and Christa Byker, 'Dialects of Nostalgia: Downton Abbey and English Identity', National Identities, 17, no. 3 (2015): 261.

76 Pimlott, The Queen.

77 Campbell, Diana, Princess of Wales, 7.

78 Andrew Morton, Diana: Her True Story (London: Michael O'Mara Books Ltd, 1992); Campbell, Diana, Princess of Wales; Nicola Oakley, 'The Toe-Sucking Photo that Drove Sarah Ferguson out of the Royal Family', Mirror, 28 May 2020, www.mirror.co.uk/news/uk-news/toe-sucking-photo-drove-sarah-13384631 [Accessed 17/06/2020].

79 Laura Clancy and Hannah Yelin, 'Monarchy Is a Feminist Issue: Andrew, Meghan and #MeToo Era Monarchy', Women's Studies International Forum, 2021, Online first, https://doi.org/10.1016/j.wsif.2020.102435.

80 Anna Clark, Scandal: The Sexual Politics of the British Constitution (Princeton: Princeton University Press, 2004); David Loades, Henry VIII and His Queens (Stroud: Sutton Publishing, 1994).

81 Stephanie Coontz, Marriage, a History (London: Penguin, 2005).

82 Repo and Yrjölä, '"We're All Princesses Now"'.

83 Ibid., 8.

84 Tom Sykes and Lachlan Cartwright, 'Prince William's Lawyer Tries to Suppress Rumors of Affair', The Daily Beast, 9 April 2019, www.thedailybeast.com/prince-williams-lawyer-tries-to-suppress-rumors-of-affair [Accessed 16/06/2015].

85 Ibid.

86 Ibid.

87 Margaret Schwartz, 'Diana's Rings: Fetishizing the Royal Couple', in First Comes Love: Power Couples, Celebrity Kinship and Cultural Politics, ed. Shelley Cobb and Neil Ewen (London: Bloomsbury, 2015), 161.

88 Peter Hunt, 'Taj Mahal Pictures of Duke and Duchess Create "New Royal Narrative"', BBC News, 16 April 2016, www.bbc.co.uk/news/uk-36062176 [Accessed 18/04/2016].

89 Rebecca English, 'William and Kate's Annus MIRABILIS: Reinvention of the Cambridges', Mail Online, 20 December 2019, www.dailymail.co.uk/news/article-7815275/William-Kates-annus-MIRABILIS-Reinvention-Cambridges.html [Accessed 04/05/2020].

90 Lara Prendergast, 'How Norland Nannies Became the Ultimate Status Symbol', Spectator, 23 January 2016, www.spectator.co.uk/2016/01/how-having-a-norland-nanny-became-a-status-symbol-for-sheikhs-and-oligarchs/ [Accessed 23/09/2016].

91 Miranda Knox, 'Kate Middleton's VAST Family Fortune Uncovered', OK! Magazine, 23 May 2017, www.ok.co.uk/celebrity-feature/1052434/kate-middleton-net-worth-family-fortune-uncovered-prince-william-princess-charlotte-prince-george [Accessed 14/05/2018].

92 Rob Cooper, 'Kate's Brother James Middleton Says Success Is All down to His Hard Graft (Although His Royal Connections Probably Don't Hurt)', Mail Online, 12 March 2012, www.dailymail.co.uk/news/article-2113755/Duchess-Cambridge-Kate-Middletons-brother-James-says-success-hard-graft.html [Accessed 16/04/2018].

93 Lawler, 'Normal People', 62.

94 Matt Bagwell, 'Spencer Matthews Will Soon Be Related to Actual Royalty', HuffPost UK, 19 July 2016, www.huffingtonpost.co.uk/entry/spencer-matthews-made-in-chelsea-pippa-middleton-engagenment_uk_578dc6aae4b0885619b10820 [Accessed 28/08/2018]; Lawler, '"Normal People": Recognition and the Middle Classes'.

95 Michael Deacon, 'Royal Baby Sketch: "Breaking News: We Have No News!"', Telegraph, 22 July 2013, www.telegraph.co.uk/news/uknews/theroyalfamily/10195749/Royal-baby-sketch-Breaking-news-we-have-no-news.html [Accessed 14/05/2018].

96 Mantel, 'Royal Bodies'.

97 British Library, 'Westminster Jousting Challenge', Text, Catalogue of Illuminated Manuscripts (The British Library), www.bl.uk/catalogues/illuminatedmanuscripts/record.asp?MSID=7238 [Accessed 17/06/2020].

98 The Official Website of the British Monarchy, 'The Duchess of Cambridge', 2018, www.royal.uk/the-duchess-of-cambridge [Accessed 17/07/2018].

99 Rebecca English, 'Prince George Meets New Zealand Babies', Mail Online, 9 April 2014, www.dailymail.co.uk/news/article-2600284/Young-prince-meets-New-Zealand-babies-families-official-public-engagement.html [Accessed 07/05/2020].

100 McRobbie, 'Feminism, the Family and the New "Mediated" Maternalism', 136.

101 Giovanna Fletcher, 'Happy Mum, Happy Baby: The Duchess of Cambridge Transcript – Blog', Giovanna Fletcher, 2020, www.giovannafletcher.com/

blog/posts/happy-mum-happy-baby-the-duchess-of-cambridge [Accessed 07/05/2020].

102 Katariina Mäkinen, 'Negotiating the Intimate and the Professional in Mom Blogging', in *The New Normal of Working Lives: Critical Studies in Contemporary Work and Employment*, ed. Stephanie Taylor and Susan Luckman (Cham: Springer International Publishing, 2018), 129–146.

103 Loades, *Henry VIII and His Queens*.

104 McClintock, 'Family Feuds', 63.

105 Smith, *Down with the Royals*, 17; Mike Woods, Elizabeth Joyce, Santa Patel and Charlotte Cross, 'Wills and Kate: The People's Wedding', *Express and Star*, 29 April 2011: 1.

106 Shome, *Diana and Beyond*, 23.

107 Nicholas Reilly, 'Prince George Looks Super Cute for His First Ever Stamp', Metro, 20 April 2016, https://metro.co.uk/2016/04/20/prince-george-makes-his-debut-on-stamps-launched-for-queens-90th-birthday-5828337/ [Accessed 05/05/2020].

108 Cooper, *Family Values*; Jensen, *Parenting the Crisis*.

109 Miranda Christou, '#TradWives: Sexism as Gateway to White Supremacy', openDemocracy, 17 March 2020, www.opendemocracy.net/en/countering-radical-right/tradwives-sexism-gateway-white-supremacy/ [Accessed 06/05/2020].

110 BBC, 'Why I Submit to My Husband like It's 1959'.

111 Agnieszka Graff, Ratna Kapur and Suzanna Danuta Walters, 'Introduction: Gender and the Rise of the Global Right', *Signs: Journal of Women in Culture and Society*, 44, no. 3 (2019): 551.

112 Briggs, *How All Politics Became Reproductive Politics*; Federici, *Caliban and the Witch*; Jensen, *Parenting the Crisis*.

113 Allen et al., 'Welfare Queens, Thrifty Housewives, and Do-It-All Mums'.

114 Eleanor Newbigin, 'Brexit, Nostalgia and the Great British Fantasy', openDemocracy, 15 February 2017, www.opendemocracy.net/en/brexit-britain-and-nostalgia-for-fantasy-past/ [Accessed 05/05/2020].

115 Caroline Davies, '"We Will Meet Again": Queen Urges Britons to Stay Strong', Guardian, 5 April 2020, www.theguardian.com/world/2020/apr/05/queen-urges-britons-stay-strong-coronavirus-covid-lockdown [Accessed 17/06/2020].

116 Helen Wood and Beverley Skeggs, 'Clap for Carers? From Care Gratitude to Care Justice', European Journal of Cultural Studies, 2020, Online first, https://doi.org/10.1177/1367549420928362.

117 Ibid.

118 Rosalind Brunt, 'Conversations on the Diana Moment and Its Politics', *Journal of Gender Studies*, 8, no. 3 (1 November 1999): 286.

119 kensingtonroyal, '@kensingtonroyal Shared a Photo on Instagram', Instagram, 4 May 2020, www.instagram.com/p/B_qQ7lDF-88/ [Accessed 17/08/2020].

120 Campbell, *Diana, Princess of Wales*, 7.

121 Chelsea Ritschel, 'The First-Ever Royal Same-Sex Wedding, in Pictures', Independent, 25 September 2018, www.independent.co.uk/life-style/lord-ivar-mountbatten-james-coyle-wedding-gay-royal-family-a8554721.html[Accessed 17/10/2018].

Chapter 7: Megxitting the Firm: Race, postcolonialism and diversity capital

1 'Suits' (dir. Aaron Korsch, USA Network, 2011-); *Remember Me* (dir. Allen Coulter, Summit Entertainment, 2010); *Get Him to the Greek* (dir. Nicholas Stoller, Universal Pictures, 2010).

2 The Official Website of the British Monarchy, 'The Duchess of Sussex', 18 May 2018, www.royal.uk/duchess-sussex [Accessed 17/07/2018].

3 Clancy and Yelin, '"Meghan's Manifesto"'.

4 Chauncey Bitette and Nicole Alcorn, 'Al Sharpton Says Royal Wedding Shows White Supremacy Is "on Its Last Breath"', 19 May 2018, nydailynews.com/news/world/al-sharpton-royal-wedding-shows-white-supremacy-ending-article-1.3998555 [Accessed 21/05/2018].

5 Helen Scott, 'The Royal Wedding: Prince Harry and Meghan Markle' (London: BBC, 19 May 2018).

6 Clancy and Yelin, '"Meghan's Manifesto"'.

7 Emily Andrews, 'Kisstory: Harry & Meg's Historic Change for Monarchy', *Sun*, 20 May 2018.

8 The Official Website of the British Monarchy, 'The Duchess of Sussex'.

9 The Official Website of the British Monarchy, 'The Duchess of Cambridge'.

10 Clancy and Yelin, '"Meghan's Manifesto"'.

11 sussexroyal, 'The Duke and Duchess of Sussex on Instagram', Instagram, 8 January 2020, www.instagram.com/p/B7EaGS_Jpb9/ [Accessed 25/08/2020].

12 Mark Landler, '"Megxit" Is the New Brexit in a Britain Split by Age and Politics', New York Times, 15 January 2020, www.nytimes.com/2020/01/15/world/europe/harry-meghan-megxit-brexit.html [Accessed 17/01/2020]; Richard Kay, 'Inside Megxit Summit: Harry Talked to Queen Alone to Give Her His Side', Mail Online, 13 January 2020, www.dailymail.co.uk/news/article-7883451/Inside-Megxit-summit-Harry-talked-Queen-story.html [Accessed 26/06/2020].

13 Satnam Virdee and Brendan McGeever, 'Racism, Crisis, Brexit', *Ethnic and Racial Studies*, 41, no. 10 (2017): 1802–1819.

14 Amna Saleem, 'Harry and Meghan Were Meant to Embody Post-Racial Britain. So Much for That', Guardian, 11 January 2020, www.theguardian.com/commentisfree/2020/jan/11/post-racial-britain-harry-meghan-tabloids [Accessed 13/01/2020].

15 Afua Hirsch, 'Black Britons Know Why Meghan Markle Wants Out', New York Times, 9 January 2020, www.nytimes.com/2020/01/09/opinion/sunday/meghan-markle-prince-harry.html [Accessed 26/06/2020].

16 Aidan Barlow, 'Politician Sparks Outrage for Posting Racist Image of Meghan Markle on Twitter', Mirror, 10 February 2018, www.mirror.co.uk/news/uk-news/trump-supporting-politician-sparks-outrage-12006200 [Accessed 13/02/2018].

17 Jessica Elgot, 'Ukip Leader Urged to Quit over Girlfriend's "Racist" Meghan Markle Remarks', Guardian, 14 January 2018, www.theguardian.com/politics/2018/jan/14/ukip-leader-henry-bolton-girlfriend-jo-marney-suspended-meghan-merkle [Accessed 12/03/2018].

18 Defend Europa, 'I Stand With Holly: Scottish Girl Becomes Unlikely Hero of the Right as She Fends Off Online Bullies', Defend Europa, 20 May 2018, www.defendevropa.org/2018/heritage-identity/i-stand-with-holly/ [Accessed 21/05/2018].

19 Communications Secretary, 'A Statement by the Communications Secretary to Prince Harry', 8 November 2016, www.royal.uk/statement-communications-secretary-prince-harry [Accessed 21/05/2018].

20 Moya Bailey and Trudy, 'On Misogynoir: Citation, Erasure, and Plagiarism', *Feminist Media Studies*, 18, no. 4 (2018): 762–768.

21 Kehinde Andrews, 'The Post-Racial Princess: Delusions of Racial Progress and Intersectional Failures', Women's Studies International Forum, 2021, Online first, https://doi.org/10.1016/j.wsif.2020.102432.

22 Sara Ahmed, *On Being Included: Racism and Diversity in Institutional Life* (Durham, NC, and London: Duke University Press, 2012), 41.

23 Landler, '"Megxit" Is the New Brexit'.

24 Kay, 'Inside Megxit Summit'.

25 Landler, '"Megxit" Is the New Brexit'.

26 Nathalie Weidhase, '"Prince Harry Has Gone Over to the Dark Side": Race, Royalty and US–UK Romance in Brexit Britain', in *Love Across the Atlantic*, ed. Barbara Jane Brickman, Deborah Jermyn and Theodore Louis Trost (Edinburgh: Edinburgh University Press, 2020), 282.

27 Mark Duell, 'Meghan Markle's Old School Headmistress Watches the Royal Wedding', Mail Online, 19 May 2018, www.dailymail.co.uk/news/fb-5748267/Meghan-Markles-old-school-headmistress-stays-early-hours-watch-royal-wedding.html [Accessed 22/06/2020].

Notes

28 Virdee and McGeever, 'Racism, Crisis, Brexit'; Gilroy, *After Empire*.

29 Valluvan, *The Clamour of Nationalism*, 3.

30 Virdee and McGeever, 'Racism, Crisis, Brexit'; Hannah Jones, Yasmin Gunaratnam, Gargi Bhattacharyya, William Davies, Sukhwant Dhaliwal, Emma Jackson and Roiyah Saltus, *Go Home? The Politics of Immigration Controversies* (Manchester: Manchester University Press, 2017); Nadine En-Enany *(B)Ordering Britain: Law, Race and Empire* (Manchester: Manchester University Press, 2020).

31 Barbara Smith, 'I Helped Coin the Term "Identity Politics". I'm Endorsing Bernie Sanders', Guardian, 10 February 2020, www.theguardian.com/commentisfree/2020/feb/10/identity-politics-bernie-sanders-endorsement [Accessed 26/06/2020].

32 Piers Morgan, 'Meghan and Harry Haven't Been Criticized Because of Her Color but Because She's a Selfish Social Climber and He's a Weak Whiner', Daily Mail, 13 January 2020, www.dailymail.co.uk/news/article-7881661/PIERS-MORGAN-playing-despicable-race-card-Meghan-Harry-libeled-Britain.html [Accessed 26/06/2020]; Piers Morgan, 'Harry and Meghan Should Stop Behaving like Spoiled Brats', Daily Mail, 14 November 2019, www.dailymail.co.uk/news/article-7686455/PIERS-MORGAN-Harry-Meghan-stop-behaving-like-spoiled-brats.html [Accessed 26/06/2020]; Piers Morgan, 'Meghan Markle's Shamelessly Hypocritical Vogue Stunt', Daily Mail, 29 July 2019, www.dailymail.co.uk/news/article-7298003/PIERS-MORGAN-Meghans-shamelessly-hypocritical-Vogue-stunt.html [Accessed 26/06/2020].

33 Tim Newark, 'I Can't Bring Myself to Vote ... Thanks to the Liberal Elite, Says TIM NEWARK', Express, 1 May 2019, www.express.co.uk/comment/expresscomment/1121295/voting-european-election-liberal-elite [Accessed 26/06/2020]; Sherelle Jacobs, 'From Meghan to Greta, Our "Woke" Liberal Elite Is Trapped in a Backwards Parallel Universe', Telegraph, 1 August 2019, www.telegraph.co.uk/politics/2019/08/01/meghan-greta-woke-liberal-elite-trapped-backwards-parallel-universe/ [Accessed 26/06/2020].

34 Hannah Yelin and Laura Clancy, 'Doing Impact Work While Female: Hate Tweets, "Hot Potatoes" and Having "Enough of Experts"', European Journal of Women's Studies, Online first (2020), https://doi.org/10.1177/1350506820910194.

35 Russell Myers, 'Queen Orders a Hard Megxit', *Sunday Mirror*, 19 January 2020.

36 Helen Lewis, 'Meghan, Kate, and the Architecture of Misogyny', The Atlantic, 16 January 2020, www.theatlantic.com/international/archive/2020/01/meghan-markle-kate-middleton-royals-culture-war/604981/ [Accessed 27/01/2020].

37 @sussexroyal, 'The Duke and Duchess of Sussex on Instagram', Insta-
    gram, 8 May 2019, www.instagram.com/p/BxNPb_9Bofn/ [Accessed
    10/05/2019].

38 Colleen Harris, 'The Day the Monarchy Embraced Britain's Multicul-
    tural Future', Mail Online, 19 May 2018, www.dailymail.co.uk/news/
    article-5748889/Royal-wedding-day-Monarchy-embraced-Britains-future-
    ex-royal-aide-COLLEEN-HARRIS.html [Accessed 15/05/2020].

39 Afua Hirsch, 'Meghan Markle's Wedding Was a Rousing Celebra-
    tion of Blackness', Guardian, 20 May 2018, www.theguardian.com/
    uk-news/2018/may/19/meghan-markles-wedding-was-a-celebration-of-
    blackness [Accessed 21/05/2018]; Afua Hirsch, *Brit(Ish): On Race, Identity
    and Belonging* (London: Jonathan Cape, 2018).

40 @MsJillMJones, 'What I LOVEd SO MUCH about This Ceremony ...',
    Twitter (blog), 19 May 2018, https://twitter.com/MsJillMJones?ref_src
    =twsrc%5Egoogle%7Ctwcamp%5Eserp%7Ctwgr%5Eauthor [Accessed
    21/05/2018]; @yemsxo, 'SORRY WHAT A TIME TO BE ALIVE! IM
    SO HAPPY!', Twitter (blog), 19 May 2018, https://twitter.com/yemsxo/
    status/997802377251053568 [Accessed 21/05/2018].

41 Erin Blakemore, 'Meghan Markle Might Not Be the First Mixed-Race
    British Royal', History, 8 May 2018, www.history.com/news/biracial-
    royalty-meghan-markle-queen-charlotte [Accessed 17/07/2019].

42 Celia Lury, 'The United Colors of Diversity', in *Images: A Reader*, ed.
    Sarah Franklin, Celia Lury and Jackie Stacey (London: SAGE, 2000),
    261; Henry A. Giroux, 'Consuming Social Change: The "United Colors
    of Benetton"', *Cultural Critique*, no. 26 (1993): 5–32; Les Back and Vibeke
    Quaade, 'Dream Utopias, Nightmare Realities: Imaging Race and Culture
    within the World of Benetton Advertising', *Third Text*, 7, no. 22 (1993):
    65–80.

43 David Crockett, 'Marketing Blackness: How Advertisers Use Race to
    Sell Products', *Journal of Consumer Culture*, 8, no. 2 (2008): 261.

44 Jennifer Fuller, 'Branding Blackness on US Cable Television', *Media,
    Culture & Society*, 32, no. 2 (2010): 289.

45 Anne-Marie Fortier, *Multicultural Horizons: Diversity and the Limits of the
    Civil Nation* (London: Routledge, 2008); Ahmed, *On Being Included*.

46 Fortier, *Multicultural Horizons*, 93.

47 Ahmed, *On Being Included*.

48 Ibid.

49 Cedric Robinson, *Black Marxism: The Making of the Black Radical Tradition*
    (Chapel Hill: University of North Carolina Press, 1983), 2.

50 Tyler, *Stigma*.

51 Janet L. Borgerson, Jonathan E. Schroeder, Martin Escudero Magnus-
    son and Frank Magnusson, 'Corporate Communication, Ethics, and

Operational Identity: A Case Study of Benetton', *Business Ethics: A European Review*, 18, no. 3 (2009): 209–223.

52 Ibid.

53 Friedman and Laurison, *The Class Ceiling*.

54 Andrew Morton, *Meghan: A Hollywood Princess* (London: Michael O'Mara Books Ltd, 2018).

55 Vogue, 'Forces for Change', *Vogue*, September 2019.

56 BBC News, 'Meghan Guest Edits Vogue's September Issue', BBC News, 29 July 2019, www.bbc.com/news/uk-49145664 [Accessed 07/08/2020].

57 Meghan Markle in *Vogue*, 'Forces for Change', 84.

58 Ibid.

59 Seth Jacobson, 'Duchess of Sussex to Guest Edit September UK Vogue Issue', Guardian, 28 July 2019, www.theguardian.com/fashion/2019/jul/28/duchess-of-sussex-to-guest-edit-september-uk-vogue-issue [Accessed 26/06/2020].

60 Meghan Markle in *Vogue*, 'Forces for Change', 84.

61 Clancy and Yelin, '"Meghan's Manifesto"'.

62 Clancy and Yelin, 'Monarchy Is a Feminist Issue'.

63 The Hubb Community Kitchen, *Together: Our Community Cookbook* (London: Ebury Press, 2018).

64 Ibid., 6.

65 Clancy, '"This Is a Tale of Friendship, a Story of Togetherness"'.

66 Sarah Young, 'Meghan Markle Speaks about Being a "Woman of Colour" as She Arrives in South Africa', Independent, 23 September 2019, www.independent.co.uk/life-style/women/meghan-markle-woman-of-colour-prince-harry-south-africa-cape-town-a9116896.html [Accessed 03/06/2020].

67 Holly Randell-Moon, 'Thieves like Us: The British Monarchy, Celebrity, and Settler Colonialism', *Celebrity Studies*, 8, no. 3 (2017): 404; Rajagopal, 'Celebrity and the Politics of Charity'.

68 Shome, *Diana and Beyond*, 121.

69 Ibid., 129.

70 Fortier, *Multicultural Horizons*, 37; Ahmed, *On Being Included*.

71 Ahmed, *On Being Included*, 43.

72 Edward W. Said, *Orientalism* (New York: Vintage, 1978).

73 Anna Duff, 'Meghan Markle "is Regarded as Difficult and Demanding" by "Family and Staff" – but There's "No Big Fallout" with Kate Middleton, Royal Expert Reveals', Sun, 26 November 2018, www.thesun.co.uk/fabulous/7829481/meghan-markle-difficult-demanding-family-staff-no-fallout-kate-middleton-royal-insider/ [Accessed 03/06/2020]; Lucy Devine, 'Meghan Markle Accused of Having "American Wife Syndrome" over

£2.4m Frogmore Cottage Revamp', Sun, 1 July 2019, www.thesun.co.uk/ fabulous/9408792/meghan-markle-american-wife-syndrome-frogmore- cottage/ [Accessed 03/06/2020]; Lebby Eyres, 'Why £5million Meghan "Antoinette" Markle Needs to Slow down Her Lavish Spending or Risk Offending the Queen', Sun, 27 June 2019, www.thesun.co.uk/ fabulous/9378150/meghan-markle-spending-offending-the-queen/ [Accessed 28/06/2019].

74 Lisa Amanda Palmer, 'Diane Abbott, Misogynoir and the Politics of Black British Feminism's Anticolonial Imperatives: "In Britain Too, It's as If We Don't Exist"', *The Sociological Review*, 68, no. 3 (2020): 509.

75 Bailey and Trudy, 'On Misogynoir: Citation, Erasure, and Plagiarism'.

76 Nirmal Puwar, *Space Invaders: Race, Gender and Bodies out of Place* (Oxford: Berg, 2004), 8.

77 Aaron Bastani, 'If a Royal Couple Can't Challenge Britain's Sick Press, What Hope Does a Progressive Politician Have?', Novara Media, 14 January 2020, https://novaramedia.com/2020/01/14/if-a-royal-couple- cant-challenge-britains-sick-press-what-hope-does-a-progressive-politician- have/ [Accessed 27/01/2020]; Sean O'Grady, 'Meghan and Harry Are Stepping Back Because of the Press – as a Journalist, Covering Their Story Was Sobering', Independent, 13 January 2020, www.independent.co.uk/ voices/editors-letter/prince-harry-meghan-markle-sandringham-summit- queen-media-a9280791.html [Accessed 14/01/2020].

78 Ahmed, *On Being Included*, 44.

79 Zoe Williams, 'I Never Thought I'd See the Royal Family as a Beacon of Hope', Guardian, 7 August 2019, www.theguardian.com/commentisfree/ 2019/aug/07/post-referendum-britain-royals-progressive-meghan-markle [Accessed 09/08/2019].

80 Bianca Betancourt, 'Meghan Markle's Black Lives Matter Speech "Couldn't Have Happened" While Still within the Royal Family', Harper's Bazaar, 9 June 2020, www.harpersbazaar.com/celebrity/latest/a32810614/meghan- markle-blm-speech-royal-family-restrictions/ [Accessed 07/08/2020].

81 Amie Gordon, 'Meghan Markle Being Welcomed into Royal Family Is "Obama Moment"', Mail Online, 21 May 2018, www.dailymail.co.uk/ news/article-5752463/Meghan-Markle-welcomed-Royal-Family-Britains- Obama-moment.html [Accessed 21/05/2018].

82 Andrews, 'The Post-Racial Princess'; Eve Woldemikael and Olivia Wol- demikael, 'From Suits to Royals: The Politics of Meghan Markle's Racial Ambiguity', Women's Studies International Forum, 85 (March–April 2021), Online first, https://doi.org/10.1016/j.wsif.2021.102439.

83 Shome, *Diana and Beyond*, 154.

84 David Theo Goldberg, *Are We All Postracial Yet?* (Hoboken: John Wiley & Sons, 2015), 1.

85 Remi Joseph-Salisbury, '"Does Anybody Really Care What a Racist Says?" Anti-Racism in "Post-Racial" Times', *The Sociological Review*, 67, no. 1 (2019): 65.

86 Alana Lentin, 'What Happens to Anti-Racism When We Are Post Race?', *Feminist Legal Studies*, 19 (2011): 159–168.

87 Ben Carrington, 'Is the British Monarchy Actually Adapting to Changing Social Norms?', The Conversation, 1 December 2017, http://theconversation.com/is-the-british-monarchy-actually-adapting-to-changing-social-norms-88285 [Accessed 04/12/2017].

88 Ruth Styles and Shekhar Bhatia, 'Prince Harry's Girl Is (Almost) Straight Outta Compton', Mail Online, 2 November 2016, www.dailymail.co.uk/~/article-3896180/index.html [Accessed 25/09/2017].

89 Christopher Wilson, 'From Slaves to Royalty, Meghan Markle's Upwardly Mobile Family', Mail Online, 30 November 2017, www.dailymail.co.uk/~/article-5130473/index.html [Accessed 01/06/2020].

90 Ibid.

91 Ibid.

92 Rachel Johnson, 'Sorry Harry, but She Has Failed My Mum Test', Daily Mail Online, 6 November 2016, www.dailymail.co.uk/~/article-3909362/index.html [Accessed 18/07/2018].

93 Shantel Gabrieal Buggs, 'Stop Projecting Post-Racial Fantasies on Meghan Markle', Bitch Media, 1 December 2017, www.bitchmedia.org/article/meghan-markle-no-post-racial-power [Accessed 04/12/2017].

94 Maxine Leeds Craig, *Ain't I a Beauty Queen?: Black Women, Beauty, and the Politics of Race* (Oxford: Oxford University Press, 2002), 46.

95 Hirsch, 'Meghan Markle's Wedding Was a Rousing Celebration of Blackness'; Hirsch, *Brit(ish)*.

96 Stefanie C. Boulila, *Race in Post-Racial Europe: An Intersectional Analysis* (London: Rowman and Littlefield International, 2019), 3.

97 Hamid Dabashi, 'The Priceless Racism of the Duke of Edinburgh', Al Jazeera, 13 August 2017, www.aljazeera.com/indepth/opinion/2017/08/priceless-racism-duke-edinburgh-170810082226234.html [Accessed 29/05/2020].

98 Ibid.

99 Ibid.

100 Patrick Greenfield, 'Princess Michael of Kent Apologises for "Racist Jewellery" Worn at Lunch with Meghan Markle', Guardian, 23 December 2017, www.theguardian.com/uk-news/2017/dec/22/princess-michael-apologises-wearing-racist-jewellery-meghan-markle-christmas-lunch [Accessed 29/05/2020].

101 Michael Billig, 'Keeping the White Queen in Play', in *Off White: Readings on Power, Privilege, and Resistance*, ed. Michelle Fine, Lois Weis, Linda Powell Pruitt and April Burns (London: Routledge, 2004), 65.

Notes

102 Billig, 'Keeping the White Queen in Play', 71.

103 Sara Ahmed, 'A Phenomenology of Whiteness', *Feminist Theory*, 8, no. 2 (2007): 157.

104 Dalrymple, *Koh-i-Noor*.

105 Diane Roberts, 'The Body of the Princess', in *Postcolonial Whiteness: A Critical Reader on Race and Empire*, ed. Alfred J. Lopez (New York: State University of New York Press, 2005), 39.

106 Ibid., 32.

107 Scott, 'The Royal Wedding: Prince Harry and Meghan Markle'.

108 Stuart Hall, 'Cultural Studies and Its Theoretical Legacies', in *Cultural Studies*, ed. Lawrence Grossberg, Cary Nelson and Paula Treichler (London and New York: Routledge, 1992), 263.

109 Peggy McIntosh, 'White Privilege: Unpacking the Invisible Knapsack', Peace and Freedom Magazine, July/August 1989, https://psychology.umbc.edu/files/2016/10/White-Privilege_McIntosh-1989.pdf [Accessed 26/06/2020].

110 Wilson, 'From Slaves to Royalty'.

111 Hillary Hoffower, 'Meghan Markle and Prince Harry Just Made Their Final Appearance as Working Royals - Here's How Much Money They'll Need to Maintain Their Lavish Lifestyle Independent of the Crown', Business Insider, 9 March 2020, www.businessinsider.com/how-much-money-meghan-markle-prince-harry-need-financial-independence-2020-1 [Accessed 25/08/2020].

112 Matt Wray, *Not Quite White: White Trash and the Boundaries of Whiteness* (Durham, NC, and London: Duke University Press, 2006).

113 Ibid., 5; 140.

114 Michael Powell, Ben Ellery and Caroline Graham, 'Meghan Markle's Father STAGED Photos with Paparazzi', Mail Online, 12 May 2018, www.dailymail.co.uk/news/article-5721959/Meghan-Markles-father-STAGED-photos-paparazzi-sold-100-000.html [Accessed 12/05/2018].

115 Caroline Graham, 'Meghan's Nephew Is a CANNABIS Farmer Who Is Planning a New Drug Called Markle's Sparkle', Daily Mail, 14 April 2018, www.dailymail.co.uk/news/article-5616449/Meghans-nephew-cannabis-farmer-planning-new-drug-called-Markles-Sparkle.html [Accessed 18/07/2018].

116 Jose Lambiet and Ruth Styles, 'EXCLUSIVE: Meghan's Uninvited Family Celebrate Her Wedding with Breakfast and CROWNS from Burger King after Getting up Early to Watch the Ceremony', Daily Mail, 19 May 2018, www.dailymail.co.uk/news/article-5748403/Meghans-uninvited-family-celebrates-wedding-Burger-King-crowns.html [Accessed 18/07/2018].

117 Fiona Handyside, 'It's All about the Poise: Meghan Markle, Doria Ragland and Black Motherhood(s)', *Women's Studies in Communication*, forthcoming.

118 Beverley Skeggs, *Formations of Class and Gender: Becoming Respectable* (London: SAGE Publications, 1997), 3.

119 Racquel J. Gates, *Double Negative: The Black Image and Popular Culture* (Durham, NC: Duke University Press, 2018); Brittney Cooper, 'Disrespectability Politics: On Jay-Z's Bitch, Beyonce's "Fly" Ass, and Black Girl Blue', The Crunk Feminist Collective, 19 January 2012, https://crunkfeministcollective.wordpress.com/2012/01/19/disrespectability-politics-on-jay-zs-bitch-beyonces-fly-ass-and-black-girl-blue/ [Accessed 22/05/2020]; Fredrick C. Harris, 'The Rise of Respectability Politics', Dissent Magazine, Winter 2014, www.dissentmagazine.org/article/the-rise-of-respectability-politics [Accessed 22/05/2020]; Sika Alaine Dagbovie, 'Star-Light, Star-Bright, Star Damn Near White: Mixed-Race Superstars', *The Journal of Popular Culture*, 40, no. 2 (2007): 217–237.

120 Enid Logan, 'Barack Obama, the New Politics of Race, and Classed Constructions of Racial Blackness', *The Sociological Quarterly*, 55, no. 4 (2014): 654.

121 Ibid.

122 Fortier, *Multicultural Horizons*, 93.

123 Logan, 'Barack Obama, the New Politics of Race', 655.

124 Luisa Farah Schwartzman, 'Does Money Whiten? Intergenerational Changes in Racial Classification in Brazil', *American Sociological Review*, 72, no. 6 (2007): 940–963.

125 Harwood K. McClerking, Chryl N. Laird and Ray Block, 'The Fragility of Racial Transcendence: An Analysis of Oprah Winfrey's Endorsement of the Barack Obama 2008 Presidential Campaign', *American Politics Research*, 47, no. 2 (2019): 305.

126 Ibid., 308.

127 Puwar, *Space Invaders*.

128 Ella Alexander, 'Meghan Markle Wore Tights and the Internet Had a Lot to Say about It', Harper's Bazaar, 23 May 2018, www.harpersbazaar.com/uk/fashion/fashion-news/a20882984/meghan-markle-wore-tights-and-the-internet-went-insane/ [Accessed 02/06/2020].

129 Ibid.

130 McIntosh, 'White Privilege'.

131 Hilary Mantel, 'Royal Bodies'.

132 Ahmed, *On Being Included*, 151.

133 sussexroyal, 'The Duke and Duchess of Sussex on Instagram'.

Postscript: The post-royals

1 sussexroyal, 'The Duke and Duchess of Sussex on Instagram'.

2 Kate Williams, 'Harry and Meghan's "Flexi-Royal" Plan Could Modernise Monarchy', Observer, 12 January 2020, www.theguardian.com/

uk-news/2020/jan/12/harry-meghan-flexi-royal-monarchy-modernisation-kate-williams [Accessed 13/01/2020].

3   Barbour, 'Prince Harry and Meghan Markle's Netflix Deal'.

4   Caroline Davies, 'Harry and Meghan's Archewell Trademark Suggests Plan for Non-Profit Empire', Guardian, 7 April 2020, www.theguardian.com/uk-news/2020/apr/07/harry-and-meghans-archewell-trademark-suggests-plan-for-non-profit-empire [Accessed 20/07/2020].

5   Mikhaila Friel, 'People Think Meghan Markle's First Movie Role after "Megxit" Is Defiant, but It's Actually a Tribute to Her Royal Roots', Insider, 3 April 2020, www.insider.com/meghan-markle-disney-plus-elephant-pays-tribute-to-royal-roots-2020-4 [Accessed 20/07/2020]; Christopher Bucktin, 'Meghan and Harry "Earn £400k Speaking at Exclusive JP Morgan Banking Summit"', Mirror, 7 February 2020, www.mirror.co.uk/news/uk-news/meghan-harry-earn-400k-speaking-21453460 [Accessed 20/07/2020].

6   Annabel Sampson, 'Prince Harry and Meghan Could Charge up to $1 Million per Speech with A-List Agency', Tatler, 26 June 2020, www.tatler.com/article/harry-and-meghan-sign-with-harry-walker-agency-high-profile-speaking-agency [Accessed 20/07/2020].

7   Sussex Royal, 'Monarchy', The Official Website of The Duke & Duchess of Sussex, 2020, https://sussexroyal.com/monarchy/ [Accessed 20/07/2020].

8   Max Hastings, 'My Worries over this Vulgar Hollywoodising of the Young Royals', Daily Mail Online, 7 September 2017, www.dailymail.co.uk/~/article-4860122/index.html [Accessed 06/10/2017]; Elle Hunt, 'Royals for Rent: Will Harry and Meghan Become the World's Biggest Influencers?', Guardian, 23 January 2020, www.theguardian.com/uk-news/2020/jan/23/royals-for-rent-will-harry-and-meghan-become-the-worlds-biggest-influencers [Accessed 27/01/2020].

9   Luke Chillingsworth, 'Meghan Markle Breaks Silence on Public Attention – "They Don't Make It Easy!"', Express, 17 July 2019, www.express.co.uk/news/royal/1154161/meghan-markle-news-privacy-prince-harry-archie-pharrell-williams [Accessed 17/07/2019].

10 Emily Andrews, 'Meg Takes Control: Maverick Meghan Markle Is "New Diana" with PR Tactics, Briefing Friends on the "Truth" behind Headlines and Defying Stuffy Palace Bigwigs', Sun, 8 February 2019, www.thesun.co.uk/news/8379391/meghan-markle-new-diana-pr-tactics-truth-palace/ [Accessed 08/02/2019].

11 Hunt, 'Royals for Rent'.

12 Graeme Turner, *Understanding Celebrity*, 2nd ed. (London: SAGE Publications, 2014).

13 Pimlott, *The Queen*.

14 Russell Myers, 'Queen Taking Legal Action Against Charles' Former Butler for "Misleading Public"', Mirror, 3 August 2020, www.mirror.co.uk/ news/uk-news/queen-taking-legal-action-against-22464243 [Accessed 04/08/2020].

15 Guardian, 'Sarah Ferguson's Busy Summer: Shopping Channels and Swiss Chalets', Guardian, 31 August 2015, www.theguardian.com/uk-news/ shortcuts/2015/aug/31/sarah-ferguson-fergie-qvc-shopping-channel-swiss-chalet [Accessed 08/06/2020].

16 Rebecca English, 'Queen BANS Harry and Meghan from Using the "Sussex Royal" Brand', Mail Online, 18 February 2020, www.dailymail.co.uk/ news/article-8018043/Queen-BANS-Prince-Harry-Meghan-Markle-using-Sussex-Royal-brand-cost-thousands.html [Accessed 20/07/2020].

17 Weiner, *Inalienable Possessions*.

18 Boulila, *Race in Post-Racial Europe*, 4.

19 Ibid.

20 Sussex Royal, 'Media', The Official Website of The Duke & Duchess of Sussex, 2020, https://sussexroyal.com/media/ [Accessed 10/06/2020].

21 Ibid.

22 Mark Landler, 'Harry and Meghan Cut Off U.K. Tabloids', New York Times, 20 April 2020, www.nytimes.com/2020/04/20/world/europe/ harry-meghan-uk-tabloids.html [Accessed 20/04/2020].

23 Sarah Arnold, 'Opinion: Harry and Meghan Need to Start Practising What They Preach', Independent, 20 August 2019, www.independent.co.uk/ voices/prince-harry-meghan-markle-private-jet-climate-change-elton-john-ellen-a9071366.html [Accessed 19/08/2020].

24 Andrews, 'Meg Takes Control'.

25 Hastings, 'My Worries over This Vulgar Hollywoodising of the Young Royals'.

26 Rojek, *Celebrity*.

27 Clancy and Yelin, '"Meghan's Manifesto"'.

28 Richard Dyer, *Heavenly Bodies* (London: BFI Macmillan, 2004).

29 Ibid., 5.

30 Paul McDonald, *The Star System: Hollywood's Production of Popular Identities* (London: Wallflower Press, 2000).

31 Charlie Lankston, 'Meghan Markle Was a Suitcase Girl on Deal or No Deal', Daily Mail Online, 28 November 2017, www.dailymail.co.uk/femail/ article-5126699/Meghan-Markle-suitcase-girl-Deal-No-Deal.html [Accessed 17/07/2020].

32 Marwick and boyd, 'I Tweet Honestly, I Tweet Passionately'.

33 Charlie Parker, 'Meghan Markle's Letter in Full: Read Explosive Letter Duchess Sent to Her Dad', Sun, 10 February 2019, www.thesun.co. uk/news/8396792/meghan-markle-letter-read-dad-thomas/ [Accessed

19/08/2020]; Sun, 'Miss Meghan Markle – An Apology', Sun, 11 February 2017, www.thesun.co.uk/clarifications/2838630/clarification-miss-meghan-markle-an-apology/ [Accessed 02/05/2018].

34 Carrie Goldberg, 'All of the Celebrities, Royals and Surprise Attendees on Prince Harry & Meghan Markle's Guest List', Harper's Bazaar, 21 May 2018, www.harpersbazaar.com/celebrity/latest/a18754442/prince-harry-meghan-markle-royal-wedding-guest-list/ [Accessed 19/08/2020].

35 Bridie Wilkins, 'Inside Meghan Markle and Prince Harry's LA Home Owned by Tyler Perry', Hello!, 15 May 2020, www.hellomagazine.com/homes/2020051589879/meghan-markle-prince-harry-la-home-tyler-perry-photos/ [Accessed 19/08/2020].

36 Danielle Stacey, 'The Lavish Ways Prince Harry Has Spoilt Meghan Markle on Her Birthday over the Years', Hello!, 4 August 2020, www.hellomagazine.com/royalty/2020080494775/how-prince-harry-celebrated-meghan-markle-birthday/ [Accessed 19/08/2020]; Liam Doyle, 'Meghan Markle's Lavish Life: Inside Meghan and Harry's £10m Mansion in Canada', Express, 29 December 2019, www.express.co.uk/news/royal/1221958/Meghan-Markle-Prince-Harry-holiday-home-Canada-Vancouver-Island-royal-news [Accessed 19/08/2020].

37 Arnold, 'Opinion'.

38 Rebecca Perring, 'Meghan Markle and Harry "Finally Start to Pay Back £2.4million Cost of Frogmore Cottage"', Express, 17 May 2020, www.express.co.uk/news/royal/1283268/meghan-markle-prince-harry-frogmore-cottage-cost-pay-back-royal-news-meghan-markle-news [Accessed 19/08/2020].

39 Clay, 'Prince Charles: Inside the Duchy of Cornwall'.

40 Pegg, Evans and Barton, 'Royals Vetted More than 1,000 Laws'.

41 Philip Murphy, 'Opinion: Harry and Meghan Are Right about the Problematic Commonwealth', Independent, 14 July 2020, www.independent.co.uk/voices/prince-harry-meghan-markle-commonwealth-british-empire-colonisation-a9616251.html [Accessed 14/07/2020].

42 Bagehot, *The English Constitution*, 59.

43 Moorhouse and Cannadine, *The Queen: Art and Image*.

44 Ann Laura Stoler, 'Colonial Aphasia: Race and Disabled Histories in France', *Public Culture*, 23, no. 1 (2011): 125.

45 Clancy and Yelin, 'Monarchy Is a Feminist Issue'.

Index

Index

Index

Index

Index